Voices from World War II

mc Marshall Cavendish
Editions

Copyright © 2007 Marshall Cavendish Partworks Ltd

First published in 1988–89 in *Images of War: The real story of World War II*

First published in 2007 by:

Marshall Cavendish Limited
119 Wardour Street
London W1F 0UW
United Kingdom
T: +44 (0)20 7565 6000
F: +44 (0)20 7734 6221
E: sales@marshallcavendish.co.uk
www.marshallcavendish.co.uk

A CIP record for this book is available from the British Library

ISBN-13 978-0-462-09911-8
ISBN-10 0-462-09911-3

Designed and typeset by Phoenix Photosetting,
Lordswood, Chatham, Kent

Printed and bound in Great Britain by
TJ International Ltd, Padstow, Cornwall

Contents

War Declared

The transition to war is never easy, particularly if the armed forces involved have not been prepared for conflict. In September 1939, the British Army was not ready for a long conventional war, having suffered economic constraint throughout the 1920s and 1930s. But at least the army was expanding. In May 1939, two months after Hitler marched into what remained of Czechoslovakia and war suddenly seemed inevitable, a form of selective conscription had been introduced in Britain. Young men were expected to serve in the Regular Army for six months – in the event, most conscripts served until 1945/6. By September 1939, they had undergone four months' training. They were going to need it.

James Palmer was called up to the Royal Tank Regiment at the age of 18, in mid-July 1939, and was one of the many who would be 'home before Christmas'. His girlfriend Muriel and widowed father waved him off at the station in his home town of Hulme in Lancashire – and a new life began.

"It was with mixed feelings that I sat on the platform bench, awaiting the train. Dad, and Muriel had come along with me, and both looked terribly upset. I felt both excitement and anxiety, and was really at a loss as to what was happening. I knew that I would not like being in the army, yet I felt a little pleased at being one of the first to go. The militia men had been the sole topic in the newspapers for the last few days, and in a way I was looking forward to the experience. It was only for six months, so the papers said, and I would be home before Christmas.

The train puffed to the platform and we walked through the

turnstile. The moment of departure was here, and Dad was very emotional and upset. I know that he was thinking of another such occasion, 20-odd years ago, when he had stepped on such a train, taking him to some benighted camp.

Muriel was in tears and clung to my arm, and Dad turned away when she kissed me. It was all so dramatic, and a lump in my throat prevented me from saying much. I remember a woman crying as she spoke to a young lad about my age, who was waiting to board the train, and I thought that my Mam would have been doing the same thing if she had been there.

Two young lads were in the compartment, but didn't say anything. They just sat looking out of the window. I did the same, but I think our thoughts must have been exactly the same. We didn't feel like talking and were all busy with our own thoughts. The train had left Manchester, and the green fields were scurrying by the windows when the dark lad in the corner broke the silence with the blunt observation that he supposed we were all in the same boat. I liked him from that moment, and did not realise that at that time what we would have to go through together.

His name was Joe, and he lived in Ancoats and had been a trolley boy with Manchester Corporation. He soon enlightened me that he was going to the Tank Corps at Warminster and that he hoped he would be home for Christmas, because they had promised to train him as a bus driver when his service was finished. The other lad was quiet and seemed a little shy, but he perked up when the Tank Corps was mentioned because he was going there too. It was good not to be alone, and fags were soon passed round.

Things happened quickly when we eventually arrived at Warminster. In charge of our hut was a corporal named Jock (I never found out his full name, but he became a good pal of mine). It appeared that the regulars had been given the honour of training the militia, and had been instructed to try and behave like gentlemen with us, on the assumption that we 'civvies' were all gentlemen ourselves. There was to be no bullying, and discipline was to be mild. It looked a cushy set-up to me, and my first thoughts were that it was not going to be so bad after all. Our beds were quite comfortable and the meals were good and ample. We had been asked if we wanted any more plum duff! The corporal gave us a little lecture and I first heard the phrase 'You play ball with me and I'll play ball with you'.

The corporal had turned out the lights when a bugle sounded, and I lay in bed thinking about the day's events and Muriel. Everything had happened so fast, it was hard to realise that I was in the army. George was in the next bed to me, and in the dark he seemed to want to talk more freely than he had done all day.

He chattered on and on, then someone at the other end of the room started to tell jokes. At first it was a low mumble of sound in the hut, but soon it developed into pandemonium. The corporal, who was sleeping at the top of the room, raised his voice to quell the noise, but no-one took any notice. At last he could stand it no longer, and his army training asserted itself. Never have I heard such a blast. The very walls shook as he told us what he was going to do if we didn't shut up. I cringed under the blankets, but one bright lad from Liverpool shouted to the corporal, 'Get stuffed'.

That did it – before I realised what was happening, the corporal was out of his bed and the lad from Liverpool was on the floor with his bed on top of him. The corporal held him against the door with his left hand, 'Did you say something?'.

The poor lad from Liverpool stood wobbling at the knees, but tried to bombast his way out of the situation. Then it happened. I don't think the blow travelled six inches, but it was straight to the chin, and I saw a man knocked out cold for the first time in my life. He slithered to the floor and the corporal picked up a bucket of water and threw it all over him.

The corporal turned and, in a frightening bellow, gave us to understand that the next who moved would find himself in a hospital bed for a month, we all believed what he said, and 'Liverpool' was left dripping on the floor. The corporal climbed back into bed and, in a voice that echoed round the hushed hut, said 'Now lads, let's get some bloody sleep'.

It was when the corporal thought that we were all asleep I heard him creep out of bed and go towards the crumpled body, and then I listened, amazed. The corporal was apologising to the lad and was helping him into bed. 'I didn't mean to hurt you, lad, but you shouldn't have said that. You'll be OK in the morning, so try and get some sleep'. I couldn't believe my ears! How could anyone be such a two-sided character? He was as gentle to 'Liverpool' as a mother, and yet ten minutes before I had seen him pole-axe the lad.

About two o'clock in the morning, I was still awake, and could hear drunken singing in the distance. The sounds came nearer until I could recognise the words. The song was about a troop ship leaving Bombay and the chorus finished with, 'Cheer up my lads … 'em all'. This song seemed to follow me about in later years, and it will always bring back memories of my first night in the army."

George Rhodes was 23 and working in a mill when the news came that Britain was at war with Germany. It was no surprise to anyone – everything which had happened in the previous five years seemed to lead to this.

"1938 was a rather peculiar year. In the cinema, where we learned all the news via the newsreel, they started 3D pictures. They gave you a pair of glasses when you went in and you put them in a large box on your way out after the film show. Everybody in the cinema used to sing with the organist, who played before the film started, in the interval, and also at the end of the film.

What used to happen went like this: there would be two 'houses', as it was called, 6pm to 8pm and 8pm to 10pm. You sat down and waved to various people that you knew. The organist would finish playing, lights would go down and the first thing would be the news-reels, then a comic cartoon – Mickey Mouse or Popeye the Sailor Man – then a song-sheet would appear on film. The organist would play the tune and a small white ball would move over each word, and move on until the song was finished. So everyone learned the latest and the old songs as well.

After the interval you would settle down for the big picture and, if you were lucky to be with a girl, you would have a quiet snog. Some-times they would have auditions, and if you could play an instrument or sing, you would be up there on the stage to do your stuff. The audi-ence would applaud and cheer – it was a happy time, even though at the back of your mind was the thought that one day war would come.

One knew that a war was impending, because the Government ordered the militia to be formed. The nearest to us at Shipley was a huge camp at Harrogate. We in the TA looked down on these militia boys, the same way the regular army chaps looked down on the TA. On the wireless, songs were being sung in praise of soldiers, such as *There's Something about a Soldier* and *Kiss Me Goodnight, Sergeant-Major, Quartermaster's Stores* and *When the Soldier's on Parade.* You could sense that England was priming her people in readiness for war.

Every day in the newspaper there would be all the doings of Adolf Hitler and his friend Mussolini – and trying to turn the British against these two countries you had the newsreels at the cinema, going at it pell mell. They tried very hard.

1939 ... what can I say, but the fact that all the people in England were now resigned to face the war that in a few months' time would happen. That year I went to camp – to Redesdale on the Scottish border. While we were there, rumours flew thick and fast that we were not going home after the camp but would be called up...

We had orders to be on parade, fully dressed, for Sunday morning at 9 am, on 3 September 1939. We were then told to stand at ease after a full kit inspection, and that the Prime Minister would speak to us all at 11 am. Loudspeakers had been placed on the roof of the barracks. The sun was shining. It was a lovely morning. At 11.15 am the Prime Minister, Mr Chamberlain, spoke on the radio for all to hear.

'This morning, the British Ambassador in Berlin handed the German Government a final note, stating that unless we heard from them by 11 o'clock, that they were prepared at once to withdraw their troops from Poland, a state of war would exist between us. I have to tell you that no such undertaking has been received and that consequently this country is at war with Germany.'

After the Prime Minister, Mr Neville Chamberlain, finished speaking, another voice came on the air, telling the nation to carry gas masks at all times and to obey the orders of the Air Raid Wardens to take cover in the shelters that were being built in the streets and parks, and that subways could be used. Also, not to hoard food, as this would only make it scarce. After this pep-talk, the colonel called us all to attention, said 'Good luck' to us, and then he and the officers went off. The regiment was then marched inside the barracks, just as the air raid siren went off. It was just about 12.15 pm, Sunday dinner time.

We were told to draw from the stores water bottles, mess tin, knife, fork and spoon, and queue up for dinner – a stew. After having this slop, we went on parade again to draw from the stores rifles (303), plus 50 rounds of ammunition, tin hats, gas masks, gas capes, gas goggles, ground sheets, three blankets and one palliasse. Then we were told to set up on the floor in the barracks (which was a huge hall) our bedding ready for inspection.

Then came the inspection. First, the sergeant, then the sergeant-major, then a second lieutenant, who passed it on to the captain, then the major, then the colonel. After various things had been corrected, he said, 'You are now going to sleep, eat and live here until further orders. No-one is allowed to go home. A guard will be mounted, and a fire piquet. Kit inspection will also be carried out daily. Any problems regarding home life, see your No. 1 first, and he will make the move for you in the right direction. Tomorrow we will be able to tell you what is expected of us. Carry on'. With that, all the officers scarpered to some hotel for a binge.

It was a peculiar first night – totally different to what we were used to at the training camp. In fact, by 9.30 pm that evening most of the chaps were in bed. Some chatted until 10 pm, when the orderly sergeant and the orderly officer came round, and all the lights were doused.

Monday morning, 6 am, 4 September 1939. We of the 70th Field Regiment Royal Artillery, 49th Division, were asleep on the straw-filled palliasses in the drill hall of the barracks at Valley Parade, Bradford, Yorkshire, when reveille was blown by a bugler, who was standing by the stables. Well, the effect of this deafening bugle-call in such an enclosed space was electric, to say the least. Bodies were being forcibly ejected from their flea-ridden palliasses by the sergeants – and especially the orderly sergeant who, with his cane, seemed to delight in giving any recumbent figure a mighty whack.

After ablutions, we all lined up for breakfast. The time was now 7.30 am. The cooks had done to the fried eggs something which no person of sound mind would have done. They had obtained a huge metal tray, which was supposed to be used under the lorries to catch the drips of oil, and in this container they had cracked God knows how many eggs, and had fried them to a frazzle. Then they tried to separate them to give each man an egg in his mess tin. I must say, they tasted like a piece of leather. I'm sure that I would have done better to eat my gas mask!

I caught sight of my father standing near the door, and with him stood my sister Jessie. She was in the ATS. In fact, Jessie was one of the very first girls to join up in Bradford as a volunteer for the ATS in 1937. For my mother's sake, Dad, Jessie and I had a photograph taken of all three of us together.

The colonel then gave us all a peptalk, including the ATS, and told us that we would, in the near future, be moving from Bradford, just as soon as the War Office had decided where to send us. It could be France, but we should all be home with our loved ones by

Christmas, as that was about as long as the war with Germany was expected to last. Little did we know that six years would slip by before we would be back with our loved ones – and that many would never return. He then gave us a run-down of the total strengths of the armed forces opposing each other. From our side, the picture looked rosy."

Josephine Harcourt, as a young woman working in London, recalls her feelings towards the news that war was breaking out in Europe, and Britain had joined the fray. She remembers how it disrupted her work in the film industry and what her response to being called up was.

"The news, on that first day of September, was that Germany was bombing Poland. At the time I was working on a film at Islington Studios with Arthur Askey, called *Band Wagon*. On that day the production was called off – just temporarily, while everybody got themselves together and prepared for what might be the worst: nobody knew then whether it might be flights of bombers coming over or what.

Then, of course, came Sunday the Third: the ultimatum to Hitler had expired, and if he didn't withdraw from Poland, we would be at war. At 11.15 am, Prime Minister Chamberlain came on the radio and declared in a solemn voice: 'We are at war'.

We had all been standing in the sitting room, it chokes me even to think of it now, and one or two of us wept a tear – we thought it was the end of our lives, and especially we were thinking of all the children. Anyway, that was it.

Meanwhile, my younger sister was already 'evacuated' down to Bourne End on the river. We went back to Edgware, where we lived, to pack up all the things we thought we might need if we were going to evacuate down to Bourne End. I then phoned the studios at Islington and was told that the production was starting up again. Everybody had drawn a second breath – nothing had happened.

The Islington Studios were very ancient and it was very difficult to create any shelters around there. But they were an offshoot of Gaumont British which was at Shepherd's Bush, where the BBC Centre is now, and so we transferred the whole production from Islington to Shepherd's Bush, and in two days we had started production again. We were called at 7.30 in the morning, because the idea was to get in as much as we could of daylight hours, so that everybody could get home by night, because the bombers might come by night. Transport and everything else was organised so that people could get home in daylight. There was this terrible threat in the air that you never knew what would happen.

On 22 September, petrol rationing caused us to give up hurtling down to Bourne End using up valuable petrol, so we retired back to Edgware, which was not exactly a town house, but anyway, a suburban house, and continued to work from there. I think the next event was the call-up. People were called up by their age/class; it is always the young men who go first.

I have always been more or less a pacifist, although not a very active one, ever since my school days. I remember reading the war poems of the First World War and being absolutely shattered by seeing a production, *Journey's End*, which was about the First World War and the ghastly trench warfare. It actually shook me to the core. I had a feeling this is such a crazy way for humans to behave, that I was naturally pacifist, although I have never been a very great activist – I didn't demonstrate or do anything like that. Indeed, I would have preferred to work in hospital services or something like that; I wouldn't have been against doing some social work, but I didn't want to be involved in the aggression.

So when time for call-up came, and I got my papers, I chose to go to a tribunal where I was interviewed; I had to explain why I didn't want to go into the services. Armed with letters from Sir Anthony Asquith, for whom I was working at the time, and Terrance Rattigan, who was the script writer, I went to this tribunal and I explained that I thought it was crazy to put me into the services where I would have to learn new skills and to bring somebody else into the film industry who would also have to learn what I knew already. Why not keep my experience going in the film industry? Anyway, they seemed to be convinced, and I stayed in the film industry – all through the war – which was quite hazardous because, of course, later on in the war we did all sorts of propaganda films that were very important: I went out on a submarine to make *We Dive at Dawn*. Another time I was based on a disused airfield up in Catterick in Yorkshire to do *Way to the Stars*, that was with Carol Reed. They're still quite popular, these oldies, I mean – they had a great message to tell.

It became difficult travelling to work from Edgware when the bombing started, then it became quite dramatic, because going by tube was OK, except, of course, the Underground was absolutely packed with people who had slept there all night. All the platforms were stacked with bunk beds. Anyway, you could get through on the tube, but the buses would probably take quite irregular routes to avoid the bomb craters that had occurred overnight, with buildings down all over the road.

I think what influenced our social lives largely was who was going to be home and when the menfolk were going to be on leave. Having this little country house down Bourne End was an absolute target for jollifications when the men came home on leave. We were all in our twenties then and we used to have some wonderful evenings if we had enough money. On a Saturday night we used to go to Skindles in Maidenhead for a dinner dance – well, I think we used to buy the minimum drinks and the minimum food, just whatever would get you on to the dance floor. But we did have some good times."

Dunkirk – In Victory and Defeat

*I*n April and May 1940, after eight months of so-called Phoney War, Germany invaded Denmark and Norway and, on May 10, Belgium and Holland. Three French armies and the British Expeditionary Force responded by crossing the border into Belgium to hold the Dyle Line. Holland, attacked by land and air, fell on May 15. The same day, tanks and infantry of German Army Group A, headed by Panzer Group V, punched through thin French defences at Sedan and began a drive for the Channel coast, reaching Boulogne on May 25. After a heroic defence by British forces Calais fell a day later. A day later at 19.00, Vice Admiral Bertram Ramsay launched Operation Dynamo, the seaborne evacuation of more than 330,000 British and French troops in northern France and Belgium, which surrendered on May 28. Although larger ships could use the harbour at Dunkirk, the Royal Navy asked small-boat owners to assist in the evacuation as they could approach the sandy coast and ferry men to larger ships off shore. By the small hours of June 4, the flotilla of vessels that answered the navy's call had helped rescue around 338,000 men, over six times Ramsay's original estimate. The cost had been high: six British and three French destroyers had been sunk, along with 56 other ships and 161 small craft; the Royal Air Force had lost 100 aircraft. But the spirit and success of the evacuation turned an English defeat into a *byword for national pride. Only when Veterans of Operation Dynamo look back does the enormity of the undertaking and the sheer doggedness and courage required to see it through emerge.*

Corporal George Andow of the 4th Royal Tank Regiment was evacuated in a ship which narrowly escaped being blown apart. In retrospect, his memory is one of being woefully unprepared for the savageness of Blitzkrieg – and of how very desperate and piecemeal the British escape really was.

"We were all very low when we reached the town, very low in spirits … but we were still getting rations from somewhere. If I remember rightly I still had some iron rations when I got to the other side.

Any organisation, at least so far as regimental organisation was concerned, was pretty non-existent. You might come across a group of chaps who had been together for a while, but that was as far it went. Not all of them had weapons. If you saw one lying around you picked it up.

By this time, the tanks had gone into this rearguard action. We did not see them again. And all the personnel with them were either killed or taken prisoner of war.

The voyage took six hours maybe, I wouldn't like to say. We just had this one bad attack with these six planes – whether they were Messerschmitts or not I wouldn't like to say off-hand now. I daresay they were floating around us for four or five minutes, in which time they could do quite a bit of damage … but for some unknown reason they just went down the port side. They never did the starboard side at all.

The thing is – and I've thought about this a lot – that whenever you were training before the war, you always got on to the objective and there was never anything in the training about being suddenly surprised by the amount of armour that was positioned on the objective that we were going to. I think the British Army learnt some lessons in France.

Back home, I think the general public was rather surprised at how fast the advance had gone; we were ourselves. But I don't think the public itself could grasp the situation until the troops had come back from Dunkirk and Calais and so on, and told them what was really taking place out there during the retreat.

When we got back to England, naturally enough the newspapers and the radio were getting information left, right and centre – and I don't think it was censored too much. After all, you can't gag thousands upon thousands upon thousands of troops, can you?"

Lieutenant Carter of the 2nd Sherwood Foresters, later to become Colonel, honoured with the OBE, MBE, MC, remembered the obedience and orderliness – and the tremendous fortitude of the men under his command.

"We marched back towards Bray Dunes and dug in on the coast there. Major Temple was put in command of the anti-tank guns. We didn't see him again – in fact he was killed; most of his force were killed or captured.

The difficulty was getting the boats to take the men to the destroyers because they were quite a long way out. There were boats there but, as they had drifted back towards the shore, they had lost their oars. We got onto this Mole and went on by companies, quite quietly and steadily. I remember putting a brave young officer in charge of getting the wounded on – there were quite a lot of wounded there. We got every man in, every man carrying his weapon, you see, and this awful Boys anti-tank rifle was taken solemnly aboard.

I don't know what the papers said but I don't think anybody knew very much what was happening. A lot of the soldiers go back for old times' sake, but it was a defeat, and that's all there is to it."

Brigadier F P Barclay, DSO, MC, then a Captain in the 2nd Royal Norfolks, recognised the debt owed by those who got away to the last defenders of Dunkirk. The British Tommies' indomitable spirit was a credit to them.

"Well, the first thing I'd pay tribute to is the men and the morale that we had in the battalion, which was absolutely wonderful. It was the most thrilling feeling to experience the spirit of the chaps who were with you.

On the other side, I think we were shockingly badly equipped. Some of the equipment we got we'd not trained with. It only joined us when we were mobilising.

So far as training in the orthodox forms of warfare went, we were fine, but we hadn't done enough movement at night by transport.

We had tremendous courage in our men and the way they held out when the Dunkirk withdrawal was going on – they never got to Dunkirk themselves – they were stopping the Germans interfering with the withdrawal of thousands and thousands of other people. Which they did successfully and I mean, the battalion was practically wiped out doing it. But, such was the determination to put the biggest possible spanner in the Germans' advance that it succeeded in letting the better part of the British Expeditionary Force get back to England."

Private Samuel Valentine Love of the Royal Army Medical Corps, interviewed many years later, recalled conditions on his rescue ship and then, later, the same man's shocked return to France without even setting foot on British soil.

"I bet there were thousands buried on them beaches that nobody knows nothing at all about, because the bombs were coming down that thick and fast. One would make a crater and a bloke would fall in it and the next bomb would cover him over.

What condition was the town in?
Burning and blowing up. We'd get in a doorway, and I used to say 'Let's go' and we'd go – and as soon as ever we'd gone that building went as well.

How was the crossing?
This boat that we got on had had a hit. We had to back out and they were after us – Jerry was after us all the while we were trying to get out. Four or five miles after we left Dunkirk harbour, we lost three destroyers in twenty minutes.

What happened at Dover?
We were turned round and sent to Cherbourg. Do you know, the troops lined up along the rail and they were going to shoot that captain if he didn't take us to Southampton.

Eventually there were 146 wounded and 26 of them that had died on the voyage to Cherbourg.

How was the Cherbourg hospital?
They fussed over me properly when they found out what I was and what I'd done. A sister offered me sleeping draught – I said I didn't need it – I'd had no sleep for a fortnight. I could sleep on a clothes line". The next day Private Love sailed home.

Pilot Officer John 'Chalky' White, of No. 32 Squadron of the RAF, saw Dunkirk from above while giving air cover to the rescue boats.

"We arrived at Wittering for a break, and learned that we had to leave for Dunkirk. We patrolled it the best we could – the town was covered by a huge pall of smoke and it was very difficult indeed to see any low-flying enemy aircraft such as Stukas. We were ordered to patrol at 15,000 ft in Hurricanes, with Spitfires at 30,000 ft.

I met two young officers who had been posted to our squadron at St Pancras. It was about 4.30 am in the morning when we finally reached Biggin Hill. We had to go straight out to the aircraft, and I remember telling them, 'For heaven's sake keep your eyes open all the time'. I was worried stiff as they were brand new to the squadron and there they were – expected to fly into the heat of the action within the hour.

Over Dunkirk we got mixed up with a whole lot of 109s. It was a question of flying around in tight turns and firing at any 109 you could, while making sure that no-one was on your tail. Those two poor youngsters were both shot down and killed on that first mission – that was the end of their war experience.

I know a lot of the troops on the ground said that there was no Air Force protection – I can assure you that whatever aircraft and men we had were out there trying to provide air cover from above the smoke.

Troops were coming back without equipment – bedraggled, grey, dusty and dirty – and I remember thinking 'My God, this is the pride of the British Army'."

Reporting back from a visit to the front, one of General Maurice Gamelin's liaison officers bore witness to the terrible rout of French Army.

"Complete disintegration. Out of 70,000 men and numerous officers, no single unit is commanded, however small … at most 10 per cent of the men have kept their rifles … Out of the thousands we sifted, it wasn't possible for me to form one company for the defence of the bridge at Compiègne. However, the losses had not seemed to be high. There were no wounded among the thousands of fugitives … they don't understand what has happened to them. The sight of an aeroplane induces terror in them. Service troops broke up before the infantry and spread disorder."

Jean Murray, a French gunner on leave from his infantry regiment, was awaiting transport to the front.

"We marched incessantly, with a surprising continuity for two long hours, and then the column suddenly stopped. A powerful light was fixed upon us at a turn in the road ... profiting from this unhoped-for halt, men sat down on the side of the road. A quarter of an hour passed, then an officer came to the back of the column, to announce that we were prisoners and that we must throw away our arms. The commander had already been taken away by the Germans ... I threw my rifle away in a ditch. How simple this had all been!"

Fritz Kanzler, a German soldier with the Panzer-schütze (tank crew member) recalled the apparent ease of the advance – it all seemed too easy...

"It's through the speed of the Panzers that we've managed to come round to the back of the English. We are travelling north-east. Our second company has been on the move all night in order to be at the arranged place to meet the artillery battalion. We can still feel a pleasant warmth from the burning town we've just come through.

The Tommies would not let themselves be taken and are still shooting at us from a distance. An abandoned English anti-tank gun stands at the fork in the road – an evil looking thing with considerable gauge and power.

Another battalion is arriving from a different attack which they had started the previous day. There are still many fallen German soldiers laid out on the road from this assault.

The artillery follows closely after the Panzers. So far, everything is going as if on the practice ground, but still everyone had the feeling that the enemy, who are holed up in positions in the hillocks over there, are only letting us advance so as to be able to wipe us out at the closest possible proximity.

Suddenly there are new orders. The Panzer division splits immediately from the artillery unit and quickly makes the crossing of the Canal at Merville to pursue the English who are in retreat...

Unfortunately we have very little cover and I'm lying near the others, out of breath and panting. Just as I raise myself up to join them, another shell whistles above us into the masonry. As I'm lying there, I cut the boot from the foot of the Lieutenant next to me and bind a splint to his broken leg."

Battle of Britain – Heroes of the Air

During ten tense weeks in the summer of 1940, thousands of anxious British eyes peered upwards towards the weaving vapour trails and drenched blue sky. With France defeated, Hitler's next objective was to invade Britain by launching Operation Sealion in mid-September. On 1 August, the Führer ordered the Luftwaffe 'to overcome the British air force with all means as its disposal, and as soon as possible'. The fate of over fifty million British citizens rested on the outcome of countless, swirling dog-fights that came to be known as The Battle of Britain. Fighting on different sides and under orders to wipe each other out, but with the same sense of duty, the aerial heroes of the Battle of Britain recall the summer of 1940.

Flight Lieutenant Peter Brothers of No. 32 Squadron, later Air Commodore, CBE DSO DFC, made flying his entire life, and was at the forefront of the action in the south east.

"The philosophy of taking on German bombers and fighters was based on the fact that the Hurricanes should attack the bomber formations and the Spitfires the fighter cover. Of course it never worked out like that. Either you weren't together with the Spitfires when the raid happened or, by the time the first flight went in to attack the bombers, the fighters were already coming down – so one of you had to play rear guard action and take on the fighters. This usually fell to my lot, although I did get mixed up with bombers on occasions.

If you had the time and the height, you got into a favourable position up-sun – but again that didn't usually work out, because one was always scrambled on the late side. This was because, until the controllers were certain that it was a raid and not a spoof to draw you into the air, there was no point in launching you. If it was a spoof, by the time you were refuelling, the main raid would come – and this was what the controllers were trying to avoid.

As a result, it was rather late when we got the word 'Go'. That usually meant that you were at a disadvantage heightwise, so you'd have to take the bombers head-on. That, we discovered, was one of the best ways. They didn't like that, as they didn't have forward-firing guns – or very few of them did.

You could break up a formation and, once you'd scattered it, you had a good opportunity of shooting down individual aircraft without being involved in crossfire from the rest of the formation. Also, by the time the fighters got as far as London, they were at the limit of their range.

The Germans had one formation where they were not in close cover with the bombers – this was with the fighters stacked up above, giving them a very favourable position. Once you were attacking the bombers, they could build up speed diving down to attack you. The 109s could dive much faster than we could. If they carried on their dive you hadn't a hope of catching them.

The 109s had fuel injection, with the result that they could take inverted load without the engine cutting. Whereas, if we pushed the stick forwards and went into a steep dive, we got a momentary cut in the engine – which didn't help build up speed. The only thing to do was a half roll, so the engine didn't cut, then an aileron turn down straight after them. On occasions we'd catch them like that, but that was usually because the chap was inexperienced.

Life was much simpler afterwards, when we were doing sweeps over France – you planned those. During the Battle of Britain, there was a lot of time for sitting around and waiting – and then there was the panic of the scramble.

The game was, you were shooting aeroplanes down – the only time I felt positively sick was when I hit a chap straight in the cockpit. I thought 'I didn't mean that – I only meant to hit a wing off'. That was the game side of it – we all rather hoped the chap would jump out and be taken prisoner of war rather than be killed.

One got very tired. When we were operating, we were at readiness half an hour before first light at about half past three in the morning, and we'd finish about half an hour after last light – say 10.30 at night.

By the time you'd gone over to the mess and had a meal (and I often used to go back and take a crate of beer for the ground crew, and had a chat with them to thank them) and were in bed, it was around midnight. Then you were back down at the aircraft by 3.30 am, with time for breakfast beforehand."

Pilot Officer R G A Barclay with No. 249 Squadron based at North Weald, kept a diary during the battle of Britain. Excerpts for 15 September read as follows:

"I followed three of our Hurricanes climbing up on the left of the bombers for a head-on attack – but lost patience and turned to do a beam attack on the leader. At the same time, the leading Hurricane turned to do a head-on attack and we almost collided above the bomber.

I remember diving earthwards in the middle of the bomber formation. I opened fire with more than full deflection and let the Do fly into the bullets like a partridge.

The Me 109s escorting the bombers were far above and behind and did not trouble us – I believe due to Spitfires engaging them. Owing to lack of fighter opposition, there was no need to break right away downwards, so I came back and did a short quarter attack. The Do 215 then broke away from the formation, and I saw that the engines were just idling as it glided down.

We were scrambled again later – and very shortly after reaching our height of 16,000 ft, we sighted fighters above us and about 20 Do 215s, for once at the same height as ourselves. The squadron went into the attack on the beam, except one, who went into some Heinkel IIIs he saw coming up behind the Do 215s.

As we attacked, I noted the cannon fire from the top rear gun positions of the Dos – little spurts of white smoke flicking back past the twin rudders in the slipstream, like intermittent squirts from a hose pipe.

After my attack, the Do 215 dropped behind the formation a bit and one parachute came out underneath. I then noticed all the Dos jettisoning their bombs. The Dos had broken up on our first attack and some dived for the clouds, but stayed just skimming the clouds and did not go right into them and instrument fly home. Inexperience?"

Group Captain Peter Matthews, then a Flying Officer with No. 1 Squadron based at Northolt, had been in France since the start of the war – so the start of the action came as no surprise.

"We came back on June 18, three days after the French packed up. We left everything behind – I left my golf clubs, saxophone, some marvellous records, a gramophone – all for the Germans to find. We were called out so often that we slept under the wings of our aircraft.

I was flying Hurricanes – there were more Hurricanes than Spits in Fighter Command at the time. We'd get to bed just after dark and try to get a few hours sleep – then up again. We spent a lot of time waiting for the phone to ring.

We were all pretty scared, really. The waiting was the worst part – we'd sit about playing poker, with that tension in the pit of our stomachs – it was almost a relief when we heard the phone ring to scramble us.

In a day we might be scrambled three, four or even five times – then you were probably only in the air for half an hour or 45 minutes. It's amazing that time went so fast. I suppose we all stood up to it because we were young.

I remember one attack we made on a big formation – we went in head-on. We wanted to get higher and avoid any fighters and shoot down the bombers from that position, but we couldn't gain the height in the time. So, we made a head-on attack on a bunch of 110s – we were very successful and must have shot down three or four.

Our Hurricanes weren't as fast as the Germans, but we were more manoeuvrable, if slower in climbing. Those Hurricanes took a hell of a lot of punishment – you could get badly shot up and still be safe."

Formal reports cite an incident on 18 August 1940 as follows: 'Spitfire N3040. Abandoned over Horsmonden, damaged by return fire from Ju 88 2.15 pm. Crashed by Tucks Cottages, near Park Farm. Flt Lt. Robert Stanford Tuck baled out and was slightly injured in heavy landing. Aircraft a write-off'. To Tuck of No. 92 Squadron, it was like this:

"Spotted two Ju 88s that had passed over me at 15,000 ft, heading SSW or S. I turned on them and gave chase. As there was no cloud, the two E/A (enemy aircraft) put down their noses and went straight on to the surface of the water.

I flew straight ahead of them as fast as possible and then turned head-on and fired at the number 2 E/A. After passing close over the top of the E/A and pulling straight up, I observed that he had gone straight into the water with a terrific splash and disappeared. (Up 'til this time, I had only been hit in the wings and through the left side of the perspex on the windscreen.)

I then flew straight ahead again to attack the E/A that was left. Just when I had opened fire on this head-on attack, I saw a large greeny bluish flash from the nose of the Ju 88. Immediately following this, there was a loud crash on the underneath front of my aircraft. This seemed to tip my tail up and I thought I should hit the water. However, I pulled straight up and left the Ju 88 heading off on the same course, leaving a trail of oil on the water. I was now approximately 35–40 miles south of Beachy Head at 4,000 ft. My aircraft must have been badly damaged, as there was excessive engine vibration and glycol and oil temperatures were very high.

I managed to reach the coast, but dense fumes were coming from the engine and under the dashboard. I could feel myself being overcome by these fumes, so decided to abandon my aircraft. Jumped clear at 800 ft. Could not say whether my aircraft was straight and level or not, as fumes had blinded me. My aircraft landed ½ mile away from me in a wood and did no damage."

On only his second bombing mission, Oberleutnant Hans Gollnisch of the German Stab II/KG30 bomber unit was grounded by an RAF fighter as he approached his target.

"In early September 1940, my unit was transferred from Denmark to Chievre, near Ath in Belgium, in order to concentrate bomber groups for bigger raids on England. It was my second mission of this kind when on September 9 we took off from Chievre to meet about 200 bombers at 5,000 metres over Cap Gris-Nez.

After a wide swing eastwards, we headed for London, escorted by hundreds of German fighters. The targets were the docks and shipping in the Thames, and could already be seen, when we were suddenly hit by a very short burst of fire from the machine guns of the RAF fighter that had evidently approached from below and behind, unseen by the escorting fighters and our rear gunner, Unteroffizier Diebler.

Our plane was badly damaged and the situation was grim – the control column didn't work any more, as a bullet must have severed the elevator cables, and both engines were hit, the right losing gasoline, the left oil.

Then, the observer, Unteroffizier Rolf, reported that Diebler was lying dead in a pool of blood, a bullet having pierced the artery of his neck. I gave the order to shed the cockpit roof in order to bail out, but then I found that I could just about control the aeroplane by the trimming wheel, which to some extent replaced the elevator. Thinking of our dead gunner, I decided to stay in the plane and make for the Channel. If our engines kept going long enough, we could get down on the water and maybe get back to France in the rubber dinghy which was carried on board. So I turned south for the shortest route and jettisoned our bombs. However, we now had no guns to defend ourselves against further attack, as these had gone with the roof, so I dived for cover in the clouds 3,000 metres below.

Unfortunately, in the clouds the engines stopped and didn't want to start again. By now we were too low to bale out, so had no choice but to make a very difficult landing with no use of the control column. I couldn't even let out the flaps, because the electrical system had failed!

I was very lucky to make a good landing as another problem was that of all the fields being covered in all sorts of poles and obstacles like old cars – as a defence against a possible landing by assault gliders in an invasion. However, I got us down in one piece and after we had lifted out the dead gunner, we set fire to our aeroplane and gave ourselves up to police and soldiers."

It was on a fighter mission to escort Stuka bombers that Oberleutnant Gerhard Kadow with the 9th Staffel, Zerstörergeschwader 76 (9 Squadron, Destroyer Group 76) became the first German brought down and taken prisoner on British soil.

"On 11 July, I flew Me 110, number 2N + EP, with my wireless operator and air gunner, Gefreiter Helmut Scholz. My squadron was stationed at Laval, and we flew from here to Dinard for refuelling and from Dinard to England at about 12.00 noon.

My squadron, together with two others, had orders to protect Ju 87 Stuka dive-bombers, which would attack targets on the south coast of England in the vicinity of Portland.

Before we started, our commander, Major Grabmann, told us that it was vital that no Stuka be lost. This meant a considerable risk to our lives.

At the English coast I counted some twenty dark spots in the distance, somewhat higher than we were. I was certain they were RAF fighters, but couldn't recognise whether they were Hurricanes or Spitfires – but knew that our twin-engined machines were no match for these single-engined fighters.

However, it was our duty to protect the Stukas, so that they could bomb unhindered. The main strength of the Me 110 was the two 20mm cannons and four machine guns in its nose. I pressed the firing buttons and bullets flew like water out of a watering can towards the enemy. The closing speed was high, and at the last minute both I and my attacker had to break away to avoid a head-on collision. Whether I scored any hits or not, I don't know.

The next moment, two fighters were on my tail and had opened fire. Almost immediately both of my engines stopped and a return to the Continent was clearly impossible. The enemy saw his success and stopped shooting, but watched me from behind.

I flung off my cabin roof for a quick escape and hoped it would hit him. I ordered Helmut Scholz to do the same. He radioed that the mechanism to ditch his cabin roof would not operate as a result of bullet damage.

I couldn't bail out and leave Scholz to his fate, and for the same reason a ditching in the sea seemed unwise. The only alternative was a crash landing on British soil.

After we had landed I found I could not leave my cockpit – a high explosive bullet had hit my seat, causing a big hole. The torn aluminium 'fangs' around the hole had nailed themselves through my parachute pack and tunic and on to my flesh.

I pulled myself forward, and suddenly was free. I left the aircraft and smashed the cabin roof of my gunner so that he could get out. He was hurt only by shell splinters. The first thing to do was destroy the aircraft. We didn't have a self-destruct charge, so opened the fuel caps and tried to ignite the petrol with the muzzle flash from my pistol.

I fired eight shots, but had no success. In hindsight, this was just as well, otherwise the aircraft would have exploded and killed us."

The Blitz – Relentless Attack

On the night of 24 August 1940, two flights of German bombers ordered to attack the oil refineries at Thames Haven got lost and showered their deadly cargoes across a wide area of London. Churchill retaliated on 25/26 August by sending 81 Whitleys, Wellingtons and Hampdens to bomb Berlin. The RAF returned to Berlin four times in the next ten nights. Hitler was furious at the bombing of Berlin and ordered the relentless terror raids on British cities that would bring 76 nights of death and violent destruction. For those both in the air and on the ground, sights and sounds they never expected to see in their worst nightmares became a reality with the onset of the Blitz.

Douglas Reader was in the voluntary fire service in Coventry, and saw his city change in one night into an inferno – and then a massive area of charred rubble.

"Unfortunately, when I was on duty there was inevitably a raid of some kind – I got the name of Jinx Reader for that reason.

That evening, sirens went around half past six – and after that it was all hell let loose. Bombs and incendiaries came down in showers. Actually, at the start it was a very, very frightening experience – you could hear the bombs whistling down, and you got down on the floor with your hands behind your neck and hoped for the best.

If you heard one go off, then counted the others, two, three, four – you could get up and walk around. At that time, around the first raid, they were dropping in sticks of four. They penetrated the ground to a depth of 10–15 feet, so the blast went upwards rather than out – which saved a lot of people.

It was a very cold night, but as bright as day, with a hunter's moon, and with all the fires raging and all the activity going on, you didn't feel any cold or anything. Some lost their nerve and ended up in mental institutions. There was one incident when a pump crew arrived from Walsall – we saw it get to the end of Friars Road, and then there was one blinding flash. The whole pump, crew and everything had gone, vanished. They had a direct hit from a 500 lb bomb – it went through between the vehicles. All we found later were bits of gumboot and a few mangled tin hats.

We went down to a shelter just off Charlesmore in Greyfriars Park, where there were known to be about 90 people. They were all dead. A bomb had fallen on the entrance, and all we got out of it was bodies. The effect of it hit you days later and you started to think 'It could have been me', those poor so and sos who went into a shelter, thinking they would be safe.

We got almost to the centre of the town around 10 o'clock, and Owen Owen was on fire from end to end. There was a turntable ladder with one fireman on the top. Another high explosive came, hit the building and the blast went up. You saw the top of the ladder bend – the fireman pitched straight into the centre of the fire. That's the last that was seen of the fireman from the top of the ladder.

Records say there were 650 killed in the November 14/15 blitz, but I would rather think it would be in thousands – a couple of thousand. A lot of people were not accounted for – they were not at home – they must just have been blasted to smithereens."

Florence Barton was an usherette at the Scala cinema in Coventry during the Blitz – the memory of the night of 14 November is still clear in her mind.

"When an air raid warning went, people in my cinema had a choice; they could either go to the top of Gosford Green or stay in the theatre. We'd got a lovely cellar at the back of the theatre for us staff, but we couldn't go there, simply because there was always somebody left in.

On the night of the November blitz there was quite a few in, but most of them went up to Gosford Green. There was a young woman with a tiny child in her arms – what the devil she was doing with a child in the cinema, knowing full well that there was bombing going on, I don't know. There was a girl on the other side, and a man next to me.

The one with the baby was killed. The blast went straight through the baby and into the mother. She was still sitting up there, with the child in her arms, but she was dead.

On the opposite side, in the centre gangway, the girl was sitting there – well, all her insides were lying on the floor beside her. So that was another one dead. The other one was the man, he died in hospital during the night."

Kenneth Turner in the Chief Clerk's Department had to deal with the administrative problem of identifying and dealing with the hundreds of bodies returned to the mortuary after the raid over Coventry.

"There was a mortuary established in Hill Street to which all the bodies collected from under the debris and so on had been taken, and the idea was that relatives should be able to go there and identify the dead and satisfy themselves in that way. Unfortunately, the mortuary itself was also bombed, and a state of chaos was rendered even more chaotic.

Three or four days after the raid, the Medical Officer of Health who was responsible for the mortuary and the Chief Constable who was in charge of public morale had a serious difference of opinion. The Chief Constable was saying that unless people could go to the mortuary and identify their dead, there would be riots and trouble, and the Medical Officer of Health was saying that conditions at the mortuary were such that it was impossible for anyone to do this.

They came to consult the Town Clerk and he asked me to go and inspect the mortuary and give my opinion of it. He sent me off with a bottle of whisky in my pocket to sustain me, and indeed, when I got there, I found I needed it.

The mortuary staff were engaged in fitting bits and pieces together to make whole bodies, and in many cases there were no means of identification or anything of that sort. The whole place was literally a shambles.

I came out and stood on a box at the entrance to the gas works and a crowd of about two or three hundred had gathered. I said I'd been in and made an inspection, and that it was not possible for them to go in. That led to great shouts and so on, in particular from some service chaps in the front row, who had been allowed home on compassionate leave. I picked a sailor and an airman from the crowd and said 'You can come in' and took them inside.

They were both violently sick in a couple of minutes. They came outside and said 'It's right, what he says', and the crowd accepted it and dispersed.

After this, people couldn't arrange for private burials – it would have been impossible for four or five hundred individual graves to have been dug – and of course they couldn't choose which was their body out of all these. So it was decided and accepted that the whole lot be buried in a mass grave."

Ralph William Howes was a clerk with Alvis, the car and aircraft manufacturer, when Coventry was flattened.

"I was on my round to Lamb Street, where there were more shelters, when someone said 'The Alvis has been hit'...

It was really ablaze – you couldn't do anything about it. You'd just got to leave it, but there were several people trying to do little bits with buckets and sand – which was hopeless – but their main job was to stop the fire spreading to the houses.

They said that the night shift had got out – that was at about 7.45, or a bit later – so I went back to the school shelters. That's where it got hit, and I was lucky to get out. I kept popping back to the works, but it was still ablaze.

I put in my report and then went back there – people standing outside the ruins said there were probably one or two still inside. Eventually Schreiber, one of the Home Guard, and Jim Seaman and I went in. We found Jones, the night watchman – we found part of his leg, that's all there was, with the braid from his trousers stuck to it. We found Alec Baker's hat too, but Alec was safe – he'd gone home."

Ballard Berkeley, actor, served as a special constable in London's West End during the worst of the Blitz, and was responsible for keeping order in the midst of chaos.

"Sometimes we were called in because of the looting that was going on. It was one of the most awful things, I remember thinking – one heard of all the bravery and courage – and then there were also some very nasty things – and some very nasty people. Some of the looters at the Café de Paris bombing, for instance, didn't have time to do otherwise than cut people's fingers off to get their rings.

One night, the City was really having a bad time – you could hear the guns, see the lovely red sky down there, and we wondered if they were coming up our way or not.

Then we heard a bomber overhead – the drone of the engine. You could always tell the difference between the German bombers and the British.

There was the usual screech, and then came down a whole whoosh of incendiary bombs, right across the road. Eventually my beat seemed to be more or less clear, and I saw a tremendous blaze in the direction of Dean Street and Old Compton Street. I went down there and it was a bedding factory that was ablaze – it looked as if the north side of Old Compton Street and Wardour Street was going to be burned down. Because the fire service couldn't cope with all this, they had decided to evacuate the area – all the people who lived there and all the shops.

It really was the most extraordinary thing – I'd just put a case of something on the pavement across the road to save it, and was coming back to get more – then suddenly everything stopped and there was complete and utter silence. It was so quiet it was incredible. I heard no bomb coming down, no explosion, but whether the explosion had deafened my eardrums or not, I don't know – but everything was silent."

Jane Clare was a waitress in London's Dickens and Jones store during the Blitz – even though her East End home was blown apart around her, she recalls that she never missed a day's work due to the bombs.

"My friend made a bed in the basement and I went on the first floor. The air raid – I hadn't got into bed at that time – started early, so I went down to the basement. All was quiet, then I said I'd go upstairs and see what was going on.

I threw up the passage window and I saw the sky – it was blood red, with long, silver chandeliers hanging at intervals all around. In fact, I suppose we were dead on target. These chandeliers were silver – they were what the Germans used to drop – and they were like fireworks which would light up London.

I was just admiring the view, when I suddenly felt shivery and thought I'd better go in and put a coat on. I'd no sooner got that coat on, then the house seemed to be torn apart, and the door, the built-in cupboard and the wall with the washstand came and hit me, all at the same time. The house continued to shake, and I thought 'Now you're going to die'. Anyway, I clambered over the door into the passage – and there was nothing there. Everything was blown out, the windows, walls and doors.

Outside, all the houses were devastated, and there was a thick fog everywhere over all the debris. It was as silent as a grave, so I thought I'd go downstairs and see my friend in the basement.

The Air Raid Warden had to force the door to get her out – a land mine had broken a water main in the road and flooded the basement. She had only a nightdress and a coat on – she had nothing with her whatever. The people next door and opposite all drowned in their basements."

Ivor Leverton, a funeral director in Hampstead, London, was in the Auxiliary Fire Service – until he was bombed out while he was working.

"We came back from a funeral to find that the coroner wanted us to move someone from the National Temperance Hospital. That meant moving instead of having lunch, so we were a bit annoyed.

We got there at half past one and went down a flight of steps and waited for the mortuary keeper, who was on the roof as a spotter.

The three of us were there with our coffin – and the bomb came down the lift shaft. It exploded and killed a woman – tore her to pieces, just the other side of the door.

Of the three of us, one was badly shocked, but he was round behind a wall and missed a lot of the blast. A second was cut badly with the glass from the door, and I was sent up about twenty stairs up a staircase. I flew through the air, presumably with the greatest of ease, although I didn't feel very easy about it.

The first thing I remember was seeing this metal coffin – split right down the middle. How we weren't split down the middle too, I don't know. My first reaction, after finding our other two men was to find my glasses. Well, the chances of finding anything at all in all the debris was pretty remote, but people did daft things then. The scene was absolutely unrecognisable from how it was minutes earlier."

London electrician Robert Rosamond was on Home Guard duty outside a power substation when an incendiary bomb landed on the roof.

"The building at the back was blazing like a blow torch and this was making the roof exit burn with it. I got a bucket of water and slung it on the roof – the lead was dripping off the roof – just to cool it down. We got the stirrup pump working and got the hose – we managed to cool the spiral staircase inside down, but as soon as I got the fire out, the flames from the building next door burned it up again.

This went on for some time, and it was getting a bit dodgy walking along the coping. I had to hold my coat to my face to keep the heat off.

After some time and many buckets of water, the building that was burning collapsed. When I looked down it was like hell – a furnace.

There was a brick building at the side of the yard ablaze – all the burning debris was falling out of the windows on to the roof of the pub at the side of the yard. I had to do something, but I'd got no water and no stirrup pump – and I was on my own.

I put the steps up against the wall and climbed on to the roof. There were a lot of sandbags there, so I ripped these open and was getting hatfuls of sand. Every time a lump of debris fell, I was pouring the sand over it with my hat."

Bomber pilot Lieutenant Walther Freiherr (Baron) von Silber, of the III Staffel First Group Kampfgeschwader 53, Legion Kondor, was sent to bomb London. His crew did not return.

"I remember that the night of 10/11 May was very clear. We were flying at 4,800 ft, low towards the target area around the Houses of Parliament. The Heinkel was hit by fire from the ground, and I immediately pressed the emergency button releasing the entire load of bombs.

We then went into defensive manoeuvres using our own weapon systems. The Heinkel was hit for a second time and we were on fire. The observer, Fischer, first of all tried to establish how the other crew members were. He called them through their headphones, which were obviously damaged, but he got no answer. In the central section of the plane, fuel had leaked out and had caught fire.

Feldwebel Fischer reported that Oberfeldwebel Meister and

Unteroffizier Schurf were obviously dead and Feldwebel Wylenzol was wounded and was unable to crawl through the narrow hatch doors, which were already smothered in flames.

The fire on board was getting worse and worse, and it now looked impossible to rescue Feldwebel Fischer. So I gave him the order to bale out over the mainland. I still wanted to try and force-land in the Channel, and hoped to reach the French coast by dinghy. But the Heinkel 111 was now impossible to steer because of the raging fire on board. She began to fall away to the left and then she went into a spin.

While it was still in a spin, I managed to clamber out through the opening above the pilot's seat. Whether the parachute was forced open while I was climbing out, or whether I unconsciously pulled the rip-cord, I cannot remember.

I was taken prisoner by members of the Home Guard, and there was a striking difference in their attitude to the enemy in comparison to the active troops. The worst experience I had was with an English interrogation officer, an emigrant in English Officer's uniform, who seemed a rogue. During five and a half years of imprisonment, I got to know and respect many English officers, but I certainly regret this particular incident of English politics."

Oberfeldwebel Alfred Sticht, age 25, was an observer in a German Heinkel 111 bomber with Kampfgeschwader 53, when they were ordered to bomb the airfield at West Raynham, Essex.

"The pilot radioed me to follow the railway line we sighted below. He turned in and we flew at about 50 m over a railway station.

I shouted for joy into the microphone: 'The anti-aircraft guns haven't identified us as enemy aircraft; if they had there'd be an air-warning siren going down there!'

According to my navigation, we'd be at the target in about one minute. Suddenly – on the left – the airfield. Rows and rows of aircraft.

Leutnant Meier did a steep curve immediately. I asked him to get up higher, as I couldn't aim my bombs accurately at this angle. He took the machine up into the clouds and performed a blind turn, and two minutes later, we were flying over again at 50 m from the ground.

We could see the soldiers between aircraft running about in panic. The bombs lay between the stationary aircraft, one 250 kg bomb fell into a large hangar. It lasted only seconds.

Below, all hell broke loose! The mechanic reported that all bombs had hit the target. As we flew away, we could see only fire and smoke. The flak shot from every barrel. They didn't hit us. My comrades were firing on all barrels.

We headed off in a south-westerly direction, but after about 10 minutes, I heard the voice of the radio operator: 'Watch out! Fighters above us at the rear'. Four Spitfires were coming at us, getting nearer and nearer.

Now began a life and death fight. Our pilot, an experienced 'blind' flyer, did the most fantastic caprioles. We opened fire on the Spitfires when we reached the next cumulus cloud. We did a 90 degree turn inside the cloud.

When we came out of the cloud, the enemy fighters were buzzing around the cloud and were getting ready to dive down on us. We turned straight back into the cloud to shake off the enemy.

It was a cat-and-mouse game – in deadly earnest. The fight went on for about 20 minutes, that for us seemed like an eternity, until we reached a thick cloud layer and were approaching the North Sea. We flew on as long as we could, blind, until we were certain we'd left the English fighters behind and reached our fighter protection area.

General Loerzer came to Vitry to congratulate us. He invited the crew to eat with him at the Officers' Casino, and awarded us with 25 bottles of Sekt."

North Africa – The Desert War

E arly in the evening of 10 June 1940 Italy declared war on the Allies. Hitler had not asked his Axis partner to join, but the Italian leader Benito Mussolini (Il Duce), seeing the French on the verge of collapse and the British Army routed out of Europe, was determined to claim his share of the spoils from a North African campaign. The desert campaign was no picnic for both Italian and British troops: scorching noonday heat, sub-zero nights, pitiless and endless terrain, blinding sandstorms alternating with torrential rain, and the constant race against time and the enemy.

Enrico Emanuelli, an Italian soldier in Libya, recalls the last days of peace before Il Duce ordered his forces into action – and then a summer of airless heat and death all round.

"I remember those days of 1940 – every day seemed to bring another painful adventure. The memories which come back are of so many men dead – right from the early days in Tobruk, through to the end.

I arrived in Tripoli just before Mussolini announced the start of the hostilities in a speech from the balcony of the Palazzo Venezia. On my arrival, I knew only Pio Gardenghi – an old trade unionist who was secretary to Italo Balbo. Gardenghi promised to introduce me to the fascist leader, and one evening took me to the castle which was the seat of the governors.

I could never have imagined that, one month later, in a burned-out valley east of Tobruk, I would meet up with him again – but this time as a corpse. I saw him reduced to a body with no legs and a deformed head, wrapped up in a blanket.

That evening, though, I met the great man, and without so much as an introduction, he told me, 'In Rome they want to make war'. He laughed. 'What will I telegraph to the *Padrone*?'. He looked at me, a stranger whom he met for the first time that evening, and showed me a copy of a telegram which went something like this: 'In view of the events which are being prepared for, I would like to make it known that I have very few aircraft and 10 tanks. I say 10 – and most of these are light tanks. Perhaps in Rome you like to have a joke'.

In those last days of peace, I was in a hotel in Tripoli, and I remember witnessing a little tragedy which stuck in my mind. My room had a window which, in part, was on the road side, rather than the sea, and I could see the flat roof of another hotel nearby. On a number of days I watched a little black cat climb up the building to the roof, then back down the other side. One day I looked out and the little cat was lying dead at the foot of the building.

After three months of war, I was sheltering in a dugout in Tobruk, waiting for the English to stop their naval bombardment, and I told the story to my Captain, Giraudi. He replied, 'We too have made a great jump – and are no longer able to get back up. All that remains now is what is termed our duty'.

The war had started – and they called it 'clean' – because we didn't destroy buildings, didn't kill women and children, and, for a while anyway, we didn't have the means or the warlike frame of mind which was necessary. We didn't have suitable equipment either. We had no pipes to run water along the tracks in the desert and we had no carburettor filters for the spotter planes – so they simply drew in sand and immediately got into engine trouble.

I remember one point, when five of our divisions had been lost, soldiers without guns, on foot, were trying to get back to Tobruk. They were all tired, silent, with bloodshot eyes, but a general, looking at them, said, 'All is in good enough order'. When I asked him what he meant, he said, 'Can't you see, they can still salute?'

Balbo saw the foolishness – one evening I remember him looking around cautiously, then saying to me, smiling, 'I won't support this clowning around for too long. I'll wait a month, then I'll go to Rome and make a scandal of the whole thing'.

Sadly he never got to do this – it was on the eighteenth day of the war that the incident at San Georgio happened, which took him away."

Sergeant Bernard Griffith left home and joined the army at the age of 17. After a few months with the Royal Horse Artillery in India, he found himself on the way to North Africa in 1939 where, as Observer Post driver, he took part in the campaign which culminated in the battle of Beda Fomm.

"At first light you stood to and then moved out of the leaguer area at about 5.00 am to prepared gun positions at certain times and new positions on others. At that stage I was an Observation Post driver-operator, so was the last back into the leaguer every night and first out every morning – so I was generally about four miles in front of the gun position, mainly attached to the infantry. At that time, our total hours of rest, if there was any, was about three per night.

You didn't draw any money in the desert – there was nowhere to spend it. You got two bottles of beer and some cigarettes – when it arrived, the beer immediately used to explode because it was hot and it had been shaken about over hundreds of kilometres of desert. So when you went back, you had all your credits, as they were called. Pay was two bob a day then – that didn't accumulate to much. The form was, you arrived in Cairo. You got a local to introduce you to a gharry – a horse and truck – and he took you to a hotel – a sleazy place in the backstreets.

The first thing you did was take off all your muck. You used to drop everything on the floor and give the bloke so many piastres to go out and buy you underwear, socks, KD shorts (khaki drill), slacks, shirts – and you lay in the bath for two hours.

The first stop of most of the 7th Armoured Division was the American bar in Fout First Street, which we called the Beaulac. You used to have steak, egg and chips and a big bottle of Stella lager, which used to blow your head off if you had too much of it. Then we used to go round the cinemas and the shows they put on – varying types of show and, to be quite blunt, fornication – as you can imagine.

After a little setback after the first Italian push in October 1940, Jock Campbell formed us into 'Jock Columns'. The ammunition used to be put inside the vehicle, the crew used to sit on top of the ammunition, and you'd go bounding across the desert at last light and do a right hook, generally, and come up behind an ammunition supply and dump the men and ammo.

You'd drop into action just before first light, provided your navigation had been good, and fire like bloody hell on the enemy concentration – then get the hell out of it. It was a hit and run thing.

If you were caught behind enemy lines, the idea was to get away fast from the enemy concentration, find a little undulation and camouflage yourself up. For the whole day, you just sat there, getting cooked by the sun. There was no light, no smoking, no noise and you just sat there for the day – and at last light you made your way back to your own lines.

Christmas 1940 I shall never forget. I was in a cave. We had started our advance on the Italians and we reached a load of caves to the west of Sollum. You had so much food issued to each truck and the driver normally was the cook. We had one tin of bully, one tin of marmalade, a lump of cheese and a tin of herrings. Our sergeant put the lot in one can. That was Christmas dinner 1940.

We moved to a point four miles west of Beda Fomm and the Italians came up and halted – the whole of the 10th Army. We got to our appointed rendezvous to learn that the Australians were on the move. The Italian Army came into view at about 4.00 am in the morning. So we just sat there and popped 'em off.

There was a shortage of water and petrol – and terrible terrain. It was raining cats and dogs, and we were soaked to the skin. Vehicles kept breaking down, we didn't get any replenishments. We were going into battle with the ammunition we had, and we'd no idea if we were going to get resupplied or not. We were down to almost nothing and morale was low. However, when you dropped into action, you knew that you were cutting off the Italian Army, and the world was your oyster.

At the end of it, it was pure elation. We found these Italian forts – full of food, chocablock. We just gorged ourselves silly for a few days. They all had water – literally hundreds of containers. We started tipping it around the place, washing our socks in water instead of petrol. They had bottles and bottles of Chianti, and we just tipped it back – we made hay while the sun shone."

Sergeant Francis McGoff, later Warrant Officer, was with the Royal Army Medical Corps during the desert campaign. His memories are of the extraordinary desert conditions.

"The men used to get desert sores – you used to wash all your clothes in petrol too – you didn't have water. The worst affected regiment was the 11th Hussars. We thought we'd found the answer to it when we captured a load of Italian anti-diphtheria vaccine – we tried using wet dressings of this on the sores – and they cleared up! But then a few days later they broke out again.

The desert sores started as a little blister. This would burst and a whacking great sore would appear. The treatment we used was to brush them with stiff nail brushes and scrub them with carbolic soap until there was a nice blood flow, then we'd dry them off in the sun. Then we used to grind up MB693 tablets – and that used to clear them up – but not permanently. We had to stop that eventually, because there were vast temperature changes in the desert, so pneumonia was a very common complaint. There were blokes having to be evacuated to base with pneumonia, but if you treated pneumonia cases with MB693, the patients were better in five days – a marvellous treatment. But, they found too, that the chaps who had been treated topically with the stuff – when they were treated with it internally, the areas on their skin went black. There were hell of a lot of deaths too – so we had to stop using the MB693 for skin treatment."

General Sir Richard O'Connor GCB DSO MC, recalls his planning and execution of the campaigns leading up to Beda Fomm – Bardia and Tobruk. As Major General, he commanded the Western Desert Force and later became Lieutenant General.

"It was absolutely vital that secrecy should be maintained, and that meant, not only keeping the project from the enemy, but it was just as important to keep it from our own men.

Only two senior staff officers were told to start with, and it was not until a week before that anything was written on the subject.

The troops were not told until they were already on the ground – only three days before the operation was to take place. Leave for Cairo was only stopped three days before, as the biggest source of danger was officers and other ranks going to Cairo and talking about what was going on – quite innocently, of things that the enemy could pick up ... and everything that happened in Cairo went straight to Italy – so we took every possible step we could to make sure, first that the enemy didn't know and, no less important, that our own people didn't know.

We'd formed our plan – we decided that we would advance between the most southern enemy camps, then we would pass right through and get behind the camp and so actually attack them from their own side.

In order to give this the best chance of success, I wanted to carry out a rehearsal – and obviously we couldn't call it a rehearsal for the operation because nobody knew about the operation.

During the day we had to enlist the help of the RAF in keeping the enemy out of the sky, because of the enormous amount of dust we produced in our advance to the forming-up places. One had to have some way of preventing being reported. Actually, one enemy plane did report, but I knew that it would take a good deal of time, a number of days, really, before any action would be taken on it, and I saw in the enemy reports that this was reported – but nothing very much was done about it.

The supply problem was absolutely vital and we were always on the edge of a shortage. Our five-day dumps very shortly ran out, and so we had to have our supplies moved in convoys – water, food and ammunition.

It was very important, from my point of view, that I should have absolute control of what was to be sent up. It was a subject that I dealt with every day – and I was absolutely *au fait* myself with exactly the situation of where these various convoys were and when one could expect them. Our operation entirely depended on how this worked out.

The forts we had to overcome were of a strength of about a division each – or sometimes more. For the original attack against the first one I was very insistent that we should attack them from the west – that is, from the way their rations would come. Secondly, I knew that by having our operations behind their front, we would be protecting ourselves against enemy air attack – they would damage their own people. So from every point of view, the right position to start from was attacking the enemy from a most unexpected quarter. That was the basis of the first one, and it was preceded by a heavy, short, bombardment which came as a complete surprise to the enemy and was immediately followed up by the Infantry tanks, which blasted their way into the camp, closely followed by the infantry.

The Bardia and Tobruk operations required an entirely different technique. Their defences were of a different quality. They were strong, actual fortresses, with a very large anti-tank ditch surrounding them – and wire. There was no way of getting the tanks in except to bridge the ditch – and we couldn't bridge the ditch while the enemy was shooting at us. So, we had to have a preliminary operation by the infantry, who would go in the night before the actual attack. They would, with the help of a very heavy artillery barrage, advance and make a bridge-head in the line at a place we selected, and immediately that was completed, the sappers would make a series of bridges over the anti-tank ditch.

Instead of attacking Benghazi direct, I decided to direct a force south west which would cut off all the enemy troops which were fighting in the Benghazi area.

It was a gamble that the Armoured Division had to move over about 150 miles of unreconnoitred land – more of a gamble than might have appeared necessary, because I refused to have the area reconnoitred except from the air. I knew that if we began sending patrols out in that area, it would at once warn the enemy that it was our intention to attack from that direction. They would have fallen back earlier and we would not have caught them as we did."

War at Sea – Atlantic Sea Hunt

*T*he British and German navies were both ill-prepared for war, but it was not long before the German forces used submarine skills to assert their power in the North Atlantic, to rupture Britain's trade supply lines and send thousands of vessels to their doom. Few men survived the terrible consequences of sea warfare, especially in the icy Atlantic. Those more fortunate sailors from both British and German battle fleets tell what it felt like to be at war at sea.

Commander Ronald Hay, later, in his own words 'head boy' of the Fleet Air Arm, was a naval pilot when the sea war started, and found himself struggling against the short-comings of out-dated aircraft – and the non-co-operation and rivalry between Britain's armed forces.

"Sinking the *Bismarck* didn't need the Home Fleet – we could have done without Tovey. Admittedly, though, the *Victorious* took a hand in it. We could have done without the Coastal Command as well, because the *Bismarck* was lost for an agonising 36 hours or so.

Before that, we had a tremendous search going on with our sorties. Eventually the *Bismarck* was discovered about 10 minutes after the flash report by the *Catalina* – in fact we got the first sighting report from our sorties long before we got any information from Coastal Command.

As for the part the Home Fleet played in it, it was a disgrace in many ways. For some strange reason, either because their blood was up or they wanted to revenge themselves, they closed the race, opened fire at about 20,000 yards and closed it down to about 6,000 or 7,000 yards – and when you've got great big guns like that, hurling shells at high velocity, they were simply going across horizontally.

Of course, the whole point of distant gunnery was that you sent it right up there, got lots of gravity to make it plunging fire, going right down the funnel to blow up in the bowels of the ship – which would cause havoc. Of course, they closed the range down to 6,000 yards because there was no opposition from the *Bismarck*, then all they were doing was firing their shells straight through, horizontally, hitting this big armour with a thump, but nothing else happened.

Naturally, the superstructure was a total shambles, but the ship wouldn't sink. At the same time, we had 21 Swordfish, each with a 19 inch torpedo, hanging around waiting to sink the darn thing, but Tovey said the *Dorsetshire* should sink it. They fired quite a few torpedoes, but nothing happened very much, and then, because there was a report of a submarine, they called off the rescue ship and left the rest of the men to die. Meanwhile, 21 Swordfish had to ditch their torpedoes safe into the sea. I mean, the whole thing was really pathetic.

I met the Gunnery Damage Control Officer of the *Bismarck* after the war, in Kiel. You can believe this if you want to – he told me that he blew charges and opened the sea-cocks down below himself, as he was one of the few survivors – I think there were only about 33 survivors, actually. This was apart from the carnage on the upper deck – so the ship was never sunk by the Navy, it was sunk by a German Damage Control Officer, presumably to stop the Navy from boarding the ship and getting secret logs and equipment.

So that was the end of the *Bismarck*, really. I can say that there were signals sent from Tovey saying he was unable to sink the *Bismarck* by gunfire. I read the signal myself. Of course it's now all in cipher in Whitehall. It had never been reported, but it was a signal I actually read. Well, you can imagine what Churchill said – 'You sink the *Bismarck*' – and eventually it was sunk by grace of the Damage Control Officer, which is all terribly sad, and all rather unnecessary. The final irony was that when the Home Fleet got back to Plymouth, they were treated like heroes. They all got 48 hours leave – and what happened to Force H, when we got back? We got forgotten."

Rear Admiral William Selby CB DFC, finished his naval training just after World War I, and as Commander of the *Mashona*, was on board when the ship was ordered to join the pursuit of the *Bismarck* to its final destruction.

"With regard to the *Bismarck* chase, the flotilla I was in was told we should provide escort for HMS *Rodney*, going over to America for what we thought was a refit, and also for the SS *Georgic* which was going to America too, to bring back trainees, I supposed. So we sailed, I think, from the Clyde, to pick up the *Rodney*.

We had been sailing west for at least 24 hours when we got the signal through that the *Bismarck* had broken out and was approaching the Denmark Strait. HMS *Rodney* kept its screen and sent the *Georgic* at full speed to the west, with her screen, who had orders to see her as far as possible. We steamed toward the likely meeting place near Iceland.

There is so much written about the *Bismarck* – and I can only say what part we played, which was to stick to the *Rodney*. There were at least five destroyers in our flotilla – the remaining four escorted the *Georgic*.

So it was the *Rodney* we formed a close screen to during the whole of the chase of the *Bismarck*, and by the time she finally finished up, there were only two of us left – the *Tartar* and my own ship, the *Mashona*. We had fuel for only a few more hours, and so the final episode was when we came in with the *Duke of York*. *Rodney* opened fire on the *Bismarck*, but we had to disperse.

However, I persuaded my opposite number in the *Tartar* to steer a certain course because I had a particularly good plot going down below – and sure enough, at the right time and the right place, the *Bismarck* appeared.

So, we were there on the sidelines, watching the first engagement at about seven miles distant and returning at about 15 knots (because of the fuel) towards Northern Ireland. I had a little more fuel than my pal in the *Tartar*, so I made a signal by light to them to let them know this, and that I had four torpedoes – and asking if I should attack. This was because you cannot attack with lots of battleships around without giving your intentions. No reply was received, so we proceeded on our way, but we did see the last hammering that the *Bismarck* had from the big ships before she fell down over the horizon.

The next day, the *Mashona* was hit just below the bridge. We lasted three quarters of an hour, then had to abandon ship and wait for *Tartar* to pick us up."

Able Seaman Henry Hutchings, a Higher Submarine Detector on HMS *Clarkia*, travelled 120,000 miles on escort duty across the Atlantic, responsible for safe passage of British ships against the U-boat threat.

"We used to do escort convoys out into the Atlantic, and then we used to leave them and they would be met by the Canadians. There was a space where we couldn't go further – we had to go back because of fuel. Therefore there was this area where the convoy was unescorted and that's where the U-boats picked off ships.

During the time that I was on the *Clarkia*, we only lost three ships under escort. One of the ships in the convoy one night said they saw a torpedo pass right under our ship, but we didn't ever suffer any losses.

My job was listening for U-boats. There were certain laid-down procedures we had to adhere to. You swept a certain angle – you didn't go all the way around. You covered an angle of, say, 120°. We overlapped each other, so that there was no space which wasn't covered. If you had what we used to call 'an echo', it was reported, and then my job was to classify it – whether it was a U-boat or not. We detected it through sonar equipment. We used to call it 'asdic' but when the Americans came in, they started calling it 'sonar', so of course, it stuck.

Of a night time, we never used to transmit. We used to listen all the time. You could only do so many hours on, then it used to be about two hours, and then somebody else took over. There were four of us taking turns.

As well as lack of sleep, the food sometimes affected morale. Once we were at sea, we could only take enough fresh food for about 10 days, and after that, it was corned beef, dry biscuits and tinned food – tinned fruit, tinned soup and tins of herrings.

You couldn't take a lot of bread because it went mouldy. Then the chef would try to bake bread – it was quite a job for him, especially with the ship doing all the antics under the sun. Sometimes he tried to make some sort of pie by crushing the biscuits and that sort of thing. It was amazing what he used to think of to cook something different for us.

Once, when we were escorting ships down at Plymouth, we came across a fishing boat, and they supplied us with a load of fresh fish for a couple of tins of tobacco. That sort of thing happened sometimes, but otherwise, it was biscuits and corned beef."

One of only three men to survive the sinking of HMS *Hood*, Able Seaman Robert Kilburn has a tale of horror which is just as terrifying today as it was then.

"Our radar had picked up two ships going south, so we turned to follow them to catch them. We expected them to be the *Bismarck* and *Prinz Eugen*, but until we actually sighted them, we weren't sure. We closed towards them and opened fire at 25,000 yards – 12½ miles. The *Bismarck* and *Prinz Eugen* answered immediately, and the third, fourth and fifth shells hit us and the fifth blew us up.

I was on the upper deck. I was a member of the anti-aircraft gun crew, but of course we weren't needed. There were only two other people with me at the time. The others were in a shelter deck – a shell had gone in there and killed all of them – about 200 men, but I didn't realise that at the time.

One of the shells hit one of the ready-use lockers for the four-inch guns and there was a fire on board the upper deck and the ammunition was exploding. The three of us were waiting for the ammunition to stop exploding before putting the fire out. We were laid on the deck, and then there was this terrific explosion. It was most peculiar, the dead silence that followed it – I don't know if we were deaf.

One of the other men was dead and the other one had his sides cut open and all his innards were tumbling out. I went to the ship's side to be sick.

I noticed that the ship was rolling over and the bows were coming out of the water, so I started taking off my tin hat, gas mask, anti-flash gear, overcoat, oilskin, so that I would have a chance to swim. With the ship rolling over, I just went into the water, and the water came up to me.

I was terrified. I had a small rubber life belt on, which you blew up – it was partially blown up. I started swimming away from the ship. I had a tight belt on, so I took my knife off and cut the belt off to breathe better. The ship rolled over and the yardarms, which had been broken during the action, hit me across the legs and the wireless aerials tangled around my legs, pulling me down with the ship. I cut my seaboots off with the knife and shot up, like a cork out of a bottle. I must have been about 10ft down by then. The ship was about 10 yards away from me, with her bows straight up in the air – and she just sank. There I was in the water.

There wasn't any down-current, which presupposes that the bottom had been blown out of the ship.

I was in the water for about 4½ hours until I was rescued. I swam around on my own at first. There was a large pool of oil with a lot of flotsam and jetsam in it. It was about three miles along, this oil fuel. I didn't want to go in the oil, but I could see small rafts – biscuit rafts – which were about a metre square. Eventually, after about an hour, I was so cold, that I had to get in the oil and swim to a raft. I was quite close to Ted Briggs – he was on a raft. He wasn't well, because he'd swallowed some oil fuel. I held on to his raft because I thought, 'if I'm going to die, I've got some company here'. Midshipman Dundas was on another raft, within shouting distance.

We were in a state of shock and very, very cold. I had read stories about when you were really cold you just went to sleep and died, so I tried to go to sleep, because it seemed a really nice way to die.

We were rescued about four and a half hours after the explosion by a destroyer called *Electra*. They heaved us over the side like sacks of potatoes. They tried to give me a cigarette and I was so cold that they had to put in my mouth, then remove it when I started coughing. We were so cold we couldn't move."

Hans Zimmermann, age 20, was a stoker on the German battleship *Bismarck*, when in May 1941 his ship was involved in the sinking of the *Hood*, then on 27 May, was itself sunk.

"At some distance, British ships were sighted. They were the *Hood* and the *Prince of Wales*, which was moving at an acute angle directly towards the *Bismarck*. The *Prince of Wales* and *Hood* opened fire shortly before 06.00 hrs. The first hit was in section 14 of machine room 4. The shot penetrated low in the outer armour, exploding in the secondary armour and in the torpedo bulkhead.

We received a second hit on the forecastle. Water poured into three whole sections, the leakage pump gave up after a short time, and electric and subsidiary circuits cut.

Then, soon after 06.00 hrs, came the third report that the *Bismarck* had hit HMS *Hood*. It had been blown up. It is easy to understand that a young crew was delighted to hear of its first victory over an enemy ship and we rejoiced. The general view in the Navy is that we fight ship against ship, not man against man.

We were bewildered as to why Admiral Lutjens had disengaged from the *Prince of Wales*. It was established later that this directive from the Admiral was, in fact, a mistake. Even from the British side, it was said later that it was our greatest error to let the *Prince of Wales* get away.

In the early hours of 27 May, I was replaced on my watch position and at about 08.45 hrs, they opened artillery fire on us – heavy fire. It also emerged that we had problems with fuel. During the night, we were told that from the German side, everything would be done so that the Luftwaffe could relieve us, and that tankers and destroyers were on their way to get us out of the combat zone. However, the Luftwaffe couldn't fly and the destroyers couldn't leave port with the wind speed at 15.

At 08.45 hrs, the heavy shelling began. The battle, which lasted for 45 minutes, consisted of direct artillery fire. Since it was impossible for us to manoeuvre the ship, we went round in a circle. The remaining turrets were only manned by us at this point 'out of respect for the enemy'. Then the order was given 'Blast open the sea-valves'. It was customary in the German Navy – if we hadn't, the British could have slung a hook over the *Bismarck* and towed her home.

I made my way from the front on to the deck where the living quarters were. What remained of the ship's crew, mostly technical staff, assembled in section 10. A number of men were ripped to pieces by isolated artillery shots or shells.

At first we thought the British were firing with gas explosives – but this wasn't the case. It was only smoke from the blasts. The first divisional officers were standing side by side – seconds later, they were blown to pieces.

The longest serving officers took over the command and ordered us to leave the ship by the shortest route. This was difficult, due to the collapse of the whole superstructure. In the area around the turret Bruno we found a way down and prised open a gap in the armour plating. From there we got to the upper deck. I managed to get myself to safety on the starboard by the turrets, to wait and see what would happen. The upper deck was smashed to pieces – a mass of rubble. After a while, the *Bismarck* keeled over to port.

We had civilians on aboard, about 25 of them. One of them leapt down from the rail and broke his neck. To be quite honest, I was too much of a coward to jump. Perhaps, you might say, cowardice paid off.

The water temperature was 9°C – I threw all my combat gear overboard, took off my sea boots and then jumped into the water. After about 75 minutes I managed to reach HMS *Dorsetshire*, where sailors attempted to rescue as many of us as possible.

One of them stays in my memory – Midshipman Brooks. Despite being ordered against it, he let himself down on a hawser to help an armless German sailor. Later I found out that Brooks was punished for this.

On the *Dorsetshire* we were treated as equals, as if we were rescued British sailors. It was a case of 'you today – us tomorrow'. A comrade of mine from the recruits company had already reached the *Dorsetshire*, but because oil had got into his wounds, he died. A day later, he was buried with every military honour."

Balkan Battlefront – Captors and Captives

Greece Crete

*G*reece – the cradle of Western civilisation – was to witness some of the bloodiest fighting of the entire war as the Axis powers strove for supremacy over the Balkan states and the strategic island of Crete. Troops from Britain, the Commonwealth, Germany and Italy flooded into this fierce battle zone by air, sea and land. For some the memories would be of bitter fighting. For others this was eclipsed by recollections of imprisonment which lasted for the rest of the war.

Gerhard Schirmer, age 28, was a Captain in the 2nd Battalion of Paratroop Regiment 2, and was one of the thousands of German soldiers who dropped on to the island of Crete as part of Operation Mercury.

"General Student had a tactical plan. He wanted to build five *Riegel* [locking positions] – one at the airfield at Maleme, which would involve capturing the airfield at the same time (which we needed as a base for reinforcements), one near Canea at Suda Bay, one at Retimo, and one each to the east and west of Heraklion. This last would involve capturing the airfield at Heraklion.

This plan was good, but reconnaissance had underestimated the strength of the English, Australians and New Zealanders. The English troops had camouflaged themselves splendidly and reconnaissance yielded very unsatisfactory results. Also, the English had unfortunately armed the Cretan population – who fought in their Cretan costumes, which was against every rule of war.

My battalion was to be assigned 48–50 Ju-52s. Well, the units which had been put in at Heraklion and Retimo assembled in the second wave at about midday. In the first wave in the early hours of 20 May, the units who had been deployed at Maleme and Canea were to jump. Because of the terrible problems with the dust on the airfields, the order of the units who were to jump was changed, and I was now the first.

I didn't get my eight aircraft as planned – only four. That meant I had to leave more than one complete company behind. This altered the whole plan of invasion. Before the start there was only a very short time to instruct the Company leaders and decide who would be left behind.

While I was doing this, running through my mind constantly was the foreboding – how could I carry out this mission without almost one and a half companies out of my four?

But, we were lucky – we were the first to jump in the area of Heraklion, and where we jumped there was hardly any defensive fire.

It wasn't long, however, before the first attacks came, principally from the New Zealand and Australian forces. The 3rd Battalion Paratroop Regiment 1 attacked the town of Heraklion, but the western edge of the town was magnificently defended by the English. There was an ancient 10 metre high town wall, in which there were few gates, and it was impossible to get in. The Battalion had to withdraw. Next day Major Schulz and I took one company from my already very tiny front and attacked Heraklion again. This time we succeeded in getting into the town along the coast. But the counterfire was so heavy that we had to pull our forces back again – it was impossible to reach the airfield.

Very heavy fighting ensued. The English attacked – we counterattacked. It was a period of uninterrupted fighting. We'd planned to bring in a mountain regiment to Maleme from Greece and from the Peloponnese, using boats – little boats, fishing boats, in fact, since there were no other ships available. This little fleet did set off, about a hundred of them, but the English Eastern Mediterranean fleet got between them and the land, and the mass of these boats were sunk. Italian cruisers and destroyers were to provide protection for these boats, but once the English fleet arrived, they turned tail and headed back to Italy. So, no mountain regiment – which was meant to pick up paratroopers and bolster the attack. No, we had to carry on alone in Heraklion. That was an unbelievably difficult situation, especially as the losses were very high.

We had a stroke of luck. A rather weak battalion of paratroopers was dropped into my position on 25 May. This battalion had been cobbled together by General Student in Greece from subsidiary people from the individual units, functionaries etc. This was a significant reinforcement. Once again, I sat down with Major Schulz, Commander of the 1st Battalion Paratroop Regiment – we had to decide what was to be done. We had to carry on. We advanced with the two battalions in a row, one man behind the other, keeping the old front line only thinly occupied.

We marched off, headed south, right up to the edge of the mountains, and then bore left, heading east. We passed south of Knossos to reach the Lion Mountain, just south of the airfield of Heraklion. We wanted to take this. The English still held it, though somewhat feebly now. We took this mountain on, I think, 28 or 29 May, and then the next day we wanted to attack the airfield from this mountain, that is, from the south, but once this attack was finished, there was no resistance at all – the English had all boarded ships, again near Heraklion, or others had gone off in lorries to the south of the island to Petra, and had boarded ship there. They were gone, and we had the airfield, but with absolutely our last ounce of strength.

When we had taken Lion Mountain, there was a little Arabian Chapel up on the top, painted white. I got in there and lay down, gave over command of my battalion to a Company Leader. For the first time in days, four days, I think, I could get some sleep. I slept for quite a number of hours and eventually, when they woke me, they told me that the English Fleet had been firing its 280 mm guns at the mountain and the hits from the shells were less than 50 metres from the little chapel. I heard absolutely nothing. That shows how battle-weary we all were.

It was a hard fight, but we knew whenever you fought against the English, it was a fair fight. We were able, and this happened in Crete also, to send over envoys and agree on a ceasefire of, say an hour, so that both sides could retrieve their wounded, put them under cover and see that they were looked after. Anything like this was unthinkable in the fight against the Russians."

Walter Wachter, Oberfeldwebel (Flight Sergeant), flew a glider during the German invasion of Crete. Despite his own spectacular valour, for which he was awarded the Iron Cross, 1st and 2nd class, the invasion was more tricky than had been planned.

"On 20 May 1941 we were on the extreme edge at the rear of the airfield just outside Athens. The DFS-230 gliders were assembled and ready to start, and it was still night.

The towing aircraft for the first *Kette* (a formation of three planes flying side by side) were rolling in front of me. Time to take off.

A huge red cloud of dust hung over the airfield. Within 15 minutes my *Kette* was all set to go with a crew of eight paratroopers. The Ju's rolled forward. The rope was secured and the dust had not yet settled when the signal came to start.

The overloaded glider rumbled along clumsily behind the towing aircraft and wouldn't leave the ground. Slowly we were pulled into the air.

Everyone was lost in his own thoughts. We flew past the Peloponnese – the open sea lay before us. We had now reached our unhooking height. It was a peaceful flight in the first light of dawn. Suddenly, the towing aircraft to our right drew ahead of us trailing a rope, but no glider. We now had 20 men: too few.

We could see a lot of mushroom-shaped smoke clouds – the bombers were at work, preparing the ground for the Luftwaffe. There were smoke clouds coming from the AA guns.

This was entirely different from the operation over the Corinth Canal. There we flew in secretly and without bombardment – we flew in the early hours of the morning and the English knew nothing about it. It's impossible to compare the Crete attack with the earlier operation. Of course, we were not told that the attack on Crete from the air would probably yield enormous casualties, but we all felt it – sensed it. It couldn't be otherwise, to attack so large a target only from the air with no back-up.

At intervals I could make out the lie of the land between the smoke clouds – it was bloody narrow and steeply inclined. A few bushes and trees and hedges were blocking the landing area. We were soon very close to the landing point, but too high. On the left of our landing site was a dry stream bed running north to the beach. We had to move very swiftly – we couldn't present any target for the AA guns. Everything was happening so fast now. After a few manoeuvres, there was the ground before me. Apparently no machine guns. Then they opened up.

They rattled out as we were a few feet from the ground, but there were not only hedges – there were terraces with hedges on top of them. We flew across them and away, almost touching down – one, two, three terraces – then smash, we landed in a bush.

The left wing struck a tree and broke off. The glider rocked and stayed still. The crew were unscathed – we all climbed out.

The second glider hadn't done so well – it smashed into one of the terraces and went head over tail. The crew were injured – now we had only ten good men out of 30. The Battle Group was ready in a very short time, but we were soon hit with heavy defensive fire and I was wounded – and, as in the paratroopers' song, for eight of my comrades 'the sun would never laugh again'."

Karl Eisenfeller, in his own words 'a simple riflemen', was with a German Paratroop Regiment, and was only 19 years old when he saw his first war action in the invasion of Crete.

"I set off, leaving everything behind which might slow down my movements. Without my steel helmet and armed only with a pistol, I got to the road at the entrance to the village without hindrance. Just as I was about to leave the road, I saw two dead comrades lying before me in a huge pool of blood – obviously dead. In spite of my terror, I tried to identify them – it wasn't the two I'd been sent to retrieve. The other two must still be in this house. I'd much sooner have turned tail, but I tried to think of another way of getting to the house. It was at the edge of the village, so I tried to reach it across the open land. I had to pass another house and I saw a woman there, washing clothes. She was terrified when she caught sight of me. She began to scream – and that was the last thing I needed, so I shoved my pistol back into my pocket demonstratively, to show I would do her no harm. She calmed down, so I carried on towards the house. A crowd of young men was there when I arrived, but my comrades had all gone.

When I asked them a question, I mentioned something about how high up we were. I got some water and tried on no account to show my fear. I picked up a swastika flag which we used to mark lines, and despite their protests, wrapped it around me and went off in the direction of our positions, expecting at any moment to be shot in the back. Luckily they only shot when I was quite a way down the road and they missed. I found good cover in a little stream which ran through this valley, then headed off to the right climbing up into the hills.

I met a comrade who wanted to get water from the stream. He told me about a group of soldiers – he thought they must have been British, and if I carried on, I'd run straight into them. After a while we threw a few hand grenades in the direction of the noises, but it was probably too late, for the next instant a machine gun fired at us at what seemed to be point-blank range. While my comrade could easily disappear under cover in the terrain and soon get back to our position, I made an error. I ran towards the hills, heading for a small sheep shed, which stood right against the hill. Between the shed and the hill there was a gap which I tried to reach. As I ran, I looked down and it was as if the earth was moving under me. My enemies had spotted me and shot off all their guns at me. When I reached my goal, I couldn't believe that I'd come through unscathed again. But then I thought 'Now I'm in a trap – and I might not get out'. There was another way in from the other side, and I felt that at any minute the enemy would come and mow me down. I didn't dare run through such fire again. They shot at the entrance, as if to remind me they'd not forgotten me. So I decided to wait until it was dark and to crawl out very quietly in the other direction. The way was now firmly imprinted in my mind, and I waited until it got really dark. It came off OK and in a short time I was being asked by one of our sentries for the password. I didn't know it, I'd been away the whole day. I called out 'Don't shoot – I'm Eisenfeller from 2 Company'. I could then walk forward with my hands up and they said 'My God, man, it is you.' "

Gino Decet was in a division of the Italian Alpini – mountain soldiers – when they were ordered to invade Greece through treacherous mountain terrain.

"On 10 October we set off for Albania, first going to Brindisi by train. Imagine 40 men and 20 mules, stuck in a train for hours on end. Not a lot of fun. From Brindisi we caught a boat for Porto San Giovanni. The boat couldn't actually dock here – there was not enough water, so what we did was to load the mules on to a smaller boat. By tying straps under their bellies and lowering them down into the boats, we finally got them ashore...

We knew of another aircraft, one of ours, which was based at Bera, or just below on the air-strip. There was one of our captains who went with this aircraft into Greece. Not long after he would return and within minutes we were being bombarded by Greek aircraft from all round. This happened on several occasions. Due to the terrain, not too much damage was done, although our ammunition dump was always in danger. A smart lieutenant became suspicious of this captain and one day followed him in his own aircraft. He noted that he landed at the Greek airfield. The lieutenant returned to base. On the arrival of the captain, all the commanding generals and officials were waiting, but unfortunately they didn't have time to question him, for as soon as he saw them approach, he realised that he'd been found out, drew his Beretta and shot himself.

Once we could hear the bombs dropping in the Verzeka valley. Anyway, we had a bridge to pass after which we knew there were some Greek supplies. Someone said to be careful, they could be poisoned. We crossed the river, got over the bridge, but through the water, in case of booby traps, and found some of these supplies. They were in boxes, about 30 × 40 cm in size. 'What have you found?' came the shout. I opened the boxes and one was full of grapes – the other full of cognac. '*Sacramento*', went up the cry – you can imagine the joy! Another box was full of beans and one full of salted sardines. Washed and eaten with nuts and beans, we had a nice meal, washed down with pints of cognac. You can imagine the state of us.

We advanced on the valley, bombs dropping all over. The lieutentant came up after a bit and said it was the Greeks firing into the valley – who would volunteer to find and destroy their gun? Twenty of us set off.

Slowly we circled round the other side of the valley – a 13-hour trek – and all of a sudden, there they were, having a whale of a time with these guns. There were two lots of them – anyway, we soon sorted them out. A few hand grenades and a shout of 'Up with your hands!' and the valley was quiet once again. It's amazing what courage a little drink can give you.

Still advancing, we reached a spot close to Ponto Peratti. We knew that there were Greeks here somewhere. One of our aircraft on reconnaissance came over and circled, not far ahead of us, and suddenly, from nowhere, Greeks started to stand up and put their arms in the air, obviously thinking they'd been spotted. Over 1,200 of them were taken prisoner. We found out that they were at their limits – no food, tired, fed up and demoralised."

Trooper Fred Veale, a Gloucester man, born and bred, was called up from the reserve to the Nottinghamshire Sherwood Rangers Yeomanry and sent to defend the island of Crete. Life was tolerable – until the German invasion.

"There we were, guarding this island. It was like going from home to home – you got treated like civilians. It was really quite nice!

The Eyeties made a raid. We captured them and put them in a prison camp – then we heard that the Germans were coming. We manned our six-inch guns – we had, and this is absolutely true, one aeroplane for spotting. We were told we'd have a lot of reinforcements…

The Eyeties had been in the camp for two or three days when the Germans came over. Not one parachute, not a hundred – thousands of parachutes came out of the sky like birds and landed on the island. They came along with all their tanks and just took us prisoner.

They put up in the camp where the Eyeties had been, then after a bit, they got us in groups of about 50, each with three or four guards.

We got treated like soldiers – they allowed us to go for water and so on. Later they rounded us all up again and they put us in cattle trucks – 50 or 60 to a truck. The further we got back, the worse we got treated. When they rounded us up, they took everything off us – watches, it didn't matter what you had – anything they could destroy, they destroyed and threw on the ground. There was this photo I had and this German, he couldn't speak English and I couldn't speak German, but I pointed to my wedding ring and indicated that the photo was of my little daughter – and he gave me that photo back again. One good German in a thousand!

On the journey, when there was an air raid, they stopped the truck on the railway, took the injured off and the guards ran off. We couldn't get away, anyway. They'd run off anywhere into shelter and if we got blown up, it was too bad.

When we got to the camp, Stalag 8B, we got put into a compound again, like sheep. We had escape committees, but we didn't know who they were – it could have been anyone."

Corporal Jack Gardner of the 1st Battalion Argyll and Sutherland Highlanders was taken prisoner on Crete and held in Germany until the end of the war. He remembers the Crete campaign as a terrible waste of time, men and money.

"My battalion was called out of the desert – Egypt – in May 1941. It was just a few days after my birthday. We were put on a ship called the *Glen Goyle* and landed on Crete in small landing craft. During the landing a lot of the landing craft were wrecked by the turbulent seas.

All we knew was that we were being sent to a place where we would see some action, but we didn't know the exact name or location. It was just a job to us regular army men.

We were marched inland overnight to take up position and we were then sent out in platoons. I was left behind as rear guard, over-looking an area near a house.

There were a lot of Stukas flying about. Then I saw the Germans going over in the Junkers. The troops below were more or less deci-mating the men that were jumping out. Some of them never came out of the aircraft because the aircraft had already been riddled with bullets, so they must have been dead or injured.

We soon realised that it was a very disjointed affair. There wasn't any cohesion in it because there wasn't any means of communica-tion. Communication was literally non-existent – it was guess-work. Where should the front be, when there were parachutists being dropped off in different parts of the island?

Most of us thought 'what the hell are we supposed to be doing?' It was totally chaotic. We were wandering about like lost souls in the night.

We had been on Crete for about four days before they tried to evac-uate us. We were waiting in the hills to be evacuated. We could hear the British destroyers at night, ramming the Germans who were coming to Crete from Greece. We didn't have much food because you couldn't get supplies. We were buying food off the Greeks.

We were captured when we were waiting to be evacuated. Somebody walked down and the Germans stopped him and sent him back with a message that the Germans had surrounded us. The senior officer decided that there was no point fighting, so ordered us to destroy every weapon that we had.

We were marched up to Heraklion. It took two days – you just kept going. I wasn't apprehensive because the Germans had taken prisoners before. Fear didn't enter our minds because they are civilised people. It had happened, and that was that. I don't think that there was a man on that march who was frightened either.

We had very little communication with the Germans during the march. They were told not to antagonise us because we were front-line soldiers, and the Germans had a lot of respect for front-line men. A German said to me that he didn't know why we were fighting each other.

We were held prisoner on Crete for four or five days in different places before we were taken to Greece. They kept us behind barbed-wire fences. You couldn't say the treatment was bad, because they didn't have much either. You got one meal a day, that was all, because they didn't have much food. When we were down at Suda, the Germans were using British stocks of food from the *York*. I was on a work party and a German asked me 'what's in this tin?'. There wasn't a label, but I guessed 'peaches' and it was. He gave me a tin, and I opened it up. They tasted good – it was the first tin of peaches I had had in over a year."

Barbarossa – Scorched Earth

*O*n June 22, 1941, Hitler launched his attack on the Soviet Union, codenamed Barbarossa. The odds seemed overwhelmingly against the Germans: with only 3,332 tanks, they were massively outnumbered by the Soviets' 24,000. But the initial Soviet resistance was ineffectual. As the German army rolled into the Soviet landmass, fighting huge battles of encirclement, it exacted a heavy toll. Of the 12 million soldiers the Red Army mustered for this extraordinary land battle, around a quarter were taken prisoner, while the Germans also captured around 15,000 tanks. Despite their own 800,000 casualties and the loss of the majority of their tanks, the Germans were convinced by the end of 1941 that the huge losses had broken the back of the Red Army. As the Reich's stormtroopers advanced, however, they found progress increasingly difficult. Poor roads turned from dust to thick mud; the retreating Red Army fought a strong rearguard action, and destroyed vital bridges and industrial sites in a scorched earth campaign that finally brought the Germans to a halt in the snow outside Moscow. Against the backdrop of the longest and most savage land battle ever fought in history, participants from both east and west tell of how they experienced the epic confrontation.

Konstantin Simonov, a Russian novelist and poet, was sent as a war correspondent to join a unit at the front. His train's progress was blocked, so he set out on foot with an artillery captain to hitch a lift and join up with his unit.

"German aircraft were circling the town. It was desperately hot and dusty. At the exit of the town, near the hospital, I saw the first corpses. Some were lying on stretchers, others without. I don't know where they came from – they were probably bomb victims.

Troops and vehicles were going along the road, some in one direction, some in the other. It was impossible to make sense of it all. Having discovered that the petrol filling point was 15 kilometres out of town, we went there, picking up a supplies officer and two or three soldiers on the way.

Everything was quiet at the filling point, although we had been told *en route* that the Germans were there. While we were filling the tank with buckets of petrol, the captain went to the commander of the point to explain something. Following behind him, I saw a strange sight; the captain with whom I was travelling and a colonel were pointing their pistols at two officers in sappers' uniforms, who had been disarmed. One of them wore medal ribbons. It turned out that they had been sent to discuss the possibility of demolishing the point, and either they had given the impression of already being on the point of destroying it, or there had been some kind of misunderstanding, but in any case, the captain and colonel took them for diversionists and for five minutes held them at pistol point. When it was all cleared up, one of the sappers, an elderly major with two decorations, began to shout that nothing like this had ever happened to him before, that he had been wounded three times in the Finnish campaign, and that after this insult, the only thing left was to shoot himself. It was quite difficult to calm him down."

Later in the day, Simonov and a military lawyer were in a wood along with some other officers. All around were Red Army men, confused by the sudden shock of the German attack. The officers banded these men together in companies and battalions.

"Half an hour after I arrived, the Germans discovered our assembly from the air and began to machine-gun the wood. Waves of aircraft flew, one after the other, at intervals of about 20 minutes. We lay down, pressing our heads against the gaunt trees. The trees were not very dense, so it was easy to shoot at us from the air. Nobody knew each other and with the best will in the world, it was difficult for people either to give or to take orders.

Finally, after three o'clock, a flight of IL-15s flew over. We jumped up, elated because our own planes had turned up at last. But they gave us a good shower of lead and several men nearby were wounded – all of them in the foot. They had been lying in a line.

We thought that this was an accident, a mistake, but the planes came back and went over the wood a second and a third time. The stars on their wings were clearly visible. When they went over for the third time, someone with a machine-gun managed to bring one of them down.

Quite a few people ran to the outskirts of the wood, where the plane was burning. Those who had gone there described how they dragged the half-burned body of a German pilot from the cockpit. I do not know how this came about. Probably the Germans in the first day captured several planes somewhere and showed their pilots how to fly them. In any case, it left a very depressing impression on us.

I walked to the edge of the wood, where the forest road joined the Minsk highway. Suddenly, five paces away, a soldier with a rifle jumped out on the highway. His eyes seemed to be crawling out of their sockets, and had an insane look about them as he shouted out in a strangled, tearing voice: 'Run! The Germans have surrounded us! We're finished!' One of the officers standing by me shouted, 'Shoot him, shoot that panicmonger'. He began to fire.

I also pulled out my pistol, which I had obtained just an hour before, and began to shoot at the fugitive. Now, later, I think that he was probably a man maddened, a psycho case, not having been able to stand the terrible events of that day.

Evidently we did not hit him, as he ran off further. A captain jumped out in his path and, trying to hold him, grasped his rifle. It went off and, frightened still more by this shot, the fugitive, like a hunted animal, turned round and with his bayonet, rushed at the captain. The latter took out his pistol and shot him. Three or four men silently dragged the body off the road."

Dmitrii Gavryushin, an infantry battalion commander, was amongst the many Russian troops cut off behind the advancing German front line, trapped by the sheer speed of their attack. His escape from captivity was to last an agonizing three months on the run.

"Having fought for 14 days without a break, I was bruised, but stayed in action. I was later wounded in the arm and hand. On 24 July I was put in the Mogilev hospital. On 26 July, the town was captured by the fascists and the hospital was not evacuated because it was encircled.

Another two days later I, and some soldiers from my battalion, fled from the hospital. We changed our clothes in someone's home and set off in the direction of our troops.

We went in the guise of civilian prisoners who had been working at the airport and had been wounded in the bombing. After five days, the fascists detained us at the front. We were held for three days, and then sent to one of the Smolensk hospitals.

Having spent three days there, and having carried out an appropriate intelligence appreciation, we ran away from this hospital and after 15 days, caught up with the front line near Shmakov, where they again detained us.

After five hungry days, they put us in a truck and sent us forwards. Catching up with a group of our prisoners of war, they put us out of the lorry, joined us to the column, and hurried us on. Hunger, and the pain of my wounds, stopped me keeping up with the fit ones, and I lagged behind, with the fascist escort all the time pushing me on with rifle-butt blows to my back. Having spent the night gathering our strength, we ran away in the morning. After several days, we reached the settlement of Stodolishche and bumped into our surgeon. We asked him to change our bandages. He uncovered our wounds and they were already gangrenous, with little worms crawling about."

Eberhard Wagemann led a platoon of 13 Company in Regiment 67 of the German 23 Infantry Division in the advance into Russia. Contrary to popular German belief, the Red Army turned out to be a formidable adversary.

"Returning to Regiment 67 in 1941, detailed to lead a platoon with the 13 Company, I would frequently go and see my contemporary from my training period, Ekkehard Maurer, who was then Adjutant to Captain Heinemann, Commander of III Batallion. He had gained a special respect from the members of the regiment because of his fearlessness, even towards leading party figures, his military prowess and soldierly bearing.

Once the news began to spread of the proposed Russian campaign, he left us in no doubt as to what he thought of it. 'This is the end for Germany' – still, he remained a soldier and a Commander, served his Fatherland and his comrades, and had no illusions about the prospects of this war. As a cadet schooled in Berlin in the Prussian tradition, he called it 'something I just damn well have to do'. All his life he remained a model for us.

We felt no sense of injustice towards the Soviet Union. We knew about the Party's monopoly of power and of Stalin's Terror. We were convinced we were superior to the Red Army, which had been weakened by Stalin's purges, and had hardly given a convincing account of itself in the war against Finland in 1940–41. But it was the great expanse of Russia we feared, in which even Napoleon had had to fight to the bitter end. We knew of the Russian soldier's courage and stamina.

The III Batallion had its first taste of this directly behind the frontier of Eastern Poland, which had been annexed by the Soviet Union in 1939. The garrison in the newly-built bunkers of Sklody defended them down to the last man. During the advance march we were confronted with the horrific effects of modern weapons of war, as we passed alongside mile-long columns of Russian tanks, which had been destroyed by our Stukas.

However, our batallion was soon to see the other side of the Russian soldiers during the attack on Brunitschi and Mogilew – their courage and military skill.

The attitude of the indigenous population towards us was one of cautious trepidation at first, but they became increasingly friendly. The people had clearly been fed horror stories about the German soldiers.

Particularly in White Russia, the old men, women and children welcomed us with bread and salt, and they would show us their crucifixes and icons, which they stashed away in 'God's holy corner'. As for provisions, there wasn't much for us to take – initially a bit of poultry, sometimes, though rarely, a calf or cow for the field kitchen, all of which we had to pay for, of course. So long as you continued to behave decently towards them, you could get along quite well with the Russian people.

However, the partisan warfare, which was just then starting up, had been prepared and orchestrated, as it were, at arms' length, by the Red Army and the Party. I had taken over 9 Company from the wounded 1st Lieutenant Petersen by the Desna. Following the battle of Wjasma, I had been ordered to 'clean out' an area of woodland with this company, after shots had been fired from there at our vehicles. As we got into the wood itself, we could see that the whole area was one large partisan camp, extended and occupied in peace-time. The paths had been covered over with camouflage netting – underground passageways linked bunkers and fighting positions, which were dug into and magnificently camouflaged in the overgrown forest floor. It was possible to mount an all-round defence of the area from the combat positions – the underground passages followed a path with various corners.

At first sight the wood looked deserted – however, as the first volunteer stepped on to a ramp, he was shot in the stomach. The operation had to be called off – Stukas were called for."

Martin Hirsch, age 28, was an NCO with the 3 Panzer Division 'Brandenburg', which advanced into Russia in summer 1941. He had fundamental disagreement with Nazi tenets, and eventually became a 'Verfassungsrichter' in Germany – one of the most senior-ranking constitutional judges.

"I was brought up in an actively democratic and republican family, and the schools I attended were run along the same principles, so that I was completely immune to the ideas of National Socialism. As a student I marched through the streets chanting, 'If you elect Hitler, you elect war. Smash the fascists wherever you find them'. Unfortunately, we were proved right, but it wasn't us that smashed the fascists – they were smashed by others, in the war, that is.

When I was first called up, I was passed unfit for military service on grounds of health, but when the war came along, the circumstances were not so favourable, and this time I was passed fit.

I was with the 3 Panzer Division 'Brandenburg', which was mobilised for Operation Barbarossa. My first recollection is of crossing the Bug in the direction of Brest-Litovsk – we were standing around waiting for orders, and there were, at that time, various rumours going round, quite absurd now, looking back on them. Rumours like, there would be no war in the east as such, instead the British would go in with us to encircle the Russians and liberate the world from Communism. This was obviously rubbish, but that was the kind of rumour that was usual then.

The first heavy barrage from the Russians that I experienced was during the advance on Brest-Litovsk. We had crossed the Bug and camped down. On the advance into Brest-Litovsk I got my first taste of the horror to come. There was a huge field full of corpses and wounded Russian soldiers. These had, I think, been hit by the advance bombing by the Luftwaffe. One Russian soldier was bleeding heavily and I tried to bind his wounds, when suddenly a soldier from another unit, whom I didn't know, came over to me: 'What are you doing here?' he asked. I told him I was bandaging a soldier. He said it was not my job to look after these 'Untermenschen' – he did actually use this word – but I remembered from my training that our instructions were that a wounded enemy soldier was no longer an enemy, and it was our duty to help.

He told me he would report me, but I never heard anything more from him. He struck me as quite a callous Nazi, and I was pleased that I never caught sight of him again.

The war went on, and my memory of the individual experiences is not very clear. My major preoccupation throughout the whole of the Russian campaign was to ensure that I would not be promoted to an officer.

There were others who felt like me, but we were a minority, and any actual meaningful resistance in such a theatre of war was impossible. Had I been at the Western Front, I'd have tried to go over to the other side.

What I remember of the daily routine of the early part of the war is mainly the sheer tedium of it all.

I remember sleeping in bedclothes thick with dust, dirt, cockroaches and lice which plagued the motorised units – I was then with the artillery – for whom, it was said, conditions were relatively good.

My worst experience during the initial advance was in August of 1941. The unit was based in a village – I can't remember which, and we were hit by heavy bombing from the Russians. We were in our quarters, and some of the men were sitting around a table. We could hear the whistling of the bombs which seemed to be quite a distance away. Then the noise was more high-pitched ... the bombs were dropping closer. I dived under the table. All the people who had been sitting at the table were killed in this attack, one had his head ripped to pieces. I don't know how I came through."

Alex Vanags Baginskis was a young teenager when Germany invaded Latvia. He recalls the people's delight at being freed from the existing oppressive Communist regime, and their subsequent disillusionment.

"I was living in Riga, the capital of Latvia, with my mother when the Soviets invaded. We woke up one morning – June 17 1940, and the tanks were in the streets. I was thirteen years old and very intrigued I looked at the tanks and the soldiers – they were scruffy, their uniforms didn't look nice and they were all armed. At the beginning, they said that nothing would change – but it did.

I remember very clearly reading in a Soviet paper in April 1941, a little, insignificant notice about German troops going through Finland. They were just passing through Finland to Norway. I was good at geography, and I wondered to myself...

People were hoping that the Germans would come. They are our historical enemies. They arrived with the Bible and the sword in the 12/13th century and subdued our people, forcing Christianity on with them. They ruled us until World War I, but even the Germans would be better than the Russians.

Early in 1941, the Soviets suddenly started increasing the number of troops in Latvia. Artillery moved through at night, the horses' hooves wrapped in rags. We couldn't hear them, but we could see them.

In spring 1941 the Russians suddenly wanted to build 80 or 90 airfields in Latvia. Most of them were bomber airfields – and you don't build bomber airfields for defence – they were planning something.

In June 1941, whispers started going around that the Soviets would deport people. These people were described by the Soviets as 'socially dangerous elements'. One night, over 35,000 people, out of a population of about 1,600,000, were deported. Quite a number were shot as well. You can imagine the shock of going to visit my uncle next morning to find the whole house empty.

A number of people, including my mother, took to the woods to stay with a family who lived near a farm. There were about 30 or 40 people living there with us in the woods.

About a week later, the war began. Suddenly, early one morning, the German aircraft arrived over Riga. We were up on the roof, binoculars in hand, watching the dive-bombers and the anti-aircraft guns firing. The Germans didn't bomb the town – they bombed gas tanks, oil tanks.

Within two days, the Red Army was retreating. Single German aircraft would fly over in the evening dusk and fire on the road. You could see the tracers. Once I saw a Soviet fighter take off, trying to catch a German plane. His aircraft was shot and exploded in the woods.

We returned to Riga a couple of days after the Germans arrived. A home guard and scout groups were organised. I was a scout. There was still some hard fighting to do – there was a lot of street fighting in Riga old town with the remaining Soviet troops or local communist militia.

There were burnt-out tanks with skeletons inside which had sunk into the pavements and we couldn't move them. They remained for a long, long, time. There were lots of things for kids to do – aircraft and tanks to look at. I remember going to a Soviet airfield with fighters lined up there. The Germans didn't want the aircraft and there were boys there with screw-drivers, taking everything apart. You could find ammunition, machine guns, rifles – I had a whole arsenal!

At first everything was very patriotic – it was a feeling of relief. We all, even us kids, thought 'We're free now'. The Latvian flag was everywhere. The honeymoon lasted for two or three months, before the German Party people came and that was it. The national front was forbidden, national patriotic songs were forbidden, our anthem was forbidden. We were an occupied country again."

Moscow – A Merciless Fight

---

*O*n 2 October 1941, the German Army Group Centre launched Operation Typhoon, the drive to capture the Soviet capital Moscow. By the 20th, the Panzer spearheads had advanced to barely 40 miles (64.5 km) from the city, where they came to a halt. Fuel was running short, the harsh Russian winter was beginning to bite, and a new Soviet commander, General Georgi Zhukov, had arrived in the city to organise its defence. Zhukov massed all available aircraft to protect the city as he waited for reinforcements and for the weather to worsen. The last-ditch defence succeeded: between November 16 and December 5, the Germans had lost some 85,000 men. The weather had worsened: as temperatures plunged to $-40\,°C$, the Germans began to fall back. Not having entered Russia equipped for a winter battle, their troops suffered badly. As his ambitions for taking the Soviet capital vanished, Hitler ordered his armies to stand and fight, relieving 35 generals of their commands and appointing himself Commander in Chief of the Army. His troops finally fell back to a line between Vyazma and Rzhev, which they held until March 1943. Zhukov had saved Moscow and turned back the German tide – but at the cost of 500,000 men. War on the eastern front was a savage, brutal affair on a scale never before conceived. Both German and Soviet fighters recall their terrible ordeal.

M E Katukov, commander of the Russian 1st Guards Tank Brigade, consisting of the excellent new T-34 tanks and some of the not-so-new KV and BT types, was intent on hampering the progress of the German troops as they launched their second attempt to take Moscow on November 16, 1941.

"The enemy was tearing towards Yazvishche village in order to cut off the Volokolamsk highway. The defence there consisted of a battalion of frontier guards, commanded by Samoilenko, two tanks in ambush, Afonin's and Leshchishin's, and two batteries of the anti-aircraft division, commanded by Afanesenko. Samoilenko reported that German tanks were approaching, and the reply came, 'Use the ambush and smash them.'

The Hitlerites tried to surround Samoilenko's battalion. Four of their tanks crawled along the highway, but were set on fire by Afonin and Leshchishin. But behind them came six more tanks and a line of Hitlerite infantry amounting to a battalion.

The frontier guards could not withstand this enemy pressure and made a fighting retreat to the village of Gryadi. Afonin and Leshchishin knocked out two more tanks and, striking the Hitlerite flank, began to crush the infantry. Some Hitlerites succeeded in climbing on to Afonin's tank from the rear and shouted, 'Russians, surrender!'.

Having seen this, Leshchishin used his machine gun to clean the enemy off his friend's tank. At the same time, Afonin saw that the Hitlerites were similarly crawling on top of Leshchishin's tank and knocked them off with his machine-gun.

Our brigade was given two armoured trains, which bombarded enemy concentrations near Lystsovo. At this same time, about 30 enemy bombers attacked the station at Chismen and damaged the track.

Although no bombs hit the armoured trains, their gun platforms were put at a slant, so that the muzzles pointed into the ground. We allocated repair squads to help, but then the enemy intensified his attack. The battalion of frontier guards again went into action and our two anti-aircraft batteries fired at the enemy tanks and infantry, succeeding in beating off the attack. Soon the railway track was repaired and the armoured trains were once more fit for battle."

Commander of the Russian 2nd Guards Cavalry Corps, I A Iliev, described a successful operation conducted by the Red Cavalry against the German troops as they advanced towards Moscow.

"At 3 o'clock all the detachments were to concentrate in a wood south of Lake Velisto, and all the commanders were to report their decisions within an hour. My voice was drowned by the roar of enemy aircraft, flying low over the wood. 'They're looking for us', observed Revin.

'We've really got them worried if they've put so many aircraft up', I heard Dovator say from behind me, as he jumped off his horse, adjusted his sword and pistol and came up to us.

The intelligence officer reported that an enemy motorised column of infantry and artillery was moving along the road from Nikulin and would cross our path. 'What does this mean? Is it a planned regrouping or is it …? No, if they were coming after us, they would be in battle deployment by now.' We instantly decided to destroy them.

I give the order to move off. Liaison officers hurry off to their units. Our movement slows down, the units tense. We stop, with the road in front of us. We can hear the sound of motors, and the German commands. I look at my watch, whose luminous hands show that it is twenty minutes to midnight. The attack signal.

Grenades explode. The babel of mixed rifle and machine gun fire. The roar of motors. Like a thousand black ghosts tearing out of the night, we rush out sowing terror and death.

It's soon over. The cavalry dissolve once more in the thick mist of the wood. All that can be heard is the dull clink of harnesses, the excited breathing of horses and the occasional Cossack voice."

M A Zashibalov, commander of the Russian 60th Infantry Division of the 23rd Reserve Army Group, recalls the part his troops played in the defence of Moscow after a speedy training as a division of the 'Peoples' Reinforcement' – a kind of rapidly recruited citizens' army.

"The enemy, having broken through the front in the Kaluga area, began to mount an offensive against Tarusa and Serpukhov. The 49th Army HQ did not have enough reserves to defend these towns and an operational 'gateway' 30–40 km wide began to form, undefended either by troops or defence obstacles.

Luckily for us, the German-fascist command was so drunk with success that it did not always carry out a proper tactical or operational reconnaissance, and therefore it had no idea of the favourable situation which was developing in this sector.

The Military Council of the Western Army Group decided that the 60th Division should be immediately transferred to the 49th Army, and by forced marches, the division moved to the Tarusa area, where its units occupied the 30–40 km sector of the defence line and busied themselves with filling the breach that was forming, so as to bar the enemy's route to Serpukhov.

With such a length to be defended, our density on the ground was not, of course, very great. We had one soldier for every 100–150 metres of front, and one heavy machine-gun for every three kilometres."

As Germany continued to push through towards Moscow on land, Flight Sergeant Alfred Sticht, Observer in a Heinkel 111 of Kampfgeschwader 53 Legion Condor, was flying in to make the first bombing attack on Moscow.

"It is a Sunday afternoon – the crews are in their tents and the sun is blazing down on the Russian soil. We will be going in from the airfield at Minsk-Dubinskaya. Nobody moves from his tent – heat, dust and mosquitoes are our constant companions.

Our truck driver, Feldwebel Panizzi and Unteroffizier Methner have been standing at the same water pump for three hours, waiting in vain for a few precious drops. We have no choice but to wait.

In spite of everything, there is a solemn quiet in our 'tent city'. The Group Commander, Oberst Leutnant Kaufmann, comes to see the flying crews in the afternoon and tells us that we will most likely be starting another raid today. My crew is sitting pensively in their tent; perhaps one or two of them are thinking of their loved ones and home. There is a request show on the radio, the one link between the front and home.

Our youngest crew member, Martin Lehner, Unteroffizier and gunner, is just writing to his mother in Vienna, telling her he'll soon be home on leave as the Unteroffizier vom Dienst announces standby III. Now there's a real commotion in the tents. The crews are getting all their equipment together. Parachutes can be seen, flying suits, helmets, maps, navigation equipment, fur boots, high-altitude breathing apparatus, and pistols strapped to belt buckles, for any emergency, particularly in case you get shot down and have to make your way through enemy territory in the dead of night. There's a more serious look on the men's faces. I look at the map and plot the flight path.

Ten minutes later, the UvD announces Standby II. We're off in about half an hour.

Once our princely meal is over, the Staffelkapitän, Hauptmann Allmendinger returns from the combat position and calls in the crews for a meeting. We get orders – night attack with strong forces on Moscow.

Heavily loaded, our Heinkel 111 A1 + AB tears over the runway into the twilight. We fly over the radio beacon on the airfield and head off on a course east. We leave Smolensk behind us. We are flying along the taxiway leading to Moscow. We pass Vyasma. Our target is the large airfield of Moscow and the nearby aircraft factory.

Our crew is one of the longest-standing of the Squadron 53 – we've done about 200 raids together. Our experience at the front has given us a certain sense of security. Nevertheless, it's a mixture of extreme alertness, conscientiousness and a large amount of solidierly luck that lets you carry out your mission.

The sun is setting. We've crossed the front – below us enemy territory. Our cannons and machine gun positions are manned, weapons are primed and ready to fire. We've passed Gschazk. Before us, shrouded in darkness, Moscow. The glare of searchlights pierces our eyes.

The altimeter reads 1,200 metres. There is little in the way of flak. The first flashes of searchlights on the run-in to Moscow – their startled fingers grope the night sky.

The searchlights have yet to pick us out. More and more flash out, the closer we get to Moscow. I can see the runway below, threading through the landscape of Moscow. I can count 50 to 100 searchlights. Pray that all goes well. Still no sound from the flak. We were told at the stand-by meeting to expect little in the way of flak. Nevertheless, the mass of searchlights is beginning to disturb me. We are climbing cautiously, at 2 metres per second. Look! What's that ahead? Another machine is caught in the brilliant glare of a searchlight. In a flash, several other searchlights pounce on the aircraft. I can see through the telescope it's a Heinkel 111 – it's one of ours. He's making frantic attempts to escape the clutches of the searchlight – in vain.

Our strategy is to pull the stick in and climb as fast as possible. Five more machines are caught in the innumerable swarm of searchlights. Meanwhile, we've climbed to 1,700 metres and have reached the outskirts of Moscow.

A searchlight grazes us, then loses us, but it's soon back again – and this time it catches us. We quickly put on our safety goggles and start to turn. Ordinary manoeuvres cannot shake it off. The glare of more than 30 searchlights fix on us. The flak fires from every barrel. Shells go off all around us.

There's a huge bang, then a flash of fire. Our machine is shaking – we've been hit. I prime the bombs and pull the emergency cord. There's a giant column of fire below us. We turn off towards the south-west. The altitude gauge shows that we're descending at 10 metres per second. The flight meter climbs to 500 kph. The engines are screaming. 'Is anyone wounded?' Everybody reports they're OK.

Meanwhile, we've dived down to 300 metres and we're roaring through the Metropolis of the East. The searchlights have lost us, we've left the environs of Moscow behind and are heading on a southerly course. Five minutes later we turn off and head course west. Sluggishly, our valiant wounded bird makes its way. There's hardly a word spoken and everyone is thinking the same – will the engines hold out?

They're still turning flat out and are not dropping many revs. The pilot checks the control panel every second. We breathe a sigh of relief when we reach the front. After five hours in the air, we land, battle-worn but intact, in Minsk-Dubinskaya."

From the cover of a *Schutzstellung* (protection position), Hauptsturmführer Dr Med. Windisch of the Small Divisional Command Staff SS Division 'Reich', watched as the battle unfolded around Moscow.

"It was afternoon and we were standing beside the Magistrale, protected by the woods, observing the enemy, who were circling around in tanks on the other side. A battery of 8.8 Flak had been put in position and was firing on the Russian tanks. Our grenadiers from the Regiment 'Deutschland' had broken through into the enemy's network of positions north of the Magistrale and were pushing on further, in a bitter struggle with huge losses.

Meanwhile, the 'firework display' began. I had never seen anything quite like it. We were standing on the hill, with three generals beside us, watching anxiously the movements of our own troops and those of the enemy.

Suddenly I heard the unmistakable noise of the Russian rocket shells, the so-called 'Stalin's organs'. They were definitely meant for us, for everybody disappeared suddenly into cover holes. Since I hadn't dug one myself, I couldn't disappear without leaving a trace. So I quickly threw myself behind a tree and watched the terrifyingly beautiful display of rocket shells crashing down. I will never forget the sinister black, red and violet flare from the shells.

The whole area, the air all around was full of the explosions of shells crashing down. Suddenly behind us all hell broke loose. I hadn't a clue what was going on there, and ran to my friend Mix, the Ic (third General Staff Officer) of the Division, who lay under cover, not far from me. He laughed and answered, 'That's our multiple rocket launchers!'.

You should have heard this terrible ear-shattering scream. It mixed in with the bangs of the Russian shells hitting, there was a whistling, a drone, a hissing and roaring from the firing and hits of the artillery, from machine-guns, mortars and multiple rocket launchers. The effect of the latter on the enemy must have been devastating. The battles lasted all through the night. The effects of our launchers had been a decisive influence on the battle."

Unterscharführer Streng with the SS (equivalent to the rank of lieutenant) was part of the Germen attack on Moscow which took place on 2 December 1941.

"We could only advance step by step towards our final destination – Moscow. Fierce cold all around us – and all this with poor accommodation and insufficient food for the fighting troops. The supply problems were getting worse all the time. These were the main causes of our crisis – without these problems, we would have been much nearer our destination.

Nevertheless, the troops forced through, advance after advance, with superhuman effort, and fought themselves through all kinds of adversity with incredible patience.

Many of the soldiers had managed to steal Russian overcoats and fur hats and were hardly recognisable as Germans any more. All our winter clothing had been infested with lice and was impossible to wear. To keep the engines running, we had to light fires underneath the sumps. Some of the fuel had frozen, the engine oil had thickened and we had no glysanthine to prevent the drinking water from freezing.

The already dwindling fighting strength of the units was depleted further as more and more men were picked off by the cold. The troops could not take on much more. The innumerable losses would completely destroy the fighting strength of the company.

Half-frozen German troops were fighting on in the merciless cold, which sometimes sank to below 45° below freezing, in their normal uniforms, their normal leather boots, no gloves, no overshoes, no scarves, facing a merciless winter.

With the Russian prisoners, things couldn't have been more different. They wore the best winter clothing you could imagine. Their winter uniforms were thickly lined with padding. They had felt boots, fur gloves and fur hats. To stop themselves from freezing the German soldiers took the precious winter clothing from the dead Russians.

Over the precincts of Moscow hung giant flash rockets like the stars of Venus, and tight packs of searchlight beams hurtled around the sky, went out again, then appeared, ghost-like, clawing the air again at other places, criss-crossing in giant packs of beams. Between them, the flashing pearl garlands of heavy Russian flak. The light trails from shells sent long threads of dark red and orange into the night sky.

Moscow roared, the loud thunder piercing the December night. Heavy German bomber squadrons attacked Moscow through the night from the air, bringing death and confusion to the centre of the enemy's power base. Along the contours of the distant hills, you could see the flash from the exploding rows of bombs, until half an hour later, the night became silent.

Moscow had opened the prisons and had armed the released prisoners. In the factories, workers' brigades had been assembled. Women and children were put in to dig trenches. Fresh Siberian troops were on their way. The streets of Moscow were filled with the Red Army, marching to the front."

Pearl Harbor – The Sword Descends

The Japanese war with China, which had been going on since 1937, had become a struggle of attrition, which the military government in Tokyo realised could only be won with additional resources. With France and Holland occupied by the Germans, and Britain at bay, the Japanese turned their attention to the now-vulnerable European colonies in South-east Asia, which were a potential source of oil, raw materials and food. The only serious threat in the area was the United States, which had forces in the Philippines and a major base at Pearl Harbor in Hawaii. On 7 December 1941, the Japanese launched a surprise attack on the US Navy and Army Air Force bases at Pearl Harbor, the objective has to leave US forces incapable of intercepting the Japanese invasion fleets en route to seize the Pacific islands and the Dutch and British colonies in the East Indies and Malaya. For all its ferocity, the attack failed to destroy the fuel storage bunkers and repair facilities at Pearl Harbor, and the Japanese aircraft were unable to locate those US carriers that were at sea on exercises. The chance to cripple the entire US fleet had gone – the carriers that survived would form the basis of the eventual American triumph against the Imperial Japanese Navy. The Japanese raid on Pearl Harbor was a major turning point in the war. For the attackers and for those who survived it would be the longest Sunday morning ever.

Mitsuo Fuchida, the commander of the Hawaii assault, led the *Akagi* Flying Corps into the fray. He recalls his part in the first wave which struck the US base.

"The enemy ack-ack was fierce. The nearer we got, the more it concentrated on the high-level bombers. The bombs sent filthy black smoke pouring up into the sky. Then a hail of bullets closed in on me. I looked down to see where it was coming from, and could see firing coming from the main fleet in Pearl Harbor, but also here and there there were flashes from the guns on shore, sparkling and glittering. 'The shore ack-ack's joined in' I thought. At that instant, the aircraft juddered, as if something had slammed against it. Lieutenant Mitsuo Matsuzaki, at the controls, yelled through the speaking-tube, 'Commander, have we been hit?' I didn't know, so turned round to look. The answer came from Mizuki in the seat behind, 'I think we've been hit aft by cannon fire – there's a big hole in the fuselage and one of the control cables has been cut. I'll try to mend it, but I don't think I can reach it'. 'Can you still fly her?' I asked Matsuzaki. 'Yes, we're OK' he said.

Closing in on our objective, it was tricky adjusting the course for the bombing run. It was time to drop now. I concentrated all my attention on the pathfinder's bombs. The instant it left his aircraft, I tugged at the release and dropped ours at the same time. Thinking we were out of range, I felt a sense of relief, then the shock of an explosion passed into me through the seat. The firing came closer. In one intense moment, I thought, 'Let the bombs go, quickly, now'. I glanced down, to one side. We were already into Pearl Harbor, and over Ford Island. Bits of broken cloud floated beneath us.

The pathfinder banked sharply to starboard, signalling, repeat, repeat. We were skimming over the streets of Honolulu, turning again into the bombing run. A patch of cloud had made us miss our aim at the very moment of release.

As the first squadron followed us again into a bombing run, there was a huge explosion close to our objective. A deep red flame burst up into the sky, followed by soaring dark smoke. Then white smoke, to a height of what looked like 3,000 feet. That must be the magazine! A shock like an earthquake went right through our formation and my aircraft shuddered with the force of it. It was the *Arizona* going up."

Kazuo Sakamaki was in command of a midget submarine in the Pearl Harbor attack. Hit by depth charges and with control problems, plans misfired badly.

"The compressed air and gas from the battery were leaking, and the air inside the submarine was becoming dangerously foul. We were very tired and weary.

It was near noon. We had not done anything. I was getting very restless. The two destroyers [patrolling the harbour] looked as if they were two big cats playing with a little mouse. I wanted to sink one of them with the last of my torpedoes – but my target was not such a tiny ship. I still wanted to get a big battleship – the flagship *Pennsylvania*.

Again, my ship hit a coral reef at the port entrance. Miraculously we got our ship afloat again. We lowered the ship deep and started investigating damage. We discovered a fatal injury to the torpedo dis-charging mechanism. No longer was the sole weapon at our disposal useful to us. My aide asked what we were going to do. 'The only thing we can do now is to plunge right into the *Pennsylvania*'. My aide knew that it meant our self-destruction as well.

I made up my mind to do just that – but the realisation that I had failed tortured my mind and bitter tears rolled down my face.

Although the ship had lost most of its power, I still had hopes of returning to fight. We tried to run the ship faster toward the island. White smoke shot up from the batteries. They had discharged all their electricity. There was danger that the batteries might explode – but we did not fear it. Death was in front of our very eyes.

At that moment, we hit a coral reef again. We immediately thought of the explosives we were carrying as a matter of self-destruction just in cases such as this. No matter what should happen, we could not let the midget submarine fall into enemy hands. The time to destroy the submarine had come. We had made up our minds."

[The self-destruct mechanism failed and Sakamaki was taken prisoner.]

Minoru Genda, on the staff of No 1 Air Fleet in Japan, was charged with the detailed planning of the Pearl Harbor raid – and solving the problems too.

"Fuchida was my class-mate, and Murata was a Shimbara man, a real hero. Murata was the top torpedo authority. He had been transferred to command the *Ryuga*'s Air Unit. However, when he was doing deck-landing exercises, I watched his landings and thought, 'Right, that settles it!' and I had him transferred to the command of the *Akagi*'s Air Squadron.

We were not convinced [about the use of torpedoes] but that was the time when all the senior officers were together – not one of them said it was impossible. Mind you, not one said he was certain we could bring it off.

There were unsolved problems with high-level bombing. It's unusual for carrier-borne aircraft to carry out high-level bombing against an enemy fleet on the high seas. Torpedo bombing is so much more effective. However, high-level bombing has its strong points. It simplifies a concentrated attack using a large number of planes – but its success rate is low.

However, something startling occurred. The aircraft-carrier *Akagi* was doing bombing exercises against a target moving away freely, from a height of around 9,000 feet. A formation of nine aircraft scored four hits. That's a success rate of 45%. And they did it three times running. If that could be maintained, it was far more effective than dive-bombing. So, I thought, if we can't use torpedo bombing, we can attack Pearl Harbor with high-level bombers. I was that confident."

Ruth L Lawson, wife of Captain Richard Lawson of the 19th Infantry Regiment, stationed in Hawaii, was at home with her daughter and mother when the Japanese struck Pearl Harbor.

"They came down with such screaming power dives that you felt surely they were going to crash. Then came loud explosions that made the walls of our stucco bungalow seem to push in and then be sucked out. We saw the Rising Sun on the planes, but still couldn't believe it.

I put Jeannie in the inside clothes closet with her clothes, told her to dress and not come out until someone came for her... the bullets and shell casings were hitting so continuously on our roof, it sounded like hail.

In the midst of the attack, someone pounded on our front door. With my heart in my mouth, I went to answer it, half expecting a Japanese soldier – but it was one of our soldiers in combat uniform. Just as he started to say something, one of the Japanese planes flew so low over the corner of our roof that I had a brief glimpse of the pilot's face. Bullets and shell casings spattered on our front walk, so close the young soldier jumped inside the door, almost knocking me down. He immediately straightened his helmet and, standing up straight said, 'As I was saying, lady, if you get dressed, I'll take you to a safer place'. It was only then that I realised I was still in my nightgown.

You think you feel very calm, at least, I did, but afterwards I realised my stomach must have dropped to my toes and my heart catapulted to my throat by the queer sensation inside, but fortunately that doesn't show on the outside. Everyone was remarkably calm and we had some good laughs afterwards at some of the silly things we did. I only saw two cases near hysteria.

That night all women and children were evacuated from Schofield by bus. It was raining and so black that I had to hold on to mother and Jeannie to keep from being separated. They used the buses belonging to the Honolulu Bus Service and several times the bright stars and a partial moon would emerge and seem to throw the whole scene into the focus of a spot light. Each felt in her heart that our buses were gleaming targets for the Japanese planes which were expected momentarily. No one can yet understand why they didn't come back and finish us off when they had knocked us to our knees. One shell exploded in a field to our left, violently shaking our bus and showering it with coral, rocks and dirt but not a person in our crowded bus said a word.

Jeannie, who was sitting on my lap, tightened her arms around my neck and hid her face in my shoulder. None of us knew where our husbands were, whether the Japs had succeeded in landing, where we were going, or where the next bomb would fall – but there was silence during that long ride. I have been convinced more than once since that Americans – women and children too – still 'Have what it takes'."

Lieutenant Commander Robert Lee Simpson was Radio Officer on board USS *Argonne*, when America was suddenly pitched headlong into war.

"I was in my cabin on the main deck, having previously been awakened by our mess boy. I had just put on my white uniform coat when I suddenly heard several terrific explosions which rocked the ship.

I grabbed my cap and dashed down the passageway for the main radio room, transmitting station aft. Some men only had time to put on their shorts and shoes in their mad rush to battle stations. The uniform for the day was white shorts and undershirts, which caused many sailors to suffer severe flash burns.

Six torpedo planes had already made their runs on the *California* directly opposite us. Great clouds of smoke poured from her hull as the torpedoes tore into the ship, tearing open huge holes in the side. The *California* sank slowly as the torpedoes entered her passageways, killing crew members as they abandoned ship.

Oklahoma, only a few yards astern of *California,* was hit by six more torpedo planes. The port side armour belt of heavy steel was torn off by the exploding torpedoes, exposing a large gaping hole about 200 feet long. The watertight compartments had not been closed. The water rushed in and she immediately capsized and went down with all hands within ten minutes. Her crew were caught like rats in a trap.

Cutting torches were used at first, but had to be abandoned because the trapped men were being cremated by the flames. Air drills were then used to gain entry into the double bottom compartments.

The navy department announced later that indications were found inside the ship that three men had lived for 16 days. They had consumed all their emergency rations and had marked a calendar with an X for each day from December 7th to December 23rd."

Ensign H D Davison was aboard the USS *Arizona* on 7 December, expecting a routine Sunday, when the first Japanese dive-bombers struck.

"It was just before colours, in fact, I had already sent the messenger down to make the 8 o'clock reports to the Captain. Then I heard a dive-bomber attack from overhead. I looked through my spyglass and saw the red dots on the wings. That made me wonder, but I still couldn't believe it until I saw some bombs falling. The first one hit up by the air station. I sounded the air raid alarm and notified the Captain. He and Lieutenant Commander Fuqua came on deck, and the Captain went on up to the bridge. About that time we took a bomb hit on the starboard side of the quarterdeck, just about abreast of Number 4 turret.

We grabbed the men available and started dropping the deck hatches and leading out hoses on the quarterdeck. Then the planes that had made the initial dive-bomb attack strafed the ship. Mr Fuqua and I told all hands to get in the marine compartment. It was reported to us that we had a bomb in the executive officer's office. Just after I stepped in the booth, we took another hit starboard of the quarterdeck, just about frame 88. The Boatswain's mate and I were trapped in the booth by the flames. We started out of the booth, trying to run through the flame aft on the quarterdeck. We couldn't get through, so we went over the lifeline into the water. I was conscious of the sweetish, sickening smell to the flame. After I got in the water, my first intention was to go the quay and then on to the quarterdeck or swim to the gangway and get aboard. But after I took one look at the ship, I decided that it was useless – she had settled down by the bow, and appeared broken in two. The foremast was toppled over – she was a mass of flames from the forecastle to just forward of turret 3."

Lieutenant Colonel H H Blackwell wrote to his wife from the United States Army base at Fort Shafter, Honolulu, Hawaii, after the lightning raid by the Japanese on Pearl Harbor. His letter was returned to him by the censors.

"I was rudely awakened just before 8 o'clock by the terrific noise of bombs and cannon... At first I thought it was dynamite blasting in a tunnel – but when I heard the whistling sound preceding the explosion on some of the closer ones, I jumped out of bed and ran to investigate.

When I got outside I was perfectly dumbfounded. Black columns of smoke were rising from Pearl Harbor Navy yard about three miles distant and the sky was filled with puffs of black smoke from AA shells. It looked like war, but I just could not believe that Japan could make an air attack from such a distance without our navy having some warning.

The attack caught both the army and navy completely by surprise. Being Sunday morning, most everyone was still in bed. Our AA guns were not in firing positions, but were parked at Shafter or other posts. We were on alert against sabotage, and in a condition of readiness which allowed three hours to go into action in case of attack. We had frequent drills on going out into battle positions and everyone had been trained thoroughly on just what to do (thoroughly should be qualified, however, since 80% of our troops have had less than eight months' service, and the organisation of the Brigade was not completed).

We had found that this took about three hours. However, as soon as we found out that this was the real thing, we cut the preparation time in half. Speed limits were ignored. Some units began firing within 45 minutes from the time they were alerted. All units began firing before the attack was ended, and we shot down four or five planes. The AA fire I first saw was from the Navy...

...The other day I saw three soldiers bringing in a suspected Japanese spy which they had caught under suspicious circumstances. The Jap was sullen and slow in following directions. One soldier was behind him with his bayonet pressing against his behind, and every now and then he would give it a slight push to speed him up. On either side was a soldier with a bayonet pressed against his ribs. Whenever they wished him to change direction, the bayonet was pressed into his off side, and he would immediately respond. He could not understand English, so the soldiers resorted to this method of directing him. From the expression on the faces of these soldiers, I could see that they would have liked to have used the bayonets more violently. They were exercising extreme self-control. You need have no fear of the fighting spirit of our soldiers."

The Fall of Singapore

At 2.00am local time on 8 December 1941 as US ships were blazing at Pearl Harbour, on the other side of the Pacific Basin, Japanese craft neared the palm-fringed beach of Kota Bahru, 400 miles to the north of Singapore – the British Empire's 'impregnable' fortress in the east. Defenders, attackers and stunned Singaporeans tell their stories of Japan's capture of Singapore.

Douglas Davis, an Engine Room Artificer, was on HMS *Repulse* off Singapore when, their position betrayed by a radio broadcast, they were attacked by Japanese aircraft.

"The Japanese attacked us with aircraft in a new style. Instead of coming in at a level where they could attack us and we could set our guns on them, they came in at various heights – it was impossible really for the gunners to decide where to fire.

Soon there was an explosion in the boiler room. It was something you couldn't understand – the place was dark, there was no shouting – nothing. The men must be dead.

I got through an air intake on the top deck, only to find that now I could only just about see with one eye. The other one had undoubtedly been burned.

I had no feelings of pain – the thing was that I felt all alone. I saw men mown down by aircraft coming in at sea level. I found myself flat on the deck, not knowing that I'd also been hit with bullets which had bounced off the deck.

I was given morphia – but it didn't work. Why, I'll never know, but it saved my life. I managed to get to my feet and leave the area to climb towards the upper decks. When I reached a porthole, it was at such an angle that it just let in daylight. There was no sign of any water, as it was at an angle of some 30°.

With help I managed to get on the outside of the side of the ship. I was pulling myself down towards the water. I had no lifebelt, and my ability to swim had gone – I just couldn't. Yet I hit the water by pushing myself down – and immediately I got into the water, everything went black.

I was pulled up by rope to the quarterdeck of a ship. It seems my clothing had been completely burned off – I was nude. On looking down, I could just see the tops of my shoes – the soles had been burned off. I was also severely burned and I had been wounded in the leg.

It was five bullets, according to the doctor. I was given another injection of morphia, and immediately it put me out until the moment I arrived at Singapore General Hospital. I was in a very bad condition. I believe I was unconscious for about three days. I had double pneumonia, and degrees of burns which were – I don't know, they used to number them off. I had lost all my fingernails and toenails. My ears had been burned off and my back, feet and legs were burned.

The nursing they gave us at the Singapore Hospital couldn't have been better, not even for the Royal Family. They were wonderful.

There were complications with my injuries due to the oil that had leaked out of the ship as it sank. It caused septic poisoning, and this had such an effect that the injuries could not be dealt with in the normal way. I found that my hands, legs and neck were being eaten away by maggots – the most horrible feeling.

They gnawed away until all the dead meat that had been burned in my hands, neck and legs was eaten. It took days and weeks for them to do their job, cleaning my hands, then finally the doctors took over and cleaned the maggots away so that they could introduce some skin grafting to cover the injuries. They did a remarkable job."

Sergeant William John Mondahl was with the 5th Field Regiment, Royal Artillery, attached to the 11th Indian Division, and fought desperately to reach the relative safety of Singapore.

"We fought all the way down to Singapore. We held certain spots for a certain time to get the infantry downwards, and then we would retire. We were under attack constantly. At times, we were surrounded and had to fight our way out with the infantry. We weren't trained for that type of warfare, whereas the Japanese were. They would send their men out into the wilds with a packet of rice and they would hang on for days.

At times it was frightening because we were being bombed from the air by Japanese aircraft. We had very little defence then from the air. I know that they had asked for a number of aircraft before the war started out, but they didn't get what they asked for. They did get some Spitfires out there, but we saw more Japanese planes than British.

We felt very isolated because even the lowest ranks knew that we would never hold out. We were going down country so quickly. On the way down we were told to burn things, so where we found a food warehouse, we would stock ourselves up and burn the rest so that the Japanese wouldn't have it.

We eventually got across the causeway into Singapore. We put up a good struggle there and we lost a lot of people. Those that died were buried there with a marked grave.

The causeway which we had come over was supposed to have been so badly damaged that the Japanese would never get over it. Our engineers had planted dynamite, but the Japanese soon overcame the problem and repaired it very quickly.

Once we were in Singapore proper, we dug trenches, put guns in the gun pits and that was our last stand. We were in action, with our backs to the water, overlooking the town. Raffles Hotel was just across the road.

Morale was not too good, although we didn't have as many casualties then as we did coming down country. We did our best, but after a while, when talks had gone ahead with the enemy, we were told to expend all ammunition. We did spike a few guns – in other words, we put a round up and a round down the muzzle, which breaks the barrel.

The men were exhausted – sleeping everywhere. The next morning we were taken over by the Japanese. We were assembled in Singapore and we had to march 15 or 20 miles to Changi jail."

Sid Walker joined the RAF in 1937 and, as a Corporal, found himself in charge of a radar team of highly technical staff operating top-secret equipment on the edge of the jungle outside Singapore.

"Once, when the whole of Malaya had been taken, we set up a unit of a receiver and transmitter on radar, and just opposite us,

about a mile away, was an army unit on top of a pineapple plantation. They came under us for admin and rations. When Salita was
taken, we were ordered to evacuate into the centre of Singapore,
so I got all the lorries – our unit was mobile – and we gave
instructions for the army to destroy all the equipment – the transmitter and receiver – and to assemble down on the main road
where we would supply transport to take them into Singapore
(they had no transport).

So they demolished the transmitter and receiver and when they
came down and assembled, one fellow was badly burned – a private.
We said we'd get him to a hospital. Anyway, when he was on the truck,
he called for me – he heard me ask the sergeant if everything had
been demolished – and heard him say 'Yes'.

This fellow turned round, all badly burned, and said 'I want a
word with your officer'. I asked him what was up – and said he
could talk to me. He told us then that the receiver hadn't been
destroyed – so I reported back to my officer. Everyone else was
assembling to get back into the middle of Singapore and the
officer said we'd better get off – and this was two or three hours
later, and we'd arranged for tins of petrol to be put in the back of
each truck.

I took one of these tins up to the site – and the transmitter
hadn't been destroyed. There were bayonets and rifles all stuck in
the ground – it was a complete shambles. It was dark and we went
to open this tin, which I had presumed to be petrol – and be
blowed, it was lubricating oil, which was no use to us at all. I remembered seeing some guncotton or something on top of this transmitter, and I thought, 'I wonder if it would blow up if you burn it'.
Anyway, the officer says 'Come on, we'll have to go down'. I said I
knew there was petrol in the wagon, but the fellow had gone and
got things messed up and put in lubricating oil. We went back to
our original site. We poured the petrol over the transmitter and set
fire to it – and up she went.

Just prior to this, there was a dog which the army had taken to and
fed, and I said to him that he should come with us. It was very wet –
raining like the Dickens. The dog went in front of us. We went
down this very narrow track through the pineapple plantation to
get to our vehicles, and I remember well, this dog suddenly started
growling. I instinctively fell back. I had a premonition that there
was somebody waiting for us. There were two Japs. We had a big

shoot up with Sten guns, then we ran like the clappers to reach our trucks. Finally we got to Singapore."

Seng Yong Ng was 25, a clerk in Singapore. With the threat of Japanese invasion ever-present, people with business dealings with the resident Japanese came in for reprisals.

"I think the anti-Japanese feeling started way back before the Pacific War, in 1937. The system was very cruel in a way, I would say – the anti-Japanese would cut off the ears of those who have connections with the Japanese. In one incident, two of these anti-Japanese people followed me up to the KPM Building – in those days, Mitsui occupied the fourth floor. When I entered the lift going up, I noticed the two youngsters followed me right up to Mitsui and waited for me at the main door. As I was coming out, they quickly entered the lift before me. Feeling a bit suspicious, I withdrew and entered Mitsui's office and went down by the staircase. I strongly suspected that those two were after me.

My first contact with the Japanese soldiers was the third day after the surrender. A sergeant came to the farm where I was evacuated. He asked me a question, and I was surprised that he spoke fairly good English. Later in the course of the conversation, I dared to ask him his occupation. He told me he was a magistrate in a lower court in Tokyo. He asked me, 'Do you know how we conquered Singapore?'. I shook my head. 'Our fighting spirit, our courage, our bravery – which the British completely lack…'.

The local population was very much afraid of the Japanese soldiers, particularly the Kempeitai, the military police. Their headquarters was the YMCA – in those days it was known as the Torture House.

I remember once, my brother-in-law was just a boy and he was hit by shrapnel. When the Japs came, he was pushed out of hospital and it took him about two weeks from GH, Outram Road, to get to Great World, which is only about say a mile or a mile and a half at the most. It was because of the Kim Seng Road Bridge, where the Japanese sentry was very strict – they didn't allow you to cross the bridge without a pass.

He was only 12 years old – and hadn't got a pass. The sentry was cruel, especially to a boy of that age. He asked him to carry a granite stone above his head for nearly two or three hours until he nearly fainted."

Wee Eng Tang, a clerk at the Singapore Dockyard, had admired the great ships of the British Navy from afar – until their sinking by Japanese air attack.

"'Britannia rules the waves' or so we were innocently taught. We used to sing all these songs in school – but when the Japanese came along, all the bubbles burst. When I heard the *Prince of Wales* and the *Repulse* had been sunk, I thought it was impossible. I was so proud of the *Prince of Wales* when I saw it – all the beautiful modern guns. We really under-rated the Japanese – that's the joke.

All our confidence in the British defences was shattered overnight. When we saw the headlines about the *Prince of Wales* I was shattered – morally, physically, mentally, all sorts. Without all that confidence, how could we fight?

There were sailors with oil splashed all over them, angry, tense, shouting and blaming the RAF, because they could not fight back against the waves and waves of kamikaze planes with their fantastic torpedoes. They came right up near the deck to drop their bombs. What chance had they got? That type of bombing had never been read about before in western books. They meant to sink that boat, the Japanese. They were dying for the Emperor, they sacrificed themselves for their chivalry – *Bushido*. It was fabulous, fantastic – the Japs really shocked the world, not only us – the whole world was shocked."

Kip Lin Lee, a Chinese student, was only 16 when the Japanese arrived and took control in Singapore.

"I saw some Australian soldiers coming down after the battle of Bukit Timah, hundreds of them. They were in a terrible state – torn shirts, torn trousers and wrapped in bandages – they were more or less retreating in disorder, as they would describe it in military terms. One soldier came knocking at the door. I opened it to see who it was, and there was this Australian who had a terrible-looking ulcer on his leg, asking us whether we had any medicine to apply to the wound. We took the tin of 'Zambuk' – the green ointment – and gave it to him. We asked him what it was like, and he was cursing the British all the time for not sending enough aeroplanes.

The first Japanese soldier I saw was coming in through the kampong after the surrender. They came, two of them, fully armed, fixed bayonets, fully camouflaged with a red arm-band, which we later learned was for military police.

They walked into the house and looked us over. To our great relief, they were friendly, smiling. They tried to make conversation and patted the little kids on the head. We said, 'Look, it's not so bad. They're quite friendly to us and to the children'. After that they came in droves, in groups of twos, fours and sixes – sometimes three groups in the house in the space of an hour."

General Sugita, an English-speaking Japanese officer, gives his account of the surrender discussions. Percival, however, never received a copy of the terms as finally agreed.

"When Yamashita took his seat opposite Percival he asked him if he had seen his terms which had been handed over to the peace envoy. Percival said he had, and was given a sheet of further details which Yamashita said he wanted carried out too. Concerned for the disturbances in Singapore City, Percival said he would like to keep 1,000 men under arms to protect non-combatants. Although Yamashita promised that non-combatants would be protected by the spirit of *Bushido*, Percival still argued for a force of 1,000 armed men. Yamashita replied, 'As the Japanese Army is continuing its assault on the city, an attack is likely to go forward tonight'. Percival asked if he would postpone the attack – 'The attack will go forward if we cannot reach an agreement'. As Percival was still asking for a force of armed British men to be permitted, Yamashita, sure he was boxing to gain time, grew irritated with the interpretation, banged his fist on the table and tried to make his own meaning clear with two words. 'The time for the night attack is drawing near. Is the British Army going to surrender or not? Answer YES OR NO! Percival replied, 'Yes, but I would like the retention of 1,000 armed men sanctioned.' The only answer was, 'Very well'.

After Singapore fell, it became received wisdom that the British Army had surrendered unconditionally, but the words 'unconditional surrender' do not occur either in the surrender document handed to the British or in the 'Items of treatment accompanying the surrender of the British forces'. Rather, it was announced that officers and men would be treated 'in the spirit of *Bushido*', as the document states. All the staff officers of 25 Army concerned were unanimous in refusing to acknowledge an unconditional surrender."

Lieutenant-Colonel Hōsaku Shimada, a regular tank officer, was in command, the spearhead of Lieutenant-General Matsui's 5th Division in its advance south to the Slim River.

"We burst straight into the town streets. Enemy trucks were parked here and there, with bored soldiers sitting yawning in the driving seats. Others, cheroots in their mouth, were fooling around with puppies, not knowing what else to do. The town was wrapped in an enormous stillness. After one second, this town out of a fairy tale turned from paradise into an inferno.

'FIRE!' The tanks tore into the town centre, aiming for a building from which the British flag was flying, hardly sparing a glance for the enemy troops falling on either side. Military vehicles were drawn up in front of the building. From a window, an officer poked his head out, an incredulous expression on his face. He stared at the tanks as they screeched to a stop. Heads peered out of windows, a dog began to bark.

Then the firing began. Shells smashed into the windows, shattering them into smithereens – the windows blew apart. The whole town shuddered as the gunfire went on, as if it had been struck by an earthquake.

The MGs were waiting for the soldiers as they came out. The shells smacked into oil drums stacked up beside the building. There was an explosion, then great gouts of flame. The fire spread to the single-storeyed houses behind, and more enemy troops streamed out of them. The MGs chattered and they fell. From inside the building too, an enemy officer hurled himself into the street. This one could really run. Then he too fell forward – bullets poured into him. Three other officers who came after him were shot as they came out on to the steps. The building seemed crammed with men. The guns kept up their fire. I looked out and selected new targets, but I could not see any more occupied buildings. 'Right. Let's go!', I shouted, 'Cease fire!'.

A puppy dashed out of one of the houses. It barked, turning towards the tanks which were heading out of the town, which looked as if a typhoon had swept through it.

An enemy which offers no resistance puts a damper on your fighting spirit, but the tank men were not concerned with this mood of mine, and the tanks stormed off once more. I watched them move off, silent. At times like these, I suddenly felt alone, as if I'd been left behind. I was overwhelmed by an unspeakable feeling of loneliness."

Hajimo Sudo was the Lieutenant-Commander leading a flight of landbased bombers of the Japanese No. 1 Air Fleet. He recalls the excitement of the attack on the *Repulse*.

"The command aircraft waggled its wings – 'All units attack!'. The time was exactly 1.48 pm. A host of shells burst in front of us. The whole plane shuddered. 'Calm down,' I said to myself, and tried to put some strength into my guts – but my body went stiff and I felt as if my insides were rising up into my gorge. 'This won't do,' I said to myself, to give myself courage, and felt better.

The white wave kicked up by the stern of *Repulse* suddenly seemed to expand. She was changing course! I turn to port, and my No. 3 which is just behind turns to port, while banking steeply. But it's only the second ship which is turning inward, the King George V class ship is turning outward. Right, I'll go for *Repulse*!

At this moment, heavy AA MG fire comes up at us as well as the AA shells and literally spatters the fuselage like rain. Star shells which seem to be weightless float up incessantly towards me. The plane backs and judders, but miraculously I'm not hit. If this AA hits me, I can still fix my target before going down. My fish will do 10,000 metres, and there's a high probability of scoring a hit.

In this instant of attacking the enemy ship, clenching my teeth and curling my body into a tight ball, all fear of death had gone. If I can swap my life for that enormous ship, I feel absolutely no regrets.

Repulse is making more than 20 knots and listing to port, turning her bows towards my aircraft which is leading the attack. The bearing narrows – I'm so close I can't manoeuvre freely. 'Ready to fire! Fire!'.

I feel a slight shock in the plane at the moment the heavy fish leaves it, and at the same time take evasive action, veering to port, almost grazing the sea surface. I've come so close that the big ship's side seems to hang over me, and I can see the flicker of a tense ruddy face beneath a pale helmet, working a machinegun. I can't be more than 150 metres from him, but at the low ceiling at that distance, either they can't depress the guns freely or they feel it's a waste of ammunition because my torpedo has already been fired. Almost nothing comes up at me.

I hear a shout, 'Got her!'. I look round and see a weird shape rise up into the air, a huge column of grey water. The one that struck her in the stern, I'm quite sure, that was mine! It was the first torpedo to hit *Repulse*."

The Philippines – Death March

*O*n 10 and 12 December 1941, the Japanese landed on the main Philippine island of Luzon, with more landings on the 22nd. Though they fought hard, the island's 65,000 American and Filipino defenders were ill equipped and at the mercy of Japanese air superiority. Luzon fell on 2 January 1942. The Americans and Filipinos continued their defence on the fortified island of Corregidor, believing it could be reinforced if their forces managed to keep a toehold on the rugged Bataan Peninsula. But on 8 April 76,000 of the 'battling bastards of Bataan', 12,000 of whom were Americans, were forced to surrender to the Japanese. The prisoners, exhausted from their heroic resistance, were force-marched some 60 miles (96.5 km) from Mariveles to San Fernando. Suffering from cruel heat, lack of food and water, and barbaric treatment from their Japanese guards, between 10,000 and 14,000 prisoners died in what became known as the Bataan Death March. Survivors of both sides tell their stories.

Sister Louise Kroeger, a nun in the Maryknoll Order, was in a convent in Baguio. On 23 December she answered the phone to an American businessman from Baguio.

"'Sister', he said, 'we've had a meeting here in the Pines Hotel, and I want to tell you what we're going to do. The Japanese are coming up the mountains and right now are in the outskirts of the city. We've sent a delegation out to meet them. All the troops have left Baguio and we want to surrender. I'm asking all Americans not to offer any resistance. We're civilians, and we'll seek the protection of the Geneva Convention.'

Unknown to us, the Japanese ran amok in Baguio. I remember looking back at the convent. It was one large building – the living quarters, a now deserted school and the chapel. High on a hill and with a courtyard of tough Philippine concrete, it was built to withstand a typhoon.

A bird, high in the trees above, gave a shrill cry of alarm, and then suddenly we heard howling and screeching; a horde of Japanese soldiers burst into the courtyard. We all stood quietly calm, but even though we had led sheltered lives, the intent of the soldiers was clear. Both groups stood their ground.

Our gardener and handyman, a quiet and unassumingly devout Filipino, stepped in front of us. At that moment, the soldiers moved aside as an officer strode into the courtyard. Tall for a Japanese, and strikingly handsome, I recognised him as a stallholder from the market in Baguio – we had regularly purchased fish from him, and never been aware of his identity.

Our gardener was a brave man. He begged the officer to explain to his soldiers that nuns were not like other women, and to leave us alone. He did – but they wrecked our convent.

Nobody was sure what they were looking for, but they tore the place apart and spared nothing. Even the beautifully hand-embroidered altar front was slashed by Japanese bayonets. Our priest, a Dominican friar who came from Belgium, was savagely beaten. We could only watch as they beat him to the ground and then kicked him near to death. The Japanese left. I helped carry the priest in and tend his wounds.

Later that evening, when we had repaired as much of the damage as possible, I went out to lock the courtyard gate. I found a Japanese soldier standing there, who asked me to take him to the priest. The soldier was humble and subdued – there was no hostility in his manner, so I took him to the bedside. The soldier knelt before the bed and begged forgiveness. I translated, and will always remember his words.

'I'm Catholic, father, and I know how I should treat a priest – but in front of the others, there was nothing for me to do but beat you as I did. I have come back to ask you pardon. If the others find out I came here, they will send me to an infantry assault company, and I will surely die – but I could not live with my conscience and not come and say I'm sorry'.

Our priest gave his blessing; we knelt and prayed. The young man wept unashamedly."

When General King surrendered on Bataan, Captain Winston Jones of the Philippine Scouts Artillery was one of the 70,000 men who trudged 57 miles to Japanese POW camps. Although he had been without food for days, he was beyond hunger. He was about to have his first experience of an unknown enemy.

"I felt very uncertain and afraid. Despite the campaign, this was the first time I had come face to face with the Japanese, and none of us knew what was expected of us as prisoners of war. There were some in our group who were very sick – we helped as best we could, but none of us was strong enough to carry anyone.

We had just come abreast of the dirt airstrip called Cabcaben Field when a battery of Jap heavy artillery opened fire on Corregidor. The island fired back, but its first rounds fell short – they burst along the road and decimated the ranks of the column ahead. Then a Japanese military policemen appeared and motioned our groups off the road into rice stubble. We were made to stand directly in front of the guns, and in plain view of Corregidor.

The Japs made us stand there for over an hour, while guns blasted Corregidor. Our boys could see us through the range-finders and did not return fire. When the time came to move on, some of the men were too ill to move. The guards bayoneted them where they lay.

From Cabcaben the road runs north and then straight up the east coast of Bataan. There were artesian wells every kilometre along the roadside. Their pure water had been used to irrigate the rice fields. Now the ground around the wells was littered with the dead, and in some, where we stopped to drink, the Japanese guards would urinate in the water first.

The worst was when a convoy of enemy trucks came down the road in the opposite direction. The dust they created was bad enough, but Jap soldiers in the back of the vehicles thought it was great fun to knock our hats off with long bamboo poles as their trucks went past. There were many men in my column who were knocked senseless into the path of oncoming vehicles.

The columns became strung out and frequently we were out of sight of the ones behind and in front. This made our guards very edgy, and they made us march double time to catch up. Some of the men couldn't maintain the pace, so they fell back through the ranks until, alone, behind the column, they were bayoneted.

We were one of the later columns, so the road was littered with dead, who were already being picked over by carrion birds. The smell of the dead is something I shall carry with me to the day I die."

Malcolm Champlin, 'Champ' to his friends, was a Naval Reserve Lieutenant serving in Manila, working as Aide to Rear Admiral Rockwell, when, on 10 December 1941, the Japanese bombed the Cavite Naval Yard.

"I rushed outside with a faceful of lather and looked up into the clear sky. I counted a formation of 54 bombers banking high over the base. A smoke bomb burst. Then nine 3-in anti-aircraft batteries opened up at their maximum range of some 24,000 feet. The Japs climbed above the shell bursts.

They turned for a second high-level pass over the base and another smoke canister was dropped, presumably to get the windage. On the third pass, the planes bombed in formation and with precision. It seemed that not a single bomb missed the base area, as the yard erupted into smoke and flame. The ground shook beneath my feet to the concussion of high explosives. The planes now dived into two formations, then came in at a lower level and dropped their incendiaries. Cavite burned.

I ran for a car and headed for the 'Commandancia' or headquarters building as floods of frightened Filipino workers hit my car like a tidal wave. Harassed Marine guards tried to clear a way through the mob, but it was no use, so I turned into a side road. This proved just as bad – fires raged and the dead lay in the streets, so I abandoned the car and pushed through on foot.

I found Admiral Rockwell – he had established a command post in front of the ammunition store. Hoses were directed on to the dump to keep the temperature down. Lieutenant Commander Whitney, Captain of the Yard, came limping up with his knee in a bandage, uniform torn and bloody, to report that some 800 gas-masks were stored in a loft above one of the machine shops. At that moment, another report came in of fresh fires near the post office and radio station. Admiral Rockwell turned and told me that the gas-masks were my problem to solve.

I flagged down a passing four-by-four and climbed aboard. I needed a working party and quick. As the truck rounded the corner near the commissary, I chanced upon a group of sailors and shouted to them to come with me.

We got as close to the burning machine shop as we dared and I led four of the men up the outside staircase and into the loft to look for the masks. They were easy to find, stored in cans like small barrels, with six masks in each of the sealed cans. We rolled the barrels down and tossed them over the balcony to the ground below, where the other men piled them on to hand carts and ran them out to the truck.

We worked like fury. I remember there was a loud crack and a beam directly above split open in a shower of cascading sparks. I ordered the men out of the building. We had saved more than 700 gas-masks, ready for the day, as we believed, when the Japs would use chemical weapons against us!

We climbed on board the truck and the driver edged out into the street. Our route to safety lay between buildings which were burning on both sides. Burning debris littered our path and there were buildings caving in all round us. My driver hesitated, but I thumped him on the shoulder and urged him forward; he was only a kid, and scared to death. He crashed the gears into a low drive and the truck ground forward over the burning timbers. The sailors behind clung on with one hand and warded falling timbers off with the other. The heat was incredible. I could feel my skin tighten and begin to blister. Then we were through the tunnel of flame and into an open area.

I stopped the truck to let the sailors down and thanked them for their efforts. One of them I remember was a bruiser of a stoker, had the sort of face that was scarred from a hundred bar-room brawls. It seemed the stoker was the spokesman. 'I'm up for a summary court martial, lieutenant', he said, 'Will you testify for me, sir?'.

I assured him that I would, whatever his crime, only to find that all the others needed the same favour. This threw me a bit, and I asked where they had all come from. It appeared they had been in the brig and released by the Marine guards when the air raid started.

There was no problem. I told them that the headquarters was a total wreck and all the courts martial records burned to a cinder. As far as the navy was concerned, the sailors had a clean slate, so we got on with the war."

John Spainhower, a lieutenant in the Philippine Scouts, wounded early in the campaign, had barely recovered when the garrison surrendered.

"I marched for two days without water and on the third, as our column approached Orani, the guards allowed us to drink from a small creek which stank from the decomposing remains that floated in it.

We stayed a night at Orani. The conditions were awful. We were dumped into fields and left until the morning – there was no food and no sanitary arrangements. The next day, I was questioned by a Japanese officer, who found out that I had been in a Philippine Scout battalion.

The Japs hated the Scouts, perhaps because we beat the hell out of them at the Abucay Hacienda. Anyway, they took me outside and I was forced to watch as they buried six of my Scouts alive. They made the men dig their own graves, and then had them kneel down in a pit. The guards hit them over the head with shovels to stun them and piled earth on top.

I was made to stand at attention over the graves until eventually I collapsed with sunstroke."

Seiichi Nishida was a Private First Class with a water purification unit in the Japanese 16th Division when the horrific 'Death March' came into view.

"Before our eyes, hundreds of prisoners of war were moving along. When I looked closer, I could see they were, in fact, stumbling along, half-naked, in broken boots. A fiery sun beat down on their heads. From mouth to mouth I could hear a babbling sound, 'Water! Water!'. At first I didn't understand what they meant, then I realised what they were asking for, so I filled my mess tin lid with clear water and gave them some to drink. A US soldier, face burned red with the sun, kept repeating, 'Thank you, thank you', with tears streaming down his face."

Hidezumi Ima was a member of the No. 1 Propaganda Team with the Philippines Expeditionary Force from Japan. His view of their landing on these lush islands belies the violence to follow.

"Someone bawled out, 'Wakey, wakey, we're there!'. Of course, everyone woke up. I folded my blanket and tidied it away with my life-jacket, which served as a pillow, and hurried out on deck.

The island of Luzon was green – so beautiful a green it made you want to cry out. A bright cobalt sky, like something by Fra Angelico, stretched away over receding mountain ranges which seemed to be piled up, one on top of another. By the seashore, clusters of coconut palms, between them you could make out, here and there, 'nippa huts', sprouting nippa palm leaves, the high-floored huts of fishermen. The sea was totally green, like molten jade, and utterly peaceful.

As far as the eye could reach, bright primary colours. The shore must be about 2,000 metres away, but everything seemed terribly near, as if we could quite happily swim the rest of the way. We were more used to scenery which was like a water colour swathed in mist, rather than a brilliant oil painting – but the island's vivid green was so lustrous that it dazzled.

I was overcome by its unfamiliarity, and quite forgot we were on enemy territory – but as I gazed, leaning over the railing of the starboard side, I saw the shape of a plane glide over the mountains. Then an ear-spitting roar as the AA guns from our ships began to fire.

Tracer shells described a red arc. In the distance another plane, hugging the ground, seeming to be sweeping the landing units with machine-gun fire. From another ship, more AA fire howled up into the sky. In the intervals of all this racket, you could hear bursts of rifle fire. The enemy planes did not seem to be coming for the convoy, which was moving into Lingayen Gulf, but were concentrating on the landing units close into the shore. Like someone passing out lines of red tape, the tracer was cast up into the sky like so many threads trying to trap the enemy planes in their fibres. They sped away, without approaching the convoy. 'You asked for it!', shouts went up from those of us who had been watching.

With that, the battle came to an end. After the enemy planes had beat a retreat, all there was was an innocent, clear morning sky."

Private First Class Kyūichirō Maeda of a Japanese Signals Unit, No. 9 Infantry Regiment, became used to operating behind the US lines keeping his superiors informed about enemy moves.

"Our boundary was the road running across the peninsula. We used to wait for nightfall every day, then slip into the area held by the enemy. I was attached to No 3 Company, and had with me a No 6 wireless transmitter set. I was responsible for following officer patrols and reporting the reconnaissance of enemy positions. If we came across an enemy patrol from the US/Filipino army, we would hide among the trees, let the enemy pass on, then open fire and attack.

Noticing that the fire was coming from their rear, what looked like their own positions, the US/Filipino troops would flee in amazement. Another time we were going through the pitch-dark forest and the US/Filipino Army wire loomed up in front of us. Everyone kept absolutely silent as I typed out my message."

Lieutenant Hirohisa Murata of the Japanese III Company, 1st Battalion, 61st Infantry Regiment, and his troops began embarking in landing craft at Limay, a town on the east coast of Bataan, to attack Corregidor.

"Our regiment was clearly marked out as a suicide unit, the whole lot of us. Because of this, we all cut our hair and nails and left them behind as souvenirs for relatives. At 7 pm we finished embarkation. I had made up my mind that I was going to die.

Before embarking on the landing craft, we received detailed instructions. According to these, while the landing craft were on the sea, the artillery positions on Bataan would continue to pour a fierce gunfire bombardment into Corregidor. It was indicated that the landings should take place after the shelling stopped, in two or three minutes. However, things were not to pan out so gracefully. On the contrary, the too-detailed arrangements caused an unheard-of number of casualties among the first wave to land.

At the signal, 'Approaching shore', everyone dashed out of the landing craft. But they had not reached the coastline, and in the pitch-black night the men hurled themselves into the sea and were soaked to the skin. Bullets poured point-blank into them, and when they finally managed to struggle ashore, right in front of them were perpendicular cliffs about 10 metres high. They put their hands out to touch the cliffs, and felt a queer, slippery sensation. When they looked closer, they saw that the rock surface of the cliff was running with coal tar. The men closed up to the cliff and tried to tackle it with hands and feet, but all they got was a slimy, slippery sensation – it was quite impossible to climb it...

Preparations had been made for an assault landing, and we expected to be placed in that sort of situation. Luckily for us, as the unit came up to the rock face of the cliff, the enemy fire could not reach us. So we threw up the ropes we'd prepared for the landing and reached the cliff top by hauling ourselves up on the ropes."

Midway and Coral Sea – Out of Sight

If the battle of the Coral Sea between US and Japanese naval forces on 4–8 May 1942 could be described as a draw, Midway three weeks later was the victory that wrested the initiative from the Japanese in the Pacific. Coral Sea, fought south of the Solomon Islands, marked a new era of naval conflict: it was the first action to be fought entirely by aircraft, with no visual contact between warships. The following Japanese attempt to land troops on Midway Island – home to a vital American airfield – was part of an elaborate plan involving a diversionary force being sent far to the north to land on the Aleutians. But Admiral Chester Nimitz was aware of the plan from intercepted signals – the US had cracked the Japanese codes – and manoeuvred his carriers Yorktown, Enterprise *and* Hornet *close to Midway and the approaching 165-ship Japanese force. The young airmen of the United States had paid an enormous cost for victory, but Midway marked the turning point of the war in the Pacific. Victory paved the way for the landings at Guadalcanal and the entire subsequent sea and land offensive against Japan.*

Rear Admiral C Wade McClusky was Air-Group Commander aboard the US carrier *Enterprise* and led the initial bombing run on the Japanese carriers. A Lieutenant-Commander at the time, McClusky's leadership was crucial in the American success.

"My orders were to make a Group attack on the enemy striking force. Radio silence was to be maintained until sight contact with the enemy was made. That was the extent of my instructions. The *Hornet* Group was likewise to be launched and, although the *Hornet* Group Commander was senior, no command relationship or co-ordination was prescribed. No information was received to indicate how the *Yorktown* Group was to participate. So, with this meagre information, we manned our planes.

At 9.45 am, by flashing light signal, I was ordered to 'proceed on mission assigned'. No information was given as to why the torpedo planes and fighters were delayed. This meant we would be without fighter protection – a serious predicament.

Climbing to gain altitude, I led this small force on a south-westerly course and figured to intercept the enemy at about 11.20 am. At our departure time they were believed to bear about 240°, distance 155 miles and heading toward Midway at 25 knots. Our Task Force was to maintain a course of 240° to close the enemy except when flight operations dictated otherwise.

Arriving at the estimated point of contact the sea was empty. Not a Jap vessel was in sight. A hurried review of my navigation convinced me that I had not erred. What was wrong?

With the clear visibility it was a certainty that we hadn't passed them unsighted. Allowing for their maximum advance of 25 knots, I was positive they couldn't be in my left semi-circle, that is, between my position and the island of Midway. Then they must be in the right semi-circle, had changed course easterly or westerly, or, most likely, reversed course. To allow for a possible westerly change of course, I decided to fly west for 35 miles, then to turn north-west in the precise reverse of the original Japanese course. After making this decision, my next concern was just how far could we go. We had climbed, heavily loaded, to a high altitude. I knew the planes following were probably using more gas than I was. So, with another quick calculation, I decided to stay on course 315° until 12.00 pm, then turn north-east-wardly before making a final decision to terminate the hunt and return to the *Enterprise.*

Call it fate, luck or what you may, because at 11.55 am I spied a lone Jap cruiser scurrying under full power to the north-east. Concluding that she possibly was a liaison ship between the occupation forces and the striking force, I altered my Group's course to that of the cruiser. At 12.05 pm that decision paid dividends.

Peering through my binoculars which were practically glued to my eyes, I saw dead ahead about 35 miles distant the welcome sight of the

Jap carrier striking force. They were in what appeared to be a circular disposition with four carriers in the centre, well spaced, and an outer screen of six to eight destroyers and inner support ships composed of two battleships and either four or six cruisers.

I then broke radio silence and reported the contact to the *Enterprise*. Immediately thereafter I gave attack instructions to my Group. Figuring that possibly the *Hornet* Group Commander would make the same decision that I had, it seemed best to concentrate my two squadrons on two carriers. Any greater division of the bomb-load we had might spread out the damage, but I believed would not sink or completely put out of action more than two. Picking the two nearest carriers in the line of approach, I ordered Scouting Six to follow my section in attacking the carrier on the immediate left and Bombing Six to take the right-hand carrier. These two carriers were the largest in the formation and later were determined to be the *Kaga* and the *Akagi*. As a point for later mention, after radio silence was broken, Lt Dick Best, skipper of Bombing Six, radioed that he was having oxygen trouble, had dropped to 15,000 feet and would remain at that altitude to commence the attack. One remarkable fact stood out as we approached the diving point – not a Jap fighter plane was there to molest us. We attributed this to the Japs' fear of the torpedo plane and the defeat they had sustained by that plane in the Coral Sea.

It was 12.22 pm when I started the attack, rolling in a half-roll and coming to a steep 70° dive. About half-way down, anti-aircraft fire began booming around us – our approach being a complete surprise up to that point. As we neared the bomb-dropping point, another stroke of luck met our eyes. Both enemy carriers had their decks full of planes which had just returned from the attack on Midway. Later it was learned that about the time we had discovered the Jap force, an enemy seaplane had detected our forces. Apparently then, the planes on deck were being refuelled and rearmed for an attack on our carriers. Supposing then, we, Air Group Six, had turned southward toward Midway, as the *Hornet* Group did – I can still vividly imagine the *Enterprise* and *Hornet* at the bottom of the sea as the *Yorktown* was some three days later.

In the meantime, our bombs began to hit home… I levelled off at mast-head height, picked the widest opening in their screen and dropped to deck level, figuring any anti-aircraft fire aimed at me would also be aimed at their own ships. All their ships' fire must have been pretty busy because I was well through the screen before I noted bursting shells creeping up behind. With the throttle practically pushed through the instrument panel, I was fortunate in avoiding a contact with death by slight changes of altitude and varying the get-away course to right and left.

It was quick work to figure the return course, and as I raised my head from the plotting board, a stream of tracer bullets started chopping the water around the plane. Almost immediately my gunner, W G Chochalousek, in the rear seat, opened fire. Then a Jap Zero zoomed out of range ahead of me. A hurried glance around found another Zero about 1,000 feet above, to the left and astern, about to make another attack. Remaining at 20 feet above the water, I waited until the attacking plane was well in his dive, then wrapped my plane in a steep turn towards him. This not only gave him a more difficult deflection shot, but also enabled my gunner to have free room to manoeuvre his guns. Then ensued about a 5-minute chase, first one Zero attacking from the right, then the second from the left. Each time I would wrap up towards the attacker with Chochalousek keeping up a constant fire. Suddenly a burst from a Jap seemed to envelop the whole plane. The left side of my cockpit was shattered, and I felt my left shoulder had been hit with a sledgehammer. Naturally enough it seemed like the end, we sure were goners. After two or three seconds, I realised there was an unusual quietness except for the purring engine of the Old Dauntless. Grasping the inner phone, I yelled to Chochalousek, but no answer. It was difficult to turn with the pain in my left shoulder and arm, but I finally managed and there was the gunner, facing aft, guns at the ready and unharmed. He had shot down one of the Zeros (probably the one that had got the big burst in on us) and the other decided to call it quits.

We found that our plane had been hit about 55 times."

Captain Elliott Buckmaster was in command of the US carrier *Yorktown* as Japanese aircraft attacked – and was witness to an astonishing victory of the US navy and aircraft against overwhelming odds, although he lost his ship.

"The *Yorktown* joined up with other carriers in attacking Jap forces. Our group immediately hit one carrier with torpedoes and bombs. Later it was reported that this carrier sank. About this time, our fighters intercepted a large group of enemy dive-bombers and fighters.

The sky was filled with falling Japanese bombers. The AA fire of the supporting ships and the *Yorktown* was magnificent. Our gunners literally chopped the enemy planes apart. Every single dive-bomber that came towards us was blown to bits, but three made hits on us before being destroyed.

By this time, our engines had stopped, but through superhuman effort our engineers got our boilers operating. A swarm of enemy torpedo planes appeared – we avoided several torpedoes, but two dropped close aboard.

I felt that the ship would capsize very soon. Reluctantly I gave the order 'Abandon ship'. The courage displayed by the officers and crew throughout the engagement is beyond my powers of expression. I believed the *Yorktown* was stricken beyond repair. Later, however, I returned with a small salvage party. With the help of the destroyer *Hammond* we were able to right the ship by $2°$. We felt sure she would live. Then suddenly, four torpedoes fired from an enemy submarine outside our destroyer screen were sighted. We were heavily hit and the destroyer *Hammond* alongside was sunk. As our destroyers were attacking the enemy submarine, our crew was transfered to a small tug to await the arrival of salvage tugs at day-break. However, the next day, from a companion ship, I saw the *Yorktown* slowly sink beneath the waves. The Japanese lost four aircraft carriers in that engagement and many of their best aviators. In the *Yorktown*'s four short years, she destroyed more Japanese planes and ships than any other single US ship. Tonight, the *Yorktown* rests on the bottom of the Pacific."

Iyozō Fujita, Flight Commander on board the Japanese aircraft-carrier *Sōryū*, was piloting an escorting Zero fighter when the Americans attacked.

"I sighted a formation of 20 torpedo bombers – but this time they had an escort of three fighter planes. I made for the enemy fighters, to get rid of that nuisance first of all, but strangely enough, they seemed to have no stomach for a fight and made off. Without pursuing the fighters, I turned and made for the assault planes.

A shell, which I thought came up from our carrier, smacked into my plane amidships – exactly where my fuselage fuel tank was. In no time, smoke began to pore out. The cockpit began to fill with flames.

Next thing, bullets began to spatter from the 7.7 mm magazine. There was going to be no time to make a forced landing on the water, and when I looked down, I saw the cruiser *Jintsū* speeding ahead below me, so I decided to use my parachute. I opened the cockpit windshield and tried to climb out, but my head was pushed against the windshield, and I could not get out.

I heard once how a man got out of his cockpit by hanging his legs over the edge and lying athwart. I spotted the altimeter as I left the aircraft – I was at 200 feet.

I could hear the wind scream past in my ears, but the parachute refused to open. The canopy stretched out, but when I saw it was not bellying out with air, I grabbed the chute with both hands and tugged at it. As I did so I felt a shock go through my whole body, as I entered the sea.

My body was entangled in the cords of the chute, and I tried to free myself. Finally I came to the surface. With amazement, when I looked round, I saw the *Jintsū* making full speed ahead. She hadn't seen me.

On the distant horizon I saw three columns of black smoke. The waves were calm enough, but there was a very big swell. I was carried to the top of the swell, from where I could see for about 20 miles, but when I came down to its base, all I could see was sky above my head.

At any rate, I thought, those must mean that's where our fleet is, and I began to swim towards them. The flying helmet was a nuisance, and I look it off and threw it into the sea. Next, my flying boots, my socks, gloves. Then I began to worry about sharks.

I remembered I'd heard someone say that sharks line up alongside you and measure the length of your body against theirs. If you are longer than they are, they don't go for you. So, I began to unwrap the muffler and tied it round my waist to make me look like a long object. But the back of my neck got so cold I couldn't bear it, so I wrapped it round my neck again.

I remembered my long-distance swim from Naval Academy days. I did 10 miles, going into the water at 7 o'clock and coming out at seven in the evening. Now, as I gazed at the black smoke, I could see it was 20 miles away, and if I kept swimming as I was, it would take 24 hours. I lost all appetite for swimming. In a mood of quiet despair, I spreadeagled myself in the water and lay gazing at the sky. I saw a 96-type sea recce plane fly over. Without thinking, I waved my hands to signal to him, but he flew off without spotting me.

About four hours must have passed like this, when I heard a noise and opened my eyes. What had been the aircraft-carrier *Akagi*, still burning, had come to within 1,000 metres of where I was. Then one of her escort destroyers, came up close.

Soon I became aware of something. From her gunwale, the muzzle of a gun was pointing at me. My hair was long in those days, and my face, burned by the sun, had turned red. 'They've taken me for an American pilot!' I realised. I trod water and began to semaphore with my arms: 'I AM AN OFFICER FROM *Sōryū*. I don't know if they followed this on board or not, but the gun muzzle moved up."

Mitsuru Iwashita was a Japanese gunnery officer on board the battleship *Kirishima*, and saw for himself the destruction of Yamamoto's aircraft carriers.

"The bugle sang out the order for anti-aircraft combat readiness. An enemy plane, apparently. Far off, the sound of machine-gun fire. Enemy torpedo-bombers came in to the attack, but our Zeros shot them all down.

Suddenly, another anti-aircraft warning. Fierce machine-gun fire. Enemy aircraft coming in to attack. They seem to be coming in quite close this time. Our anti-aircraft gunners are all keyed-up. 'Fire!' comes the command, then an appalling roar from our guns, with the MGs chattering away. Everyone makes for the shelters. When I take a look outside, I can see the sky filled with AA gun bursts and puffs of smoke. The enemy planes drop their bombs, and the roar of the explosions splits the sky apart. First one plane, then another, swoops over our ship, then skims away again.

After them come our Zeros, in hot pursuit, and a burst of AA fire hits the sky from close to me. The MGs cease fire. The enemy planes have all been hit, but there seems to be little damage on our side.

Then a signal comes in, reporting the sighting of enemy aircraft-carrier force. We all feel the tenseness of anticipation. A voice – 'Aircraft-carrier hit!'. I make it fast to where the voice is coming from, and look out from the deck. A sea of bright red flames engulfs the deck of our flagship *Akagi* which was making speed far off to port.

Then they say another carrier's gone – and gazing far astern I can see *Sōryū* turning, her decks a mass of smoke and red flame. The first carrier to be hit, *Kaga*, is now only a distant column of black smoke.

Whether or not it was the result of induced explosions, I don't know, but the fire on *Akagi* looks frightful enough to blow her sky high. So our carrier force is reduced to one, *Hiryū*. With no more than *Hiryū's* carrier-based planes, we mount an attack on the enemy's task force.

Enemy aircraft coming into the attack again. Now we have no fighters to go up and meet them. Apart from the random firing of the MGs and AA guns from our ship, there's nothing, but they manage to spread a curtain of fire across the sky. At length the attack begins to flag, and I can see the *Hiryū* making speed on our starboard side. Everyone is wild with joy that *Hiryū* is still in good shape. Then we notice black dots appearing in a gap in the clouds above her. Enemy dive-bombers. In an instant, the decks of *Hiryū* are a sheet of crimson flame. That's it, then, they have had it. Our fleet is now running completely naked before the enemy task force. When night finally comes the fires are almost out on the *Hiryū*, but she can't manoeuvre and comes to a dead stop, listing. The fleet quietly watches over the blackened shapes of the ships. The Battle of Midway is over, and fortune has not been with us."

Akira Tendo was special correspondent for the Japanese newspaper *Asahi Shimbun* and navy correspondent at Wake Island when US aircraft sank his ship, the *Shōhō* – in the Coral Sea.

"I felt the ship give a shudder. What looked like blackened fragments of burned wood swept past our eyes as we stood on the bridge. Then the ship was enveloped in a great noise, like a steel curtain being hit by some great force. That can't be, I thought, nothing can have gone so wrong. 'They're bits of enemy planes', I tried to convince myself. It was no enemy plane, I soon realised, a bomb had done for our rudder.

The enemy pilots must have jumped for joy when they saw our carrier, like a man paralysed from the waist down. They came at us with renewed strength, harrying us, closing up, then dropping bombs.

On they came, sweeping over our heads. As we watched, we wondered if their attack would hurl them into the sea, then we saw them roar up into the sky again. These were not the American lushes we'd learned about in Japan!

I felt a sensation as if I'd been struck with a whip. 'So, we've had it, at last. That must be the third or fourth bomb that's hit us'. The instant I had time to think 'that's close', something smacked into the deck, and there was the blast of an enormous explosion.

'Bastards!' I turned round in amazement at that voice, ablaze with rage, and saw a petty officer with his cheek torn away. He was holding it with both hands, and from between his fingers the blood was flowing. A sailor was standing close by, his right arm almost torn off. He had a cloth at his waist and, taking the shrapnel fragment between his teeth, he staunched the blood from his right arm, using his left hand. Then he went into the signals cabin. His gait was steady, as if he were not seriously wounded at all. Then, with his left hand, he began to tap on the key of the W/T set.

Another sailor started to his feet, quite near me. I looked at his leg and was aghast. The flesh of his thigh was scooped away, and the white bone was clearly visible. He stood in front of the telescope, trying to support himself. He began to report what he saw. In these conditions, to collapse would be shameful.

The bombs and torpedoes kept coming. When a torpedo hits, the ship does a pitching and tossing movement. They work together, and the result is like an earthquake. The sound's dull, but it makes you feel as if your intestines are being drawn out. Suddenly I had the impression that I was wounded too. I looked down at my leg. Blood was flowing from it. Was I going to die from loss of blood? My instinct at first was to go down to the ward-room and have it treated. But what was happening around me stopped me. Men with worse wounds than mine were still at their stations. I stayed.

After a while, I noticed my wound again. I was increasingly aware that the blood was still flowing from it, but all I could see was a scratch on my kneecap. 'Is that all there is to it?' I comforted myself with that thought, and stayed on the bridge.

The ship finally began to settle into the sea, bows first. I hurried from the bridge to the bridge deck. I saw our photographer, Yoshioka, taking pictures of enemy planes coming into the attack.

'You press men, get down below, it's dangerous!'. The gunnery officer was concerned for us, but we did not listen. An enemy plane released its torpedo. 'Still alive?'. We shook hands. 'Let's go!', 'Yes, let's both go together!'. But where did I intend to go? Perhaps my mood was, 'If we're going to die, let's die together'. The deck below was already awash, and the waves swirled in front of my eyes.

Although the ship was on the point of sinking, the men were still at their stations. As one man, they had refused to leave. The ship's bows plunged into the sea, and she came up by the stern. By now up in the air, the screw kept turning. The engine room, went on doing its job to the end.

A petty officer climbed up a mast which was beginning to go under. Someone said he was trying to keep the ship's flag flying. Then, along with the ship, he vanished from sight.

Although the ship had gone down, you could still hear the sound of machine-gun fire. It was very odd, as if the firing were coming from the sea bed itself. The gunners were all dead. What happened was that the gunnery officer – the one man left alive – went on firing until the very last. The paymaster crewmen all remained at their stations. From the portholes of the sinking ship, they waved their white caps in a gesture of farewell.

Apart from us war correspondents, there were three non-combatants on board – the barber, the cook and the laundryman. These too, stuck to their posts, moving badly wounded crew, giving medical aid. Like the sailors, they too died at their posts."

Malta – An Epic Struggle

*O*f enormous strategic importance to the Allies, the group of small islands known as Malta lie 200 miles from Tunisia, and 985 and 820 miles respectively from the British ports of Gibraltar and Alexandria. In 1942 Malta was still part of the British Commonwealth. It had witnessed much conflict and many conquests in its long and turbulent history. But the ultimate test of its people's endurance and bravery was to come when the Axis powers would attempt to 'wipe Malta off the map'. For residents, the defending British forces and the attacking Germans and Italians, the siege of Malta was a time of mixed comradeship, stoicism and courage.

Sergeant John Mason of the Cheshire Regiment was based at Floriana. While working to clear rubble and help the civilians after air raids, he formed a lasting memory of Maltese fortitude and staying power.

"Most of my work was civil defence, which involved rescue work and first aid. The planes would come over at meal times and at night, and we would go out as soon as it had quietened down to help where we could. Then we would go back and await the next one.

We used to be a bit over-anxious to try to get out to help. Sometimes we didn't wait for the bombing to finish because by the time we got there, people were already staggering in the streets. If we'd got there five minutes earlier, we would have saved their lives. People were losing limbs unnecessarily because they weren't being attended to soon enough.

One case which I always remember was when the Regal cinema was bombed. It had already been bombed on four occasions, but this time it was particularly bad. The cinema had been crowded, and when we got there, people were making their own way out of the rubble to the nearest hospital in Floriana, with their faces cut away and terrible injuries.

In my regiment alone, we buried 21. In my own company two died, and one of those boys hadn't been out with us long. He was on his way to the dining hall to get a cup of tea. We found him sitting by the railings, not a mark on him, still holding his cup of tea. It was the bomb blast that had sucked the air out of him.

There were very few ambulances in Malta, particularly towards the end, because they were getting worn out. We used the old army ration trucks and 15-hundredweights.

We also did guard duties on the water front against U-boats. We had machine guns situated in sandbaggage or brickwork, sited almost everywhere around the coast. We also helped at Luqa airport, filling the craters in. As the bombers made the craters, we used our 15-hundredweights, containing all the damaged brickwork from the air raids and piled it into the craters to be steam-rollered.

The bombing wasn't perpetual – they would give you a break and then give you a real hammering. They picked meal times, and then the middle of the night. That was how we got the casualties. People would think they were getting a break and leave their homes – then the planes would come over.

People had to go out shopping – they had to go to work. It was impossible for them to stay indoors in the shelters all the time. After about six or twelve months of air raids, there weren't many residential buildings available for them, and what there were were just hovels.

I've never seen people like the Maltese for stamina and fortitude. You would see them weep and wail, but immediately after they were marvellous. Everyone would come out after the raids to see if the neighbours were all right and then they would get on with their lives."

'Laddie' Lucas, later CBE, DSO, DFC, was a Flight-Lieutenant, without 'gongs' (medals), on his way to Burma, when he found himself joining 249 Squadron on the beleaguered island of Malta in the company of the war-weary Canadian pilot, Stan Turner.

"We landed at dawn at Kalifrana, near the Fleet Air Arm base. We got

out of the Sunderland flying boat on to the jetty and walked up along
to the mess at Halfar. I can still see old Stan, his pipe turned down in
his mouth – it never had anything in it. He suddenly saw these half a
dozen Hurricanes clambering up – they were really clapped-out
things – the engines were like some old banger. He looked up and,
right over the top of them at about 10,000–15,000 feet were two lots
of Messerschmitt 109s, flying in that sort of finger four thing they
used to do well. Looking askance, he simply said 'Good God!'.

In the first fortnight I reckon but for Stan and all his experience, I
should have been knocked off. Apart from the pilots, there were two
other people who were terribly important. One was the AOC, Hugh
Pughe Lloyd, who was an Air Vice-Marshal. He was a buccaneer,
really – he didn't play to the rules. The Air Ministry wouldn't have
had any of it, I'm quite sure. There used to be aeroplanes going out
to the Middle East and India, and Malta was the staging post where
they refuelled. We used to get so short of aircraft (we used to lose
them on the ground, with the bombings) that he used to comman-
deer them as they were going through. He was the original hijacker.
A good friend of mine, Ivor Broom, arrived in Malta late one
evening, and Hugh Pughe Lloyd was there. 'Sergeant Broom, you'll
be staying here for one or two days'. 'But I'm supposed to be going
on', he said. My God, when he woke up next morning, he found he
was on the next detail for an attack on a convoy. He was there for
weeks, and he was dead lucky to survive.

The other chap who was absolutely invaluable and essential to the
operation was Group Captain A B Woodhall. He was the Group
Captain Operations, and as such was in charge of the fighter control
– directing the aeroplanes and talking to them, the radar plots and
so on. He was a First World War pilot and had a hell of a lot of experience. Not only did he understand all the ordinary operations stuff
and talking to the pilots, he could read a battle.

To give you an idea, it was awfully difficult when the Spitfires
arrived off the carriers, before we got even a reasonable number of
aeroplanes, and we were operating sometimes four, six or eight aeroplanes against raids of a hundred. If we hadn't had really experienced pilots and been really well controlled by this chap, we would
have simply been murdered.

I remember a single raid I was on with my squadron and we had
eight aeroplanes serviceable. Woodhall got on to me on the operations telephone in our dispersal hut, such as it was (about three

chairs and an old roof), and said that there was a raid building up over Sicily. 'I think perhaps if you get off in about 10 minutes – I'll send the word through. Then climb up and get plenty of height – 25, 28 thousand feet, south of the island. That way you'll have the sun behind you and I'll give you a running commentary of these aeroplanes coming in across the Sicilian Channel. We'll play it like that'. We got the word to go off, eight of us – two Englishmen, the rest all New Zealanders, Australians and Canadians. I got up right over the south of the island, about 15 miles south, the sun behind me, at 26 or 27 thousand feet. He was giving me a running commentary of the planes. He started, 'It's 50 plus ... a lot of little jobs (fighters) and not many big jobs (bombers)'. The thing built up slowly, from 50 to over 100. 'They're coming in over St Pauls Bay – there are now about 100 plus – about 80 small ones, the rest big jobs. I suggest you come in now, and come in fast.' Just as he said it, I could see these things down there, and with the sun behind me, there was marvellous visibility. We got it absolutely right – it might have been like Wembley, with say, 100,000 people there, and we'd got all the height in the world. We were above the fighters, so we were able to come right in through the fighter screen, and in point of fact, there were three Italian bombers – that's all. They obviously hadn't intended for this to be a bombing raid. What they'd intended was to knock down the remaining fighters we'd got. We went right through and shot all three of these Italian bombers down, and broke away."

Robert Porter was a marine on board HMS *Aurora*, based on Malta. The ship's task was to intercept enemy convoys travelling between Italy and North Africa.

"The *Aurora* arrived in Malta at the end of October 1941, and the blitzes started in November. There were just two cruisers – us and the *Penelope* – and we were the senior of the two. I remember the *Penelope* became known as 'the Pepperpot' because of all her shrapnel holes.

We, along with two destroyers, were the only striking force operating from Malta during the blitz. We would get a message that a convoy had left Italy and was on its way to North Africa, and our job was to intercept. We always seemed to work on a Saturday night – we called it the club run.

The run I remember best occurred when the Admiralty decided to send us a big, heavy cruiser from Alexandria, called the *Neptune*. Her more senior captain took charge of our force.

We were told that there was another German or Italian convoy coming from Italy, so we had to leave Malta with the *Neptune* in charge, and go to intercept it. We missed the convoy and somehow ended up within eight or nine miles of Tripoli. We only found out that we were in a minefield when it was announced over the tannoy that we were in a 'tense position' at about two o'clock in the morning.

About ten minutes after that, there was a hell of an explosion. We looked around and realised that we were still all right. It was very, very quiet, and we didn't know what had happened. Then we heard someone shout that HMS *Neptune* had hit a mine and had sunk. There would be no survivors. There were probably a thousand men on board.

Our captain, Captain Agnew, took command again. He talked to us very calmly and said that we were still in the minefield. He sent a light destroyer that was with us in to see if they could pick up any survivors. Five minutes later the destroyer blew up. I think that there were some survivors which a submarine picked up. Then there was another explosion – and that was us. The bows were blown off the ship, but nobody was killed.

The ship could now only do about 9 knots, and we had to get out of the minefield and back to Malta before light. We wouldn't have stood a chance in daylight – the Luftwaffe would have picked us off immediately. We did get back before daylight, but we couldn't go out to sea again until the end of March. We had to stay in Malta in the dry dock.

Before we hit the mine, it had been my job to work with the gun crew up top with the 6-inch guns. They were for surface ships. Now that the ship was in dry dock, they took the 6-inch ammunition off the ship and left only the 4-inch guns on board. This meant that when the Germans came over, all the men who were on the 4-inch guns had to stand to their guns, because they were specially for aircraft.

There wasn't any use for us on the ship then, so the ruling was that if you were on the ship when a blitz came over, you had to leave and go into the undergound shelters in the rocks. The shelters were only yards away from the ship, but me and my friend, Johnny, would never go into them. I think we thought it was sissy. We used to stay on the deck while the blitzes came over – there would be maybe 30 or 40 aircraft at a time coming over, dive-bombing like birds.

I remember one particular afternoon when I was just walking past the turret, and I heard 'All men to blitz stations'. People ran to their guns or left the ship. I thought to myself that I would have a little sleep on deck. I got my little cape down and laid it next to the turret. It was a lovely hot day. I didn't worry – I was young, I suppose.

Our Sergeant-Major was on top of the turret, firing at the Stukas. He happened to notice me and called out, 'Marine Porter, you get in that shelter. That is your duty!' All the time, he was facing the enemy, firing at them. I have never seen coolness like that in a man. I felt very sheepish going into the shelter.

I used to go ashore whenever possible. You could get a little bed and breakfast hotel for sixpence a night. I stayed on the seafront on one particular night in a little place called 'The First and Last'. The seafront at Valletta hadn't been bombed then. It had been one of those days when the Germans had followed a convoy and sunk practically all the ships. I think three or four ships had got to the harbour, but that was all. I was the only marine ashore that night.

I fell asleep and in the morning, there was only my hotel and two other buildings on the front still standing. The Germans had blitzed the lot. Everything else was rubble."

A specialist gunner in the Regia Aeronautica, Nicola Patella attacked the Pedestal Convoy – which won him the Bronze Medal for Military Valour.

"I remember the Stuka's peculiarities such as having an all-metal structure, unlike our Italian aircraft of the period. It was strong and had a very strong landing gear, so it could operate from primitive landing fields near the front line without structural damage. Its horizontal speed was rather slow, but in the vertical dive, with its aerodynamic underwing dive brakes extended, it could reach 1000 metres in 7.21 seconds.

The bombs carried varied from 500 to 1000 kilos, according to mission, and were usually released after diving to about 700 to 1000 metres. On coming out of our attack dive, the aircraft's speed was again rather slow – and it was here that we were vulnerable.

Against naval targets we found the use of our Stukas very difficult, as we had no extensive training in this type of attack. We found the lack of datum points (as against attacking ground targets) and the determination of wind speeds and drift difficult to calculate and allow for.

Because of the unique wing shape, we found that even a slight wind over the target during the dive could shift the Junkers Ju-87 from its trajectory. The defensive armament was also limited with a 6.65 mm machine gun with 1000 rounds of ammunition in the rear cockpit and two fixed machine guns with 1200 rounds in each wing.

On the morning of August 13 we flew against the convoy and we personally attacked a big oil tanker, the *Ohio*, dropping a 1,000 kilo bomb at the end of our diving attack.

However, one of the escorting cruisers opened up her anti-aircraft artillery and my Stuka was heavily hit. We crashed into the sea, about 10 kilometres from the convoy. My pilot friend Savini (later to die in 1945) and I escaped death and got to the life raft. We stayed there for three days and two nights, along with a British Beaufighter pilot, Ron McFarlane, whom we found in the sea, before we were rescued by a German seaplane on the evening of the 15th. Ron and I are still good friends since those days and still write."

Hauptmann Gerd Stamp of I Luftgeschwader 2 flew a Ju-88 from Gerbini in the Pedestal attack – their main target the aircraft carrier *Indomitable*.

"At the time of Pedestal, only I and II Wings were stationed at Heraklion. There were no other dive-bomber units in Crete and none at all at Eleusis airfield near Athens.

I well recall how none of us were very pleased about things when we had to move from our well-established quarters on Crete and transfer over to Sicily in readiness for the Pedestal battle. Any temporary move of this nature to Sicily always involved a great deal of discomfort and upset, because our technical requirements, our personal needs and our servicing was all in the hands of strange ground crew who did not know our squadron, our machines or us. It was not their fault, they were already fully committed to servicing their own squadrons – we were extra work for them.

On the attack, our pilot approached the target ship from her port side. He wanted to make sure that at least one bomb would be a direct hit.

'Ready for diving!' – the pilot would enter his dive within seconds. It was a textbook attack, as now I saw the big ship down there coming closer to the red mark ahead of my feet. This mark showed us when we were in the 60° angle for the dive. The pilot closed the radiator flaps of the engines. I saw the propeller indicator being moved back to the half-past-eight position, and now the air brakes came out, and our Ju-88 was shaking like a chained stallion.

All of a sudden everything was literally flying in our cockpit. My heavy leather navigator's portfolio was moving around in suspension as the Ju-88's nose went down. I hung in my belts – all I had to do was keep my eyes on the altimeter. At 1500 metres altitude, I had to knock my pilot's knee, shouting 'Fifteen'. At 1200 metres, a second knock – 'Twelve hundred!' At 1000 metres a final clout to his knee, 'Thousand'. We now had our maximum diving speed of 600 km/h and we would lose another 400 metres while flattening out automatically – so the bombs had to be dropped right now. The pilot pushed the red button on the left horn of his steering controls. One could physically feel the loosening of a total 1000 kilos of bomb weight, as the Ju-88's automatic pull-out returned the aircraft to level.

Six Gs were pressing us into our seats and made our heads bow as if an invisible heavyweight had sat on our necks. My stomach, which had almost come out of my throat when we started diving, was now somewhere else. My chin was torn downward and so was my tongue. The pilot did all he had to to bring us back to normal flying."

Maria Gazman was married to a Nationalist Party member – a man dedicated to strengthening Malta's bonds with Italy. Suddenly it is Italy who is bombing their home on Malta.

"The feeling I remember most about the bombing of Malta is the shock and disappointment of being at war with Italy. Before the war, there had been many Italians living on Malta – among them my best friend.

Many Maltese felt the same horror when they realised that the Italians were our enemies. There were British living in Malta too, but most of them kept apart from the Maltese people. I think that what really made us Maltese feel closer to the Italians was our Roman Catholic religion. When you have the same religion as somebody and you go to the same church, it is very hard to think of them as an enemy.

Before the bombings the British told the Italians to leave Malta. I remember saying goodbye to my friend and being very, very sad. At that stage, it was very hard to imagine a war – and impossible to picture what was going to happen to the Maltese.

A lot of British soldiers arrived in Malta by boat and paraded around Valletta in their uniforms. Some of the Maltese boys joined up too, and they were also marching round the city, looking very pleased with themselves. I was glad that my daughter was only nine as a lot of families had problems with their daughters wanting to go out with soldiers. I was also glad that my sons were not old enough to join up.

We were issued with gas masks and told that the Italians would attack us with poisonous gas. My husband and I had four children, and we didn't have enough gas masks for the whole family. We began to get very worried about what we would do if the Italians did drop poison gas on us. Our church was more and more full of people, praying for an end to our problems.

I remember clearly the day of the first air raid. It happened very early one morning in June when I was shopping. I heard a very loud noise, but I didn't know that it was an air raid siren, although it certainly frightened everybody. When the bombs fell, I was so shocked – I had only thought about gas attacks.

We were very lucky – nobody in our family was hurt. We saw and heard terrible things around us and my husband decided that we should leave our home and stay with cousins in Rabat. We didn't want to leave, but as the bombings got worse, we knew that we had to think of our children.

Our relatives lived a village life and only had one room for our whole family. We did have plenty of food with them, and they were very, very kind – the most terrible thing was worrying about what had happened to our home, and if it was still standing or not.

When the air raids became less frequent, we moved back home. Then, one terrible night in January 1941, hundreds of planes came over – this time it was the Germans. Valletta suffered terribly – there were piles of rubble everywhere, dead animals and dead people in the street.

Again we fled inland. We walked for hours. Although we had left our home behind, we knew that it would not stand up to the attacks for very long. We had left a lot of things behind, but we were glad to have all our children with us, safe."

Tobruk – Desert Furnace

Tobruk, a port in Italian-controlled Libya, was captured by the British on 22 January 1941. When Erwin Rommel's Afrika Korps counter-attacked across North Africa, rolling towards Egypt, the Seventh Australian Division dug in behind the abandoned Italian-built defences. From April 1941 the city remained under ground and air siege from German and Italian forces. But the garrison remained a thorn in the Axis' side, making continued raids into occupied territory. In May 1942, Rommel launched a fresh offensive, this time determined to take Tobruk and the garrison (now comprised of 35,000 troops, drawn largely from the South African Second Division with some British and Indian troops). On 20 June the Germans breached the defences and reached the harbour and on the following day Tobruk surrendered. The town would remain in Axis hands until it was taken for the last time by the Eighth Army under General Bernard Montgomery following the Second Battle of El Alamein. During the fight for Tobruk, both the Allies and Axis forces had to deal not just with persistent onslaughts from each other, but with the relentless, wearying battering by the desert elements.

South African Sapper Wesson was with the 5th Field Engineers when, after the battle at Sidi Rezegh, the survivors of his unit were left to try to join up with any other group they could find.

"Our company found itself right in the thick of it, with Jerry tanks and armoured cars everywhere. The only protection we had was under our trucks.

Having spent all our ammo, trying to shoot Jerry heads as they appeared from tank turrets, we found our shallow slit trenches were of no use, as the tanks and armoured cars rode over them, firing at random. One of our men, Andy O'Grady, was shot at point-blank range in a shell slit. The three lead bullets all hit his tin hat and bounced off. He still had the helmet months later, as evidence of his lucky escape.

Some of our men held string attached to landmines and were pulling them across from truck to truck, trying to get the Jerry tanks and armoured cars to go over them.

And, in all this, our Malay cook went about his business out in the open, making pancakes over a fire made by pouring petrol into the sand. The Jerries seemed to take no notice of him – and he brought around to each truck some of his cooking.

At dusk, an officer shouted, 'Into your trucks, and join the convoy to the east'. Most of our trucks had been destroyed, so we got on anything that moved and headed east. I think the driver went over every shell slit in the desert that night, while we were bashed around in the back. As soon as we found the convoy we tagged on.

A German armoured car came up, not certain where it was. When they realised they were in our convoy, they opened up with everything they had, but fortunately all went high and through the canvas of our truck. Then they made the quickest getaway I have ever seen.

It was late afternoon, and we were still under our trucks, when I saw General Erwin Rommel. A line of German tanks came straight past our position. In the middle tank, with the hatch open, stood Rommel himself. The battle was over, and he knew it. He was right out of the turret, saluting to both sides."

Ian Quarrie was a Sub-Lieutentant RNVR commanding an experimental boat in October 1940, when he was given an order which seemed nothing short of suicidal. It was to be the first incident in an uncanny coincidence which concluded in the sea off Tobruk.

"In 1940 I was a Sub-Lieutenant, commanding HMMTB 106 – an experimental boat with one torpedo and a speed of over 45 knots. On a dull, cold October morning I was suddenly ordered to take her to sea to explode an enemy mine by going over it! Off Southend, a convoy was waiting to sail with cargoes desperately needed up the east coast. The Germans had just begun laying acoustic mines, and that night an aircraft had dropped one in the narrow channel the convoy had to take.

There was no known antidote and it was considered worth risking us to get the convoy away, hoping our speed would carry us clear of the explosion. We managed to pass directly over the mine. The reaction was instant, and we were blown out of the water. The launch sent to pick us up in this eventuality had stopped and couldn't restart her engine – and we had a long swim waiting for MTB 107 to come and rescue us. Her First Lieutenant, Sub-Lieutenant Johnny Wolfe RNVR pulled me out of the water.

Four months later, my father's ship, HMS *Rosaura*, an armed boarding vessel, was also sunk by mine, close to Tobruk. A strong swimmer, he too survived.

In the spring of 1942, I also found myself in Tobruk, commanding a new boat, MTB 312. Our flotilla spent some months there, carrying out offensive sweeps up the enemy coast, landing agents behind the lines and so on. We were a well-knit, happy unit but oh, how we hated Tobruk! Stukas by day and night were bad enough, but my own pet hate was the appalling water supplied – too brackish even to brew a drinkable cup of tea. We left just before the town fell to the enemy. I hoped never to see the place again.

I was back again on 14 September, MTB 312 being part of a Combined Operation intended to hold Tobruk for a day and destroy the enemy's ammunition, fuel and other military targets. Unfortunately our operation failed, and our losses were high.

The attack was abandoned shortly after dawn, and soon after setting course for home, we were attacked by several Italian Macchi fighter planes. Despite our manoeuvrability and fire-power, augmented by the Bren guns of the soldiers we were carrying, we were eventually set alight from end to end by incendiary bullets. The boat burned long enough to enable us to take to our collapsible boats or jump into the sea and swim some distance away before our ammunition, 3,000 gallons of petrol and four torpedoes, blew up with quite a bang. And there I was, swimming for my life again.

To my relief, two MTBs came across and took us all aboard, though not all were to survive the running battle back to Alexandria. As I was hauled aboard MTB 265, her captain looked down from the bridge and said with a wry smile, 'Haven't we done this before?' His name was Lieutenant Johnny Wolfe – and I later confirmed my suspicion that we had been sunk within yards of where my father had swum for his life too, 19 months before."

Dennis O'Brien, Petty Officer Coxswain on Motor Launch 1048, was trapped inside the port as it fell. Escape seemed less and less possible as the enemy fire grew more intense.

"One night we were on patrol off the boom when a submarine must have spotted us – our boat had a very clear silhouette. They fired at us and the torpedo must have been very, very accurate, because the ASDIC operator threw the headphones off because of the noise of this torpedo. However, being a coastal forces launch, our bottom was hardly below the surface of the water, so the torpedo missed.

We never knew our status at Tobruk. The only way we could judge our situation was by going out to sea at night and listening to the Home Service. We could sense the situation was getting worse – you could feel it. One particular day, as we came in to the port, it seemed very serious. The enemy seemed to have made a pincer movement on the port and the air raids were very intense.

We went alongside a beached ship, awaiting orders from Navy House. Messages were delivered from the Admiralty by the despatch boat called the *Eskimo Nell*. The firing went on all day, and despatches came over telling us to go easy on the ammunition.

Towards the evening, the situation was getting very bad. There were enemy tanks appearing out of the sand, around the perimeter. We were called over to Navy House and went alongside *Eskimo Nell*. She was released and we were told to leave and tell a minesweeper to proceed to Alexandria and not return. We could see German tanks arriving on shore.

We delivered the message to the minesweeper. The firing was getting worse all the time, so we sheltered around the other side of the *St Georgia*, an Italian cruiser which had been sunk and was resting on the bottom. The shells were hitting the other side of her and we didn't know what to do. We turned around and proceeded back towards Navy House. Another motor launch was coming down towards us. One of the heavy shells hit it. ZAP – it was gone.

When we saw this, we decided to go back to the shelter of the *St Georgia*. We saw some sailors on the jetty in the distance. They had a large dog with them. They yelled across to us, '1048, 1048!' We replied, 'Not on your life – you swim it!' After some discussion, we moved alongside and picked them up with their dog.

It was the best thing we ever did, because among this naval group was the Boom Defence Officer, who knew a particular point where the boom dipped. All the MTBs had departed and we were the last ship there. The fire on the boom was so heavy that you couldn't have lived.

We nipped through the point that the officer knew, and as we went through, a German tank hit us in the wheelhouse. Our captain was hit in the face and suffered bad injuries. The tank shell hit the chart box and destroyed half our chart, but God was very kind to us. The half of the chart that we didn't need had been blown off, the rest survived!

Another fairy tale happened as we went on our passage. Fog came down – which is very rare in the Mediterranean. We heard the high-revving engines of the German mopping-up craft, but we were safe in the fog. All our MTB pals had been mourning us for lost."

Private Robert Brady was a nurse with the 22nd Field Surgical Medical Team which, when drafted out to Tobruk, was attached to the First Armoured Division. Their duty was to help the wounded, whatever their nationality.

"My duties were general nursing work in the operating theatre, but every man did what he could. There were seven people in each medical team, but often you were understaffed – a lot of good men got killed getting the wounded back, or when working in the operating tents.

Half the time we were level because as the enemy advanced, you couldn't keep moving backwards, so he was bound to come within range – they were advancing all the time. I remember once, when our tents were pitched and there was some shelling – and they were ours. It carried on until they got the word that it was our hospital there.

All the members of the team used to go out and take the wounded back. If you saw a bloke go down, you would go and get him. We took the Germans in as well – a casualty is a casualty. He's just a soldier. They picked up ours – we picked up theirs.

You knew when shells were coming because you listened – and

from listening you could tell whose fire it was. Ours had a sharp noise – with the Germans you could hear a sigh as the belt was going through.

We had terrible casualties – legs blown off, arms blown off, tummies opened up. We would stop the bleeding if we could, and we tried to stop infections by cleaning the wounds. We gave people morphine, if we could get it. We had medical supplies, but we were in the lines, so you couldn't always replace what you'd used. We had plasma from England, but the soldiers were giving blood for the wounded.

We laid the wounded out on stretchers. They were kept under canvas, as best we could, but there were no guarantees. If the tents were full, we laid them outside as close to the tents as we could. We did what we could for them, and then they were taken back to base hospital. Until you've been through a battle, you can't begin to understand what it was like."

Bill Bebbington had joined the Royal Warwickshire Regiment and was in an anti-aircraft unit when, in 1941, he was drafted out to Egypt. From having a relatively quiet time at home, he was suddenly in the forefront of the battle.

"I'd never heard a shell fired or anything, and within two hours, we were in action – we had walked slap into the lion's den. We knew where we were going, but had no experience of it, and we arrived on a very fast minelayer and just leapt ashore. Stuff was flying everywhere – it was hair-raising.

In two hours, we were firing like hell. An air raid over there consisted of one Stuka after another, coming straight down at you, and if they were Germans flying them, they used to come down very low indeed. My Sgt. Major, Nobby Clark, had a pile of stones and he used to throw the damn things at them – they were that low. The Italians didn't like that – they used to stay a bit higher – sometimes they had Stukas too. We always knew when Germans were flying them, they used to come so low. It was bad enough seeing them coming straight at you and dropping the bombs, but later they had screamers – and they made a hell of a row.

It would start early in the morning – you'd have your morning raid, then they'd stop for breakfast. You'd have six or seven air raids a day – sometimes we never got undressed, because they made a dead attack at the AA sites, and we were protecting the place without any help from the RAF. There had been some Hurricanes there – but the two we had left couldn't do much.

It was incessant – there was no way of having a couple of days off. They did considerable damage, killing men and knocking out guns. They did tremendous damage to the town – just one church spire left. It wasn't just the damage – they denied you rest too.

My first day was 20 September, though the siege started on 11 April, 1941. I remember the first two casualties – deaths – we had. We used tiles from a bombed bathroom in the town and made a proper grave.

One day, after Tobruk was relieved, we were sitting having breakfast in my dugout. Shells started appearing out of nowhere. We thought the army was miles away – but the Germans were knocking on the door. We fled – just packed everything up and fled. I had one thing in mind, and that was that I was going to be in an Alexandria night-spot as soon as possible. We did not stop until we got to Alexandria.

The tank boys and infantrymen fought a rear-guard action all the way back – and a bloody fine one too. We were getting our equipment out of the way and on the way back, I had to do without a hat. A shell landed while I was talking to the sergeant. It didn't go off, but it hit a brick, bounced off and hit me on the head – knocked my hat off. I scarpered!

Another funny episode was when we had newspaper men with us. J L Hobson came, and others – Chester Wilmot stayed with me for three days in my dugout. We sat in these little holes and the mice and rats came in too – it was terrible.

This chap Wilmot was a great character. Somehow, he got hold of SRD Naval rum – special reserve something – stone-bottled. You know, I've never touched rum since. I can't even be in the same room as someone drinking it. He and I, one night, drank a complete jar of this really strong stuff. The last thing I can remember was a sentry saying to me, 'Are you all right, mate?'. I was out for the best part of 24 hours.

I remember my favourite food was Libby's corned beef. We lived on Maconochies canned stew and corned beef. We had no greens – we had ascorbic acid tablets instead.

We had Bill Bowes posted to us, the Yorkshire cricketer – and he was taken prisoner. We left him behind. I remember his last words to me, in a broad Yorkshire accent. 'Just my bloody luck, I should have kept my bloody mouth shut and stayed in Cairo'. He got taken prisoner because he couldn't run fast enough!"

Australian Private Bob Swanborough with the 2/3 Infantry Battalion was in the drive to take Post 57 – part of the attack to take Tobruk in 1941. His job was to go in after the engineers put the 'Torpedo' charges under the wire.

"We knew about land mines around there – they were like a Thermos flask, filled with fragments, obviously from a munitions factory floor – and there were four of them inside a box. They were attached by a grey cotton in among the sage brush, and the idea was that if you hit one with your foot it would set them off.

As we moved up to the start-line, we suddenly walked into a nest of these bloody things. Two sections were immediately wiped out … I'm on the ground and my first reaction was, 'The bastards have got my leg.' There was blood, but no feeling.

The stock of my rifle had been blown away and I was ripped, right across the front of my uniform, and had bits and pieces stuck in my webbing. I had a steel mirror stuck in my pocket and lodged in that was a piece about the size of a large coin. I found out later that my leg had a fragmentary wound which did muscular damage more than anything.

About then, the Italian bugle sounded, calling their troops to arms. Eventually I got up and used my rifle as a crutch and hobbled forward to the tank trap where the Company was. By this time, our platoon had been reduced to one section, the platoon commander had lost a leg, and my mate had been wiped out.

When the 'Torpedoes' discharged, we all went forward, what was left of us. I was limping into the show, and we hit the first position where the bugler had been – and took that. The remaining section attacked the next post. By this time it was daylight, and the brown-shirts had the idea that they would use their bayonets. Immediately, our fellows swung into line, stretched out a bit and went in with a bit of a bayonet charge… we took those two posts."

Hauptmann Adalbert von Taysen was Company Leader of the German 3rd Company Machine-Gun Battalion Tank Grenadier Regiment 104 as his men went to retake Tobruk.

"We crouched in the dark, the tension enormous. You could only detect the presence of the next man by the cigarette behind his hand.

The question was, 'Would it work this time?' We had maps of the fortress, but would we be able to spot the bunkers, machine guns and gun emplacements quickly enough?

The veterans among us remembered the fateful days of last April … At about 00.30 am hours, the Company broke up to push forward towards the barbed wire. There was an eerie quiet in the battle zone. The peace of the night was then broken by a brief exchange of fire. The 4th Company overpowered an Indian advance group.

Time passed too slowly – it seemed like an eternity until the first glimmers of dawn appeared. A light ground mist blinded us, but the British were in the same boat.

Five minutes later there was an earsplitting roar. Stukas flew in, dropping their bombs on the fortifications about 100 metres in front of us. The last machine had scarcely turned away when there was an almighty bombardment of shells raining down on the British positions. Before us was an almost impenetrable wall of mist, dust and smoke.

The commanders and platoon leaders gave the signal to attack. We shot up and stormed through the barbed-wire and minefields ahead. In front of us were tank traps – we jumped in and climbed up the opposite wall. Anti-tank gunners raced through a sloping passage, intended for the British reconnaissance trucks. The men worked their way through under the protective fire of the machine guns, threw hand-grenades and took the combat positions. Then came the first British, running towards us, their hands in the air."

Hans-Dietrich Arberger was Platoon Leader/2nd Lieutenant of a German machine-gun company with Tank Grenadier Regiment 104. His group made an attack on the Tobruk fortress in June 1942.

"The 3rd and 4th Companies broke through and built a bridgehead. The 1st Company, far ahead of their own artillery fire, stormed a British artillery position to find Tommies peering out, nonplussed. They hadn't expected to see the German infantry so far behind the bunker lines!

Isolated counter-attacks by British infantry were fought off. We found out they were 11th Indian Brigade. We'd probably have encountered stronger resistance had they been New Zealanders or South Africans.

The men lay in the positions, drenched in sweat and exhausted, but still full of attacking adrenalin. 'Now the tanks can come', they were thinking – and there they were, as if summoned, coming out of the layers of dust behind them. At the road fork on the way to El Adem, we dug in until our armoured cars arrived. We drove down the Djebel to see the town which had been so bitterly contested.

Now there were only a few dozen buildings left, mostly in ruins. In the harbour we could see masts and funnels sticking out of the water from the ships which had been sunk. On the west side of the harbour, a black wall of smoke was rising up, where the British had set fire to fuel stores. Several small ships made their way laboriously to the open sea, peppered by shells from our artillery and AA guns. Behind us the noise of battle had died out, but in the south and west, a dogged fight was still going on. That was where the core of the defensive troops were – the 2nd African Division. We got the order to turn south-west to break up the resistance.

In the evening, a British Brigadier General appeared at the battalion combat post and surrendered his troops to the Regiment Commander. Despite the darkness, we went on booty raids. There was nothing in the way of food that the mighty stores did not have … The night was full of rejoicing, despite the day's efforts. Tobruk had fallen. We'd our revenge for April!"

Leutnant Fritz Starke of the German 1st Company Machine-Gun Battalion 8, Tank Grenadier Regiment 104, was at the Gazala Line in June 1942, when some British troops tried a last-ditch break-out.

"A few athletically built Tommies tried to fight their way out with fisticuffs. One warning shot fired in the air ended this little sporting endeavour. A few stray Arabs appeared and led us into hiding holes and camps. In winter they had led the Tommies to our hide-outs. They applauded in April 1941, when we marched into Derna, in December they applauded the British on their march west, they rejoiced when we came into Derna again two months ago, and they would be clapping again when…? Who could hold it against them? After all, the Arabs were not Italian citizens!

An old Arab took Oberleutnant Pfeiffer to a wadi. In front of a cave stood an armoured truck, the engine still warm, which meant the crew could not be far away; then three Tommies came out. After we'd searched a bit more, Oberleutnant Pfeiffer and Feldwebel Sievert found three freshly bathed men sleeping, and judging by the uniforms on the ground around them, they were officers. They got quite a shock when they woke up – less because they were now being taken prisoner, but more because they were stark naked. This is not how the English gentleman likes to be seen."

Battle of the Atlantic – The U-Boat at War

On the same day – 27 May 1941 – as the sinking of the Bismarck (pride of the German fleet), the Allies notched up another less spectacular – but perhaps even more important – success in the Battle of the Atlantic. Convoy HX129, which left Halifax, Nova Scotia, on the 27th, became the first ocean convoy to be given anti-submarine escort all the way across the Atlantic, arriving in Britain without loss or damage. Until this time, the situation in the Atlantic had been critical for the British, as Donitz's U-boats were charged with the task of starving out the British nation, whose vulnerable convoys were forced to run the gauntlet of submarine attacks in order to bring in vital supplies. The men who went out to sea in the convoys and the pilots who flew marathon 17-hour sorties to protect them, remember those dangerous days, and the U-boat crews who stalked them look back to their long patrols in cramped conditions under the surface of the icy oceans.

Squadron Leader Terence Bulloch, DSO and bar, DFC and bar, was personally credited with four U-boat kills. With his unorthodox and inspired tactics, he became the top anti-submarine ace.

"The Liberator was a marvellous aeroplane for long-range anti-submarine work – especially the Mark I, which didn't have much defensive armament. Somebody had put four cannons under the nose, firing forward, and it carried eight depth charges, and we had an early type of radar which worked very well. We started operations in September '41 in the North Atlantic.

The radar was Mark II ASV – Anti-Surface Vessels, with Yagi aerials under the wings – and we had what was called a Christmas Tree down the top of the fuselage and beam aerials just below where the beam gunners' positions were.

We only had ten Liberators – one of those got written off while taking off with a full load. We were very pushed, and the Americans were very tight and didn't want to let us have them, even after 'Lease-Lend' went through. There was only one VLR (very long range) Liberator squadron, which was 120. We were mainly in the North Atlantic, doing convoy work and sweeps, looking for these blockade-runners and also these odd cruisers and battleships that got loose out there.

We escorted convoys *en route* from Halifax – and where the convoys were you always had submarines. I had a squadron of Libs up in Iceland, end of '41/start of '42. We had to get into 'the Gap' off Greenland. No aeroplanes could get near before from the mainland, Northern Ireland, or even from Newfoundland, and we used to cover that gap. That was when everything improved and we started killing them.

People thought I was very lucky. I was on a Liberator squadron from the middle of '41 to the end of '42 – and a lot of people won't believe this either – I sighted 28 U-boats, attacked 19, and the Admiralty credited me with four as definitely sunk. I'm not going to argue with them, but I know lots of people in my own squadron who flew for two years and never saw a U-boat the entire time. It wasn't luck, it was shrewd assessment of where they would be – and crew training. I had a marvellous crew. My flight engineer and two of my WOP/AGs (wireless operator/air gunner) stayed with me for the whole period – two and a half years. 120 squadron was the first VLR squadron in the RAF, and it's still going today.

The way I usually found submarines was by radar. My eyesight was very good – they used to call me 'Eagle Eye' – and I could spot the wake of these things quite a long way off. Then we used to manoeuvre around – we didn't just go hell-for-leather at the damn thing, as we were instructed. I devised a different way to stalk and attack them, up and down a track at an angle of about 20°. If you were attacking at 20° across, instead of at right angles to the U-boat, you had a much better chance of getting at least three depth charges doing some damage. They were only 270 pounders, Torpex filled, and you had to plonk those down. They were set to go off at about 25 feet, so you had to get them before the U-boat went down, preferably while it was on the surface or in the act of diving. If they got below 25 feet, you hadn't a hope. Not only that, the DC [depth charge] had to explode within about 10–15 feet of the hull to do any real damage. They were very well made – tough. So it was difficult, and we had no fancy bomb sights or anything, it was all done by eye. We used to come down to within 50 or 100 feet and the pilot used to plant a stick of six DCs.

We used to take photographs of every attack. You had to bring back evidence. The Navy were very hard to convince – they were so stuffy.

There was one U-boat which sank in 'the Gap' behind the HX217 convoy on December 8. On that day I attacked eight U-boats and sank one – I only had eight DCs. I sank one with six, then had another go at another with the remaining two. With this one, there was an enormous oil patch which got bigger and bigger after it went down, then suddenly sea birds arrived and you could see bits of wood, floating about in the middle of this oil patch. We took photos of that – and of the sea birds which appeared from nowhere, and that was the only evidence. One of the escorts went through the oil patch and took a sample back to Newfoundland. He said we'd killed it – they found some parts of dead bodies in the wreckage. But the Navy wouldn't credit us with it."

Air Vice Marshal Wilfrid Oulton, CB, CBE, DSO, DFC, was a trained fighter pilot – then chose to change to flying boats. However, he found himself Wing Commander in charge of 58 Squadron of Halifaxes, facing the marauding U-boats.

"Submarines were operating mainly from French ports, so they had to get through the Bay of Biscay before they could get into the Atlantic to do their job. They couldn't go all the way through the Bay without surfacing because they could only go so far on their electric batteries. Then they must surface for a number of hours to recharge their batteries by running their diesel engines – then they could dive again. Our plan was to cover the area with aircraft so that they could not stay on the surface long enough to charge their batteries. If they did try to stay on the surface, we had to try to catch them and attack.

There were two squadrons of Halifaxes at St Eval in Cornwall (there was one Liberator squadron too). The Halifax hadn't got a very long range, so in one squadron, 502 Zulu Squadron, they took out the main gun armament, which was a four-gun turret in the top (really for defending against fighters on bombing raids) and it gave them an extra fuel tank, so they went further out. My squadron, 58, kept all its guns and would operate close in to the French coast and tangle with the German fighters as necessary.

The first day with the squadron I said, 'Show me how this aeroplane works', and the second day I flew by night, making sure I could do that. The third day I went on a long trip with the maximum load, because there's a lot of difference between a light aeroplane and one that's absolutely loaded up, that could just clamber off the ground. On the fourth day I was on operations. Then, after a week or so, I decided to go out with each of my crews in turn, because it wasn't for me to be glorious – I wanted the whole squadron to be glorious. I said 'Right, I'm going to judge every captain by the way his crew performs, so I'll leave the captain out – I'll be captain, and see how the crew works with me'. I flew with each crew in turn – and they were awfully good.

May 8, I was off with a couple of good chaps and a crew of ten manning the guns, radar, wireless, taking turns, as after a while your eyes get tired and you can't see any more – at least you don't see, and you think you see what isn't there.

Just as dawn was breaking, there in the murk was a submarine. It was much too close to get in a reasonable attack, and the depth charges missed, but we were going round in a D pattern – what is called a creeping line ahead, and you fly a rectangular box, then you move beyond a few miles, and then move on again a few miles, so that you sweep the way through an area. With aircraft on each side, we swept through the whole of the Bay westward, to cover the whole area in which a submarine would have to surface. You stood a fair chance of one of the aircraft spotting one or two submarines.

Then about two hours after the first attack, there was another submarine – in fact it turned out to be the same one, and we attacked it. It turned out that this attack was successful. I was having kittens doing this, because as I stalked it and then came up and dived at it, there was a light flashing at me. I thought, 'Oh my God, is this one of theirs or one of ours?' There had been one nasty incident when one of our aircraft had sunk one of our own submarines.

I looked at this thing, and it was just a steady flashing light – it wasn't a recognition letter – so I went on. Then a piece fell off the aeroplane, so I thought, 'It looks as though it's not one of ours', and I carried on with a successful attack. What it was, in fact, was the 3-inch gun, firing at us. When you're looking right down the barrel, what you see is the flashing light as it is fired."

Leading Signalman Bert Wade joined the Navy as a scout and took over from regular Navy staff who had been allocated to commodores of convoy. It was on PQ17 that his luck ran out.

"I was on the bridge, fortunately, when the torpedo hit us. I'd just come on watch about an hour before, and it was about 6 o'clock in the morning. The torpedo hit the aft end, where the men were accommodated – the gunners, naval personnel who were on the ship. The lifeboats had moved away on one side, because the ship couldn't stop – the engines' special stopping valves were all jammed and she was travelling at about 8 knots, sitting down at the stern. Two of us managed to get off on the port side in a small boat, which was lowered by the gunnery officer. As he lowered it down, he let go of the rope and the thing hit the water and filled up. We slid down and managed to get in. I fell in the water alongside the boat, but my friend pulled me in. The other signalman jumped over from the deck. He'd managed to get out from below where he was trapped – but he was covered in smoke and tar. In his hurry to get over the edge, he'd caught his legs and thighs on the hooks of the rails – but fortunately the blood froze.

Then the submarine came up and came alongside us, filming all the time. The captain ordered us to join the other boat, which looked to us to be about a mile away. There was an argument about who was captain and who the people in uniform were. They settled it by taking the army cipher chap off the boat. He went in the submarine and we didn't see him again. The Captain, who was sitting in ordinary clothes, everyone said had gone down with the ship. We scrambled aboard two boats, about 60 of us, and we were there five and a half to six days. The Arctic is unbelievable. In the cold, there was the rumbling of icebergs – the colour is unbelievable and, to a young bloke of my age, fascinating. You didn't think about where you were or what the problems were. When I went into the water, I had a big overcoat on, which was drenched. The people who had been in the water, in waterproof suits, which were supposed to be the essence of survival – they were worst off. There were two stokers in these suits, and they weren't too well at all.

They used to row an hour on and two hours off, but no-one was quite sure where they were rowing to. The corvette picked us up on what was, more or less, my 21st birthday.

In the open boat there was water collected from what was left from each of three boats. Most of the water was mucky stuff, but there was pemmican and biscuits. They rationed us to two ounces of water every eight hours.

I remember it now, there were 30 people sitting in a boat, passing a beaker down to the other end with two ounces of water – and passing the same beaker back through the boat. It was unbelievable. Everybody tips it up on the way back and it's ages before it comes out with the next two ounces. I made up my mind never to be thirsty or wanting again.

I don't remember, as a 20-year-old, being very cold or very tired – I think it was excitement more than anything. The chap alongside me kept on about what it was like to die – and in trying to make him change his mind I obviously managed to change mine. Most of them were quite happy. Two or three of them died – because as soon as you got very cold, there was no way of recovery. You had to try sitting on people to recover them. We held a church service for two or three of them, and there were two boats together trying to sing 'Abide with me'. It still sends shivers down my spine if I hear it now.

It was a young kid of about 18 – a wireless operator – who had died, and the captain decided to have this service. We couldn't clothe the bodies, they went over as they were.

Rowing, I suppose, took most of the time, and a lot of them didn't want to sleep – they thought if they went to sleep they wouldn't wake up.

Captain Wharton had the idea that if you rubbed some whale oil on to your feet, it protected you against frostbite. But we only proved then that it was the wrong thing to do. I took my left shoe off and couldn't get it back on again. Frostbite made it swell up like a sprain, and you find you're walking on a lump.

When we went into Archangel the reception from the Russians was more or less negligible. We hadn't brought them anything, and they didn't want to know."

For Maurice Tither VRD, a Sub-Lieutenant telegraphist on HMS *Shearwater*, a corvette in E-Boat Alley (Channel and east coast of UK), Christmas 1940 was a bleak one.

"Action stations sounded. Cursing, we all closed up. Seconds later, we had an E-boat come dashing through the convoy. Then there was a terrific bang – the first ship was hit. When a torpedo strikes a ship, it's a tremendously loud noise as it reverberates through the sea surface – then it goes dead quiet. A very eerie sort of feeling. A Dutch steamer called the *Staad Maastricht* was lying helpless, her hatch covers blown off with a gaping hole under the bridge.

Everyone got away on one boat – the whole crew of 20, including a woolly dog, all covered in soot. We took them on board and gave them food and clothes.

Someone on shore with more rings on his sleeve than our skipper radioed that the ship MUST NOT be allowed to sink in the channel. All we could do was send for tugs and wait for Christmas.

As a party took the towing hawser on board her, a rating found all these bottles of gin and whisky and turkeys in the chart room. The chap in charge of the boarding party was a merchant service officer. Our skipper was straight RN, Dartmouth trained. The RNR chap shouted back to the ship, 'There's all sorts of hooch and stuff over here'. Then a clipped Dartmouth accent came back, 'No loot please – get the hawser aboard and get back here as quickly as you can.'. So we left it – but turned in much comforted, just knowing it was there.

Just when the folks on shore were sitting down to their austerity Christmas pud, the *Staad Maastricht* decided she'd had enough. She had slowly taken water and it became too much for one of the bulkheads. She just parted company like tissue paper. She sighed, wallowed and lurched, then down she went – with all that stuff on board. Our Christmas dinner was corned beef between slabs of dry bread."

Ernest Charles Goodwin saw action on the Russian run as a 'gun sweeper' on a First World War escort ship, HMS *Westcott*. His ship was one of many U-boat victims.

"The Germans had what they called an 'acoustic' torpedo, which worked by picking up the vibrations of your propellors. They would get within a mile of the boat, then fire. To counteract them, we attached two trailers to the boats called 'rattlers'. We towed them half a mile astern and the torpedoes would be attracted to them. We had both ours blown off several times.

We couldn't spend too many days in Russia – only enough time to refuel, because there was always a danger of being iced in. We saw lots of Russians, but most of the guards on the jetties were women – the men were away, fighting.

The people seemed very poor – I remember seeing an old woman dragging a sledge across the snow with her husband's body on it. She had to dig a grave to bury him herself. There was a cinema, but of course, there was no way we could understand the films. The first time there were about 18 of us, all smoking. They turned the lights down and put the film on – then the lights went up again. Smoking wasn't allowed, but we hadn't been able to read the 'No smoking' signs.

In winter there was about one hour's daylight, from around noon to 1 o'clock. There was one particular winter storm which was worse than all the U-boat attacks. We ran into what's called a 'stern sea', which means that it's coming up behind you. On a destroyer such as ours, it's particularly dangerous because you've got a low deck. If the water comes swilling over and the water-tight doors aren't closed, it will go in and take the ship down immediately.

The storm got so bad that the skipper decided that the only way to get through it was to head into the storm. We did a hard starboard turn. As the ship rolled, I could have reached out and touched the water with my hand.

The storm went on throughout the four hours that I was on watch. After I had gone off watch, I was called back at 2 am because the direct-hit shells had got loose and were rolling around all over the gun deck. When you wanted to use a direct-hit shell, you took off the cap, and they exploded as soon as they hit something. Nobody knew if the covers were on or not, and there was a big danger that they might explode. I knew exactly where everything was, so they tied two safety ropes around me, as the storm was still going on, and I had to throw all the shells over the side – very hairy!"

Third Officer Joe Wharton left New York with the British merchant ship *Empire Mersey*, as part of Convoy SC104. His ship encountered U-618 in the dark Atlantic night.

"At about 2.30 am hours on the morning of the 14th October, some 400 miles south of Cape Farewell. Greenland, the *Empire Mersey* met her fate. With an unholy crash, the ship shuddered and lurched over to port. Slowly she recovered, but started to go down by the head. 'Sparks' sent out the SOS and the order was given to abandon ship. My boat was being lowered down into the water with heavy seas running.

Inadvertently, the forr'd fall was let go, and the boat crashed down into the water with the after fall still secured. We were all flung into the water and it was every man for himself.

I was wearing a pair of long-johns, a sweater and a uniform, together with a duffel coat on top of which I had my lifejacket. My thoughts were dreamy ones of home – my mother and sister, how they would be asleep in bed, and here I was, with some 5000 fathoms of water beneath my feet, on the point of drowning in the north Atlantic.

To hell with that for a game of soldiers. I kicked off my boots, tore off my panic bag and paddled about desperately until I came across the canvas cover containing the boat mast and sail, which I clung to grimly. Around me in the water were some other crew members, crying for help – some were just floating in the water dead, but the red lights on their jackets were still burning. I was joined by one of the sailors, Batchelor. After what seemed an age, we were carried alongside the 2nd Mate's boat, and hauled aboard.

The boat's crew whistled to attract the attention of the rescue ship. She made some kind of lee, and our lifeboat came up on her port side, where she had the scrambling nets out. Searchlights were playing over the whole scene and as we were washed alongside, one of the survivors made a grab for the net – but just a fraction late. Before he could get a firm footing, the boat had fallen away, leaving him dangling. Up came the boat, broaching hard against the side of *Gothland*, crushing his head to a pulp.

Due to exposure and cold, having been in the icy water, I was unable to stand, let alone climb the scrambling net. A rope was passed under my armpits and I was hauled aboard, seized by two able hands and then carried down below to the fuggy warmth of the sick bay. After being stripped of my sodden clothing, I was towelled down with a rough Turkish towel. The air was blue – not to mention my skin!"

In command of the German U-618 was Leutnant Commander Kurt Baberg. As Convoy SC104 trailed across the Atlantic from New York to London, his boat sank the *Empire Mersey*.

"We still had no further reports of sightings or reports from the shadowing boats, and I had left the bridge for a short time to consult maps with the first mate, to decide on which new course we would follow. There was a shout from above, 'Commander to the bridge – we're right in the middle of the convoy!'.

As far as the eye could see, dark shadows of freighters were visible all round, quite a distance between each, and amongst them, the slender silhouette of a destroyer. Visibility was poor again when U-618 broke through the convoy's escort screen, undetected.

The convoy of ships was sailing in a three-column formation, widely spaced. We didn't feel at all bad, right in there, relatively secure, for the ships which towered high above the water could hardly spot us. Their attention and that of the surveillance craft was directed outwards, where they would have expected any attacks to come from.

We moved on in the middle of the convoy for about 90 minutes, following every tack and change of course, so that we could find a good firing position.

At about 02.00 hours we finally fired the 'tin fish' from the rear tubes, which should then have been followed up by a salvo from the front tubes. But nothing happened, despite perfect firing conditions, and we decided to wait a while before making the next attack so that we would reload the empty tube at the rear, which we did in what seemed like record time. Half an hour later, we steered back on course for attack, held back the 'tin fish' at the rear as reserve, and at about 02.30 hours, fired off a volley of four torpedoes at a group of steamers, overlapping in the central and starboard column.

We saw two of the torpedoes hit one of the ships (about 6000 tons of her) in the outer column. Black smoke rose to the top of the mast-heads from the exploding shells, and then quickly fell away. A few minutes later, nothing was to be seen of this freighter – it was the *Empire Mersey* (5971 tons of her). We heard that the other two torpedoes had hit, but we couldn't be certain we'd sunk another ship.

It was a long time after the war that I found out that the U-618 had sunk the *Empire Mersey* in the early morning of 14.10.42. The Third Officer on that ship was Joe D Wharton, now a retired Captain of a merchant ship, with whom I had my first contact early in 1986."

Leutnant-Commander Reinhart Reche was Commander of the German U-255, which sank 25,544 tons of shipping from PQ17. He holds a Knight's Cross for his service in the Atlantic.

"We were to join the U-boat group *Eisteufel* (Ice Devils) and the 5th Air Fleet in Norway to stop the massive supply operation.

The sea was smooth as silk. Brown banks of fog were blocking our view. At around midday, two escort ships emerged briefly out of the fog, which we reported immediately with a short signal. We pressed on into the fog to get nearer to them. The Admiral for the Arctic ordered the group to make a patrol line half way towards Bear Island the next day. Visibility was down below 500 metres. We dived and picked up a narrow band of sound on our hydrophone – however, sound carries far in those waters. We pushed forward above water in a northerly angle to take a sound bearing and then took another sound bearing under water. This gave us an approximate location of the convoy, which we then reported over the U-boat frequency. Behind us! In the constant brightness of the Arctic summer, we had to mount an underwater attack from the front.

Suddenly we came out of the fog, and there was the whole of Convoy PQ17 on a plate before us. Behind us an escort ship came out of the wall of fog, pumping black smoke. We had to radio a message before diving.

We worked forward in a wide arc. An attack by torpedo aircraft was announced for the evening. We fired off a twin torpedo blast on the outer escort screen. But it was spotted – no surprise in such smooth seas. Then came our 'baptism of fire' – 40 depth charges. After this unsuccessful attack by the aircraft, we surfaced and set off in pursuit.

We took another sound bearing in the north, where several explosions could be heard, and set off towards the noise. We met *U-Siemon* and then saw a sinking ship on the horizon. But as we drew closer, we were fired on and we submerged.

At 19.00 hours, Ju-88 bombers roared overhead. We heard their bombs exploding and watched as one of the aircraft was hit and burned up in the sky. Then, from behind, a swarm of He-111 torpedo bombers appeared flying close to the surface of the water, and roared past to the north. We reported the weather conditions around the convoy for the aircraft. It seemed that the large ships were no longer attached to the convoy.

Uncle Joe Stalin must have been in serious trouble if he was ordering convoys to sail at this time of year. For the Allied seamen, the winter storms would have probably been preferable."

Dieppe – Blood Beach

By April 1942, Allied planners were beginning to think seriously about the prospect of a cross-Channel invasion of occupied Europe. If a full-scale invasion was to be mounted, the Allies needed to discover as much as they could about the practical problems involved as well as the likely German response. The only way to do this was to organise a limited incursion into occupied Europe, putting an assault force ashore and then recovering it after only a short time. The success of the St Nazaire raid in late March 1942 acted as a boost to such thinking. In any full-scale invasion, it was believed a port would be essential for resupply. Dieppe was chosen as being typical of the size of port required. But the assault on Dieppe, on 19 August, turned into a blood-drenched disaster for the Allies. For the defending Germans, it was like shooting fish in a barrel. Veterans of both sides describe the Dieppe massacre.

Denis Whitaker was a platoon commander with the Royal Hamilton Light Infantry. As a Brigadier General, DSO CD, he recalls the confusion and horror of the Dieppe raid, when almost every man in his platoon was killed.

"On 6 July, we were all set to go but unfortunately the weather turned very, very bad and we stayed on board the ship for four or five days. By then the time had expired when the tides would be right for the operation, so it was cancelled.

Everybody was talking about where they had been and what they were training for. If there had been any enemy agents around, they would certainly have known that we had been planning to go to Dieppe. Then, all of a sudden one afternoon, we were told that we were off, and the next thing we knew, we were in Southampton.

It was 18 August. We were loaded on to our ships and told 'It's on – you're going to Dieppe'. Again, we were on the mother ship which carried assault landing craft. We would go most of the way on the mother ship and then we would get into the assault landing craft and proceed into Dieppe.

Some of the personnel had been changed and had therefore not been trained for the operation, and the special weapons which we had been issued with and trained to use had been taken away from us when the operation was cancelled. On board we were issued with new weaponry which was in grease. We had to clean it and had no opportunity to test it.

As we approached the beaches we came under fire. The ramps went down and we proceeded on to the beach and ran forward, into a line of barbed wire. My platoon had a Bangalore torpedo which is a long pipe filled with explosives. You put it underneath the wire, light a fuse and it blows up. The first fellow to put it under the wire was shot through the head and killed.

We were under such heavy fire than the operation became rather disorganised almost immediately. By this time the Germans had started to mortar the beaches. There were two headlands on either side of the beach and the Germans were up on top of them. They also had machine guns in the caves in the cliffs.

I decided that if we didn't get off the beach, which was a shale one, we were all going to die – a lot of people never did get off that beach. I led my men into the Casino, which was just a little bit to our right in front of us. We broke through the wire in front of the Casino and knocked out a pill box which was right on the beach. Naturally there were Germans in the Casino, defending it, and we had to clear them out before we could go any further. By this time, we had lost a number of men.

There were some trenches on the other side, which the Germans were in. We cleared them out of those and we then had to cross a great, wide esplanade which ran between the beach and the hotels. We ran across this esplanade and ducked behind a little wall. There was a machine gun behind us which opened fire. I was very lucky, because shots went underneath my stomach and in front of my head, but missed me.

We were able to get into one of the buildings on the front and then through it to near the cathedral. We got inside the cathedral, which was where we were supposed to establish our headquarters. But the people who were supposed to be in there hadn't yet arrived. This all sounds as if it happened very quickly, but it took several hours. There were now only five or six of us left; originally there had been over 30 of us.

We had to withdraw the way we came. Just as we got there, we received information that the landing craft would come in at a certain time – I think it was around 11 o'clock, but timings can be confusing. We were only waiting on the beach for 15 or 20 minutes. It was full of injured people. Three or four tanks had got on to the esplanade, but the rest of them had been knocked out on the beaches.

Just before the landing craft arrived, an RAF plane flew along the front and made a beautiful, solid smoke-screen. We had some smoke containers and hand-grenades which we used to create more smoke. When the boats came in we made for them, helping those who were still alive. I was lucky – I got on a boat.

We had taken a German prisoner at the Casino. He said that they had been expecting us for a week. The morning after Dieppe I was awakened at 6 o'clock and told that Admiral Mountbatten was having a meeting in London and I was to be there at 9 o'clock. Mountbatten had masterminded the attack and he was trying to prove that the Germans weren't forewarned."

Jack Brewin, 19½ years old, was trained up as a member of the Special Sea Service. His group has informed by Lord Louis Mountbatten that they would man new craft – the brainchild of Churchill – in heading an assault on France.

"On the afternoon of August 18, things really began to take shape. I think our own force left Newhaven at about 01.00 hours. I recall it to have been a very dark night, the sea was swelly and no lights were visible. We were under strict orders not to fire, even at suspicious targets. There were several near collisions between craft and we ourselves missed hitting an LCT which actually was beam on to our approach. Movement was very hazardous in the dark.

Naturally we were at action stations and I was gun-layer on No. 2 pom-pom. I now have the impression of feeling very lonely when I cast my mind back to that stage of the operation. I was not afraid of the events which would undoubtedly lie ahead. I do not think any of us were, but we had time to think and contemplate on what might be in wait for us. The average age of the ship's company was 19 to 20 years, and none of us had seen previous active service. I myself was just 19½ years of age.

At about 03.00 hours, the sky suddenly filled with tracer shot and it was obvious that some attack was taking place. We immediately altered course to starboard to avert, and eventually the action was left behind. I now know that this event was the unfortunate chance meeting with a small German convoy. We did not participate in any way, neither did I realise that this encounter had already contributed towards the terrible outcome of the operation.

As dawn broke, we had our first glimpse of a hostile shore. Strangely at this stage, it appeared quite normal – not at all like I had envisaged. I saw some white cliffs and a town, and apart from some distant thuds, nothing seemed other than commonplace. However, as the morning light grew I began to see the magnitude of the operation. The foreshore was obliterated by many craft, the sea around us occupied by many ships.

Maybe it was not actually like I now imagine it, but it now seems that with the coming of full light, the scene changed. The air was suddenly filled with aircraft and we fired madly at them. We were about half a mile from the shore, and so occupied with our fire that whatever was happening on the beach escaped us.

I estimate that we were so engaged for about two hours. There appeared to be hundreds of planes swarming everywhere, and identification was difficult. We just fired at everything that came near. When a plane was shot down, we all cheered and claimed responsibility. That day the RAF were operating Mustang fighters for the first time, and the resemblance of this aircraft to the German Me-109 was such that we most certainly shot one of these down.

It was about 08.30 hours when there appeared to be a change in our role. We began to steam closer to the shore and whatever we had already experienced under air attack was nothing to the holocaust which now presented itself. It now all seems to be one mixed impression of terror and nightmare. I can but try and describe that impression *en bloc*, so to speak.

Withdrawal of the landing was now taking place and landing craft, mostly LCPs, were streaming from the beach filled beyond normal capacity with badly wounded men. Our own craft lay all but on the beach, broadside on, and it seemed that every gun, light and heavy, was directed on us from the shore. I seemed rooted to the gun platform, possibly because I imagined the shield would give some protection. Tracer flew in all directions, and a great piece of metal from the ship's side landed at my feet. I heard terrible screams all around me, the gun had jammed and the wounded were being lifted aboard from the shore. The sights were ghastly – a Canadian minus an arm climbed aboard unaided, calmly smoking a cigarette. I wouldn't have believed such courage. Terribly mutilated bodies all around, the sea full of debris and floating dead, tremendous noise and the air full of stinking smoke. I remember looking towards the bridge seeking some renewal of strength from our officers – and seeing nothing but white faces as frightened as my own.

The officers' mess deck was being used as a sick bay and the orderlies were almost throwing the wounded down to the surgeon, who was doing an impossible task of mercy that day. Almost as continuously, the dead were being arranged on the deck. One of these Canadians was covered in a Union Jack which had been found inside his jacket – surely not the purpose for which it had been intended.

I have no idea how long this terrible episode lasted – it must have been several hours. The ship's guns were now all out of action and our only purpose was as some misplaced haven for those returning from the beaches. A Canadian actually tumbled aboard cursing and screaming before he turned around and dived back into the sea. I remember a dead Canadian being eased with my foot over the side to make further room aboard. It all added to the general impression of noise, smoke and utter disaster.

Orders were eventually given for our withdrawal. I have no idea of the actual time, but I do know that we were among the very last to leave. A wave of Boston bombers swept in very low as we departed. The skies were by now clear of enemy planes, but the fire from the shore was still active until we were out of their range. A heavy cloud of smoke enveloped the town, the beach filled with immobilised tanks and landing craft.

The returning force must have looked a sorry sight. We were all bearing the scars of battle and even now I noticed craft sinking or being abandoned. A steam gun boat slid alongside us and transferred to our keeping a German pilot picked out of the sea. I remember him to be naked apart from a blanket, and some of the Canadian survivors attempting to kill him before being restrained. He was to be confined in a paint-store, little larger than a cupboard, for his own safety. No-one was in the mood to respect conventions at that moment.

The journey back was one of utter misery. The mess deck was crowded with survivors and wounded lay around everywhere – a stench of mutilated humanity prevailed. I myself was in a state of utter shock. I lay on the deck and tried to gather my shattered wits together. I had no knowledge of what our role had been. I knew even less of what, if anything, we had achieved. I suppose someone, some-where was able to make a pattern of the day's events – I couldn't.

Later a war correspondent came aboard and approached me. 'What did you think of Dieppe?' he asked me. 'So that's where we've been', I replied. How ridiculous that must have sounded to him – but the name meant nothing to me."

Richard Schnösenberg was Captain and Battalion Commander of the German 3rd Battalion Infantry Regiment 571 of the 302 Infantry Division, based at Puys at the time of the raid, and wit-nessed the whole disaster.

"Effectively the day began for me the night before – I was engaged in a manoeuvre and during the alarm practice, we heard the first artillery fire from the sea. A German convoy had run into the English fleet. The fog dispersed for a moment, and we could make out a Union Jack on a warship, and saw that the ship had sent out landing craft to the beach.

It was about 6.00 am when the first wave of landings came from the Royal Regiment of Canada – an incredible number of boats – there was a barrage of fire going on during the landing until the men were actually on the beach. Then came the second wave – tanks. Some of them couldn't get over the tank wall and some got stuck in the shingle. The other tanks overran the beach company and we suffered relatively serious losses – but they couldn't get into the town because of the other tank walls. The infantry who were with this wave were severely hit by the heavy infantry guns, and were more or less wiped out.

This was the first time the English had used the Churchill tanks, and with the anti-tank weapons we had in the infantry, we couldn't deal with them. I reported this to the Division. In the newly formed anti-tank division they had the latest 7.5 cm anti-tank guns – which we had used so successfully against the Russian T34s. That was a big surprise for the English. Eventually it was these which dealt with the Churchills.

Our defences were so strong that within half an hour the first decisive blow had been struck. The enemy now knew they couldn't take the harbour of Dieppe by surprise.

I'll always remember, shortly before the first landing, there was an air attack and several hundred British planes came over, dropping fire canisters which set the cornfields on fire. But we were prepared for this. We were surprised that our fighters were not there and had to be alerted. Then they came – well, we had a few men on our side at that time! From 11 o'clock onwards, the air space above us was clear. That was the first decisive point. The final blow was round nine or ten o'clock. We knew then that if the British didn't send in a huge armada, the forces they had landed had no chance of taking the port.

The Royal Regiment of Canada in Puys were under such a heavy barrage of fire that any incursion into the town of Puys was impossible. Most of them were taken prisoner, but one group, under Colonel Catto – and I have to admit that this was an amazing feat – attempted to scale the cliffs, about 30 of them. But they were spotted. Colonel Catto was brought to me at my combat post, since we were the two senior men of our sections. Something happened which you would never have seen in 1945 – the two of us offered each other our hands, wished one another a safe return home – and maybe this helped, because I know that Colonel Catto got home safely after the war too. I've never forgotten this gesture made at Dieppe. When I too was taken prisoner in 1945, things were quite a bit different.

I spoke to a friend of Catto's after the war – he was about 19 at the time of the raid. He told me that this had been his first taste of action, and that he had lost his entire regiment in the space of 20 minutes.

If I was asked to give a judgement on the mission, I'd have to say that the Canadians did all that any soldiers could do, but the mission failed because we were already in such strong, secure positions – and above all, the support from the artillery from the sea was entirely insufficient to take a stronghold such as Dieppe. This was 1942 – we still had some men then. In 1945, OK, then we were bled dry. It might have succeeded then. Bear in mind that until then we hadn't suffered any great defeats in the West.

We'd been told that a dawn landing was entirely possible any time, and were told to be especially vigilant from 18–21 August across the

whole of the Atlantic coast – and this we were. But I can say this in all
certainty – we didn't know *what* was to come. If we'd known that, the
whole front would have been on full alert. In actual fact, there was
just my battalion, because I happened to have organised a practice
manoeuvre – but that was not because I knew there was going to be
an assault from the sea. My battalion was on full alert, but my neighbouring battalions in Dieppe and Pourville had only the normal
night crew operating – the rest were asleep. The second battalion,
under Major von Bodin, were close by their combat positions, but
they were sleeping – except, of course, the sentries, who were on
watch all the time. We, however, had all our heavy weaponry ready
and in position. As soon as the first boat came, we could shoot, and
we managed to dig in for long enough for the second battalion to get
into place.

I stress, we were prepared for this. We'd been practising manoeuvres
in these positions for about one and a half years. We had enough ammo
stockpiled to keep us going for days on end if it had been necessary. All
we needed to do was take the machine guns in our hands and fire.
We'd had so many practices with live ammo, we knew what to do. I
can't deny once we saw the huge fleet approaching, we had to rub
our eyes, but the order to fire came, and away we went.

There was another gesture – and this was still possible in 1942.
Once we'd dealt with the wounded (you have to remember it was
August), we had to get rid of the dead. So we had to dig huge graves
to bury them in. We held a requiem service for them, about two or
three days after the battle. On the afternoon of that day, at about
3 o'clock, we got a radio message from the English, asking if they
could drop some men off to attend the service. We told them they
could send an unarmed Red Cross craft, which we would intercept,
and it would be accompanied by German fighters as far as Dieppe.
There they could drop the men and turn back. I have to mention the
remarkable fact that there was no disturbance from the English Air
Force during the requiem service for the Canadians, or the subsequent service for the German dead."

El Alamein – Final Onslaught

*I*n tough fighting during the first week of September, 1942, General Montgomery's Eighth Army – helped by decoded German signals which exposed the Axis' plans – brought the joint German and Italian forces to a standstill close to the Alam El Halfa Ridge in Egypt. On the defensive, the Axis troops constructed a deep line of field fortifications and minefields that stretched from the Mediterranean coast west of the railway station at El Alamein to the saltmarsh depression of Qattara, about 60 miles (96.5 km) to the south. Despite pressure from Churchill to take the offensive, Montgomery calmly amassed troops and equipment. A fierce tank battle at Tel El Aqqaqir on November 2 resulted in estimated Axis casualties of at least 2,300 killed, 5,500 wounded and 27,900 captured. The battle marked the most eastern point that Axis forces were to reach in North Africa. At the cost of 13,500 men, Montgomery had signalled the beginning of the end for the mighty Afrika Korps.*

Brigadier George Roberts – later Major-General CB DSO, MC – was given command of the 22nd Armoured Brigade immediately before the Battle of Alam el Halfa as he returned to the action after being wounded.

"At the time I was commanding the Third Royal Tanks during the battles at Gazala. I got rather burned and had to recover for about four weeks.

A shell came into the tank perhaps. There was a terrific explosion and I was in the turret, with a gunner below me to my left. He got out with only his boots on – everything else had been blown off. He died – he was burned all over. I was burned on my face, arms and legs – I was wearing shorts at the time. It was a Grant tank we were in, just the two of us. I don't really know what hit us – whether a shot came in and exploded one of the shells from the inside, I don't know, but there was a terrific bang. I was lucky – I wasn't anything near as badly burned as the other chap. I went to hospital and was covered in plaster – one arm and both my legs. Cutting the stuff off was almost worse – the man took my skin off while he was doing it. I was in plaster for three weeks, so my legs got very thin in that time.

I was very surprised to find I was asked to go and command the 22nd Armoured Brigade. I'd only commanded a regiment for about six months, so I was astonished when we got up to Alam Halfa. Monty hadn't joined us then, and we were about the only armoured brigade left – everyone else was getting re-equipped. There was one regiment of Valentine tanks up in the north, otherwise it was just the 22nd Armoured Brigade.

As soon as Monty joined us, things were entirely different – he saw exactly what the situation was, and went on from there. There was a very clear view in his mind what the situation was, and how it should be handled. The whole atmosphere changed, without any doubt. Alam Halfa went satisfactorily, and so he was thought of as the chap for us – everybody was very impressed after that.

We were expecting the enemy to attack us at Alam Halfa – so everything was adjusted to that. Alam Halfa was a feature, and it was where the main battle would probably have to take place. Before Monty arrived, there were three possible plans for what we would do. When Monty arrived, there was one plan – that's all there was to it, and we put that into operation and were ready to go to certain positions when the balloon went up. We knew the Germans were going to attack – it was inevitable in order for them to get to Alexandria and Cairo. It was quite an important situation which dominated the area. He who had Alam Halfa was all right.

On the first night, the Air Force was sent over to deal with their supply situation, and they bombed them very heavily. That was pretty well the deciding factor. All the guns and tanks had their places to go to, and on the word, we took up our situations, and there we stayed, waiting to be attacked. They came up and we were waiting for them.

The Germans had put a much bigger gun on their Mark IV tanks – they didn't have many of them, but the ones they had were much better than any of the guns we had. But, fortunately we'd disposed our small anti-tank guns behind little hillocks: they came on and, as they came to a hill, they had to tip up to climb – so we could hit them from below as they reached the tops.

During the attack I was in a tank a little further back, watching the battle, and telling people where to go. One regiment was almost knocked out in their first attack, and I had another in reserve, which I hurried down to take their place."

Ray Kennedy arrived from New Zealand with the 22nd Battalion three weeks after Dunkirk, to work in the desert. As a stretcher-bearer – 'body-snatcher' – he helped retrieve the wounded at Alamein, as the numbers of his own battalion were steadily whittled away.

"War had become a way of life. New reinforcements were always horrified at the handling of the wounded, which was no better than in Nelson's day. At least then the badly injured were chucked over the side – here some had to be left to die a lonely death.

It wasn't pleasant having to decide who was going to die – we have to live with these memories now. There were never enough body-snatchers, we lacked medical skills and there was always a shortage of bandages.

There was a long walk to the start line, the stretcher being carried on the shoulders of two men, in the hope that the enemy would see it. The start line was a strip of ribbon on the desert floor. At the precise hour, the infantry started off, behind the artillery barrage.

We started collecting the wounded. The enemy made the job very difficult. Streams of incendiary bullets floated by at chest height. Trip wires at instep level glistened in the moonlight, about 12 inches apart. Stretchers bearing the wounded had to be carried by two men, crawling crab-like, counting the wires they stepped between. Any pressure set off a booby trap, which would cause appalling injuries.

The only protection we could give the wounded were the sand bags which made up part of the machine-gun pit. The walking wounded were rounded up and sent to the rear. With no landmarks in the desert, it was difficult to tell north from south, so they were faced towards the flares that were sent up at regular intervals from base HQ. They were given water bottles and sent across the desert.

I wondered who would bury the dead. It was eighteen hours before we were able to get back to the badly wounded. I can still see the look in their eyes – they thought we had deserted them."

Captain W Cobb MC led a patrol of 13 Australians by night. They had moved 1,500 yards forward of their own positions, when suddenly they were challenged by a German sentry...

"Everyone knew that surprise had been lost. All talking and digging had ceased. They were waiting for us.

We crawled for about 60 yards and heard the bolt of a Spandau ripped back, about 15 yards in front. I pitched my 69 [grenade] at him and he fired at the same time. One bullet got me through the leg, one got Munckton through the foot and one got Cooper in the body. We then followed the others into where the Spandau just fired from.

The gun was not firing, but there was movement in the fairly large trench behind it. Munckton emptied his rifle into it, then Corporal Else yelled out, 'I've got a prisoner, and all my men are safe'. The patrol withdrew to where Corporal Else and party were. Just then the prisoner had a bit of a scuffle and threw himself to the ground, shamming dead. Private Woods reminded him that he was alive with his bayonet and he moved off with us.

We had gone about ten paces when someone fired from the ground at us with a Tommy gun. I got him twice with my pistol from about ten feet, but not before he had put one into my arm and killed our prisoner. I began to realise that the bullet through the arm was going to be a different matter from that in my leg. I got Private Pickup to give me a hand along but just as we reached the Bren gunners, I blacked out and Corporal Else threw me over his shoulder.

He remarked when I told him that I could stumble along behind, that he'd carry me home even if I were bloody well dead. For about 1,000 yards, they took it in turns to carry me until some particularly close medium machinegun fire forced us to ground. When I got to my feet I was feeling much better and was able to walk most of the way to the road where we found a stretcher and I rode home."

Captain Ian Quarrie's Motor Torpedo Boat set sail with a small force on the eve of the main battle. Signals would reach Rommel to lead him to believe that this force carried vital supplies for the Allies – but the force's job was that of a decoy to draw the Luftwaffe from the main assault.

"As soon as darkness fell, the landing craft were left plodding on, while the MTBs moved out to sea a bit and increased speed to get well behind the enemy lines before the battle began. Our aim now was to make a feint landing at Ras el Kenayis, a promontory on the African coast, just behind Fuka. The RAF would provide a smoke screen as we approached the shore and meantime it was hoped the landing craft would still be in a position to attract the Luftwaffe.

When we were a mile or two off Ras el Kenayis, we turned inshore and reduced speed to something under 10 knots. In the leading boat, MTB 309, I had not only Lieutenant Denis Jermain, DSC, Royal Navy, now my Flotilla Senior Officer and overall commander of this operation, but also two soldiers with equipment resembling an enlarged version of the old HMV gramophone logo (without the dog of course!). As we slowed down, they assembled their sound machine and prepared for their part in the battle.

We began to look out and listen for our friendly aircraft to lay us a smoke screen. Temporarily we wanted to be neither seen nor heard by the enemy. Suddenly, there the aircraft was, right overhead and dead on time. The Beaufort started laying her smoke-screen along the shore and we followed slowly with our two Pongos pointing their sound-machine shorewards, playing sound-tracks of fleets coming to anchor – depths of water being called by the navigators, then 'Stand by' and 'Let go', followed by the roar of cables rattling out through big ships' hawsepipes, then more shouting – all this repeated as long as the smoke-screen shielded us. The MTBs to seaward were dropping depth charges to give the illusion of big guns firing.

While all this was going on, we all threw into the water a number of homemade rafts to which we had taped electric torches pointing upwards, suitably waterproofed, hoping to entice the Luftwaffe into thinking they were lights on our Landing Force, and to go on bombing and firing at them long after we had left. Finally, with the smoke finished and our sound-machine once more below, we formed up together and bombarded the shore with our Oerlikon and .5 guns nobly assisted by our splendid Beaufort.

Then we all set off for home at something over 30 knots this time, as we wanted to make all the noise we could and show a good bright wake to those damned aircraft up top – they were meant to find us.

It appears our rafted lights were seen and not only attacked from the air, but reported from shore to the Germans. We were certainly bombed and fired on by the Luftwaffe on our way to Alexandria, although I do not remember it quite as the 'running fight lasting three hours' when 'time after time the planes roared down on the ships, blazing away with their cannon and hurling bombs' as reported by the *Egyptian Gazette* next day. To the best of my memory, only one of our MTBs suffered a little damage, and we had two ratings slightly wounded. But what had our decoy achieved?

As a result of our little jaunt, the German 90th Light Division consisting of three Panzer Grenadier Regiments, one Artillery Regiment, one Anti-Tank Battalion and a Heavy Infantry Gun Company, said in all to total some 15,000 troops, were held back from the battle for over 48 hours. I like to think it was to us that General Montgomery was referring when he signalled his 'gratitude for the valuable assistance afforded by the naval operations on D-Night', as to the best of our knowledge, there were no other naval operations in the vicinity of the battle on the opening night."

Henry Byrne, 18, a gunner with 154th (Leicestershire Yeomanry) Field Regiment, Royal Artillery found himself among complete strangers – on the way to fight in the desert.

"Where was I going? What was I doing on this troop ship, risking my life at sea, manning a Lewis gun, watching the sky on August Bank Holiday and remembering my picnic in the Dublin Mountains only a year before?

Last year a junior salesman – now a highly trained field gunner. Is it fate or madness? My comrades must have thought the latter, since compared with these men of a pre-war yeomanry regiment, I was only a boy. Gibes abounded and for the first time in my life I felt isolated and at times near to tears. Instinct told me not to lose my individualism. I too had my culture, and my father and uncle had served in the First World War in an Irish Regiment. There must have been some English among them – so how did those poor souls feel among all the Paddys?

Young though I was, I decided to do what the Irish do best – laugh at myself – little knowing that in weeks of becoming the local come-dian, the lads would seek me out to cheer them up with my jokes and a smile. Suddenly I was one of the lads. This came back to me at Alamein, remembering my solitude. Suddenly all our lives depended on each other.

Three days before the battle, our regiment moved up to the front. With evening drawing in, the sun disappeared and we were faced with a dull, dreary and eerie scene, our faces grey with dust in an empty, cold wasteland. Here and there were the burnt-out remains of vehi-cles and the odd crane. The rumble of gun and machine-gun fire told us we were near the front. Suddenly we were ordered to halt. In the distance we could see Stukas dive-bombing our lines – our war had begun. We had to wait until dark to take up our positions, so we ate our 'desert chicken', otherwise known as bully beef, and waited. No fires – no tea. I shall always remember, in the dusk of that day, feel-ing I would never come out of this.

That evening we took up positions under light, intermittent fire which indicated that the enemy was just feeling out the ground on hearing transport movement. We dug into our holes and for the next two days it was as though not a soul was in the desert. Over a million men hidden deep in the sand, not a sound anywhere 'til sunset, when the Stukas came, followed by a repeat at sunrise.

On the afternoon of October 23, leaflets were distributed, giving Monty's eve-of-battle message. 'Fight as long as you have breath in your body'. It seemed unreal in the quiet afternoon. Where were the tanks, infantry, planes and guns?

At 21.40 hours, the desert shook like an earthquake. For as far as we could see, the sky was ablaze from the guns. Such was the deafen-ing noise that we could see enemy shells exploding on our positions, but could not hear them. Our gaunt stares said it all – we were scared stiff, but oddly enough, not frightened. In the hours that followed, the tension eased. Our barrage was having the desired effect, but the infantry and engineers had it rough.

In the glare of the guns, men could be seen falling and groups being blown up by mines. Cameramen were moving forward with the infantry, but to no avail: Jerry held a strongly fortified line.

By morning we were veterans, or so it seemed. Gippy tummy reared its head, and though painful and distressing, it provided a comic relief watching each other going back and forth with a shovel to dig a loo.

We got our bottle of water in the morning and each put some in a petrol can for washing. We then got another tin, pierced holes in the bottom, put some holes in and sifted the water after every wash. After two days, one of my quips was 'It's cleaner to stay dirty'. Most of us went for bald heads because of the sand lice.

The cook-wagon, when it could provide a hot meal, did wonders with bully stew, bully fritters, cold bully (which melted in the tin), biscuit porridge, biscuit date pudding and good old cocoa. They were few and far between, but most welcome!

They occasionally gave us Carnation milk, tea and sugar when they couldn't cook and, thanks to the petrol can, we made the famous 'Benghazi' fire, made by cutting the can in half, filling it with sand and piercing holes in the sides. We then poured petrol on the sand and lit it. Our shirts and shorts were dropped into a petrol can, dipped, removed and dried in two minutes in the sand.

Of course the war was in full swing though static, and with all the above, the shocks of the 23rd became a bad dream. Stukas came over and we came out of our holes and fired rifles at them. Although no advance was possible yet, the whole picture of war changed. Morale was high, and as the days passed with the endless bombardment and bombers and fighters soaring above, the warning came that if we didn't break through soon, we may have to withdraw into Palestine. None of us accepted this – we had been too stirred by Monty's message. On the tenth day, the Axis collapsed and the breakthrough came. We were on the chase, moving up and down the line of advance to give support.

Soon we caught our first glimpse of POWs. The Aussies were throwing stones at a group of Italians, telling them to go back and fight. I found this to be in bad taste, though on the surface it was comical. On we went, and at the famous Knightsbridge, thousands of Hitler's supermen, dishevelled, dirty, some in stockinged feet, all thoroughly dejected and apparently starving, were taken, escorted by a handful of Scots Infantrymen. This is what we waited for – a victory for the British, finally breaching Hitler's master-race.

In the event, I couldn't hate. We stopped and watched these men pass by. I thought what heroes these men were to have withstood this bombardment from land, sea and air for ten days. I wished I could be sure I could be so brave. For a moment I imagined they were British and I was one of them. I thought of my family at home, and I'm proud to say it brought a tear to my eye. I was to see more of the Nazi element of Hitler's men in Italy, which did fill me with hatred – and a determination to destroy that evil empire.

However, remembering Alamein, and I often do, I feel there is a certain affection between the *Afrika Korps* and the Eighth Army. It was a man's war and I had become a man. We fought soldier to soldier, no civilians involved, and though we all lost friends, I feel sure we will always have a healthy respect for each other for the manner in which we conducted ourselves in that war."

Cathleen Violet Chidley was working in a shop before she joined up. After a few weeks with the Army Pay Corps, she found herself posted to the Provost Corps in Cairo.

I was 23 and very excited when I was told I was going. We went around the Bay of Biscay to Alexandria and the convoy was attacked by U-boats. It was most uncanny – when you looked out, you couldn't see any of the other ships, but you could hear the depth charges.

We were put on to these cattle trains almost as soon as we reached Alexandria, and sent to Cairo, where we were billetted next to an Egyptian army place. They were always cadging cigarettes. Their conditions seemed very over-crowded compared with ours. We had lovely billetting and the food was always good.

We used to patrol the streets in groups of two men and two women. We would go out at about 7.00 am and work until midday. We would work again in the evening from about 5.00 pm until 9.00 pm or 10.00 pm. In the afternoons we used to sleep – it was so hot that you couldn't do anything else.

There were some nasty incidents when we were patrolling, but when you're young, you don't feel fear of anything. On one occasion, a knife was dropped from a window and landed inches away from me. We also heard rumours that some police who had been patrolling with us had been mixed up in a drugs deal – the incident had something to do with that.

We women would be hassled a lot by the local men when we were on patrol, and we never went out alone. King Farouk used to invite the English girls on to his yacht. I went there once, but some girls went often.

There used to be a saying you'd hear at get-togethers, that we were the 'officers' ground sheets' – but you always get that sort of mentality, and it was only a minority of the men who were like that. Most of them regarded us as equals.

We were very, very naive. One of the girls was pregnant and she kept telling us she felt sick. We were all very concerned, but it didn't occur to any of us what was wrong.

Another girl I used to patrol with used to dance in a night-club. She was a Greek, and absolutely lovely. I think they knew what she was doing, and used her as a sort of spy for any information she could pick up. She was short and stocky, but when she danced, she was beautiful – I can still see her now.

It wasn't fun really, but a lot of the time we looked on it as such. We joined ENSA and used to go singing. I appeared in a play called 'The Old Mill'. In the evenings we went to places which were like beer kellers, and they were full of mainly English people. There weren't many incidents of drunkenness, although I can remember one, where I jumped on the table and started blowing my whistle to restore order."

Major Tom Bird MC commanded the six-pounder anti-tank company of the Rifle Brigade in the 'Snipe' action on October 26 and 27, earning him the DSO. Here, he tells of the courage of members of his company.

"The battle for Alamein had come to an impasse – neither side was winning. We, a motor battalion of three rifle companies and one anti-tank company, were instructed to carry out a night attack and take what was thought to be a ridge, some 2,000 yards in front of our line. At the point from which we were going to start there was disagreement as to where we were. The infantry holding that line were part of the Highland Division, and they were fairly confident that they knew where they were. We, on the other hand, had been in the desert for about two years and thought we knew all about navigation there – and we thought we were somewhere different.

The Colonel decided we would form up as if *we* were right, and he was then going to ask the gunners to put down a round of smoke on the area which we were to attack. To our embarrassment, the Highland Division were correct, so when the smoke came down, we had to switch around in the middle of the night.

As we met almost no enemy resistance, the rifle companies' attack succeeded and the anti-tank guns were sent for and dug in during the night. But at dawn, to improve their field of fire, some had to be re-sited. I think probably the majority of our casualties were at that moment and it's always one of the remarkable things in the desert, that if you were just below ground in a slit trench, you could have a fantastic amount of bombing and shelling and not come to a great deal of harm – unless they actually hit you. But if you moved about, that's when you got casualties.

All day we found ourselves under fire from our own men. As far as they were concerned, we were 2,000 yards ahead of where they thought there were any of their own troops. Added to this, during the night, various German tanks and guns had come through our posi-tions, and we'd knocked them out. Looking through the haze from quite a long way away, all they could see were some jeeps and some enemy tanks, so they assumed that we were the enemy. Once when we were being attacked very hard indeed by our own side, our intel-ligence officer, Jackie Wintour got in his jeep and drove straight at them. Luckily they didn't fire. He went right up to them and stopped the leading tanks firing, but the rest went on unabated.

The most memorable occasion was when we were being attacked by nine Italian tanks – but only one of our guns could fire at them. This was manned by the Colonel, Vic Turner, the Platoon Commander, Jack Toms, and Sergeant Calistan. They'd shot six when they ran out of ammunition. Jack Toms got in his jeep and drove to one of the other guns. Tanks which were still coming on were shooting, and everyone else was shooting at us, so he drove through very heavy fire. Then he loaded the ammunition from one of the other guns on to his jeep and as he drove back, his jeep was hit and caught fire. But he managed to drive as far as the gun and he and the colonel, and Corporal Francis, unloaded the ammunition – and of course, with the fire, this was liable to go off at any moment – and managed to get the ammunition to the gun. Calistan then hit all the rest of the tanks and knocked them out. Vic Turner was wounded in the head in this action.

I was hit in the back of the head but was more or less *compos mentis*. Vic Turner and I were more or less knocked out. Two German tanks got within about 100 yards from where we were. There was one gun in a position to fire but the gun crew were in a trench a little bit away from the gun, and they couldn't get to it because every time they made the slightest movement, there was a huge burst of machine-gun fire. The platoon sergeant, Sergeant Swann, managed, by using dead ground, to creep up to the gun to shoot at the tanks. They were within such short range that one exploded, more or less. I can remember the cheer which went up – it was a very, very brave effort.

Monty came to give the battalion a talk – I suppose it was before Alamein. I remember him telling the men that they were 'a fine body of men' – which was such a cliché. If I'd said it to my company, they would have roared with laughter and they'd have known that I was pulling their leg. However, it seemed to go down quite well. It didn't seem to matter that he talked in clichés."

Heinz Erdmann volunteered for the 'Sonder-Stab F', a special German staff unit, and he set up Special Unit 288 – a medical unit in which he served during the early part of 1943.

"We had erected a first-aid post between the coast and the road, marked with a huge red cross and situated away from the combat troops. We had made it through the so-called 'six-day race' from August to September '42 and waited to see what would happen. As a medical unit, we had relatively little to do. Then we were woken in the night of October 23/24. We suddenly heard ahead of us at the front (some of us had started to bed down for the night) a terrible roar and rumbling and crashing over a broad area, and saw a long, wide flickering gleam of light in the background, from the sea right over into the desert. It went on and on, sometimes stronger, then less. And this rumbling went on for days and nights, sometimes further away from us, sometimes nearer.

Now we had more than enough to do from the medical point of view. The first returning vehicles and smaller units were blocking the road and tracks. It became difficult for us to get our wounded back to the post. Sometimes we had to force our way through. Once our first-aid post was bombed. The fighter/bomber attacks on the road and the tracks were very bad.

Around the 30th October, we had to up sticks and move back. Then on the 3rd November the front collapsed and we began to retreat. This was definitely the worst for us, the sand blowing in our eyes, the air and the fighter/bombers, to say nothing of the artillery and tank fire. At night the coast road and wide strips to the left and right were lit up by flares.

Everything blocked up, terrible chaos, screaming, cursing, running about, burning vehicles, rescuing the wounded between them, treating them and carrying them off, and burying the dead. All this went on for days and nights – about 10 days. Then, at the Halfaya Pass, Sollum, things got more or less back to normal (for us at least). I was, and still am, grateful that my unit and myself got through this period relatively well."

Leutnant Heinz-Dietrich Arberger, with the German 3rd Company of the 21st Armoured Division recalls the start of the battle, while Adelbert von Taysen, Commander of 1 Company Machine Gun Battalion 8, remembers the final stages.

"The previous evening we were playing cards and chatting. Shortly before 22.00 hours there was a rumbling and roaring, and flashes to the north of us. We stared at the horizon, which had turned a pale colour. Were the Tommies ready to attack? Around midnight it had quietened down, and we went off to sleep. The next morning the noise of fighting could be heard. Everything was quiet where we were, so we thought this couldn't be anything to worry about. The 3rd Company were enjoying their afternoon, presenting medals, roasting gazelles – there was a jovial atmosphere. Then the alarm came: 'Prepare to march!'.

On the evening of October 25 we marched off, initially to the west, then in a wide arc behind north section, which had been heavily burned up by the enemy. After an extremely wearisome night march, during which night bombers inflicted heavy losses, we reached the telegraph strip south of Tell el Aqqaqir. We found an area of dunes which it was impossible to see over. This was already occupied by the enemy in unknown strength, but should have been occupied by Italians.

The commander ordered us to attack on the spot to clear out the area. There was a brief exchange of fire with British reconnaissance units, who immediately withdrew to the east. While chasing after them we came upon unoccupied Italian positions, some with primed 88mm Flak. The Italian battalion which should have been there, turned up afterwards from areas at the rear or from deep bunkers into which they had retreated.

The adjutant reported location and intentions to the Corps over the headphones, and got a lengthy whistle back, because our intentions had been greeted with disapproval. The Corps obviously still had faith in our allies. The events of the next 24 hours were to prove them wrong.

At about 21.00 hours there was a heavy barrage from the enemy, the like of which we'd never witnessed before. Fortunately, we had been able to find useful cover in the sandy landscape. About half an hour later, the firing suddenly stopped. It was suspiciously quiet. Then suddenly voices could be heard. We released the safety catches on our guns. With loud shouts, the Italians hurtled past us to the rear, some on foot, others on overloaded trucks, like a phantom – then silence.

On the morning of the 28th, British forces were gathered in strength in front of our sector. Without bothering too much about cover, they got into position for an attack – obviously completely aware of their superiority. However, before they could take position, our heavy artillery section fired on them. The attack ceased, but it was a gruesome sight, watching the British orderlies toiling without a break to rescue their wounded and dead. In the twilight, we scoured the battlefield behind our position and came across a badly wounded captain. It was very moving to watch the efforts our men made to bandage up the unfortunate chap, who had been lying untreated for a day and a half. They gave him food and drink and carried him off."

Adelbert von Taysen describes the night of November 2nd.

"A 60-minute barrage rained down in the night on our positions by the telegraph strip. At about 1 o'clock the fire stopped. A few minutes later, British soldiers stormed the 1st and 2nd Companies on foot and on carts. Six of these agile little gun carriers managed to destroy the anti-tank guns at point-blank range, then the enemy was on top of us. A battle for the cover holes ensued, with rifle butts, spades, handgrenades and bare fists. All you could hear was the sound of panting, groaning and whimpering. You could just see the silhouettes of the attackers against the night sky. The best way to recognise who was friend or foe was by the flat steel helmets the Tommies wore. After a half-hour battle they disappeared eastwards. Only a few dead were left behind. By some sort of miracle, we got away with only a few wounded."

North Africa – The Final Act

The six months following the defeat of the Afrika Korps at the Second Battle of El Alamein in November 1942 saw the turning of the tide in the Mediterranean war. Even while Field Marshall Erwin Rommel was beginning his long retreat out of Egypt on 3 November, a British and American armada (Operation Torch) was steaming towards the North African coast. On 8 November, the Afrika Korps was back at Mersa Matruh when the dreaded news arrived that strong Allied forces had landed from the sea in Vichy French Morocco and Algeria – in the Afrika Korps' rear. As soon as Allied troops landed, the business of clearing the Axis from the whole of the heavily contested desert region began in earnest. Vicious hand-to-hand fighting and gruelling hot days took their toll on the men of both sides. As the campaign wore on, losses increased. Axis supplies dwindled and forces endured some of the worst conditions and the bloodiest fighting of the desert war.

After the Malta campaign, Royal Marine Robert Porter trained in West Africa at Freetown to carry out bombardments. Unbeknown to him, this was in preparation for Operation Torch, to which his ship, the *Aurora*, took a large number of US troops.

"We left Liverpool on 4 July 1942 and sailed to Freetown, West Africa, where we carried out bombardment practice to train the new crew. Although we didn't realise it at the time, we were being prepared for the North African campaign. We came back into the Mediterranean at the end of October and went into dock in Gibraltar. Although it was British, you had to be very careful, because there were a lot of enemy sympathisers there.

While we were docked, massive troop ships, two or three thousand men on each, arrived. Most of the men on the ships were American – the general idea seemed to be to make the campaign appear to be American, so as not to offend the French. The day before the invasion, we got hundreds and hundreds of American Rangers on our ship. They were wearing enormous armbands showing the Stars and Stripes, so that they would easily be identified as Americans. It got very crowded, but we didn't mind because we were used to not having much space. They slept on the deck, like the rest of us. You didn't have bunks in those days – only the officers had bunks.

These American Rangers were the crack force of the American Army. They were all armed with guns and bullets – we weren't, of course, because we weren't going ashore. There was one Ranger there, a real comedian – we all took to him. His name was Dizzy. He was showing his guns off to us, and we were all fascinated, looking at these American weapons. He was getting very excited – you have to remember that these men were full of tension because they knew they were landing the next day. Unfortunately, there was a live bullet up the spout of his gun, and it went off as he was showing it to us, and hit the deck-head. The incident caused a terrible commotion and he got a real telling off from his sergeant.

In the evening, just before it got dark, the troop ships sailed right into the Mediterranean. Our destination was Oran, but we sailed right past it, as if we were heading for Alexandria. The idea was to give any spies the impression that the invasion wasn't going to be in French North Africa. When it got really dark – at about two or three in the morning – we turned around and went back towards Oran.

There were some coastal guns in Oran harbour, and some Vichy French destroyers. We had some trouble breaking the boom, which is the gateway into the harbour. There were two little ships in our force, rather like frigates. They were sent in first to break the boom, but both got hit and most of the American troops on board were lost.

From the 6-inch gun turret and looking through the cabinet, which was like a spy hole, I could see a search-light from the shore that was shining directly at us. We immediately got the order to fire, and the light disappeared – we must have hit it.

Three of the French destroyers that were in the harbour tried to get out. The captain of the first one decided not to fight us, and instead of firing, he ran it aground. We left them alone then, because they had surrendered. The second destroyer managed to get out of the harbour and escape. Then another destroyer came out and we sank it. I don't know if there were any survivors, because we started firing at the coastal batteries immediately after that had happened.

There was very little opposition to the actual landings. There didn't seem to be much heart in it, and we were on shore a day or two later, in the town enjoying ourselves. It was like a real holiday for us – it was like going to a fantasy land, seeing the old market place and the French buildings and the young French girls. It took my breath away."

Peter Allbeury, a pilot with the Fleet Air Arm, was catapulted from the deck of HMS *Renown* in his Walrus, with his crew of two, to carry out an anti-submarine patrol and to protect the invasion fleet attacking Algiers.

"We had our British markings painted out with American ones, because it was thought that the French would give the Americans a better welcome than they would the British. When we got to the end of our patrol, we were told to 'proceed ashore', as the ship was not in a position to recover us. We found an airfield at Maison Blanche, about 20 miles to the east of Algiers, so I flew there to see what sort of reception we would get.

The place was well supplied with French fighters, but to our pained surprise, there was a German Junkers 88 and an Italian Savoia Marchetti three-engined transport too. The petrol situation was now critical, so we had no option but to land there and hope for the best.

No-one came out to greet us – but it was about 6.00am, so we assumed that everyone was still abed. We could see an estaminet down the road and wandered off to see if they were serving breakfast. Much to our surprise, a lot of people were gathered there and we were right royally received. The breakfast became more liquid than solid and eventually we staggered back to the airfield to find hundreds of American soldiers. They were astounded to find that we spoke English, and more so when we explained that we were British Fleet Air Arm aircrew, a little out of our element. They were not keen to let us back on to the airfield, as they had come to capture it.

We stayed at Maison Blanche for a few days, and the place filled up with RAF personnel. We took it upon ourselves to do dawn anti-submarine patrols, until a British Army Major asked if we would do tactical reconnaisance for the army. We were delighted to help and flew him about 20 miles east to the town of Bougie, hoping that it had been captured, so that he could see how things were going with the army – especially the tanks. This meant flying very low, and zooming down wadis in the hills, to see if there was any opposition waiting for allied tanks around the next corner. We had great difficulty in estab-lishing good relations with the RAF and consequently had basically to steal petrol to keep us going in our more-or-less freelance operations. When we were joined by other Walrus crews which had 'lost' their ships, we moved to Algiers and arranged to take over the Air France base. Our army had always been most co-operative and provided us with clothing and other necessities. The army Base Ordnance Dump was to be found in an area shown on the maps as the 'Ravine des Femmes Sauvages' – there was great competition to go there in the first place, but no-one was lucky enough to ever discover any wild women there.

We also found that during an air raid, we were able to pillage the heaps of supplies being unloaded from the ships, especially boxes of rations, while others were in air-raid shelters. We lived this very unorthodox way for some time before we came under the control of Allied Supreme Headquarters at the Hotel St George in Algiers, who eventually arranged for us to hand over our Walrus aircraft to some Free French pilots. By then we had carried out 176 sorties and flown 388 hours, attacked two U-boats and rescued 19 people on air-sea rescue duties."

Peter Stainforth, a Lieutenant with the Royal Engineers in the 2nd Parachute Brigade, was leading a patrol in the area round Tunis when they stopped to rest in a farm. He combines his account, with hindsight, with that of Hans Teske, whom he met after the war.

"The first bucketful of crystal-clear water had just come up when the French farmer, Monsieur Albert Rebourg himself, came running out to us in a state of great agitation. He explained that German armoured cars and tanks patrolled the district, and it was very unsafe for us to remain in the open. He offered us a large barn in which to rest and lie up, while he personally would see that we had everything that we required. We left the immediate area of the well as though it were infected with the plague.

He showed us an outbuilding with sliding doors at the back of his farm which would just comfortably take our party of 70 men, and then instructed his farmhands to bring several bales of straw for our comfort. He brought us water in a galvanised water-cart and said he would get his wife to boil us a large kettle so that we could make tea. Finally he gave orders for a meal of cous-cous to be made for the whole party.

That French farmer was goodness itself. He gave us valuable and very accurate information regarding German activities in the neighbourhood and pointed out on our maps exactly where the Germans maintained posts and standing patrols. Above all, he strongly advised us against going into Massicault, saying that, although British patrols had once or twice visited the place, the town was more likely to be occupied by the enemy. Our main line ran much farther to the west – exactly where, he could not say for certain. He also undertook to supplement our own lookouts by keeping watch from one of his upstairs windows – where his activities would not arouse suspicion. We were now satisfied as to his bona fides, so we gratefully accepted and lent him a pair of binoculars."

Five miles away near La Mornaghia, Lieutenant Schuster's 1st Company of 5th German Paras began a day of search and destroy. Heavy armoured cars armed with four-barrelled 20mm guns were posted at vantage points on the plain to watch for the dust kicked up by marching British troops, and one was located just one mile south of El Abbaci. Lance Corporal Hans Teske went out on a motorcycle patrol, riding pillion behind Schuster, a holder of the Knights Cross. Their mission led them inevitably to the largest farm in the area at about 10 am.

We had finished our drink of tea and a very rough and ready meal of biscuits and had just fallen into a delightful doze, when suddenly we were awakened to find the farmer bending over us. 'Do not wake the men,' he said slowly in French, so that we might understand his meaning perfectly, 'it may only be a *canard* – a false alarm, you understand? I have just seen four German motorcycles with soldiers on the road half a mile from here. They are coming this way. Get your weapons ready and don't make any noise'.

The four other officers and myself got up quickly. We seized a couple of Bren guns and some grenades and had a cautious look out of the doorway, keeping well in the shadows.

Schuster dismounted and immediately questioned Rebourg about a report of British soldiers in a nearby farm. Rebourg said that a small party had called there at dawn, but left immediately. Schuster's French was not very good and both had difficulty in making themselves understood. Meanwhile, Hans Teske, an 18-year-old in action for the first time, went behind a haystack to relieve himself. In his urgency he left his rifle propped against his sidecar.

The watching British officers kept their Bren and Sten guns trained on the three Germans, staying well back. Teske, now more comfortable, was suddenly aware of some Arab children playing close by and then, to his horror, of a British soldier standing in the shadow of the barn door, covering him with his gun. Meanwhile I was leaning back in the shadows, hoping desperately that I had not been seen, and held my fire.

Teske was a quick thinker, and I later learned that he reasoned that if he gave no sign of recognition he would probably walk away alive. Hopefully this British soldier was merely covering a wounded comrade, for out of the corner of his eye he could see a pair of boots further back in the barn, as though someone was lying dead or wounded. Perhaps the British soldier shared his concern for the safety of the Arab children and the farmer and his family, and he had decided not to fire. So Teske buttoned up his flies and sauntered off, knowing full well that a false move would result in a holocaust of shooting.

The Germans re-mounted and drove off, Teske still feeling hot and cold. He was also in a fearful quandary. He could not now admit what he had seen for fear of the consequences, even though his silence had undoubtedly saved all their lives. He decided to say nothing, and the patrol continued on its way.

We were now in rather a dilemma. We could not overlook the possibility that the patrol would come back – this time with an escort of armoured cars and tanks. The farm itself afforded a hopeless defensive position. It stood alone in the middle of a plain, completely bare of trees or cover of any sort. To try and fight tanks on such terms would be positively suicidal, they would simply stand back well out of range and blow the farm to pieces with their heavy guns.

We had just made up our minds to move when our problem was solved to everyone's satisfaction. Some passing Arabs informed the farmer that there were English soldiers in the next farm about half a mile away. Immediately he sent his foreman over on a mule to confirm this story. The man returned in a little while with Charteris, the battalion intelligence officer, perched uncomfortably on the animal's withers. Charteris told us that the Colonel and about 50 men of Battalion HQ were in a farm close by and were to join him immediately. His place offered a much better and safer hideout, and a perfect defensive position from which to fend off a German attack.

We roused all the men quickly and then left the farm in open order as fast as we could go, as we had no idea who might be watching from the hills. Soon we started to climb into the foothills by a narrow sandy track, and then quite suddenly came upon a small Arab farm, standing on a slight rise and screened from the rest of the country by a convenient rim of hills. Thus it was that we came to Cactus Farm."

Corporal Paul Beck of the 1st Battalion of the 5th German Parachute Regiment, was a runner, travelling in a motorbike sidecar to carry vital messages throughout the battle zone. At the time of his account, German forces were in possession of Cactus Farm, formerly in British hands.

"In the middle of March 1943, I was seconded to the 4th Company, the HQ being at the Cactus Farm near Peter's Corner. Here it was like a holiday centre, disrupted only by the odd run to forward positions such as Point 107 or Point 133. However, on 27th of April, a British attack on Point 107 and Point 133 succeeded, changing the situation completely. Point 137 (Sidi Abdallah) and the Cactus Farm became the German main line of defence on the important Tunis to Medjez-el-Bab highway. The Cactus Farm was held by a total of 48 paras under Sergeant Schafer.

That evening I experienced the first attack on this farm. British infantry, supported by artillery, advanced towards us. We held fire until the enemy was a few yards away. Surprised by the heavy fire which opened up so suddenly, they withdrew. Next morning, we observed sappers clearing a passage through the minefield. We were unable to do anything about it, lest we display our own weakness. We also had to conserve ammunition. Soon we understood the meaning of the sappers' efforts – 16 Churchills, supported by infantry, advanced towards our farm.

Again, we only opened up at very close range. Our sole anti-tank gun destroyed or immobilised several British tanks. A few British infantrymen who had succeeded in penetrating the farm defences were again ejected. In the desperate situation, we asked our artillery to shell our own positions. The enemy withdrew. We picked up enemy wounded and took some men, who were hiding, prisoner.

We succeeded in rescuing the crew of a burning Churchill tank. They were all seriously wounded and one of them died during the night. He kept asking for water. Water we didn't have – the only liquid we had was wine, and plenty of it.

In the afternoon, the enemy attacked in several waves, supported by tanks. They managed to penetrate in places; however, this time, Tiger tanks arrived on the scene – just in time. It was sheer hell – it was night before we were in control of the farm again.

In the early hours of 30th April, British Infantry and tanks came in force and penetrated our positions. Desperately we defended ourselves. Again, we requested our own artillery to shell our positions. A lone Focke-Wulf 190 flew in to our aid and destroyed a tank through a direct hit with a bomb. In the afternoon, the enemy sent over a man protected by a white flag. He asked us to surrender honourably. He did not get a reply and departed. This was followed by a large British attack. Our positions were penetrated in places and only after more hand-to-hand fighting, destruction of tanks by 3kg charges, magnetic charges or Molotov Cocktails, did we succeed in regaining control of the situation.

By the evening of 30th April, a new defensive line had been completed and HQ ordered us to leave Cactus Farm and take our place in the new line. We left the farm under cover of darkness. To our knowledge there were over 300 British soldiers who lost their lives and 30 tanks or armoured vehicles littered the battleground. We had lost three men killed."

Lance Corporal Hans Teske, also a runner with the 1st Battalion 5th Parachute Regiment, survived the decimation of his battalion and later met his 'enemy', Stainforth, whom he had unwittingly encountered in Tunisia.

"It was January 11, the beginning of the Battle of Two Tree Hill, a battle honour for many British regiments, and my personal initiation in the real war – trench warfare with all its horrors and cruelties. Most of us were between 18 and 21 years of age. This type of war made men of all of us. It formed a comradeship which became eternal for the few who survived.

Two Tree Hill was situated near the British lines. It had been left unoccupied for many weeks. Now that we took an interest in it, this hill became important to the British – yet only two days earlier they could have taken the hill without bloodshed, and dug themselves in.

Our opponents turned out to be members of the Inniskillings, now forming part of the 6th Armoured Division. Ceaselessly they were thrown into the attack. They were brave men, taking very heavy losses – but despite all this, they were unable to gain any ground.

Artillery was peppering our positions. British tanks were in action. Some wounded arrived, blood over their faces, some shot through the lungs, gasping for air, German, Italians, British. One German was seriously hurt, his skull was shot open. I was to take him in the side-car to the first-aid post, only about two miles away. Alas, I could not: a piece of shrapnel had smashed the fuel tap of the motorcycle.

So one of my comrades and I carried him on an improvised stretcher through murderous shell fire to safety. It was so different to the training when there was an umpire who made sure things went along according to the text book. We couldn't shout, 'Stop it, some-one might get hurt,' nor would the battle stop to enable us to carry wounded back. However, we finally managed to get him back alright.

On my return to the front, I learned that during my few hours of absence we had advanced, but at a terrible cost. My company had lost every officer, either wounded or missing, presumed killed. Lieutenant Fleming had just been brought in, shot through the hip, the last of our officers, so Leutnant Kleinfeld of HQ company, formerly of the 1st, was brought up and given command of the 1st Company.

I reported back. Nowacki, our observer, came down the hill past me. He gave me the news we all dreaded – Leutnant Schuster was dead. Schuster, commanding officer of the 1st Company, who had survived the war at Eben Emael, Crete and Russia, and who won the Knights' Cross as a sergeant in Crete, was dead. His body had been recovered.

The war was ferocious and the hill, now strewn with bodies, changed hands many times. During the night, with some tanks in sup-port, we took the hill. Many prisoners were taken. I remember a dazed British artillery observer sitting on the edge of a trench, hold-ing his head, as if he were on exercise. His comrade was dead beside him. Bullets were whistling past, yet he sat there as if this was of no concern, completely shocked. Later that day, when German paras prepared for an attack, our artillery fired short. Hermann Geerz and Heinrich Krauter were blown to pieces.

Unknown to us, the enemy had brought in a large concentration of artillery. They wanted to break through in this area and thrust into Tunis. Into this build-up we advanced on 18th January. Our men with battle experience from Russia and Crete said they had never experienced anything like this. The ground shook. The whole area became full of craters and was littered with shrapnel. At the end of the day, we had gained very little. Losses were heavy. The 3rd Company suffered most – 31 killed, three times as many wounded. Infantry battalion A24 was almost wiped out."

Stalingrad – Frozen Hell

After the German Army's failure to take Moscow in 1941, Hitler rearranged his objectives. The attack on Moscow would not be resumed; instead, the weight of the German spring and summer offensive in 1942 would fall in the south. The initial aim was to complete the capture of the Crimea, followed by a two-pronged drive towards Stalingrad, 300 miles east, and the Caucasus Mountains further away. Stalingrad's factories were churning out roughly a quarter of all Russia's new tanks and other armoured fighting vehicles. The Germans looked forward to a fast victory. But the defenders of Stalin's city spoilt their hopes for an early return home. As the snows of the Russian winter close in, blanketing the besieged city of Stalingrad, civilians, Red Army defenders and German attackers found that hunger, cold and the eerie winter environment took a very heavy toll on their health and general morale.

L Ovchinnikova was a young Russian girl during the battle for Stalingrad. With three women and three other children, she hid out in a cellar for 163 days, not far from the ravine which divided the city.

"That day I had to go into the ravine for bread or soup. Mother and my little sister were completely laid out by hunger. I had to walk, run and crawl about 200 metres over open ground. The snow was coated with ash because the factory zone had burned for several days. The flames swallowed the wooden houses with their wooden carvings, the apple and cherry orchards and the tree stumps and fences on which samovars used to simmer on summer evenings.

The wind blew snow between the still-standing factory chimneys. Along the way to the ravine I knew all the craters where I could shelter during a shelling. It was terrifying, crawling past the body of Nastya, the old woman who was our neighbour, lying not far from a scorched pear tree where the children of our street used to play.

I crawled through deep snow towards the Volga. Somewhere behind were the enemy trenches. The snow covered me from the head downwards: this snow was my salvation. If the Germans spotted anything moving, there would be a bang and the slash of a bullet...

The ravine had been transformed into an ordinary trench, except that it was on a massive scale. Soldiers were walking about, rolling guns around, getting their wheels stuck, carrying boxes of grenades and cartridges, laying a telephone line. At the bottom of the ravine, enemy mortar bombs were exploding here and there.

I trod past a field kitchen. There was an unusually tasty smell in the air. Pea soup, probably, made from concentrates. I couldn't make up my mind to knock on the door of the dugout. We knew that soldiers rations had been cut from day to day.

'Where have you come from little girl?'. In front of me stood a soldier in a white sheepskin coat and fur cap. I was used to that question. What was there to say? Our story was quite ordinary – we hadn't had time to get across the Volga. Where was our cellar? On a tiny patch beyond the ravine. The captain took my small, empty bucket. We made our way up a steep climb, with me crawling on all fours, gripping heaps of soil and bunches of dried grass.

It was warm in the dug-out. It seemed I had already forgotten what this kind of warmth was like. I suddenly grew happy. I saw the captain take a string bag off a nail in the wall and put out some ration concentrates – gruel, pea soup. What riches there were on the table! The officer slid the food cubes into my bucket. I looked at him and suddenly understood. He knew how cold and terrified I had been when I was crawling to the ravine. At first I wanted to cry, but in our cellar there had been a kind of unwritten law against crying...

In exposed places, even a ruined house seemed reliable armour. I lifted a board so as to make my way to the cellar, and suddenly saw a machine gun over the entrance. Two soldiers were taking machine-gun belts out of a box. The gun was one of ours, its muzzle turned towards the fascist positions. They were our soldiers – they stayed silent and I, silent as well, went down into the cellar.

Above us the machine gun was firing. Cartridge cases flashed past. The empty saucepan on the stove trembled and the pipe leading to the window was whistling. Silently, and not taking our eyes away, we all watched the door. If the fascists broke into the house, they'd throw grenades into the cellar without warning. Many families in our district had perished that way.

The machine gun fired away. We knew that so long as the machine gunners stayed alive they wouldn't go away – wouldn't leave our cellar unprotected. I was convinced of that, in the same way as I believed in goodness and truth. Everything depended on one single thing – the thudding of that machine gun above us."

Sergeant Ivan Ivanovich Morotskii commanded a mortar detachment of the Russian 277th Infantry Division, one of the units taking part in the encirclement of the Germans besieging Stalingrad.

"On December 3, while repelling an attack, our mortar company cut off some German sub-machine gunners from their tanks. They opened up with a storm of fire. Shrapnel sang through the air and a mortar bomb exploded near us. Vanya Bochkov, a mortar layer, and Galib Setulaev, an ammunition carrier, were wounded. I merely had my greatcoat lapel torn off. I rushed to help them, but was then knocked down by two automatic-rifle bullets in my rib on the right side. Bochkov was carried off on a ground-sheet and Galib and myself crawled our own way to the first-aid point, which was quite close.

This consisted of a kind of tent whose corners rested on the heads of the people holding it up. Hasty bandaging was done here, under the illumination of lanterns. One felt sorry for the nurses…

I remember meeting some local women along the way. 'We don't need anything', they said, 'except something to eat. The Germans here have eaten the last cat and dog.' It was painful to look at these worn-out and exhausted victims. We gave them our last crusts of bread – but there was no more we could do for them.

The surrounded units of Paulus tried to break out of their encirclement at various points, but they were mercilessly crushed. One dawn we saw German aircraft flying low, and they mistook us for their own beleaguered troops. They dropped provisions by parachute and this 'manna from heaven' was just what we wanted.

In one settlement we captured a motorised battalion and the head-quarters of some German formation. There were vehicles loaded with safes containing Iron Crosses.

Along the road, broken and holed, here and there stood wrecked enemy equipment, and piles of abandoned belongings. The one-time immaculate all-conquering Hitlerite army was in retreat. On the way in we often met columns of prisoners escorted by our men. It was quite a sight, how they looked. Some wore womens' dresses and blouses and substitute over-boots made of straw. They were dirty, with frozen faces, and without the slightest spark of life shining in their eyes."

Pavel Ivanovich Doronin was one of the multitude of Russian Communist Party propagandists mobilised to become the political officers attached to all Red Army units. He saw his role as strengthening the troops' morale and from September 1942, as a major-general, he headed the political department of the army group defending Stalingrad.

"The nature of street fighting determined the form of our mass propaganda work. Usually it was carried on after dark in cellars, trenches and shelters. Leaflets, dropped into dugouts and buildings, were the most common medium. Sometimes these leaflets were the only form of political information, telling the soldiers about the most important events on the fronts, about military activity in their neighbourhood or by their own formations.

Often our soldiers were only a few metres from the enemy, and there were houses in which Germans and Russians were on different floors. In these conditions, the political officers kept our troops informed by means of powerful loudspeakers, and care was taken to ensure that these transmissions were varied with war songs, poetry reading and excerpts from front newspapers.

Special attention was paid to developing the sniper movement, which became very widespread with the fighting in the city. The army groups, as well as the political instructors, busied themselves with the selection of snipers and the organisation of their training. Armies, divisions and regiments held sniper conferences for the exchange of experience and activities involving the study of the optical sight, the theory of rifle fire, practice in camouflage and observation. The best snipers trained their pupils to become masters of rifle fire, without, as soldiers joked, 'taking time off work'.

The most popular sniper of the army group was Sergeant First-class Vasili Zaitsev, about whom legends abounded. There was one story which said that a forward observer ran to him to report that in the factory-zone the Germans were bringing up reinforcements. Zaitsev took six of his pupils and went to meet this reinforcement. He killed 11 Germans and in total they killed 40 of the fascists."

Major Friedrich Lang trained as a cavalry officer in 1928, retired from the army eight years later to complete a law degree, then transferred to the Luftwaffe in 1939 to become one of Germany's most famous dive-bomber pilots. He served in the Stalingrad campaign as Commanding Officer of II/StG2.

"We normally flew with a full bomb load of one 500-lb under the fuselage and two 250-lb bombs, one under each wing. As for the famous screaming sirens, the so-called 'Trombones of Jericho', we first had these with the I/StG2 (No. 1 Wing, Stukageschwader 2) when based at Cologne/Ostheim airfield. There was a home-made whistle and siren, but they did not work very well until the small, special-shaped wooden propeller was fitted to the undercarriage leg above the wheel spat. We did not get proper industry-built sirens until later. They turned in the wind as we dived, which created a noise that became louder as our speed built up. Incidentally, you should know that the howling sound distracted and upset not only the enemy, but also ourselves, the Stuka air crew. It became more endurable when you could turn off the propeller by means of a switch and therefore cut the noise.

Our best speed in straight and level flight with the Junkers Ju-87B (*Bertha*) was about 250 kilometres per hour. This speed built up to about 450 km/h with our powerful dive brakes extended in the attack dive configuration, and, for those who tried it without brakes, it was strong enough to withstand 600 km/h at a diving angle of 70 degrees or more.

By the summer of 1942 and just prior to the fighting in the Don bend, the I/StG2 was fitted for towing *Lastensegler* (cargo gliders). At our German home base of Graz-Thalehof, where we had been sent to freshen up after the first Russian winter of 1941/2, we practised towing them. We had 15 of these assigned to us and those Ju-87s assigned to towing them were fitted with a new hook attachment and a lever release. I then had the not very easy task of leading the towing formation from Graz back to our war station via Brno, Krakow, Lvov, Zhitomir, Konotop and to the airfield at Ochotschewka, north-east of Kursk, from where we then started the June offensive towards Voronezh. These cargo gliders were not altogether successful. Too many of them came adrift while being towed and still lie somewhere in the countryside with their loads inside them. Recovery of both gliders and cargoes was time-consuming and difficult.

While we were based on the Don bend in the summer of 1942, II Group of the StG *Immelmann* had as its group emblem the 'Bamberger Reiter' (Bamberg Rider). This was a copy of the famous stone sculpture at Bamberg Cathedral that our leader, Dr Kaufer, had painted when he was commander of the Group. Like myself, before he joined the Luftwaffe, he had been a cavalry officer, stationed at Bamberg. The 7 Staffel which he previously commanded, he called his 7th *Schwadron* as if it were a cavalry unit, which we were, in a way – airborne cavalry!

For a short period while operating over the Stalingrad front, we had fighter cover provided by an Italian fighter unit with MC 200 aircraft. They were not very fast, but then again, nor were we! However, as we expressed a lot of dissatisfaction with their cover and escort, they gave our *Staffelkapitanen* a silver medal for bravery in order to soothe our feelings.

The normal Stuka method of attacking such pin-point targets as those presented by the Russian positions in the maze of rubble and blasted factories in Stalingrad itself needed refining. Fighting each day was literally house-to-house and street-by-street.

There was no room for error in case friendly forces were hit by mistake. Blown up photographs were taken and copies were marked in red ink to show the targets. The Stuka crews then flew, photos and maps in hand, to carry out their attacks. They were forbidden to release their bombs until absolutely certain of the target. Often as many as five or six dive-bombing sorties were flown each day.

The I/StG2, which belonged to the VIII *Fliegerkorps*, was officially notified, in November 1942, that we were to be transferred from Staritsa on the Volga river, to Böblingen near Stuttgart. We had desert camouflage painted on our Ju-87s and were fitted out for

Africa. But at the beginning of January 1943, when things got really bad at Stalingrad, we received orders to cancel everything, respray our Stukas white, and transfer in the quickest possible way, Group by Group, to Dno (between Plaskau and Lake Ilmen) as the position at Volkhov and around Demyansk was becoming disastrous. In the transfer, 3 Staffel lost two or three planes in a snowstorm near Elbing."

Leutnant Gilbert Geisendorfer, pilot of an He-III with the German II Wing of *Kampfgeschwader 53*, Legion Condor, recalls the mission in early January 1943 when he and his crew were sent to deliver supplies to the encircled area of Stalingrad.

"The group assembled at Krakow to hear the order from Reichsmarschall Göring. Stalingrad had been declared a fortress and was to be supplied from the air, until the encircling ring could be broken open.

Among other things the order said. 'You, my supply airmen, have shown your mettle on all fronts, and I know that here also you will perform your duty. Stalingrad must be supplied until relief arrives from elsewhere. The Führer has prepared the highest honours for you'.

It was a great problem keeping the machines ready to fly in these extreme conditions or repairing damaged aircraft. Our technical personnel had set off with the FBK (airfield operations company) by train together with all equipment – it took them about ten days to reach the Kirovograd area. The local facilities were overstretched. So we had only two to three days clear for take-off and two to three days free between engagements, a recuperation period that was really needed under such conditions of physical and psychological stress. Mostly it was the same experienced crews who flew, but nevertheless, the losses were high. In the first ten flying days, we lost five crews. We did our best, but we just did not have enough men.

As the situation was getting more critical and dangerous, Field Marshal Milch arrived in Taganrog with special authorisation from Hitler to reorganise the supply operation. Court martials were brought in, and every crew was interrogated after it had returned from a Stalingrad mission – this was shameful for us, as if we were not carrying out our duty to the full.

We had to fly 300 km over enemy territory to get to the airfield at Pitomnik in the encircled front. We were accompanied for a short part of the way by German fighters, but then we were left to our own devices. Below us was a white winter landscape, the Don bend and behind that the smoking rubble of the town of Stalingrad. The flight went relatively smoothly, until we were at about 4,000 metres in the proximity of the encircling ring. Here there was heavy flak fire. We went down in steep spirals and, in spite of all the freshly filled-in bomb craters, we were able to land OK.

A few other aircraft had already unloaded and some of them loaded up again with wounded men. This apparently orderly situation, we discovered, changed from hour to hour. As we turned the engines off and got out, we were confronted by the whole force of this murderous battle. The din could be heard all around us – explosions one after another, fires here and there. Russian artillery fired on the airfield, the shells threw up black clods of earth on to the white covering of snow and made the hard frozen earth shake. Commandos were hard at it, filling up the shell craters again quickly. Wrecked aircraft lay all around, between them dead soldiers, also airmen in their flying suits, frozen stiff in snow and ice, like wax dummies. Aircraft were roaring overhead, but we couldn't see whether they were friend or foe.

Our wounded soldiers were waiting to be transported off, their faces exhausted and expressionless. Others, their eyes flickering in desperation, still preserved a spark of hope because of the aircraft which had landed. Their wounds had only been given emergency bandaging and pus and blood seeped through the torn rags of the bindings. They were shivering in their scanty uniforms in this icy storm. Others were walking on their knees, having no shoes, their feet wrapped in rags.

At first this inferno seemed to us unreal, like a play in which we were only extras. This is perhaps what we were, because when we came here, we had the chance to escape once more. In the meantime our machine was unloaded, then loaded up again with 15 wounded men, and after we had allowed petrol to be siphoned off from the tanks, we were ready to go again. We kept only enough petrol for the return flight. Because of the wounded men, we couldn't put on our parachutes. If we were hit, we would have had no chance."

Siegfried Melinkat, age 18, was a corporal (Unterscharführer) in the German 2nd Company, 5th SS Panzer Regiment, 'Wiking'. Late in 1942, his regiment was advancing towards Stalingrad through the grim Russian winter landscape.

"We were set down in Proletarskaya. This was a chaotic scene: abandoned trucks and weapons, scattered soldiers wending their way back, Rumanian soldiers in a pitiful state. Fighter bombers hung in the sky and attacked everything that moved below. Our armoured column was the only formation which was heading north. We felt lonely and deserted. The company rolled on into the gathering darkness, in the endless, undulating, snow-covered plain, treeless and shrubless. Suddenly the engine started to sputter. The tank jolted, then jolted again several times and came to a halt.

The company continued on and we remained behind, stuck all alone in the snow-covered steppes, waiting for the tank breakdown unit to tow us away Some 200 metres ahead of us, right near the railway embankment, there was a little hut. This was a ray of light in this wilderness. We could bed down there and heat the place up. We might even have been able to take off our winter gear and sleep in only our shirts and trousers! Two of us stayed back at the tank – the rest of the crew went ahead to the hut. In the pale moonlight, our tank stood out like a silhouette against the steppes. An icy wind was blowing from the east and brought snow with it. In a northerly direction, where Stalingrad must have been, I could hear the rumble of fire and the staccato sound of machine guns. Balls of light shot up in the air and fell slowly to the ground. What would happen to us if the Russians advanced further and were suddenly here? I couldn't get this thought out of my mind. If only the night was over, the terrifying moonlight in this white wilderness.

When I returned from guarding the tank, the fire was crackling in the stove – the smell of toasted bread and sunflower oil filled my nostrils. I unpacked the 'dead man' – a large bundle wrapped in a sheet of canvas, which contained our driver's cloaks and quilts. We'd got the quilts in the Caucasus and hadn't slept in them for ages. I now had four hours to get some sleep until the next change of guard.

Someone shook me by my shoulders. I leapt up, looked around and breathed out, relieved. It was only a dream, which had made me start. But there was no time to ponder this anymore, it was time for my guard duty. I got dressed, forced on my winter gear and shoved my loaded 08 pistol, tied by a strap to my belt, into my trouser pocket. Then I reported for duty and went outside. A howling wind blew snow into my face. I pulled my head guard over my mouth, nose and eyes and pulled my fur cap lower down my forehead."

The RAF Bombing Offensive

The RAF's strategic night-bombing of Germany was one of the main features of the war. There was constant debate as to how effective this really was. It was not until the Lancaster, with four Merlin engines and huge wing area, arrived in March 1942 that the RAF had a truly satisfactory strategic bomber. The eventual formation of the Pathfinders in August 1942 brought further improvement, and the introduction of the Mark XIV bomb sight helped as well. During the Battle of the Ruhr, which lasted from March to July 1943, Dusselforf, Dortmund, Bochum and Duisburg suffered, and the attacks also spread far into Germany. In all, 24,355 sorties were flown in 43 main attacks; 1,038 bombers were lost, excluding 2,216 damaged or lost after crossing the English coast – a daunting rate of loss. For the men dealing it out and for the civilians on the receiving end, this was a time never to be forgotten – a sustained spell of endurance where no-one could afford to lose his nerve.

Flight Lieutenant Frederick Saunders, at the time a Flying Officer, was with 627 Pathfinder Squadron, flying Mosquitoes on vital missions to locate and mark targets for the bombers. He describes the form of operations.

"When our briefing was over, the duty aircrews would know their specific role, who was to wind-find and who was to mark, and so on, and what the target was to be.

Later in the morning, the duty air crews would assemble in the operations room, and there learn of the specific routes we were to take, code call signs, radio frequencies and timing of the events that comprised the operation.

The route out for us would be different from the main force and the pattern would also be different. For instance, neither we nor the main force would fly the direct route to the target. A number of 'dog legs' would be flown to keep the enemy guessing.

Of particular interest would be our final run-in route at low level, on which would be marked various prominent land marks, like a particular chimney stack, stretch of water, railway line, church tower etc. More often than not, there would be blown-up photographs of these taken from reconnaissance aircraft at the heights we would also be flying at.

We would not be able to make notes of these, but they had to be committed to memory, and you could visit the ops room any number of times from now until the final briefing time to refresh your memory. This would take up to about midday, and then it was just a question of lunch and await the time of the main and final briefing some time late in the afternoon or evening.

At the final briefing, all the latest information would be given, like where to expect opposition, and in what form, and so on. Times of take-offs, what petrol load, what colours of TIs (Target Indicators) and dozens of other important details. When the final briefing was over, the next main event would be the 'Op supper'. For some aircrews it would be their last supper. The op supper never varied – it was always egg and chips. The medics said it was a substantial enough meal for a tensed up stomach to absorb, yet not too substantial that a fluttering stomach would reject it. Bomber Command fought its war on egg and chips, and I truly believe, somewhere in our battle honours, there should be a reference to the chicken and the egg.

Very often we would witness the forming up and departure of anything up to 800 heavy bombers in the Lincolnshire skies. Then we would take off and fly our devious routes, overtake the main bombers and reach the target 12 minutes before the first bomber was due to arrive.

Simultaneous with our low-level arrival in our Mossies, would be a number of high-flying Lancs and/or Halifaxes (Halibags) also of the PFF (Pathfinder Force) Group. Their purpose was to release 'candles' as they were called. These were high-powered flares, descending on parachutes, which burned for about five or six minutes. The purpose of this was to illuminate the countryside and to keep it illuminated until we, the low-fliers, could sight and properly mark the target.

This part of the operation would be controlled by the Master Bomber, also in a Mossie, watching progress. When he was satisfied with the marking, he would call both us and the high-flying Lancs/Bags off away home."

Pilot Officer Tony Bird of No. 61 Squadron and his crew were on their sixth mission together, bombing Hanover, when their Lancaster was attacked by German fighters. The action which followed earned Bird an immediate DFC.

"Shortly before arriving over the target we were attacked by two Messerschmitt 109 single-engine fighters, one after the other. I took violent evasive action and our gunners fired repeatedly.

The third fighter to attack was a Focke Wulf 190. Our aircraft was almost impossible to keep straight due to a large area of the tailplane and rudder having been shot away and the port outer engine was on fire.

A cannon shell from the Focke Wulf exploded in front of the fuselage and I was knocked out by the explosion in such a confined space, although saved from serious injury by the armour-plated steel back to the pilot's seat.

I evidently slumped forward over the control column, causing our aircraft to go into a steep dive, and at much the same time, a further cannon shell seriously wounded the mid-upper gunner in the chest.

The navigator quickly assessed the situation, seeing the engine on fire and the plane diving down out of control. Assuming me to be dead, he gave the order over the intercom to bail out. The bomb-aimer in the nose of the aircraft quickly released his escape hatch and parachuted safely down, as did the navigator.

Seeing the mortally wounded mid-upper gunner attempting to crawl from his gun turret to the side exit, Jim Kemish, our wireless operator, helped to clip on the gunner's chest-type parachute and pushed him out.

As he was poised to jump out also, I regained consciousness and started to pull the Lancaster out of the dive. With great coolness, Jim reconnected his intercom to enquire if he should still bail out. As I had given no such order, he received a rather emphatic negative. 'Three of them have already jumped out', he replied defensively. My reply was unprintable.

Each engine had an emergency fire extinguisher operated from the pilot's position, and the flaming port outer engine was soon smothered in foam, which extinguished the fire, although that engine was now useless, and we had no hydraulics.

Witnessing our Lancaster diving down out of control and with an engine on fire, the three German fighter pilots who had attacked us were justified in claiming that our aircraft had been destroyed, especially when they saw the three crew members escape by parachute. They would have assumed that the remaining crew were either dead or too badly wounded to escape.

Fortunately for the remainder of us, the Germans decided to return to the main bomber stream above, rather than lose any more precious altitude by following us down any further. Had just one of them elected to ensure our destruction, he could hardly have failed to have done so, as we were, by this time, completely defenceless, with no hydraulics, our gun turrets immobilised, with no mid-upper gunner, the aircraft almost impossible to control, and a bitter stream of ice cold air blowing in from the gaping hole in the nose where the bomb-aimer had jettisoned his escape hatch.

The target was now visible ahead, and as I checked the altimeter, I realised that we were down to 10,000 feet – half of our normal operational altitude. The main bomber force was ahead of us at 20,000 feet, their bombs exploding on target. Although it would have been more prudent to abandon all thoughts of carrying on to the target, it seemed a shame to have got so far only to fail at the last moment, and we had to dispose of our bomb load in any event.

By the time we reached the target some five minutes later, limping along on three engines at 110 mph, ours was the only bomber still in the area, and despite our problems, we were amused to see the flak shells bursting harmlessly at 20,000 feet, way above us. As we had no bomb-aimer, we jettisoned our bombs immediately over the target area, which was well illuminated by the incendiary bombs dropped by the main bomber force minutes before.

The chances of us getting back to England, without a navigator and with the aircraft almost impossible to keep straight, seemed remote, especially as we were already lost. I had turned west off the target towards home so that at least we were heading in roughly the right direction. It was impossible to turn to starboard, but the slightest slackening of pressure on the starboard pedal caused the Lancaster to swing violently to port.

'Ken' Kendrick, our enterprising flight engineer, found a metal bar, which he succeeded in jamming in front of the starboard rudder pedal so as to relieve me from the need to maintain continuous foot pressure on it, and for the first time I was able to stretch my legs and relax slightly.

We were now somewhere over the North Sea – but just where? Jim, our wireless operator, had for some time been taking radio bearings with his 'loop aerial' of transmissions from known stations in England, and by drawing on our chart the reciprocal of each bearing from the radio station, gave us a position line along which we were flying. Where the position lines crossed gave our approximate position. From this fix. Jim was able to give me an approximate heading to steer back.

As we crossed the English coast, we were momentarily fired on by our own anti-aircraft guns. We had forgotten to switch on our IFF, but almost immediately we switched it on, the firing ceased.

Ken began winding down the landing gear by hand as the hydraulic pump from the useless port outer engine was not working, and he then removed the metal bar which had been jamming the starboard rudder pedal. I found that by using both feet on the pedal I was able to exert sufficient foot pressure to keep the aircraft straight during the approach.

It was not until later that I learned that Ken had sustained a shrapnel wound to the back of his head when the cannon shell exploded, but he was saved from more serious injury by his leather helmet. Harry Aspinall, our rear gunner, had been suffering from frost-bite on the return journey, but had remained cheerful, despite being in great pain, never once complaining.

Soon the runway of our aerodrome came in sight and the lights had never looked more beautiful. They had been kept on especially for our benefit, the main force having landed some time earlier.

As we entered the debriefing room, the Station Commanding Officer, who was probably anxious to get off to bed, enquired irritably to know why the remainder of our crew were not with us. He was rather a disciplinarian and took a poor view of any stragglers who kept him waiting. 'They jumped out over Hanover', I replied. I continued to walk over to the debriefing officer leaving the Group Captain momentarily at a loss for words.

Eventually he came over to me and asked. 'Did you mean that?' I assured him that I had not been joking, and although he said very little else at the time, next day he recommended me for the immediate award of the Distinguished Flying Cross, and my three remaining crew members the Distinguished Flying Medal."

Sergeant Pilot Rupert (called 'Tiny' due to his considerable height) Cooling of No. 9 Squadron was involved in operations in various campaigns, from bases in Britain and abroad. His impressions of the British bombing of Germany are poignant.

"May 12, 1940 was the beginning of the bomber offensive, the first attack east of the Rhine – 37 aircraft of Bomber Command struck at Mönchengladbach. Three were lost. Ironically of the four people killed, one was an English woman living in the town.

Wellingtons of 9 Squadron went to Bottrop on 15 May. The weather outbound was rough though the target was clear and, to our surprise, there was no opposition. Homeward bound was a different story. Electric storms rendered the wireless useless – St Elmo's Fire circled the spinning tips of the propellers in a garland of lilac blue flame, whilst an arc seemed to span between the gun barrels of the front turret. The compass needle swung from side to side as we stood or sat within the geodetic and fabric cocoon which was our immediate world – 8,000 feet up in the dark, we were well and truly lost.

Who it was that suggested we might be back over England is irrelevant. We descended to some 3,000 feet and switched on the navigation lights. The blackness below was total. Tap out the aircraft's letter on the downward signal lamp – there was no response. Then suddenly a pool of light spread fanwise until the darkness soaked up the last grey glimmer. It was an airfield – but where? We touched down, rolled to a halt, then moved towards some dimly beckoning torches. The second pilot stood by with the signal pistol to set the Wellington afire, should we be in enemy territory. Happily it was Shoreham on the Sussex coast.

Three days later, we were one of six Wellingtons to attack Cologne and, with other crews, reported searchlights apparently flying above broken cloud. We never saw them again. On August 25th, about 50 aircraft went for the first time to Berlin. Six Hampdens were lost. The only bombs to fall within the city limits destroyed a summer house and injured two people. These were puny efforts returning puny results.

Costs too were small – but costs then were. On 19 June a distress signal alerted 9 Squadron to the plight of one of its aircraft. We took off to search the North Sea, almost to the coast of Holland. To and fro along the sides of a steadily expanding square we flew, peering at the relentless sage-green sea. A shout, a sighting, something on the waves. Elated, we flew towards it to find a barrel, a baulk of timber and a snarl of rope. We turned away, deflated, and resumed our search. The crew were never found. Each year, at the Runnymede Memorial, I look at the name of the navigator, whose room was next to mine, and remember that he was 20, and so was I."

Flying Officer Bill Ansell, an Australian, joined the RAF and was posted to a Lancaster squadron as an upper-turret gunner. It was on 19 February 1944 that he and his crew were briefed for their first bombing raid on a German target. As it turned out, even the best-planned operations can go wrong.

"Finally it was evening, and when we were all assembled in the briefing room, we were informed that instead of Berlin, as we had expected, tonight's target was Leipzig. It was to be saturation bombing and, in order that the target would be just as big a surprise to the enemy as it had been to us, we would set off on the usual route to Berlin and at the last minute, alter course for Leipzig. This was to be an 800-bomber raid in which Halifaxes and Stirlings would also be taking part, and we would all be going in at different ETAs (estimated times of arrival) and heights.

At the aircraft we stowed our parachutes, did our last-minute checks and were ready to move out. We finally taxied slowly out of our dispersal area and took our turn in the queue ready to take off. At a signal from control, we were off and rolling – we lifted off. 'Crack goes the whip, chaps', said the skipper, then, 'Undercarriage up!'.

This had all the hallmarks of a copybook operation with surprise, maximum impact and minimum losses, but for one small detail – as we crossed the German coast, our navigator realised to his consternation that we were way ahead of schedule. He discovered that the forecast of a 50-knot headwind should have been a tailwind. We had to throttle back to a minimum safe cruising speed and go through endless circling and dog-legging in order to waste some time. Finally, after this frustrating delay, we arrived over the target and at the right height.

The bomb-aimer, having dropped all his radar-confusing strips of Window, was getting ready to do his stuff. The target was already well alight, and at our level the flak was 'well concentrated' – this is just a fancy term for bloody awful. It was finally time, and bomb doors were open, master switches on and bombs fused.

We were now completely vulnerable – a sitting duck. I could hear Frank saying, 'Left, left, hold her steady', then 'Bombs gone. Bomb doors closed.' The aircraft did its usual bounce upward as the bombs dropped away, and we all heaved a sigh of relief as we turned for home."

Flying Officer Roderick Learoyd of No. 49 Squadron was the first living Bomber Command VC of the war for a raid on the Dortmund-Ems Canal. Two aircraft preceding him were blown up, but he stayed on target then coaxed his badly damaged plane back, keeping airborne until daylight to land with no flaps or landing gear. His own memories are more modest.

"It was just routine really, as far as we were concerned at that time. We didn't like it very much. When we'd been on a trip we were always debriefed – sometimes it was about 2 o'clock in the morning. I remember sympathising with those people who were in France – we came back and after every debriefing we went and had a cup of coffee, or breakfast, and then into nice clean sheets to sleep until about 11 o'clock. We really had quite a comfortable war, apart from the actual flights themselves.

It was for the Dortmund-Ems Canal operation I got my gong. Two or three of us were chosen and we had to do night exercises over the Lincolnshire fens and practise low-level night-flying and try to locate a little light in a canal, and do low-level flying round that. Then we were told what it was about. We were all supposed to volunteer, but we couldn't very well do anything else – it was 'You, you and you'.

The day came and there were five of us on five aircraft. I was the last of the five. There was an aqueduct carrying the canal over a river, and the idea was that we had to fly at very low level, about 150 feet above. We had special bombs – mine bombs, I think. The point was that the first one dropped his bomb, then we all came in at intervals. The first one went in at zero, the second at two minutes after, and I would have been at eight minutes after. The first one's bomb was supposed to go off in ten minutes, so I had to be accurate, otherwise I got blown up by the damn thing.

I remember going over there and we circled round at 7,000–8,000 feet. We'd all set our watches beforehand, of course – and I checked my watch. You could see what was going on, especially I could, because all the searchlights were flashing and all the guns were firing on the first ones, and I had time to get down and get really lined up, and go down to my low height. It was then that I realised that it wasn't the flak that was going to worry us so much as the searchlights. You couldn't see a damn thing! I mean, you'd got the searchlights straight in your face! I had to put my head down in the cockpit and try to see the instruments as much as possible.

Then the bomb-aimer was saying, 'Left, left, right.' You know they weren't very sophisticated bomb-aiming arrangements – they sort of stuck out forward and you adjusted it if the wind was blowing such and such a way. After a bit the bomb-aimer would say, 'Bomb gone' and the blokes in the back would say, 'Yes, right in the middle!' or something like that.

Then I did a very steep turn to get away from everything – they see where you're going, they have you lined up, whether they've seen you or not – but if you do a quick turn you hope to get away with it. In the meantime, I'd seen other aircraft being shot down – two, actually. One pilot was killed, the other taken prisoner of war. They were both Australians, strangely enough. I got up higher and realised there were a few holes in the aircraft, and later, when I got near home, the undercarriage wouldn't come down. The hydraulics or something had been hit.

And so it was not far off daylight when I got back to Scampton. I was the most damaged of the aircrew who did get back – I think the others came in alright. I had to circle around for a time to get rid of fuel, then it was daylight, so it was much easier to have a smooth landing. They didn't have proper lighting equipment, you had a thing switched on at the last minute. You had very dim lights – it was all grass.

The flaps came down and the undercarriage came down, but I think there was no indicator that it was down. Anyhow, I landed and had no trouble about that. I was debriefed, then a few weeks later I was posted as PA to Sir Robert Brooke-Popham, who was Inspector General of the RAF. One day he came in and said, 'You're wanted on the telephone'. 'This is Air Chief Marshal Harris' – Bomber Harris – and he told me I'd got the gong. I didn't take any notice as I thought it was one of my pals. Then I began to wonder, because it was Popham who had told me. And it was true.

I was the first living VC – there were two in the RAF before me, but they were both killed at the time."

Michal Leszkiewicz, a Polish pilot, escaped with his aircraft from Poland, went to Rumania and was a POW several times before finally reaching Britain, where he completed two full bombing tours with 300 Polish Squadron.

"First of all we'd usually have about 15 operational aircraft in one squadron, but after operations you came back full of holes, absolutely riddled with bullets. Goodness gracious – I was terrified of moonlight because of the German fighters. At first they were not night operational, but eventually they picked up night flying skills and got quite good. They could spot you – and they were so much faster. We had only about 210 knots and they had about 400 and could outmanoeuvre you. We would try to go as high as 20,000 feet – but when you lost your height, you went down into searchlights and anti-aircraft fire. You had to throw your aircraft this way and that and dive.

I started my operational flying in 1941 and finished in 1943 after 53 missions. I had such adrenalin up while I was there, so after the first tour of 30 missions and the second of 20, they let me do another two trips. A squadron leader debriefing us at headquarters was very impressed with my knowledge and asked me, 'How many sorties have you done?' I told him 52, and he said, 'That's impossible'. I was a warrant officer – not even commissioned.

Coming back from a mission there was this wonderful elation – 'I've done it' – and that's when the danger came, and you cannot help but relax. You were tensed up going over the target, then you'd done it and you relaxed – and by Jove, that was the danger.

I had a nervous breakdown when I went out of the squadron. I lived with no tomorrow. I watched all these people disappearing – my friends. You thought to yourself, 'You may be lucky to make another trip, but your time must come'. So you were not quite yourself – it was as if you were on drugs. I didn't sleep at all. When you finished, you went to bed and you lived through it all again in your mind. I never felt I was killing people – all Germans were sworn enemies of the Poles. They started it all, and it was so unnecessary.

I was already a trained pilot in Poland. On 1 September [1939] we just heard that this airfield was bombed and so on. We couldn't believe it – it was without warning or a declaration of war. They jumped on us like an animal in the jungle which you don't see and which lands on you.

All this is with me deep down, it is my personality. I want to run away from it because it completely ruined my life. I am a war casualty. The things which happen to me at night. I lived so much, it has ruined me, squeezed me out – drained every bit of juice out of me."

Angelica Toms, née Söhn, was a girl of only 11, living in Düsseldorf, when war broke out. The bombing of her home town was so traumatic that it has left permanent scars – she admits that she still can't hear a thunderstorm without the old fear returning, just as it did in those days of the war.

"Düsseldorf was not made up of little houses – it was high flats. One cellar was made into an air-raid shelter and fortified – they made a soft wall in them so that if something happened, you could knock through to next door, or the other way around.

It wasn't so bad until 1942 – then it really started. Don't forget, we had three enemies, the Americans in the daytime, the British at night and the Gestapo every day. If you saw a stranger, you treated him with mistrust – say even someone who came from a different part of Düsseldorf. You never knew, if you said, 'This damn war,' if they would report you. People had been arrested for showing a bit of light in the blackout. They were accused of guiding the RAF in – but we didn't need to tell them – they knew where we were. All they had to do was find the cathedral of Cologne, go up the Rhine, and there they were. Everything you said was picked up – even if you grumbled about the food. You had to be careful – you were really afraid. In the factories they put Gestapo in among the workers in boiler suits. If there was a meeting, if someone voiced a wrong opinion, they were arrested.

Within yourself you felt resentful about having to suffer the war, but you could only talk to the family – but sometimes you couldn't even trust them. There were no squeakers in my family, but there were occasions when children had reported their parents.

The drive to recruit young people was towards the end of the war. I was involved in that. I learned to shoot – after the war I could go to the fairground and win prizes – and I taught my children to shoot with air rifles. But I never fired a shot in anger.

The difference between our two countries was not hate. You see, the British always classed the army as the Nazi Army – but we looked on the Nazi Army as the SS. Even the Germans were afraid of them. The *Wehrmacht* was just the same as your army – conscripted people. You would hear old soldiers after the war saying that the SS stood behind them and pushed them into the front line. Officers had been shot for disobeying orders from the SS. You nursed the myth that all Germans were bad – but we didn't want the war. I didn't want to lose my friends. My school was bombed – in my street there were 144 houses, and after the war there were just three shells left.

When the bombings started, I went down to the Rhine where I felt safe – I didn't want to be buried alive. I was in a flat with an air-raid shelter underneath, but it was claustrophobic – which was why I wouldn't go down there. As soon as the siren went, it was only five minutes to the Rhine, and there was a big green there, where we felt safe. If a bomb dropped it was a million to one chance it would drop on you – but for a big house to drop on top of you, that's a bit different.

I had no hate, even in those days, and I have none now. We knew that someone had been given a job to do, and they were doing it. The Americans came over during the day at the sort of height that you see aeroplanes flying over now. They always did carpet bombing – never target bombing. In the winter you would see a great vapour trail – then you knew there was a load coming towards you. If you heard something whistling while they were coming towards you, you ducked – if they were passing you, you knew you were safe. The RAF tried to hit the target, but in our street there were just the three houses left standing. Two streets further down it was the barracks, but it was our street which was obliterated. We all said we thought it was the bomb-aimer's fault. It's an easy mistake, at night in a wind. We put it down as a mistake.

When you came out after a raid, the first thing you did was make sure who was underneath, who you could help to get out, and you counted your friends – so and so had not come out – they must be under the rubble. The soldiers in the barracks came and helped – an elephant from the zoo came and helped – and the zoo was bombed too. Police, air-raid wardens, army, civilians, anybody who could possibly help, helped. If a dog heard a knocking, you'd dig until you found where that knocking was coming from. Quite a few got killed, but you tried to get out as many as you possibly could. The only places where the cellars were actually damaged was where the landmines went. We lost our water supply and had to go down to the Rhine to get a bucket of water to wash. The Rhine was beautiful in those days – but I wouldn't put my toe in it now. We call it a cess pit now, but in my days it was really lovely."

Hildegard Teal, née Burr, was 10 when Hamburg was bombed. As an unwanted child when her mother remarried, she was put in a children's home at the age of two and was moved from one home to another throughout childhood. In the home she was strangely cut off from the bombing.

"In 1943 I was in a children's home run entirely by women, somewhere outside the centre of Hamburg. I don't think the women were in the 'Party' – I think it was just a local authority home. Of course there were pictures of Hitler everywhere, and we had to salute the picture, and sing *Fahne hoch!* (Raise the Flag) and *Deutschland Über Alles* and we celebrated Hitler's birthday.

Neither my mother nor my grandmother ever visited me in the home before, but a few months after the bombing when my grandmother took me to the station that I saw for the first time what had happened to the city, a lot of ruins, a lot of flattened buildings, burned out houses or just rubble. It was sad to see it all gone, but in a way this had all happened as if at another time – I was there but it was as if I wasn't there. It was different being in a 'home': if I'd been at home with my mother and half sisters and brothers I would have felt it all much more directly.

But I do remember one bombing raid in the home. We were woken up at night by one of the 'teachers', I don't know what time it was, nobody had a watch then. We were just told *Schnell, schnell,* out of the beds, everybody down the cellar. Alarm, but quietly, quietly!' Of course, we were all excited, not scared at all, just excited. Everything was dark upstairs, all the lights were off, but there were lights in the cellar. We got used to this, it happened several times, of course, in the home you didn't actually *see* anything that was going on outside. So, we were taken down to the cellar, settled down there, told to be quiet, and, of course, you *were* quiet – there was no answering back in those days – and then you went back up again. In the cellar there were straw sacks, blankets, it was fairly big. There were about 30 kids and the grown-ups.

I don't know how long we were down there, it seemed like a long time. We went back to sleep. I vaguely remember being woken up again, it was still night, it must have been about three in the morning. They told us, when you finish breakfast, get your coats on, you're being taken to another home. I must have heard about this bomb which hadn't exploded from the grown-ups. Of course we were all excited again – this was like a day trip. We didn't have any gear, only one set of clothes, and we just put a coat on top and were marched out to the lorries.

I don't actually remember seeing anything outside the building – nor could we see anything out of the lorry. The journey must have been about an hour. I think we were there about three weeks, then went back to the other place – I don't remember seeing anything of the town even then."

Ludwig Wiener was a schoolboy of 15, living in the German town of Schweinfurt at the time of the American raids. He was fortunately in the countryside for the first attack, but during the second raid he was in the thick of it. Wiener now works for the local Schweinfurt newspaper.

"On 17 August 1943 the fairy story that 'as far as the English and Americans were concerned the bombing of Schweinfurt wasn't worth the candle' came to a sudden end.

It was a sunny day during my summer holidays, and I had gone with my mother and sister to Kreuzberg, 65 km away in the Rhön area. We were about 1,000 metres up in the mountains when the silver bodies of the bombers roared by over our heads.

We first heard about it when we were travelling back on the train. The train stopped at Oberwerrn, 7 km away from Schweinfurt. We could see the town burning like a flaming torch. Thousands of Schweinfurt people were drifting out of the town with their belongings on to bicycles and little carts. 'There's no point in going any further', they said, 'the whole town is in ruins'.

We didn't hang around and hurried towards Schweinfurt. It was true, every little street seemed to be in flames. But when we got to our house, it was still standing. My father was already there, putting in new window panes and sweeping out rubble.

This first attack had claimed 203 lives: 70 men, 77 women, 48 children and eight foreign workers. It was a long time before life got back to some kind of normality. The worst thing was the water shortage – water had to be pumped from the wells.

The Wehrmacht report made almost no mention of the attack. All it said was, 'Enemy bomber squadrons, which flew into South Germany yesterday, lost 51 four-engined bombers and five fighters, shot down by German fighters and anti-aircraft guns. The population of two South German towns suffered losses'.

On 14 October 1943 the name of Schweinfurt appeared once again in the Americans' timetable. At about 13.30 more than 250 bombers attacked the town. We survived the attack, sheltering in the cellar at home, which escaped damage. This time Schweinfurt was named in the Wehrmacht report, 'American bomber squadrons attacked the town of Schweinfurt yesterday in strength, inflicting considerable damage to residential and commercial areas of the town. German fighters and destroyers engaged the enemy planes, and in the course of a fierce air-battle inflicted a heavy defeat on the enemy with help from anti-aircraft artillery. 121 of the around 250 to 300 bombers taking part in the raid were shot down.'

In the basement of our house, which had space for eight tenants, steel doors were put in, and apart from that there were just sandbags, piled up against the windows. When the bombs fell they made a hellish noise. Dust was thrown up, and it felt like the house was falling down. One of our tenants was a theology teacher, who worked at the grammar school in Schweinfurt. He prayed and everyone else joined him. About half an hour later when things had calmed down again and the barrage from the anti-aircraft guns had stopped, we went upstairs. It was always vital to search the attic for incendiary bombs, which the enemy dropped in huge numbers, together with high-explosive devices. We did in fact come across two smouldering bombs, which we doused with sand. We rushed across to our neighbours in the town – fortunately no-one had suffered any damage. But the flat where my grandparents lived had been completely destroyed and the poor souls were inconsolable. We took them in, until they were later evacuated to the countryside.

We learned of a very tragic case: a teacher's family, who were good friends of ours, had been buried alive under the fallen rubble of their house. The grammar school was also totally destroyed in this raid. The old building of the school, founded in 1631 by King Gustav Adolf of Sweden had burned down, and so it wasn't until the end of the year when teaching resumed, and this was in a village called Veitshöchheim, 50 km away near Würzburg. All the children were evacuated from the town.

This didn't affect my classmates and me anyway – like all the other pupils in our year at the grammar schools and high schools in Lower Franconia we were conscripted into the Flak-artillery 'on the home front' The 'final battle' fought by the Nazi regime with 15-year-old schoolkids manning the guns had now begun.

No wonder, one might add – Schweinfurt, as the centre of ball-bearing manufacture in Germany, was, relative to its size, the most heavily protected town. Two railway flak-batteries with 10.5 cm guns, over 20 batteries with 8.8 cm guns and just as many batteries with 3.5 cm guns were put in place all around Schweinfurt."

Sicily – Rugged Test

*O*nce the last Axis forces had surrendered on Cape Bon in Tunisia on 13 May 1943, North Africa was in Allied hands. The next objective, the southern Italian island of Sicily, would require the Allies' first amphibious operation of any scale in the war, directed by US General Dwight Eisenhower. The island was defended by 350,000 Axis troops – about a third of them German – under the command of General Guzzoni. Although outnumbered, the Allies enjoyed air superiority: 4,000 aircraft against 1,500. For the landings on July 9, 1943, codenamed Husky, 160,000 men landed from 3,000 vessels. On 12 July the British captured Syracuse and then Augusta on the 14th. On 17 August, British and American forces reached Messina, a strategic position which lay opposite the toe of Italy. Although the Axis powers were able to evacuate troops, equipment and aircraft to the mainland, they lost 178,000 killed, wounded and captured, compared with relatively low Allied losses. With the capture of Sicily, Allied shipping could operate more freely in the Mediterranean, a substantial area of enemy territory was under Allied control, and the way to Italy was open.

Shipped out by boat from Africa, Sergeant Herbert Parkin arrived in Sicily in July 1943 with the 2nd Battalion London Irish Rifles, as part of the massive Allied assault on the island.

"We disembarked and came up the beaches. There was no opposition at the beginning, because the Germans had already landed and pushed inland. We moved in, towards Mount Etna. The Germans were moving back, but slowly – they were good soldiers and they fought every inch of the way. They were always on the hills and we always got the middle. We had to get them off the high ground, as we called it, which involved climbing the mountains. It was amazing that we got up them.

Our tanks could only go up so far and you've got to remember that once they get up, they have to get down again. They had to be very careful, but they would come up and give as much supporting fire as they could. The crowd we had was very good.

Eventually, the Germans would withdraw off the hills, and as they withdrew, you had to prepare for them to come back, because invariably they would push a counter-attack in. They didn't just walk away.

We would have to dig in straight away, and HQ would try to push a fresh company up to strengthen our position, but it wasn't always possible because there might have been a lot of casualties. It was always very fluid until we got settled. You could take a position and then lose it. It looks nice on these pictures with the little arrows and things, but it wasn't like that. It was very hard work, especially for the infantry – they had the worst of the lot.

As we moved along we had to be careful of the mines. You couldn't just wander along. The infantry would come up first and then the engineers would go along and put notices up of where the mines were. They used to lay white tape down. The infantry had to take pot luck, because they had to go first. A lot of people got blown up.

The mines were in little wooden boxes which were about three inches square. Because they were wood, you couldn't detect them. If you trod on one, it took your leg off. There were S mines too, which were like a flower pot with prongs which showed above the ground. If you trod on that it would explode like a fragmentation bomb. There were a lot of them about.

On one occasion, we were moving up with the transport at the back and we pulled up around the base of Etna. We were told to get our heads down and get some rest while we could, before we moved off again. All of a sudden, someone shouted, 'Don't move, we're in a minefield!' You could see them all over the place and every one of us had missed them. We were so lucky. The engineers came in and shifted them.

Sometimes we moved forward at night and we would get in position, waiting for the dawn, which was when the Germans were supposed to attack. Sometimes they did, sometimes they didn't. You waited there, and you could feel the tension as everyone was wondering what was going to happen. People tended to get very bad-tempered. You could laugh and joke, and then suddenly someone would shout or swear. It was the tension.

Everybody moaned in the line, including me. This was wrong, that was wrong. One of our officers used to say, 'Oh they're happy enough. When a British soldier isn't moaning, there's something wrong'.

Once the Germans had left, we got refitted and had a good bath and took it easy for a bit, but at the back of our minds we knew that we had Italy to come."

Captain Ian Quarrie, on Motor Torpedo Boat 670, was speeding up the east coast of Sicily towards the Strait of Messina when he encountered a U-boat. His objective was to close the Strait to traffic by night and prevent interference with Allied supplies.

"We increased to full speed, the submarine still on the surface and guns blazing on both sides. We could only assume that our SO's signals had confused the U-boat into believing us to be an Italian unit, as never before had British forces been sighted so close to Sicily in broad daylight. The attack appeared to be unsuccessful, though.

We turned directly towards the U-boat at full speed and opened fire with every gun that would bear, striving to get alongside her before she disappeared below the surface. Her gunners, brave fellows, were still firing at us and presumably took a last-minute dive down her conning-tower hatch – or not, we would never know. Even so, they managed to score the odd hit and wounded one of my young gunners, not seriously, but quite painfully. The sea around the enemy bubbled as the air was forced out of her ballast tanks and she disappeared below us. We dropped our four charges, set at 50 and 100 feet, close around her... and then waited. In a hurry to press on and reach our patrol area, we could not stay long looking for signs of damage or destruction, and we saw none. Later we learned that we had, in fact, sunk the [Italian] submarine *Flutto*.

We had been told that there were two small Italian destroyers operating from Taormina, and as we took up our stations for the night, I caught sight of them in the darkness to the east. We moved into our positions for the attack – I signalled to the SO when I was beginning my stealthy run in at low speed to fire. No sooner had I begun my run in than all hell was let loose! I could just see the enemy in my torpedo sight, and my firing levers in front of me on the bridge were 'ready'. The enemy's first salvo straddled us and the second was just as accurate – not at all what we had been led to expect from a small Italian destroyer! If we were to survive to get our 'fish' away, it must be now or never. Pulling hard at my firing levers, I held my course until the torpedoes had leapt out of their tubes and away, then throttled to 'full ahead'. Wheel hard aport and with lumps of shrapnel all over the place, we were off on a reciprocal of the enemy's course.

At that moment, I caught sight of my First Lieutenant on his knees at the foot of the ladder leading from the bridge to the charterhouse. I asked him what the devil he was doing there and he gave me the perfect answer by showing me his tin hat, the front edge of which had been bent down vertically. 'And I think it got you on the shoulder on the way', he said. I was lucky – my shirt needed quite a bit of sewing, but the cause of the damage, a piece of metal the size of my fist, had hardly drawn blood. As the destroyers sped on their way, our SO gave us a course and speed to rejoin him and together we followed them down the coast towards Catania. It was not long before the unexpected reply came back, 'Forces being followed are friendly. Disengage immediately!'

The ships we attacked were, to the best of my memory, HMS *Aurora* and HMS *Penelope,* two of the crack gunnery cruisers in the Mediterranean Fleet. We were supposed, of course, to be patrolling well to the north of them, so they took us to be enemy. With no accurate radar available, a cruiser at 1,200 yards (the range at which they opened fire on us) looked to us very like a small destroyer at 600 yards – our poor torpedoes must have been at their last gasp when they passed astern of their target. The next time we met one of the cruisers at sea, in broad daylight, we took great care to identify ourselves early and received the daylight reply, 'Let's be friends this time!'".

Petty Officer Dennis O'Brien was Coxswain on motor launch ML 1048, which played a vital role in the landings on Sicily, guiding the landing craft in to the shore.

"We picked up our buoy and started patrolling. Another ML was also patrolling the beaches. There was a dogfight overhead, which a young lieutenant was watching through binoculars, when he suddenly dropped down dead. Nobody could understand what had happened, until they found a wound from a ricochet under his arm.

We went on to Syracuse harbour and went alongside the jetty, where a group of locals were standing. There was a very old lady, dressed in black, who gave us the fascist salute. The others stopped her very quickly – she didn't realise that we were on the other side!

While we were at Augusta, one of the merchant ships, an Empire boat, was bombed and sunk. We got as close as we could to pick up survivors. The sea was on fire, and there was one character swimming away from the ship still in his tin hat. Things were getting quite close, and a Geordie yelled out to him, 'Take your hat off, mate'. He yelled back, 'No fear, I want this as a bleedin' souvenir!'.

One survivor stayed on the bridge – he looked very tired and kept very quiet. All he said was, 'I'm Royal Navy'. The other sailors were pouring all sorts of curses on the head of their chief engineer. Apparently he had manned four ships and he had never returned with any of them. They had all gone out from the UK and been blown up. They all blamed him for the bad luck. As I was in charge, I got permission from the captain to splice the mainbrace. I got the rum out and I offered the young navy man a drink, which he refused. We went alongside a cruiser to transfer the survivors, because they had better medical facilities than us. As we were putting them aboard, the young fellow collapsed on the deck. He had the most horrible injury in his back. He hadn't said a word about it, he had just sat there quietly."

Fred Jordan was a medic with the 217 Field Ambulance, attached to the Royal West Kent Regiment and was involved in action at Bronte in Sicily.

"We landed in Sicily in July 1943, arriving by boat from Algiers. It was a quiet landing with no opposition. We marched up towards Mount Etna, where the terrain was very hilly. The Germans were already there, dug into the hillsides. We had a lot of casualties because the Germans, being higher up than us, had the advantage, and our men had no protection. Their mortars were deadly accurate, and they were just hailing down on to the infantry.

We were attached to the infantry, so that wherever they went, we went with them. On Sicily we were doing the attacking, so the infantry would go in first, and then we would follow up behind and pick up the men as they got wounded. We would evacuate them on stretchers to the next post down.

Out of all my experiences on Sicily, the incident I remember most vividly happened in a town called Bronte, which had been badly shelled by the Germans. They were mortaring the town and casualties were occurring. We moved up into a railway tunnel where the civilians were taking refuge.

Our Corporal was called Bill Lea – a very good man, very well liked. He said to us, 'You stay here and I'll just go up a wee bit and see what's happening'. He went up and there was an almighty bang. We ran out, and he'd been hit. We picked him up on a stretcher and managed to get him back to the ambulance.

After the Germans had moved out, we went to the hospital that he was in and asked for him. They said, 'He's there'. There was a blanket covering him! By all accounts, the blast from the mortar bomb had burst his lungs. When you get a blast, it doesn't blow in, it sucks out, and he'd simply died.

The sad thing was that a chap who was with us was a big friend of Bill Lea. Whoever had covered the Corporal up had left his feet outside. It's a simple little thing, but when you cover a body up with blanket, all parts of the body should be concealed. This poor chap went absolutely berserk – almost hysterical – when this happened."

Sergeant Pilot Rupert Cooling with No. 9 Squadron was flying exhaustive attacks on Pantelleria in their over-worked Wellingtons when the situation in the Mediterranean pointed to some major event taking place.

"We knew something would happen soon. Axis forces had been expelled from Africa, and the bombers were switched to round-the-clock attacks on Italy's 'Malta' – the island of Pantelleria.

Our Wellingtons were doing three trips a night, the crews two one night and one the next. On our last sortie, hours before the island surrendered, we watched the man ahead go down in flames. As we left, the rear gunner called up. 'There's another on fire behind us!'. Nightfighters – but somehow we had slipped through undetected. The air was never silent – aircraft buzzed like a swarm of bees. We watched as drones of troop-carrying Dakotas moved like skeins of geese against the blue. Something was cooking, and when the Ops board listed every crew, we knew for certain.

Sentries stood at the entrance to the walled courtyard where we assembled for briefing. Unusually, the display was covered. 'Tonight, gentlemen', said Group Captain Powell, unveiling the maps, 'we return to Europe. The Army is landing in Sicily at 02.45 hours. Airborne forces, gliders and paratroopers will go in ahead. Our target is Syracuse and four aircraft will each carry 18 flares to be dropped exactly on time from 10,000 feet. Our troops will be on high ground waiting to move in. Bombing lines must be strictly observed.'

Many aircraft would carry flares and six 500 lb bombs. It was good to be chosen for that specialist task – to know that tonight we would make a little bit of history.

Take-off was at 23.45 hours, on course at midnight. It was quiet until, ahead, pin-pricks of light then massive fire, flashes, spurts of flame. We reached the target area with twelve minutes to spare, then turned to circle just off the coast. At 02.16 hours the first flares blossomed. Syracuse lay white and naked against the dark seas, like a photographic negative. Sweeping inland, Y-Yorker headed for our dropping point. Right on time, Bill's finger stabbed the release. At 02.20 hours, our flares opened up, spot on schedule. Down to 7,000 feet and run in over the bay towards the inner harbour, our aiming point. There was a little flak and we were jolted once or twice by heavy bursts, then, 'Bombs gone'. I turned to starboard, out to sea and watched great pillars of smoke rise gradually to spread a white shroud over the target area. A few fountains of water erupted as an occasional bomb over or undershot into the sea. The flares died down – Syracuse once more retreated into the darkness. A few threads of light flak hosed into the night then ceased. The navigator was back at his charts whilst Bill the bomb-aimer stood beside me, thumbs up and a nod of approval. Our part in the drama was over – it hadn't been all that different from any other trip."

Franz Strnad was only 18 years old when he joined the Hermann Göring Panzer Division as a recruit from a flak brigade in Vienna. His story starts when he was 'selected' and concludes with a remarkable coincidence.

"On the way to Block 4 we bumped into NCO Müller, who had a sergeant with him. 'Who wants to go to Sicily with this sergeant? His name is Peter Romme', he said.

We were flabbergasted. We were not used to this sort of speed of events. Since neither of us said a word, he asked the sergeant, 'Which one do you want to take with you?'. He weighed us both up and pointed at me. I had to report straight away to the orderly room to get my marching papers, and got myself ready for the journey. We were to set off that very evening.

The train journey went via Munich and Rome to Naples. The further south we got, the more unbearable became my blue Luftwaffe uniform. Even at the posting office for the front, where we had to wait to be taken on the rest of the journey, I still couldn't get my hands on a tropical uniform. We finally set off, this problem still unsolved. With a convoy of five Opel-Blitz, loaded with tank-engines, spares and tank shells, we travelled on to Santa Maria Capua Vetere near Caserta. Our division had a base here in the Italian army barracks.

We were sent on from there and four days later arrived at Villa San Giovanni, a coastal town in the vicinity of Reggio di Calabria, right down on the toe of the 'boot'. We were then taken by ferry across the Strait of Messina to Sicily.

The first day in Sicily was my birthday, so I had to drink a bottle of Marsala with Romme and the CO, an old policeman. It was a lethal brew in the unaccustomed tropical heat. It was only when we were attacked by fighter bombers that I was able to move myself – with glazed eyes I looked at the two Spitfires, firing at us on all barrels.

While my comrades dove for cover, I stayed on the truck, which had just been loaded up with 5 cm tank shells. The two planes only launched one attack on us and nothing happened. Later, when I'd sobered up, the policeman told me that a volley of shots had hit just in front of the truck.

That night the attacks continued. When dawn was breaking, we took off into the surrounding countryside, camouflaged ourselves and lay down under the bushes for a sleep. At about midday the driver woke us, and got the truck ready to start. He explained that the Tommies would be taking a lunch break between 12.00 pm and 2.00 pm, and we would have to take advantage of this interlude.

I was assigned that lookout position at the front again, and made with 'looky-looky', as we said then. Peter Romme was assigned the lookout at the rear. None of us looked at the time for ages, and when I finally checked, it was five minutes after 2.00 pm – and as I looked up, there in the sky in front of us were two dots – fighter bombers heading straight at us!

I immediately bashed my fist down on the driver's cabin. We were just on the outskirts of Catania. The truck stopped and I guided it backwards into a side street. Then I jumped down, went back to the main street and watched the fighters, which, as they got close, I could just make out as Spitfires. One of the machines, whose pilot had obviously spotted me, made directly for me. I quickly leapt behind a garden wall and took cover.

It fired at me, but the wall provided enough protection. Once it had flown by, I jumped out and looked up at the plane flying away. To my horror, the two Spitfires did a huge curve and came back, firing on all barrels again. So I jumped over the wall and stood there for a few seconds. When one of the machines headed straight for me again, and I could see the pilot. I waved to him. Was this defiance of just plain bravado? Then I threw myself to the ground. I got up again once the planes were out of sight.

This little game happened twice more. Whenever a plane came straight at me, I waved and then dived for cover as quickly as I could behind the stone wall. On the fourth occasion that they flew straight at us, they held their fire and just flew by. This time I could see the pilot of 'my' machine clearly, and this time he waved at me.

Twenty-five years later, in 1968, I was working as a porter in the big department store in Graz. One day, a Jaguar with English number-plates drove into the garage. A woman got out and went in to see the manager. The driver, meanwhile, came up to me and in the middle of the conversation asked, 'Were you in the war too?', 'Yes, I was with the Luftwaffe, with the Hermann Göring Division.'

The Englishman was startled and said, 'So you were in Sicily, as well?'. I told him I was. He said he had been with the RAF in Sicily, and said what an amazing time that was. Then I asked him, 'Why did the RAF pilots only fly from 8.00 am to 12.00 pm and from 2.00 pm to 6.00 pm?'. With typical dry British humour, he replied calmly, 'Oh, we already had the 48-hour week by then!'.

We chatted further and I told him of my experience with the low-flyers in Catania. His eyes widened, he threw his arms around me and danced around in a circle with me. 'That was me in the Spitfire!' he was shouting."

The Fall of Italy

On 25 July 1943, the Italian Fascist leader Benito Mussolini was ousted by King Victor Emmanuel III in what really amounted to a coup from above. The King appointed Marshall Pietro Badoglio to lead the government and secure peace with the invading Allies. The Italians may no longer have been fighting, but it was in their countryside and towns that the Allies continued their struggle with the Germans. Men from both sides found themselves in very different circumstances. Here, they recall what it was like in war-torn Italy in autumn 1943. For some, the continual attrition meant the loss of many friends. For one Englishman, a prisoner transported from Africa, escape was the only route to sanity, while one German found himself fighting to take the HQ of his former Italian allies.

Royal Marine Robert Porter was serving on a ship which took troops into the harbour at Taranto for the invasion. He recalls the intense fighting at Salerno and the stubborn resistance of the Germans.

"Before going to Salerno, we called in at Taranto Harbour to drop off a lot of paratroopers and members of Popski's Private Army. The harbour was heavily mined, and the first ship that went in hit a mine and sank. We left as soon as we had got our landing parties ashore and arrived at Salerno on 10 September. The initial landings didn't seem too bad, but what we didn't realise was that the Germans were waiting inland on the hillsides.

There were a lot of ships at Salerno, including battleships and little flat-bottomed monitors, which could sail right up to the shore and bombard the enemy with 15-inch shells. All the ships were supposed to keep bombarding the shore, so that the invasion army could move inland. However, we just couldn't budge the Germans. They seemed impregnable.

All the ships had a FOO – a Forward Observation Officer – who was an army man. He would go ashore with the troops and keep in touch with his ship by portable wireless, giving the ship directions of where and when to fire. He had to be more or less on top of the Germans. The FOOs were essential, because otherwise we would just have been firing randomly at a lot of hills and mountains. We worked entirely upon their directions, firing at the German gun batteries.

This situation went on for weeks and it got so bad at one stage, that we were nearly pushed back into the sea. A Panzer division had been sent down from Rome as reinforcements, and their troops very nearly got the better of us. We could tell how bad things were by the intensity of the bombing. We lost our FOO – in fact, most of the ships lost their FOOs too.

We hung on, and gradually we got the upper hand, but it was very bad during those weeks of fighting. I remember one particular American cruiser called the *Savannah*, noteworthy because she did so much firing. We used to laugh and say, 'There's the *Savannah* again' – she seemed to be having a private war of her own.

Towards the end, our captain told all the fleet that we were going to witness the biggest barrage that had ever happened in the annals of war. The American Fifth Army, the British Eighth Army and all the ships, were ordered to fire at the Germans simultaneously.

However, there was one particular German gun battery which neither the army ashore nor the navy seemed to be able to silence. We called it 'Wilfred'. We would think that we had subdued all the Germans with the shells and the barrages and that it was impossible that anyone could be left alive – then Wilfred would start firing again. He would be quiet for a day and we would think that it was over, and then he would start firing into the sea again. This went on for days. Eventually poor Wilfred copped it too. We felt quite sad because we had developed a respect and an affection for him."

William Ernest Wright, a private with the Royal Irish Fusiliers, landed in Taranto from Sicily. His platoon marched to Bari, then went to Termoli by landing craft – an awesome experience.

"I was the commanding officer's company runner, carrying messages. The life expectancy of a company runner was six weeks, though I didn't know that at the time. If a message had to be got from here to there, and the area between was being swept by machine-gun fire, you still had to go. Most of the messages would be verbal, but sometimes they were written – and sometimes they were people.

In Sicily I once marched a German major with a lump of his brain hanging off, for three miles, to take him to the Intelligence Officer. He never got there – he died on the way. I had to ask for a receipt for his body – I couldn't just go back to my company commander and say the prisoner had died on the way – he would only have had my word for it. He could have thought that I had taken the German around the corner and killed him for an easy afternoon.

The landings at Taranto were quite peaceful. All the gay Italian matelots came out and waved at us. This was something really new to us. They asked us if we were looking for boyfriends. This young matelot came up to me and asked if he could buy me a drink. I had been through all that fighting and yet that young boy had really frightened me!

We were at Taranto very briefly. We more or less marched up to Bari with troop carriers, lorries, everything. Then we hopped two landing barges up to Termoli. They were Yankee craft and, although they were good, they had been thrown together. We got on board these troop landing craft. They were launched sideways – like tins. The crossings took a matter of hours, from dusk to dawn.

It was a terrible experience. Some of the things I remember are best forgotten really. We came under fire and these blinking landing craft were like tins. The caps were coming through the sides and killing people and those on the outside were being blown apart. You couldn't get out because they had locked the hatches on us – they didn't want a load of panicky soldiers on deck. What went on in that landing craft, I'm ashamed to think of. People were fighting with each other to get out and treading on top of each other. You can imagine being under fire in the dark, in the middle of the sea, and they won't let you out – it was like the end of the world.

Once we landed at Termoli, the commandos had already got a foothold. We were only there for 48 hours, but it was very bloody. It was the big breakthrough for the north."

Sergeant George Rhodes, 277 Battery, 70th Field Regiment, Royal Artillery, 46th Infantry Division and his gun crew had landed in Italy and were ready for action on D-Day Plus One – 10 September 1943.

"That night, hordes of giant mosquitoes descended on us in the orchard. They settled everywhere, on the dead bodies, excreta – and on our biscuits. They even ate the cream we had rubbed on our arms, legs and faces to keep the blighters away.

Dozens of men were, by now, incapacitated by violent diarrhoea, because, during the day they had been eating the fruit from the trees and bushes. I had taken my mepacrine tablets in the usual way. As I cannot swallow tablets, I used to eat them like sweets or pop them in my tea.

That night, General McCreery reported to Clark that, even though we in the X Corps had not taken all the objectives, we had established a bridgehead and were holding firm. The Yanks, on the other hand, farther south, wanted to go back to North Africa. Once again, the British had to face the blunt end of the German might. As soon as Jerry fired a few shells at them, the Yanks wanted to be taken back to England. (We had by now no confidence in either the Yanks or their officers, so we had the tendency to carry on the fight without them.)

On my side, we had by now dug our slit trenches on the shore side of the trees to give us extra protection from the shells which kept coming over all that night. I had told my men to get some shut-eye if they could, and to put their tin hats over their faces for protection from the shrapnel and the bullets from the Schmeisser machine guns. The Durham Light Infantry had moved to a position just in front of us, so we left it to them to protect us for the night so that we would be fresh for the dawn offensive.

I sat there under the tree and brewed up again. As I sat there, with my gun resting on my knees, my thoughts turned to home and the Pennines that I had often walked and cycled, and to the odd girl-friend or two.

Everyone was agreeing that the Yanks should never have been allowed to be in charge of this invasion. Even the big-wigs were having second thoughts. Major-General J F C Fuller said, 'The war in Italy was strategically the most useless campaign of the whole war. It prolonged the war, wrecked Italy and wasted thousands of American and British lives'. Even Field Marshal Alexander asked, 'Who is containing whom?'. Another factor of this brilliant cock-up was that Eisenhower kept us short of landing craft and, indeed, wanted back those that we already had.

At 6 am, No. Ones were called to the Command Post, where Captain Haslam briefed us on the plan of attack for D-Day Plus One. We No. Ones had map cases which we slung round our necks. Inside the case we had Chinagraph pencils and we could draw both ours and the German positions. Our object was to advance and drive Jerry off Hospital Hill and hold for the Durhams to come through – but Jerry had other ideas. He had orders to push us into the sea – and he nearly succeeded. We had to call on the Navy for quick and accurate gunfire. They were simply marvellous. They broke up the German tank attacks and silenced the German gun batteries. We couldn't praise the Navy enough – they were the tops.

Over on our right, the 9th Battalion of the Royal Fusiliers were having a hard time trying to capture the tobacco factory at Battipaglia. The 3rd Battalion Coldstream Guards, the 201st Guards Brigade, plus the Grenadiers and the Scots Guards, were on the other side of the factory. They had been shelled all during the night, and when Tiger and Mark IV tanks advanced on their positions, they found themselves in the same situation as us, with nothing to stop the tanks with except a few 6-pounder anti-tank guns, whose shells bounced off the Tiger tank like peas off a brick wall.

Lieutenant-Colonel Ted Hillersden was wounded in the chest. A shell dressing was applied and he was given a jab of morphia. A letter M was marked on his forehead and he was left there in the hope that he would be rescued. Major John Van Gelder and Major Sandford and their Fusiliers had to surrender. They were marched off by the German Infantry into captivity. I am sorry to say this, but the morale of the Grenadiers and the Fusiliers had been so shattered, they started to panic under the intense bombardment by the Germans. They tried to go back to the beach, just the same as the Yanks."

Tony Davies, a Lieutenant in the Royal Horse Artillery, 6th Armoured Division, was captured in North Africa, taken to Italy and moved by train to a prison camp at Chieti, near Pescara.

"Two of us planned to jump off the train… We were being guarded by a sentry who was standing in the corridor, looking into the compartment in which there were six of us. It was one of those trains where you could pull the whole window down. At a given moment, when we considered the train wasn't going too fast – or too slowly, for that matter – one of the chaps gave the sentry a cigarette and struck a match to light it. As he did this, the sentry couldn't see a thing and we went out, one after the other. We immediately scrambled up the mountainside, separated by some ten seconds between one and the other going out. The train, doing 35 mph, dropped us a considerable distance from each other.

I stopped to regain my breath in the shadow of a rock and watched the proceedings going on below. The train had screeched to a halt because the sentries on the back had seen us go and were firing wildly all over the place. The soldiers got off the train and started to climb up the mountain looking for us – but they hadn't a hope in hell of finding us as long as we kept still. After about 25 minutes they called the whole thing off and got back on the train – then it puffed off into the darkness. I went back down and shouted for Michael Gilbert – but all I could hear was the echo of my voice.

It had all turned out to be a tremendous adventure. We were dressed, really, as German soldiers – the British and German khaki drill were very much the same, the only difference being the Africa Corps cap, and we had managed to get two of these through bribery.

In the jump off the train, I cut my leg very badly, so I was looking a pretty average mess really. My trousers were torn, but that didn't deter me very much, and I walked throughout the night, over the mountains, in the hope of reaching a railway line. Eventually I came to a small country station, where I sat and waited until a train came for Benevento, some 100 miles away. Here I had to get off. I left the station about 9 o'clock in the morning and walked through this typical small Italian town, full of people. No one took any notice of me until, going down a small alleyway, I was faced with a German company marching towards me. I had no chance to turn and run for it. I wondered what on earth I could do, and decided to walk on as if nothing had happened. The sergeant-major in charge halted the column – someone was shouting at me in German. It suddenly dawned on him – he was arresting me as a deserter – that I was one of the two British prisoners who had escaped. He burst out laughing and said in very good English, 'You are one of these two officers who escaped, I think, aren't you?'. And I said I was – there wasn't any point in doing anything else really. He was jolly nice, and took me off and gave me breakfast, but then, with regret, he told me he would have to hand me over to the authorities, which he did.

I was kept in a police cell for a day and all the local peasants used to come and stare at me like something in a zoo – they brought some fruit and food too. Then the sergeant of the guard came in and said, 'We've caught your companion', and in due course he was brought in as well. He came in by truck, but he had started to walk and hadn't taken the train at all.

We were both taken back to Naples by car, and court-martialled. This was really a most comic affair. A very charming and dignified Italian general called Radice heard the case. In the midst of the proceedings, there was an air raid and American Flying Fortresses started to bomb the place. We all rushed down into the cellars. It was quite obvious when it started again, that although they were court-martialling us for escaping, which they were entitled to do, the real culprit was the poor bloody sentry who had been on our train. They wouldn't believe our story that he didn't see us go. He said to us, 'You are trying to shield this poor man. It is quite obvious that you bribed him'. He sentenced him to two years in jail. Then he turned to us and gave us each 30 days solitary confinement in the cells of the camp in Chieti."

Colonel Walter Gericke was commander of the German II Battalion Paratroop Regiment 6, who were sent in to conduct a do-or-die raid on the Italian HQ at Monterotondo, after the Italian surrender. Gericke describes the preparations, plannings and carrying out of the mission.

"My order from General Student ran as follows, 'I have a special mission for you and your battalion – secret Reich business. In the event of Italy capitulating, you and your battalion shall conduct an air raid against the Italian HQ in Monterotondo, and take out the whole Italian centre of command. On this mission, you will be left entirely to your own devices. For reasons of secrecy, you will be given no air support'.

The area around the HQ had long since been declared a no-go area by the Italians, but the next day, I flew in in a 'Storch' to see where the operation would take place.

Everything went OK at first until the Italian flak turned their barrels upwards and a couple of warning shells exploded not far from my machine. The pilot signalled that he had got the message, and turned to leave. I had not had enough time to get a good look at the area. So I drew up a plan myself, and gave myself the order – my regiment would march into the area as part of the reinforcement of the German troops there. I wanted to meet up with them and order them to take another route. I sketched out the route which the regiment would take on my map and set off for Monterotondo.

Soon I came upon the first Italian post, where there was one Italian officer and four Italians. It was difficult explaining to them what I had in mind. Finally he asked his superior whether he could let me pass. The reply came that an officer from the HQ would escort me through town.

This time everything seemed to be working out, but I was still unsure whether I would see what I wanted to see under Italian escort. The officer arrived with an escort and the journey through the town began. The HQ could not be seen from the main street – roadblocks and bunkers had been constructed all around. I also saw that all the side-streets crossing the main street had been blocked off. I dismissed the Italian officer, who cleared it that when I returned, I would be let through without checking.

So, I drove further, had a look at the terrain surrounding the town and searched out a good place for the battalion to drop, hung around there for a while and then headed back. With the aid of aerial photography, I was able to explain the exact plan of the operation – then came the delay.

One evening, a motorcycle messenger came from Foggia and before he'd even reached us, he shouted out 'Italy has surrendered!' The town was lit up and the bells rang out. Everyone was dizzy with the onset of peace.

The order to go had yet to come from General Student. I telephoned time and again, since the radio link was out due to the bad weather, but I couldn't get through. The Störtrupps (communications squads) went out to take a look. They discovered that long stretches of cable had been cut by the locals. It took until midnight to put it right, and even then, it was still difficult getting a decent line. General Student came to the phone and gave the order, 'Treason of Badoglio and the Royal House proved! Commence alone! Break a leg!'

As we neared Monterotondo, we were greeted with heavy anti-aircraft fire. The order came, 'Get ready to jump'. The pilots sought out their dropping points. I was standing in the door of the machine and could make out all the details of the area which I knew from my reconnaissance. Then came the signal to jump. I hesitated a bit, because I wanted to land exactly by the house in the vineyards, which I had picked out as a combat post. Unbeknown to me, it was the command post of the flak units of the high command. It was in our hands after a brief shoot-out.

All companies had arrived at the outskirts of the town and held Monterotondo in a pincer movement, as had been the plan. This was a slow process as the enemy, superior in number and arms, resisted fiercely. Courage and steadfastness counted for more here than numbers and concrete.

Each house had to be taken individually before we could begin storming the *Castello*. The garrison there put up a desperate fight, but by 14.30 hours it was surrounded. We were now within sight and I gave the order to move forward quickly. After bombarding the *Castello* with a captured 8.8 cm flak gun, my adjutant requested the garrison to surrender and threatened 'If you do not accede, we will send in German Stuka squadrons immediately to bomb the *Castello*'.

This, of course, was a bluff – we had neither radio contact nor any other with our superiors. We were totally out on a limb. But our enemies in the *Castello* could have no idea of this. However, before the request to surrender, the enemy launched a relief attack from an easterly direction, which we had to repel before we could finish taking out the *Castello*.

Then we went in with all the weaponry we had. Some of the braver men had dropped beyond the forecourt of the *Castello* right up to the heavily guarded main door. The main portal crashed down from a blast – the *Castello* surrendered. Before the smoke from the blast had dispersed, the defending troops came out, their arms raised. The white flag flew from the tower and 150 officers and 200 men were taken prisoner."

Kursk – Beginning of the End

*T*he winter fighting on the Eastern Front, where Field
    Marshal Erich von Manstein halted the Russian offen-
sive after its victory at Stalingrad in February 1943, created
a huge salient 100 miles wide and 70 miles deep, with the
railway junction city of Kursk at its centre. That summer the
Germans planned two simultaneous attacks from north and
south to destroy the Soviet forces and stabilise the front. The
operation, called Citadel, used 2,380 tanks and assault
guns, 10,000 guns and 900,000 men supported by 2,500
aircraft. Although senior German officers had reservations
about the operation, Hitler was adamant that it go ahead.
But Ultra intercepts of German signals had been passed to the
Soviet High Command, giving them full details of the plan.
Consequently, the Red Army turned the salient into a huge
fortress, laying deep and dense minefields protected by
artillery, supported by 3,300 tanks and assault guns, 2,650
aircraft and 1,337,000 men. In heavy rain and under
heavy artillery fire, the German attack in the north soon
became bogged down. In the south, however, tough Waffen-
SS troops made headway and on July 12 at Prokhorovka,
700 German tanks of the Fourth Panzer Army clashed with
850 of Russia's Fifth Guards Tank Army. The encounter
was the biggest tank battle in history. On July 13 Soviet forces
launched a counter-offensive that crushed the German
salients north and south of Kursk and rolled their forces back
over 150 miles. The retreating Germans lost around 1,500

> *tanks, 1,400 aircraft and 70,000 men; although Soviet losses were probably only slightly less, the victors had taken the tactical and strategic initiative. They would retain it all the way to Berlin.*

Georg Berger was First Ordinance Officer from the SS General Command with the division *Das Reich*. Almost surrounded at Kharkov, they were ordered to hold the town, but commanding general Paul Hausser decided to withdraw – an initiative which proved successful.

"The decision to disobey an order from the *Führer* was a rare occurrence and in this case testifies to the civil courage of one of the most important commanders of the Waffen-SS.

The SS Panzer Corps with the Divisions *Leibstandarte* and *Das Reich* was virtually encircled in Kharkov. Awaiting it was the same fate as befell the Sixth Army in Stalingrad – that is, unless, at the eleventh hour, an order to withdraw and evacuate the town was issued.

On February 13 Russian tank units broke through to the outskirts of Kharkov – only the arterial road to the south west, direction Poltava, could be kept clear. As First Ordinance Officer of the SS General Command, I experienced those fateful hours before the break-out from Kharkov, and witnessed first-hand how Hausser was thrown into a terrible crisis of conscience by a senseless order from the *Führer*.

The order from the *Führer* of 13 February was curt and simple, 'Kharkov is to be held'. In a situation report to the Army Section Lanz, Hausser requested permission to evacuate the town, which was rejected, citing the order from the *Führer*. Following a number of telephone conversations with the High Commander of the Army, General Lanz, Hausser was permitted to speak personally.

I passed this conversation on in the evening of 13 February. Hausser, unfortunately, had been unable to get Manstein's consent, on the grounds that we were dealing with an explicit order from the *Führer*. However, Field Marshal von Manstein empowered Hausser to seek direct contact with the *Führer's* HQ, in order to give his own explanation of how precarious the situation was.

I succeeded in relaying this conversation to the *Wolfsschanze (Führer*

HQ near Rastenburg), and the Chief of General Staff of the Army, General Zeitzler, promised Hausser that he would persuade the *Führer* to change the order during the *Lagebesprechung* (situation meeting) at 02.00 am the next morning.

In the meantime, on 14 February, the orders to the Divisions *Liebstandarte* and *Das Reich*, instructing them to withdraw from Kharkov, had long since been written up, and the Ordinance Officers of the Divisions were waiting impatiently for the orders to be distributed.

In the late afternoon of 14 February, Paul Hausser came out of the cramped farmhouse into the shivering cold and paced up and down in silence. Turning, he said calmly, 'Give out the orders to the divisions to withdraw'. I held my breath then said, '*Obergruppenführer*, the order from the *Führer* states quite clearly…'. Paul Hausser interrupted me, 'An old man like me is no loss, but I can't do this to the young boys out there. Give out the Corps order.'"

Herbert Brunnegger was an *Unterscharführer* with the *Totenkopf* Division of the Waffen-SS in the tank battle at Kursk. He had no illusions as to the futility of the Germans' task in this merciless battle.

"The most destructive battle in the history of the war had now begun. In the prelude to the battle, a matter of only hours, more shells and bombs were used up than during the whole of the French and Polish campaign.

Beside us our comrades from the *Leibstandarte* and the Division *Das Reich* were preparing to attack. We were waiting in our positions far ahead in the advancing front and at midday we watched from some kilometres away as their heavy Tiger units, guns blazing, broke through the Russian anti-tank and tank cordon. When we got the order to dismantle, they were moving up closer to our hill and were about to push past us. At around 16.30 hours we clambered into the troop carrier in what was previously the main battle-line, and we were whisked off to one of the main parts of the battle. The same evening the infantry attack began. Resistance was slight. The enemy had already withdrawn his main forces and his second and third lines were lying in wait for us.

We trudged uphill and downhill lugging the heavy equipment, under constant fire from Russian machine-guns, which were nailed to the ground. As evening fell we reached our marked destination and set up camp in the open air, while the engineers set about laying down a cordon of mines in front of us. They also took over guard of the resting troops, while we wrapped ourselves in blankets and tarpaulin. In the gathering dusk, half-asleep, I heard my name called out, and that of my comrade, Schulz. Schulz, like me, was a newly commissioned *Unterscharführer* [Second Lieutenant]. In the hope that I had been dreaming, I dozed on, until I finally had to accept that my name really was being called out. My company chief, *Obersturmführer* Schmoelz, explained to us what we had to do from his tarpaulin-covered hide-hole: we were to reconnoitre the enemy territory as far as the runway Bjelgorod-Kursk by two different routes. 'Toss for who takes which', we were told. We quickly agreed on this. Schultz would take the left, and I would take the right sector.

I took half of the group with me. We took with us machine pistols, hand grenades, gas masks and bayonets, but we would be without steel helmets. Our order – to form a line of infantry, spaced out just so that the man in front was in view.

It was pitch black all round us as we left the *Igelstellung* (position of all-round defence). I set the bearings on my field compass. I picked out a glow of fire on the eastern horizon as a provisional marker … As long as it continued to glow, we wouldn't lose our way and, despite the darkness, we would be able to find our way back to our departure point.

I was at the head of the group, trying to make as little noise as possible, when suddenly we were stopped in our tracks by loud shouts from behind us: 'Stop, stop, you're standing right in the middle of a minefield!'. Christ, this was too much, and we'd only just set off. One false step could mean instant death. I ordered everyone to get down on their haunches without touching the ground with their hands. Then, the last man in the line took the first step back out of the minefield along the path indicated by the engineers. We got out without losses. Once we finally got under way again we had wasted half an hour.

We crept quietly through the darkness. Not a sound of guns or the rattling of equipment, only the breathing of the men and the soft rustle of the stiff blades of grass in the cool night. We could expect to stumble upon the enemy at any moment.

The wind carried an aroma of Machorka tobacco. We waited a while without being able to make out a thing, but we knew now that 'Ivan' was around. We were smack in the middle of the enemy lines, but we had to go on, we had to get to the runway and complete our mission to establish whether defensive preparations had been made there.

As we crept further forward the aroma of Machorka grew stronger. I had our Russian speaker brought up to the head of the line, and instructed him that should we stumble unexpectedly upon the enemy, we would quite brazenly pretend to be Russians. I told him that he was to go on ahead alone and speak to the Ivans in their own language, while we would hang back. A few minutes later I spotted a dark cluster of people lying just below my feet. As I crouched down I noticed that it was two Russians sleeping in a hide-hole behind a light machine gun. Karp raised his machine pistol, but I gestured to him to put it away. That's the last thing we needed on a nice summer evening like this. I carefully lifted the machine gun out of the hole and gave the signal to continue…

At about 2.00 am it dawned on me that the flame beacon I had taken for a marker had strayed a good way to the right. There was only one explanation for this: the flame was coming from a burning ship moving down a river. This could only be the upper reaches of the Don. It was clear to me now that we had lost our way, and finding the way back would be a matter of instinct rather than a compass. I ordered my men to withdraw immediately, and we wasted no time heading back, since we had to be out of enemy territory before dawn broke. The anxiety that the greying light of dawn could prove to be our captor quickened our steps. I found the departure point with great accuracy, and thus also the guard company, who had been waiting impatiently for us to return. The shout of 'password' from their sentry relieved all the tension.

The reconnaissance unit led by Schulz had got back before us. He had strayed into a Russian minefield. Schulz was at the head of his men and had had his leg blown off up to the thigh, and his other leg was also seriously wounded. His men had risked their lives to get him out of the minefield, and had carried him back to the departure point. The ambulance driver came back an hour later with the news that my comrade had died.

Around 8.00 am we attacked without advance artillery fire, and with little resistance from the enemy we advanced swiftly and reached the runway around midday. We'd arrived in the nick of time, because Franz Huber was stuck fast with his light 2.2 cm anti-tank gun – a novelty. We all mucked in and pulled the tiny gun – of which the most striking feature was the hugely out-of-proportion barrel – up the slope. 'So much sweat for a little toy like this', we quipped. 'You wouldn't believe what a thing like this can do', Franz said, defending his weapon. And we'd have plenty of opportunity to find out. We dug ourselves in in the road ditches by the runway, Franz's anti-tank gun beside us. Our task to hold the position no matter what.

Right in front of us was a long line of enemy installations, still completely intact. According to statements from prisoners there was yet another carefully constructed locking installation beyond this defensive cordon. And behind this were massed colonies of tanks, ready to launch a massive Russian break-through offensive. I could not help thinking that the enormous mass of hardware assembled on our side was a gigantic drop in the ocean. This would only put pay to the first cordon, which, as I saw it, had been left empty or was occupied by only a few men. The second bulwark would bring us to a halt and stop us reaching the core of the enemy installations, the ultimate target of our offensive.

The night grew cold. It began to rain. Once again, I couldn't snatch even a few minutes sleep. I kept on wishing I'd be transferred to a new observer corps or fireman unit. The *Oberdeppen* (total idiots), as Franz Huber called them, brought the artillery fire down on us promptly the next morning by mucking about as usual, and one of these suicide cases strutted right past me. Whenever I saw one of these characters, proudly displaying their 'heroic' coldbloodedness, I couldn't stop myself shouting to him whether he thought he was in some kind of Punch and Judy show. One of them shouted back: 'What is your name? I'll report you', which left me completely cold. I thought to myself, fat chance of that, you idiot; if you carry on like that you won't survive beyond midday."

Sergeant Grigorii Sgibnev had started his career in 1941 with the Pacific Fleet, but in July 1943 was a platoon commander in the Russian 44th Guards Infantry Division. He recalls the fighting at Izyum, an action for which he received the Hero of the Soviet Union award.

"At first everything went well. After an hour's artillery preparation when, it seemed, not a single survivable place remained in the fascist positions, we dashed into the attack. So long as we were running among the trees and bushes, the Hitlerites remained quiet, but as soon as we appeared in the open in front of the fascist positions, their trenches became alive. Machine guns and automatics rattled out. Grenades also flew to meet us – one of them spun around beneath my feet.

Everyone who has been in battle knows the feeling, when it seems that one is in the space between life and death, a space, so the saying goes, that would be too narrow for a mouse to jump. One acts automatically, half consciously. I also, quite instinctively, seized this grenade without thinking and hurled it back towards the enemy trenches. It exploded as it reached them. 'Smash them with their own grenades!' I shouted.

All this happened about 20 metres from the enemy defence line. It was too close for us to get artillery or mortar support, but the fascists could not use that kind of support either, without risking being caught up in it. A grenade battle flared up. Moving towards their trench, we bombarded it with the same grenades that the fascists hurled at us.

Having overcome the first defence line, we moved on to the second trench on the village outskirts. We had to take this by storm also – and once again we threw back the enemy's own grenades.

I can remember that I had managed to pull off the firing ring of one of my own grenades and was preparing to throw it, when a German grenade fell at my feet. I seized it with my left hand, and it exploded … From hospital I went home. My father met me and said, 'You've come back alive, that's the main thing'."

Semyon Belozvertsev, aged 18, was a private in the Russian 887th Infantry Regiment when, to capitalise on the German defeat at Kursk, his unit pushed forwards through the Ukraine. He recalls the problems of crossing the rivers which divide up the area.

"Usually, when people talk of their first battle, or of the period waiting for it, they speak of some feeling of anxiety, but at the beginning, I did not experience this. I was young, full of strength and confidence…

In the night of 19–20 September, our unit reached the Desna. It was the darkest of Ukrainian nights, and the river was frightening in its mysteriousness. The order arrived to force the river in darkness, using whatever was to hand – or, simply speaking, force it one way or another.

I went down to the edge, overgrown with short bushes, to feel if the water was warm or not. I bumped into a dugout canoe. Soldiers were all around. Using the seat as an oar, and baling out water continuously, three of us (the limit of the boat's capacity) managed to get across to the other side. And in the water, the whole width of the river, we could hear splashes, talk, orders, quiet swearing ... we also heard several screams. On the whole, the crossing was successful, helped by the presence on the bank of an abandoned village, which in a flash was converted into rafts of boards and beams.

At 11 or 12 o'clock, German aircraft came and began to bomb our crossing place. The bombs fell with a terrifying scream, which at first pulled our nerves almost to breaking point and was really more psychologically effective than the acutal explosions. Having released their bombs, the aircraft began to circle and machine-gun us. Sitting in our little dugout, I watched with great interest everything that was going on around me. Soon after the aircraft came light tanks, which fired at us and began to outflank us. We came under crossfire and abandoned the village with heavy losses, because our infantry weapons had no success against the tanks.

We lost many officers, and a sergeant-major took over. He already had battle experience. He ordered us to dig in and act on the defensive. We could not retreat any further, because the river was at our backs. Going away for a while, the sergeant-major came back with dozens of anti-tank grenades which he handed out to the more experienced soldiers. The village we had abandoned was now burning.

During the night, some 45 mm anti-tank guns were sent over to us. At dawn the next day we captured the burned village and pushed on."

Tarawa – Island Graveyard

*T*he tiny Pacific atoll of Tarawa was to be the Calvary of the US Marine Corps. Earlier landings at Apamama and Makin had been achieved with relatively light casualties and, although there was limited information about the coastline at Tarawa, American planners were confident. The landing on 20 November 1943, by 5,000 men of the Second US Marine Division under General Julian Smith marked the first tactical use of amphibious tractors. However, the landing went badly. A heavy but poorly coordinated sea and air bombardment left many Japanese positions, well constructed and camouflaged under layers of felled coconut trees, intact and able to fire at the Marines as they waded towards the beach or advanced in Amtracs, many of which were unable to cross a sea wall of coconut palms and became easy targets. By the close of the day, the Marines had only a tiny foothold in the lee of the sea wall, and the next day a second landing also incurred heavy losses. The Marines, however, supported by artillery fire from nearby Bairiki Island, relaunched attacks on two fronts with the small number of tanks they had landed. In a final, furious banzai counter-attack, the Japanese threw all their remaining strength against the Marines, but were fought off. By the morning of 23 November, the atoll was declared secure. No-one from either side could have foreseen the carnage (1,000 US Marines were killed, whilst the Japanese suffered 4,600 casualties) which took place in the blistering heat of the equatorial sun.

Lieutenant-Commander Donald J Ramsey, Captain of the destroyer *Hughes*, was at hand with his ship when US 'jeep' carrier *Liscome Bay* was sunk by torpedoes from the Japanese submarine I-175 off Makin Island at 5.13 am on 24 November 1943. He rescued some survivors – but 712 men perished.

"Apparently bombs, torpedoes, gasoline and ammuntion all went up together. The whole ship was enveloped in flames so rapidly that damage control and fire fighting appeared to be out of the question. The personnel who did manage to escape were all very badly shaken up and some of them had suffered bad burns, broken limbs and shock.

Nearly every man aboard had some bruises and cuts. One man died while the medical officer was administering blood plasma – another died in the water before being picked up by the motor whaleboat. This ship has rescued survivors from the old *Lexington*, the old *Yorktown* and the old *Hornet*, but it was unanimously agreed that the sinking of the *Liscome Bay* and the condition of the comparatively few survivors constituted the most heart-rending disaster yet.

Inspiring is no word for the conduct displayed by the men picked up in the water, and the absolute courage of these men was electrifying. One man, who had been operated on for appendicitis just two days before not only scrambled up the life net without assistance, but on arriving on deck, asked if there was not a rubber boat handy for him to take out and assist others whom he knew needed help.

It was common comment on this ship that though the personnel losses were horrible enough as it was, it was a miracle that *anyone* managed to escape the inferno."

The scene of destruction seen from the comparative safety of the battleship *New Mexico*, which lay 1,500 yards off the carrier's starboard quarter, was described by a young lieutenant as follows in his combat report.

"A few seconds after the first explosion, a second explosion which appeared to come from inside the *Liscome Bay*, burst upwards, hurling fragments and clearly discernible planes 200 feet or more in the air. The entire ship seemed to explode, and almost at the same instant, her interior, except for the extreme bow and stern sections, glowed with flames like a furnace.

The ship was showered from forecastle to quarter-deck with oil particles and burning and extinguished fragments. The whole central section of her starboard hull seemed to be blown out and she immediately took on a heavy list to starboard. About a one-hundred-foot section of her flight-deck had blown clear off of the ship. One of her Helldiver aircraft, already ablaze, was also blown clear of the ship and in turn set on fire the floating oil fuel that had leaked from her shattered hull. The floating flames spread over a wide area, making rescue attempts of the survivors in the water a difficult business.

Lieutenant-Commander Ed Owen, senior officer of VF5 (Fighting Five, as they were known) from the US carrier *Yorktown II*, and his team took off in Hellcats as they were jumped by 18 Japanese Zeros, 4 December 1943.

"This was a first-line team, and they knew what they were doing. Six Zeros positioned themselves on each of our two-plane sections, with two of their planes always firing on each section. When we headed for them, they would make a violent pull-out and climb at a 60° angle. Then the next two would come at us.

We pulled into the standard protective 'thatch weave' formation, with each of our sections swinging back and forth to protect the other. It was a case of hit them with all you had, reverse, and do the same again. We were giving them everything we had with no quarter asked on either side. There wasn't time to see what happened to the Japs we hit. I would have given ten years of my life for another gun (I had only one operating, and my sight was out of commission), and for 5,000 more feet of altitude.

This continued for several minutes until one of the Jap bastards set Si Satterfield's plane on fire, shooting him on the outside of his weave. Both his wing tanks were burning, with flames reaching half way down the fuselage, apparently out of control. Why they didn't shoot us all down is more than I can figure out. Maybe they would have if they had been better gunners."

Carl J Moore, later to become Rear Admiral, was Chief of Staff to Admiral Raymond Spruance during the campaign in the Gilbert, Marshall and Mariana islands. His view of the Tarawa assault was from aboard the cruiser *Indianapolis*. From this

vantage point he observed the bombardment – but later landed on Tarawa.

"The particular job of the *Indianapolis* was to bombard suspected gun emplacements and ammunition dumps on the east side of Tarawa Atoll, while the rest of Harry Hill's outfit bombarded Betio, at the south end of the atoll, and while the troops disembarked from the transports. We made a run the length of Tarawa's east side and along the south coast, firing at lookout towers in the beautiful palm groves and at Japanese barges. We started a few fires, one of which burned for a couple of days.

By the time we reached Betio it looked like a shambles. It had been bombarded and bombed for two hours. Fires were burning everywhere. The coconut trees were all blasted. It seemed that no living soul could be on the island. Then we joined with Hill's ships in the bombardment of Tarawa and the troops approached the beach. It looked like the whole affair would be a walkover.

We saw the first wave reach the beach. Then we saw the next two or three waves get stuck on the edge of the reef that fringed the island. We saw the troops disembark and advance for about 400 yards in water that was waist-deep. It was in this phase that we had our greatest losses, for with all our bombardment, the Japs had not been routed out of their beach pillboxes. For the next 24 hours they made it hell for our Marines.

The destroyers remained in close support and the big ships continued to bombard all the next day. Finally, by ingenuity and by taking advantage of the breaks, the Marines managed to beat down the opposition on the main beaches and to land on a couple of others. By the night of the second day we felt pretty secure. The fighting continued hard, however, for a few days longer. It must have been awfully tough on the men ashore and those in the boats waiting to get ashore. We couldn't see much from the flagship except the raging fires, the shells and bombs falling, and the destroyers and small boats manoeuvring about the harbour. We had to keep moving because of the threat of submarines. But the destroyers did a fine job and good luck kept us all safe from the enemy subs. Through it all we on the flagship kept in pretty close touch with what was going on and had a general picture of the situation.

One week after the first assault, our flagship entered the lagoon at Tarawa. Raymond went ashore to meet Nimitz and his party, who had come out from Pearl Harbor. Raymond got separated from them and didn't find out the things I had hoped he would. I went ashore for an hour that afternoon but had to hurry back because Raymond and I couldn't both be away for long.

The place was swarming with Marines. I had never known that men could look like they did – dirty, burned, ragged, hot, a week's growth of beard, tired, hungry, thirsty. They were about as fine a lot of men as I ever have seen. What they had been through that week! I have never seen such a shambles – coconut logs everywhere, sheet iron, guns, ammunition, smashed tanks, equipment, shot-up cars, bicycles, carts. In fact, everything that goes with war was scattered all over – pillboxes, tanks, traps, slit trenches dug up through concrete strongpoints in such numbers they couldn't be counted. Some were smashed to smithereens. Others, still good, had contained live Japs the day before.

When I was ashore that day, all the dead Marines had been properly buried and most of the dead Japs had been thrown into bomb craters and bulldozed over. There were many Japs lying about in an advanced stage of decomposition. I contented myself with smelling them and avoided any closer examination. Some of the strongpoints were still full of hundreds of them. No-one knew it was so thoroughly defended."

Tadao Onuki, a Japanese Naval Chief Petty Officer attached to No. 3 Yokosuka Special Base, found himself preparing for battle on the island of Tarawa, having asked to move to a tank unit. From a mood of confident optimism, his comrades' morale was to receive a heavy blow. The arrival of overwhelming numbers of US Marines and constant bombardment would finally take their toll and leave him stranded.

"I went back to Japan from our base at Rabaul, and in June 1943 I was transferred to Tarawa after expressing a wish to serve in a tank unit. Tarawa is the main island of the Gilbert Islands, and is surrounded by many other islands, large and small, such as Makin.

Our unit was called No. 3 Yokosuka Special Base Unit, and we spent day after day busy with constructing positions and in battle drill. Air-raids by large enemy aircraft were a daily occurrence, but they never hindered us in any way. We were once raided for 24 hours. by a combined force of fighters and bombers, but they didn't do us any harm – in fact, they raised our morale very effectively. Here and there on the island we built some really tough positions making skilful use of the natural features of the terrain. The construction went on without a break, night and day. Our tank unit was completely combat-ready and preparations for the encounter battle went ahead.

At dawn on 21st November, a great fleet of enemy ships appeared on the distant line of the horizon. So the time had finally come – the enemy's destroyers' naval guns soon began to fire simultaneously, and their shells rained down on the Japanese positions. One of the shells scored a bull's-eye on our magazine and started a huge blaze. This in turn offered a prime target to the enemy guns. In addition, bombers and aircraft from the ships attacked us from the air, setting ablaze the food dumps and other key installations, one after the other. Soon the entire island was covered in flames and black smoke.

The enemy's naval gunfire and aerial bombing went on for several hours, while we waited in the air raid trenches like sheep in a sheepfold, expecting the order to attack. Soon, under a full-scale covering fire, hordes of enemy landing craft approached the shore. They looked likely to swamp the Japanese forces completely.

In the face of fierce, ear-splitting small-arms fire, the enemy landing-craft began to run aground, and the US soldiers began to fall into the sea. I think we damped their ardour, but they had guts and, although they received the full impact of our small-arms fire, they crossed the shallows to the shore, and then trod over the bodies of their fallen comrades, one after the other, until they finally managed to install themselves at one end of the island.

Inside my tank, I poured out shot until the barrel of my gun was red-hot, but it was impossible not to be aware of the threat of the enemy's numbers. Our men had seen our magazine and food dumps go up in flames, and from the material point of view, they were already no match for the Americans. But we moved here and there on the island and gave the Americans something to think about. Hunting for tanks, I burst into the enemy positions and ended up by penetrating deep into them, almost before I knew what was happening. I tried to withdraw, but for some reason, the engine refused to budge. I was frantic, and couldn't find the cause of the stoppage. There were signs from outside that enemy troops had begun to gather round the tank. I thought I'd had it, then I kicked my foot down on the axle in sheer desperation and the motor sputtered into life – to my intense joy! As if in a dream, I scattered the Americans who were swarming around my tank, knocked them out of the way and put on speed until I got back to our own position.

It wasn't long before the battle turned against us, and Major-General Shibasaki and his HQ moved from No. 1 Command Post to No. 2. Our tank unit was ordered to give them covering fire. At the time, the tank unit couldn't move, because we hadn't enough fuel, so we acted as gun platforms. When we finished that assignment. I clambered down from the tank. In that instant, shells from one of the enemy's naval guns came down with a shattering roar and burst all round us. My two comrades who were just emerging from the tank were blown to pieces in a split second.

On the 25th we separated into No. 1 and No. 2 troops and resolved to carry out one final attack. The report of our fight to the finish was sent off to Japan beforehand.

At that time, the number of US troops who had come ashore was several hundred times greater than that of the Japanese who had survived, and bit by bit, they began to encircle us. We were no longer masters of the seas or the skies, we had no food or ammunition left, and there was no longer any hope of a force coming to relieve us. There was only one way ahead for the Japanese on Tarawa – a fight to the finish and total annihilation.

We said goodbye to No. 1 troop as they moved off for their first attack, and those of us who belonged to No. 2 troop waited in the air-raid trenches until the evening hour when the attack was expected. But in the end, we were spotted by a keen-eyed enemy pilot, who came in to the attack. In an instant, the inside of the trench was turned into an inferno by his bombs and the explosives hurled at us by US troops – and by the flame-throwers which poured flame at us before the smoke from the bombing had cleared away. Everything was incinerated.

In that burned-out trench, where everything was totally destroyed, no human being could have survived other than by a miracle. As it happened, there was a miracle.

I don't know how long it was before I was aware I was still alive. I could not move my hands or feet freely, and my body felt as if it were being pressed by something heavy. All I was sure of was the fact that I was still alive. Then I regained consciousness completely. I was lying under a heap of blackened corpses, and around me in the trench I could see hands and feet scattered all over. It was a scene of such disaster that, without thinking, I wanted to cover my eyes, even though I was quite battle-hardened by this time.

Of the 15 of us who had sworn to live or die together, I was the only one left. There was no sign of any of the others, and my insignificant life had only been saved because I had been sheltered by the dead bodies of my comrades. I could feel there were burns on my face, but I was still not sure I was all in one piece and for a while, everything went blank.

When I came to again, I tried to crawl out of the trench. It was already dark, and all round me everything had gone uncannily quiet. Tarawa felt exactly like an island of the dead. Apart from a few lights which seemed to be in the US positions, far off, the deep blackness stretched everywhere. The sound of guns which had made the whole island shake, had completely died away.

Had the fighting come to an end? If that were the case, and I was on an island where the Japanese forces had been completely wiped out, and I was the sole survivor, what was I to do? There was no-one to give me orders. I was unarmed, I hadn't even a rifle to fight with. There were no comrades to give me comfort or spur me on. How was I going to stay alive on this island which was filled with enemy soldiers? And supposing I stayed alive, there was absolutely no hope of ever going back to Japan. When I thought about it, an indescribable feeling of loneliness pressed in on me, the terror of it almost stifled me.

Then dawn came. If I can keep alive, then that's what I must do, I thought – and at the same time, I became aware of the gnawing emptiness in my belly. I began to go round the island from then on, looking for something to eat, prepared to take the risk of being captured by avoiding being spotted by the Americans and watching out for any signs of other Japanese. But I found nothing to eat, and there was no sign of any Japanese either. All I was left with was my empty stomach and a feeling of unbearable solitude.

One night I crossed the sea channel secretly, and moved across to a small island nearby, about half a mile away. There should have been Japanese garrison troops there too – but that island also had been occupied. Since I might be spotted by an American sentry, I hid during the day in deep foliage or under the shadow of rocks, and then at night-fall, I pottered along the shore in search of food. Small fish, prawns and crayfish which could be caught in the shallows were important articles of food. On rare occasions, there would be a feast – a coconut fallen from a palm tree.

As the days went by in this fashion, I was joined by other survivors – Japanese soldiers who began to gather in ones and twos from the other islands. In the end, there were seven of us. In a way, that gave me strength and encouragement, but the way ahead was gloomy. We thought that if we were taken prisoner we would be killed, in which case, we preferred to take our own lives. So, all seven of us tried to hang ourselves, together. But the rope was weak and it snapped, so we ended up unable to kill ourselves.

On this island, if you dug down about a foot, salt water came out, so there was no drinking water at all. I found thirst harder to bear than hunger, but I knew that if I drank the water I would pay for it. Of course, there was nothing to eat, and every day rather than look for food in order to live, we lived in order to look for food. The seven of us had come together with great difficulty, but in the end we split up and went off to different parts of the island in the search for food. In the end, I was left on my own again.

This miserable existence went on for three weeks, until one day, being unable to endure my parched throat which felt, as usual, as if it were on fire, I went out along the beach, by the water's edge, almost without knowing what I was doing. US troops on patrol found me. By that time, I had absolutely no physical or spiritual strength to resist left in me.

After they had captured me, the US troops seemed to begin a search of the whole island, every nook and cranny, and one by one, my six comrades were taken. Once again, our seven faces were brought together – but this time we were no longer free men – we were prisoners of war.

The destruction on Tarawa at an end, the seven of us who had secretly survived but were weak enough to drop, were soon transferred to a US Navy destroyer. We were helped and looked after at first rather than interrogated, and they gave us food. However, since we had resolved that we would be killed sooner or later, when the next day dawned we said to ourselves. 'This is our last day', and then when the sun went down, we thought. 'We've lived one more day today', with some surprise. It was a complicated feeling. Although for the past three weeks we'd had no fear of dying at all, we began to think we'd been lucky, and as we continued to stay alive, life began to seem a desirable thing.

The Americans treated us with amazing politeness, giving us injections to give us strength, and masses of food to eat, which restored us.

It was perhaps a bit late in the day, but we were gradually made to feel the enormous gap in combat strength between the US forces which could have enough food like this, even in the midst of a battle, and our army which depended on hard tack and dried bonito. Our weakened bodies were restored to health – but the wound in our hearts would not heal.

Afterwards, the six of us were split up and I was sent by ship to a camp in Hawaii, then to New York, then again to a camp in Wisconsin and finally one in Texas. That was where I heard the war was over. It was a pitiful defeat. But the fact that the earth of my mother country still remained was a consolation for me. If the war had gone on any longer. I might have become a man with no mother country at all."

Cassino – Mountain Inferno

*I*n battles spanning the months from late 1943 to May
1944, Italian locals and British, Polish, American and
German soldiers witnessed the effects of steady attrition on the
town of Cassino. The town and sixth-century Benedictine
monastery of Monte Cassino were the key to the Gustav Line,
or Winter Line, dominating the approaches to Rome. Here,
the Tenth German Army made a successful stand from
January to May 1944. On 22 January in an attempt to outflank the Gustav Line, British and American forces landed
at Anzio south of Rome but, despite having the advantage of
surprise, were successfully contained by the Germans in a
cramped and dangerous beachhead. On 15 February, the
monastery was heavily bombed and immediately afterwards
the Fourth Indian and Second New Zealand Divisions made
limited gains. On 15 March the town was pulverised by
1,000 tons of bombs and the fire of 600 guns, and the New
Zealanders captured Castle Hill after fierce fighting with the
German First Parachute Division. Gurkhas of the Fourth
Indian Division captured the exposed position of Hangman's
Hill, but were forced to abandon it on the 24th. A lull followed and the Allies looked for a way of breaking the dead-
lock. The new plan included a decoy operation to convince
the Germans that there would be a breakout from Anzio, and
then at 23.00 hours on May 11, 2,000 guns opened fire. The
Polish II Corps isolated and captured the monastery, the
British XIII Corps crossed the River Rapido, and the French

and US II Corps attacked south of the Liri. The Allies'
advantage of surprise won them the breakthrough but
General Clark's obsession to capture Rome meant that many
German troops escaped to fight on.

Douglas Lyne, age 20, was a gunner in the Royal Artillery, acting as Observation Post Assistant in the 57th Field Regiment, part of X Corps. To him the destruction of the Cassino Monastery had a special significance, his ancestor Father Ignatius of Llanthony having founded a Benedictine monastery in Wales based on this very edifice.

"Suffice it to say that by the end of January, beginning of February, no real progress had been made towards the capture of Cassino Monastery, without which it was impossible to proceed along the road to Rome. It was about this time that my own regiment of artillery was posted into the line there, in support of the 201st Guards Brigade. Monte Cassino was on the height of about 1,500 feet and we had to climb up to an observation post at about 2,500 feet.

From there we could see across the valley, whenever weather permitted, this shining monument of Cassino Monastery, which I must say, did look in a way menacing and odd, in so far as it was the only undestroyed object in a vast waste of destruction. It was rather like seeing Buckingham Palace in the middle of Passchendaele.

On 15 February we'd been up there about a week and were feeling absolutely miserable – it was terrible weather. In the occasional breaks in the clouds we saw this monastery all the time, and it got on our nerves, to be quite frank. It became, from being a thing of beauty, a thing of monstrosity – an excrescence – and somehow it was the thing which was holding up all our lives and keeping us away from home. It became identified in an obsessional way with all the things we detested.

Remember, I had been about two years in almost continuous action, and action is barbarising and our sensibilities were blunted. Suddenly out of the mist of the south, on this really rather nice morning, just after breakfast at about 9.30 hours, appeared this vast armada – a huge bomber force – mainly Flying Fortresses, some 250 of them.

We were wondering where on earth this vast armada was going, when all of a sudden, the bombs started dropping out of these things, and came bashing down on the jolly old mother of monasteries of St Benedict, about ten miles away over the valley. I must confess it was a gigantically stimulating sight, to suddenly see this sort of Barnum and Bailey's kind of Brock's benefit – it must have been comparable to seeing the early Christians being eaten by lions in the Colosseum, I suppose. We all started cheering wildly and hugging each other. We went mad and everybody thought it was the greatest thing since the eruption over Pompeii. But there was, with me, a remarkable Welshman called Tom Roberts, who'd been my constant guide, philosopher and friend since the earliest days when we went around the Cape of Good Hope to get to Suez. He was a man of great spiritual merit who knew all about my connection with Father Ignatius of Llanthony. After I'd stopped trembling and the laughter and hysterical gaiety faded, he sat me down at one side and said, 'Steady on Doug – I mean, it's all very well, but are we really in this war for the business of bombing monasteries. What would old Father Ignatius think of that?'. Suddenly, I had a sort of complete bloody double-take. I thought, 'What the hell are we doing, up on this bloody hill and surrounded by destruction and mayhem, and everything gone to pot? What are we fighting for or against? Here we are, cheering the destruction of one of the great monuments of Christendom.' One's mood changed from exultation to a peculiar sort of horror and self-questioning, which was very disturbing..."

Sergeant Herbert Parkin with the 2nd Battalion of the London Irish Rifles was based at a holding position high on a mountainside, facing Cassino. His company depended totally on mule trains getting through for all their supplies.

"We landed at Taranto naval base towards the end of 1943 and we reformed just outside Taranto to move forwards through Italy. The terrain wasn't easy – it was all valleys and ridges and you couldn't advance too fast in case that you had no back-up. We came out of the line at a place called Inferno Valley, which was a mule point. Inferno Valley was the start line and from there we got into position on a mountain facing Cassino. We were well within firing distance of the enemy. The Germans were up in the monastery with a bird's eye view of everything. You couldn't move without them seeing you. The Royal Engineers used to put up smoke screens from the valley – pots and pots of smoke – but you could only blind the Germans for so long before the wind carried the smoke away.

The Germans would let the ambulances through, but everything else was shelled. They used the old moaners – we called them 'Moaning Minnies' – which were six-barrelled mortars. There were six at a time and they moaned like anything. The Germans were pretty accurate with them, and they did a lot of damage. Our mortars were with different companies at the time. I was therefore acting as infantry on the forward slope, in case the Germans came through.

Although the Germans were in the monastery, they were right the way around as well, dug in. You had no idea where they were. It was worst at night because, of course, you couldn't see anything in the dark. You had to listen and try and make out what the noise was. You couldn't start firing, though, because you didn't know if you were going to hit one of your own patrols.

Everything came up to us by mules – our water, rations, first-aid – everything. We could see the mules clearly from where we were, coming along the valley. If they got shelled or started misbehaving, they would dance about and sling their loads off their backs.

It was uncomfortable on the mountain, but we always got our meals. Our cooks were very good. They would send hot food up to us in boxes and looked after us very well. We couldn't dig in to the soil because it was too stony and scrubby. We built sangars instead from the loose rocks. Although the ground was uncomfortable, you managed to sleep. You had a blanket and a ground sheet and you just put your haversack down and pulled your blanket over you and your tin hat over your head, and tried to get down.

When the Poles came to take over from us, we picked up the rest of the battalion and marched across to Inferno Valley where we had a mug of tea and formed up to move back behind the lines."

Army medic Fred Jordan had gone down with malaria at the end of the Sicilian campaign, but rejoined the 14th Field Ambulance who were attached to the 6th Armoured Division, dug in at the base of Monte Cassino.

"Anybody who was there will always remember the monastery at Monte Cassino. We were there for about two weeks before we were pulled out and the Poles took over. The Germans were in the monastery, firing down at the men on the hill. They could see all the area around, which made it very awkward to get anywhere. Our front was halfway up the hill. The medics were at the foot of the hill, evacuating the wounded as they came through, back to the roads and the general hospitals. We dug in as best we could. There was no cover – you just made your own slit trench and stayed until you got the call for stretcher-bearers.

Italy should have been quicker, but the rains came. It was continuous rain. Nothing could move. The guns and tanks couldn't move because they were stuck in the mud. We used the tank drivers as stretcher-bearers because we didn't have enough men. I can remember one chap saying 'I wish I was back in my tank'.

The rain held us up a terrible lot. We had casualties because of mud slides. You could see the mud gradually moving, and all of a sudden it would come down like an avalanche. People were buried underneath it and suffocated. The strangest thing was how they were stripped of their clothing – shoes and shirts missing.

The trenches filled up with water and you had to bail it out. You slept as best you could. Eventually you came to a point when you're so tired that you could sleep anywhere.

We were being attacked by Stukas. They're a really frightening plane. They dive-bomb, and they scream as they come down at you, which is terrifying.

The morale was pretty low. You can see it in a man's face – fear and quietness. It's something you can't explain."

Private Harry Courcha of A Company, 1st Battalion, Royal Fusiliers, was sent as a reinforcement into the final crossing of the Rapido River at Sant' Angelo on the Cassino front. For him it was a baptism of fire.

"I was called up in April 1943, when I was 18 years old. After basic training I was sent to the Physical Development Centre at Richmond-on-Thames for 12 weeks as I was considered to be underdeveloped. This was probably due to the effects of malnutrition during childhood. After that I was sent to training camp on the Isle of Wight until my group was sent overseas at the end of March 1944. You weren't allowed to be sent overseas until you were 19. I had my birthday on the boat, so they were cutting it a bit fine. The voyage took two weeks as you had to try to avoid the U-boats. We arrived in Naples – Vesuvius had been active and it was still smoking. It was a tremendous sight for someone who'd previously regarded a penny trip to Hampstead Heath as 'living it up'.

We were sent for two weeks to a training camp where we were told the most horrendous stories about the front by the old sweats. We were reinforcements, as there had been very heavy casualties in the Fusiliers. They selected which company you'd join by initials, and I was sent to A Company. All my mates had later initials and almost all of them went to B Company. They only seemed to be a few feet apart. Our objective was to force a crossing of the Rapido.

The Americans lost thousands trying a similar stunt. We moved up under the cover of darkness and when we reached a certain point, we were told to pick up these canvas boats. At a given sign the whole of our artillery erupted – every gun as far as the eye could see. They also put smoke down so we couldn't see.

We discovered that the Germans were firing on fixed lines, which meant that they'd mapped out their fields of fire before-hand. The bullets started whizzing round our heads and we just kept stumbling forward to the sound of the river. Some people were already dead.

We could hear the water a long way down in the dark, running very fast – hence 'Rapido'. Many of our blokes pitched over the bank and drowned as they had full battle-kit on. I heard a voice down below, but I couldn't see a boat. Well, I was hanging on to the bank and kicking out with my feet and someone dragged me into the boat and we went across. Many of the boats were just swept away because the river was so fast. We eventually made it and found that the fire was even heavier than before. Luckily there was a ditch there and it seemed like the whole battalion was in it. It was rough. The German artillery was pounding away at us, but they couldn't hit the ditch. Machine guns were buzzing away. One of the hero types put his head up and got a bullet through it. We were pinned down for 24 hours until a Bailey Bridge was put across at St Angelo for the tanks to come across.

Our next objective was a heavily fortified farmhouse on a steep hill. The Germans had lined a hidden road between steep banks with machine guns on the flank. These couldn't be seen from our posi-tion. B Company had tried it first, and we were told that they'd suf-fered heavy casualties. They hadn't waited for tank support. I suspect it was sheer bravado on the part of the officers. As B Company had gone forward, they'd just been cut down from the side. Well, the tanks arrived and sorted the Germans in the ditch out. I was a machine gunner, and he's always the first to go in. There was I, 5ft 4in, charging up the hill with this heavy American 'Thompson', almost as big as myself. I was really expecting to die any second. Well, we got to the top and the remaining Germans surrendered. We'd stumbled over the bodies of B Company. All our friends.

After a while, when it was all over, we were ordered to bury our comrades. You have to take the identity disc and all their personal possessions and put them on a stretcher to carry them down. These were all my friends. They were the same age as me, just wanting to enjoy life. I'd been with them through training and on the boat out. Now they were dead, and I was searching them and carrying them down. I was devastated. I'd lost all my friends – I was alone."

George Rhodes, a sergeant with the 70th Field Regiment, Royal Artillery, had been through the fighting at Salerno and now found himself at Cassino. His story starts as the final attack is planned.

"April 20, 1944. The Germans came up with a new idea at Anzio – they started using human torpedoes. Thirty-seven were used and 24 were lost without any damage to the Yanks. I have gone round firing flashless shells and captured two German thunderflashes as thousands of troops are gathering behind my gun position. All are told to take their shoulder flashes off in case they are taken prisoner. You see, Alexander does not want the Germans to know that he is quietly building up a mighty army behind Monte Trocchio. Everything is heavily camouflaged.

Thursday, 11 May 1944. General Alexander issues order of the day, 'We are going to destroy the German armies in Italy. No armies have ever entered into battle before with a more just and righteous cause.'.

At exactly 11 pm, 16,000 guns opened fire. We were attacking on a 20-mile front. On my left, the two American Divisions, the 85th and the 88th, moved straight into the attack to capture Damiano Hill. Forty minutes later, the two French Divisions captured Monte Faito, which was 3,000 feet high. They were on the Yanks' right side, but my left. Five minutes after the French, the 8th Indian and the 4th British Divisions on the French right side, splashed into the fast-flowing

Rapido river, into a hailstorm of German machine-gun fire. At 1 o'clock both divisions of the Polish Corps swept up to Monte Cassino. Two hours after we had opened up, the entire front for 20 miles was now locked in combat.

The Poles on my right were doing fine. Their commander, General Anders, had studied our previous three attempts and he decided to attack everything in his path at once and no mercy to be shown to the Germans. However, as daylight came, the Germans picked them off one by one, so he had to withdraw to his start line.

The planes, 3,000 of them, came over during the day in 2,750 sorties. It was hell on earth. The Germans, even so, launched a fierce counter-attack along the Gustav Line. What a day – my gun was red hot!

Sunday 14 May. The French break through at Monti Aurunci. The 8th Indian, the 4th British, the 1st Infantry, the 5th Canadian Armoured and the 78th British Divisions all moved in for the kill.

General Juin let his hawk-faced Moroccan Goumiers loose. Their job was to climb mountains and come on to the Germans from their rear. They did not use rifles – only knives – and many lopped off the German's ears and put them into sandbags.

Tuesday, 16 May. This morning, in a beautiful classic attack, the 78th, the 6th Armoured and the 1st Canadian Divisions broke through. All we wanted now was for the Poles to deliver the *coup-de-grace*. Everything is going well and to plan. I am being kept informed every half hour as more gunfire is called for and of course, after five years, the War Office had decided that Hitler's blitzkrieg is the best method of attack. So now we have RAF officers in our observation post, and when the Infantry call for an air strike, it can be delivered within minutes. The Germans used this method with their tanks – it certainly works.

Wednesday, 24 May. The Poles attack Piedimonte. They did very well, even though they had lost 281 officers and 3,503 other ranks and 102 missing. They were all buried on the slopes of the hillside that we knew as Point 593, behind the Monastery Hill as you come from the south. On their memorial, these words are printed.

We Polish soldiers,
For our freedom and yours,
Have given our souls to God,
Our bodies to the soil of Italy,
And our hearts to Poland."

Guido Varlese, now a lawyer in Cassino, was 19 years old when the bombardment of his home town began. He was evacuated soon after Italy signed the armistice with the Allies, after the first bombs had fallen on Cassino.

"The first bombs fell at 9.00 am in the morning. We were not expecting this at all, due to the fact that the armistice was already in effect. For us, we thought that the war was over.

I was in the piazza with a friend when we saw Flying Fortresses, going towards Rome from Naples, which unloaded their bombs on the outskirts of the town. We were all amazed at these marvellous flying machines, when we realised what was happening.

This first bombardment caused enormous damage and killed many, many people. I took refuge in the shop where I usually had my hair cut. While in there, in came a German soldier with his ear shot to pieces by shrapnel. I put a towel, the first thing I could see – around his head to stop the blood pouring from his ear. He certainly would have died otherwise.

There were two more bombardments that day, the first was down by the station, the other was on the outskirts of the town, destroying mostly the road to Rome from Naples. They had spotted retreating German columns and decided to attack these. After this, my sister and my sister-in-law decided to retreat to the mountains, just under Monte Cairo. Here we thought we would be safe, as the road came to an abrupt end.

We were wrong. We found ourselves near the front lines of the German Army. This was the position of the German Alpini troops who had been fighting around this location during the winter months when several attacks were centred on Cassino. Due to the bad weather, the terrain was very muddy and the attack in December by the Allies was staved off. Tanks just got stuck in the mud and were unable to cross the fast-flowing river. The Germans had blown up all the bridges.

15 March was the total bombardment of Cassino, which I watched from a nearby village. The abbey was destroyed on February 15. The day before the bombardment, the Allies dropped leaflets telling everybody to leave the church and that they would be bombing the area. The Germans at this time were not inside the church – they were outside, around it. Freyberg, the Allied commander on the spot, was worried about the Germans using the abbey as a stronghold, at

which point the Allies would be confronted with a huge task to get past that point.

A German lieutenant decided to tell everybody that they would not be able to leave the abbey until the evening after. The bombers came and 300–400 people, still waiting to leave, were killed and buried alive.

When we were transferred from Terelle to Montforte by the SS, who wanted all civilians well away from the front lines, we witnessed a dog-fight between an English and a German aircraft. Due to the sun it was very difficult to tell which was which, but all of a sudden, one caught fire and started to plummet to the ground. We saw the pilots jump out with their parachutes. Then we noticed that the remaining aircraft did not go away, but turned steeply and shot the two flyers in the air. This has to be the most horrific thing I have ever seen. We were under the misapprehension that there was a certain camaraderie among even opposing pilots. The flyers fell from the skies to crash against the rocks below – I will never forget the sound of these poor flyers as they screamed and shouted."

Kazimeircz Gurbiel was 26 and a Lieutenant with the 4th Platoon, 1st Squadron, 12th Podolski Lancers, 3rd Carpathian Rifle Division, when he led the first Polish troops into the ruins of the monastery.

"Point 593 was captured, over-run at about 7.00 or 7.30 am on May 18. Maybe an hour later, I was sent out on patrol with 13 men. I left some men on guard at the foot of the monastery and took half the men with me towards the ruins. There was no shooting and we had heard that the Germans had gone.

Everywhere you looked among the rocks were poppies, blood-red poppies. It must have been about 9.30 when we entered the abbey ruins. I had a Silesian with me who spoke very good German. I told him to call out that 'it was not in our minds to kill them' – after all, today, they are prisoner – tomorrow it may be me.

The commander of the Germans, a cadet officer, came out. He asked for a half hour's time to get ready to become a prisoner with dignity. One minute before time is up, he comes to me and says it is time for us to go. In that time, one of my lancers said, 'Lieutenant, here is a hole'. I said, 'Come on, boys', and took about six or seven men to St Benedict's crypt. I look in and there were three wounded boys lying there.

What I see in their eyes is fear. I said, through my Silesian, 'Don't worry, boys, nothing will happen to you'. There were 17 or 18 Germans, and enough food to feed an army. We raised our flag, made out of bits and pieces, at about 10.00 am – after all that fighting, all those months, the monastery was captured without a shot being fired."

Corporal Cadet Officer Zbigniew Fleszar with 3 Co., 1st Bat. 1st Brig., 3rd Carpathian Division, 'deserted' from a temporary post in a rear echelon to join his own company at the front line to see some action.

"We knew Cassino would be a very significant battle. We simply didn't want to miss it. After breaking relations with the Polish Government, Stalin accused us Poles of not wanting to fight the Germans, so, however small our contribution, we had to be there. The victory at Monte Cassino was to be our gift to Poland.

We were assigned the task to take the Gorge. My company was to reach the slope over it and protect the march and attack of the following company. We were loaded with equipment and already hot. I don't think we were scared – just apprehensive.

The company left the Big Bowl immediately after dark, passed the Small Bowl and slowly progressed over the rocks and bushes. Then a whistling shell flew low overhead – and another, and another. I felt as if a bridge of iron was being erected overhead, and wondered how it was that shells did not collide. Over a thousand guns were firing. The noise reverberated over the mountains. One could pick out whistles, crying and sobbing and roaring of shells. Then it all changed. The Phantom Hill in front of us was suddenly on fire. There was an explosion every split second. The mountain trembled.

Sweat running down our eyes, battledress wet, chests like smithies' bellows, we pushed forward on the slope. Then all hell broke loose. We did not expect it. The heavy shells started breaking among us. At first we thought it was our own artillery firing short. The code for this was 'Oranges'. This went out over the wireless – but the explosions were not oranges. This was German artillery. The explosions sounded like an enormous giant clearing his throat. I had an extraordinary wish – to be one of the smallest pebbles under one of the biggest rocks.

My company was lucky. The barrage caught only our tail. The following companies were not so lucky. As a result of this first shelling, the first battalion lost almost half of its complement killed, wounded and shocked. We chased away some of the advanced German posts and sat just over the Gorge, waiting for the following company to pass over.

Towards the evening of 12 May, the Corps Commander decided that the attack must be called off. The taken ground was evacuated. Somehow it was left to me and a few others to perform the final action. Our 3 Platoon, together with the company commander, for some reason did not receive the order to withdraw. They sat on the edge of the Gorge the following night and throughout the next day. My platoon commander, looking me straight in the eye, informed me that volunteers were needed to fetch them.

A small group of us was formed with a lieutenant, second in command of the company. 'You going for a cross?' someone said. 'Yes – maybe a wooden one!' I replied. We went back and found the missing men. On the way back the lieutenant was killed and a few were wounded.

Now, on the Calvary mountain, on marble tablets, there are the names of the fallen soldiers of the 3rd Carpathian – 1045 graves facing the Abbey. At the centre of a podium, a huge carved cross of Virtuti Militari, the highest Polish battle honour, has at its centre an eternal flame. Around the circle is written, 'Passer-by, tell Poland that we fell faithful in her service'."

As the American pilot leading the raid to destroy the Cassino Monastery, Lt.-Colonel Bradford A Evans remembers the view of the scene from above as the fateful bombs dropped, sealing the fate of the ancient building for the fourth time in its history.

"The monastery of Monte Cassino unquestionably looms ahead. Sitting 1,500 feet above the valley floor directly above the town of Cassino, the abbey is a welcome sight – welcome in the military sense that the pilot, navigator and bombardier are assured that they have the correct target in sight.

In seconds the 96th Red Devils, led by 'the Beast' 666, will unleash the start of the bombing that will turn out to be the largest ever directed at a single building in World War II. 666 suddenly lurches upward and the proverbial 'bombs away' was heard over the intercom system...

Snapping on a portable sausage-like oxygen bottle, the commander worked his way back to the bomb bay section from where he could observe the initial impact of the ship's 12 bombs, and those of the following aircraft a fraction of a second later. Suddenly a small puff appeared in the south-western portion of the monastery, which was the explosion of the 12 bombs, and then a gigantic blast occurred which covered the entire abbey. In another fraction of a second the bombs from the other squadrons of the 2nd Group added their weight to the fatal blow, but by now the smoke, dust and debris were so heavy that they covered Monastery Hill, precluding further observation. At the same moment an act of providence took place in the monastery where the Entrance Cloister and the Cloister of Bramante were joined by an archway, for here was the impact point of the bombs.

Moments before, a refugee, 24-year-old Oslavia Pignatelli, her parents and another family from Cassino were secluded in the small post office (now the gift shop) at one end of the Entrance Cloister. When they realised that danger was just around the corner, they wanted to descend into the depths of the monastery for better protection, but they were prevented from doing so because the passageway doors were locked. When the first 12 bombs from 666 exploded, the blast blew open the locked doors and the refugees fled to the lower levels of the abbey during the 15-minute lull between the first and second wave of bombers. Also at the time of the first bomb impact, Abbot Diamare and eleven of his monks sat helplessly, reciting the prayers of the divine office, in a long and narrow room in the bottom level below the monastery's college. It was an act of providence that some of them had not ventured to other parts of the monastery.

Nearby, German soldiers scattered to places of seclusion to escape the blasts. They looked on in disbelief, wondering, 'Why are they bombing the monastery – it is not being used for military purposes?' Allied soldiers hooted and hollered when they saw the first explosions. To them, those observing eyes of the enemy in the abbey would be prying no more."

German paratrooper Robert Frettlohr with 15th Company 4th Regiment 1st Division Fallschirmjägerpionier (Paratroop Engineers) recalls the final moments of the battle for Monte Cassino and his capture in the ruins of the monastery on 18 May 1944.

"The 4th Regiment was in reserve when the monastery was bombed in February and many civilians were killed. Then on March 15 it was Cassino's turn and 470 bombers dropped many tons of bombs, but I remember seeing the bombers going over, wave after wave. There must have been several hundred or so. It was the first time that a front line has been bombed like that.

On April 1, I was posted to the Rocco Janula (Castle Hill) and I was up there until the order came to retreat. They were shelling us all the time as we were going up. As a young man of 20 years old, it was impossible to know what you felt. They kept telling you that you had to fight for your country. Forget it. You fight for self-survival. If anyone gets killed you say, 'It's not me'. Anyone who says they weren't scared is lying – 'cos you were scared, all the time.

After we'd rested, we waited to time the shells – one... two... then two of us – always by two – would go. Off... gone. Then it was my turn. We waited for two shells – always the two – and we were off.

Then there was a flash close by and my left leg ... I don't know, I must have been stunned... I passed out. When I woke up it was like a balloon. I was off again. I crawled up to the monastery – literally crawled – and I got to the first-aid post which was in the old Roman part, where St Benedict was buried. The doctor there put a bandage round my leg and said, 'That's it, you're not going back'. If there had been a road and I'd had a stick, I would have tried to get back – but there was no road, only rock.

It was 10 o'clock in the morning when the Poles came into the monastery. Lieutenant Gurbiel came in with some men. I don't know what we were expecting – a grenade to be tossed in, maybe. There were three of us wounded and 14 men trying to take us back, but that didn't materialise. Anyway, one of the Poles with Gurbiel spoke very good German to me, and I remember him saying, 'Are there any mines?' I said, 'There are no mines. This is a first-aid post'.

We talked, in German, about this and that, and about midday the 14 were taken down to the command post, Gurbiel said. There was no massacre as had been reported – I wasn't there. Later, all these reporters arrived. You can imagine a soldier who has been fighting for weeks, dirty, filthy, unshaven, full of lice. We must have looked a terrible sight.

Later on we were taken down the hill to a Polish first-aid post, where a British ambulance took us to a big Yankee tent hospital, six or seven miles behind the line. We were treated there, but I don't know what happened to the third badly wounded man. A few days later we were transferred to a POW hospital camp at Aversa near Naples."

Overlord – Falling into France

*P*lanning for eventual landings in occupied Europe began soon after Dunkirk, but it was only when the full resources of the American shipyards became available to the Allied war effort that an invasion became realistic, as large numbers of ships and landing craft were needed to cross the Channel. Of the potential targets, the coast of Normandy was selected because it was less well defended than the Pas de Calais, and its large shelving beaches would allow landing craft to beach and offload troops and vehicles. The Germans, under the leadership of Field Marshal Rommel, built bunkers and obstacles to defend the beaches, while coastal batteries were installed under thick concrete protection. Allied planners decided that the best time to land was at half tide, when many of the obstacles would be exposed. From west to east, the designated beaches were codenamed Utah and Omaha for the US Army, and Gold, Juno and Sword for the British and Canadians. As the tide would rise up the Channel from west to east, Montgomery's British troops would be landing later than the Americans, so in order to compensate for the loss of surprise he lengthened the offshore bombardment of German bunkers. The Germans had flooded the land behind Utah, so paratroops of the 82nd and 101st Airborne divisions would land to secure the causeway exits from the beach. In the weeks before the planned landing, Allied aircraft attacked the road and rail links to Normandy to prevent the Germans moving men and equipment to the area. British paratroops of the

> *Sixth Airborne Division would land at the eastern edge of the beachheads to secure or demolish the bridges that gave access eastwards, and prevent German reinforcements attacking the beachhead. Bad weather prevented the operation, codenamed Overlord, from taking place on June 5, but in the early hours of June 6 paratroops and gliderborne soldiers landed in the darkened French countryside. Here, the invaders, the spearhead assault troops and the defenders fell at the run-up to D-Day.*

Sergeant Pilot Rupert Cooling, after flying support missions for the Sicily invasion from bases in Africa, returned to England to train for the big invasion. With 516 (Combined Ops) Squadron he found himself in Western Scotland.

"Our squadron was equipped with a motley mixture of machines – Mustangs, Hurricanes, Blenheims, Ansons, two Lysanders, a Miles Master and a Tiger Moth which we flew mainly for fun.

Exercises simulated both air support and attack during practice assault landings. Blenheims carried cardboard case bombs with the blast and noise effect of a 250-pounder. We dropped sticks of four ahead of the troops as they hit the beach. Care was needed – these could kill at seven yards. Mustangs and Hurricanes strafed the shore with cannon.

One Blenheim was fitted with a siren which howled like a banshee as one dived to attack – its purpose was to put the vertical breeze up any brown or blue jobs below. For an encore, we laid smoke. As the landing craft headed for the beach, we would level out at some 50 feet and head straight across their bows. Press the bomb-release tit and a long, dense white sausage of smoke would blot out the view all around. It was hazardous, but we were away in the clean, clear air above – except once.

Loch Fyne forks at its eastern end. The shorter spur thrusts into high hills which plunge down almost to the water's edge. The target beach lay in the lee of this high ground.

Approach from the west was barred by these 2,500 foot plus mountains. No way could a Blenheim clear those – it had to be a run in from the east. By the time I was down to 50 feet, the aircraft was travelling at about 250 mph. I throttled back to kill excess speed then pressed the firing button which blew the seals on the smoke cylinders in the belly. What happened next is uncertain, but the effect was cataclysmic. The cockpit, instruments, flying controls, even my hands on the stick disappeared from sight within a brilliant dense white cloud. I sat and waited to die as the aircraft plunged into the water or exploded in a ball of flame upon the surrounding hillside. After an aeon, perhaps three or four minutes, suddenly the smoke cleared. The Blenheim was in a gentle climb ten miles from the target, flying at 1,500 feet down the centreline of the loch. High ground lay on either side. After landing, I went first to the medical section for treatment, and then to the Padre – it seemed appropriate.

We lost three pilots, four aircraft on various exercises. Not many in the total cost of that mighty enterprise, but they were just as much casualties of the D-Day operation as those who died on, off or above the Normandy beaches."

Lt-Colonel Michael Forrester DSO, MC, was serving with his regiment in Palestine when war broke out. Joining the 7th Armoured Div., he fought through Greece, Crete, the Western Desert and the Italian invasion before returning with the 'Desert Rats' to train for the European invasion.

"We didn't know, of course, when D-Day was going to be – in fact we knew very little about anything. We were given training directives and facilities in Norfolk at that time were quite good. But there were things other than training to be dealt with. Everyone had been abroad for a very long time. Leave was the first thing. I remember we got as many people as we possibly could away on leave. I forget how long they had now, but this was the first time they had seen their families for a long time.

One other aspect which I'd like to mention is the fact that we were back in England again for the first time after a considerable number of years, and this meant being at home as opposed to being in the desert where there were virtually no inhabitants, so all needed reminding of the importance of local public relations, which in our case included the people of Kings Lynn and the villages around it which we would be passing through for training. We were trying to weld ourselves into the community and become part of it, although we knew we weren't going to be there for very long. The people of that part of England were open-hearted and kindness itself and they gave us a marvellous welcome – they could not have made us more at home.

There was also a memorable day which General Erskine, our divisional commander, arranged specially for the division, and that was an investiture at the Palace, when every member of the Division who was due to receive a medal, won during the previous months and years abroad, was included, so it was very much a family affair at Buckingham Palace. All these things, including the visits, tended to raise our spirits and morale, and made us feel we were in for something very important.

Training directives indicated that we were going to be fighting in fairly close country, and in the event, when we got to Normandy, we found the so-called *bocage* country there even more restricting and close than even we had anticipated. It was, because of its nature, almost as great a change from Italy as the desert had been to Italy, because the fields were so very, very small, with high banks with hedges on top of them dividing up the fields, making fields of view and tank movement very, very difficult indeed. Of course, the Germans had the advantage over us there – they were familiar with it.

Of course we were aware from the start that we were going to take part in the invasion of Europe, but we didn't know where we were going, and I remember very late on, all the officers had to assemble at some cinema somewhere, and the Army Commander, General Miles Dempsey, was to address us. I had served under him for a short time when he was commanding XIII Corps with his headquarters in Syria.

He very kindly spotted me in the audience, and had a few words with me, and something I said must have caused him to say, 'But surely you know you're going to ...' and he got 'Nor' out, and then he checked himself. He said, 'Didn't you know?' He had stopped at 'Nor', so I thought Norway. Then he realised we didn't know – weren't supposed to know – so he deftly changed the subject. I went round in a haze for the next day or so, wondering if we were going to Norway or Normandy!

So it was as closely kept a secret as that, right up to the end, and when our time came to get ready finally, we moved out of our areas in Norfolk down to camps, very sparse, primitive tented camps – but perfectly adequate for the purpose, in Essex. It was there that our camps were sealed, or we were sealed into them, and we were briefed properly, and allowed to brief right down to soldier level – but up 'till then, no-one had known.

It's very relevant to talk about fear. The unknown, which we were going into, meant uncertainty. You don't know, and uncertainty very naturally leads to apprehension, and so the adrenalin is flowing, quite rightly.

I don't think fear actually comes into one's thoughts until one is confronted with something dangerous, but the apprehension is there all the time. I would say I felt really frightened on several occasions. I think too, that the definition of war (which is anonymous, though someone may lay claim to it) that 'War consists of long periods of intense boredom, punctuated by short periods of intense fright', is a good one. I think it was coined for the First War, it was very relevant for the Second War too.

Once confronted with a situation, there are certain sorts of fear. I think the predominant sort of fear, in the case of some, is 'Am I going to be up to this myself?' I think it's awfully important to recognise that – it takes a certain amount of personal drive to overcome it, and to say, 'Yes, I am'.

Certainly, while people were very frightened, they went on because they felt they couldn't possibly *not* go on. *Esprit de corps* is very important for morale because you drive yourself to meet the challenge, and you know other people are meeting it too, and you are going to be in it with them."

Flight Lieutenant David Warner, a navigator with 296 Squadron, had returned from North Africa late in 1943, and started to train in towing gliders, dropping paratroops and supplies in accurate zones, and using Gee radar. All this was in preparation for the D-Day assault.

"In between training and the invasion we were sent out to France to drop supplies to the Maquis. That also gave us training for map-reading at night. A typical exercise was to go to somewhere where the mountains start, in the middle of France, where the Resistance were.

We would fly over from England to Fécamp, and then gradually reduce our height from about 6,000 to 2,000 feet and descend to about 1,000. I used to aim for three little islands in the middle of the Loire, which always reflected in the moonlight and gave me the confidence of having a pinpoint, then we would come down to 500 feet.

All the searchlights would be out looking for something, but at 500 feet they couldn't get you, because as they came down, they would go out, and you could duck underneath the lot. Usually we would be over the top of the flak before they could get organised, but there would be quite a lot of things shooting behind. Then you would come to the rendezvous and the dropping zone, where there would be the reception party.

We would go round and acknowledge the fact that we were there, then we would lower the flaps and the wheels, reduce speed to about 80 or 90 mph and go 600–800 feet above the line of torches to drop the goods. Then up again, go around, flap our wings, wish them good luck and away.

When it came to D-Day we were given lots of pictures of the French coastline. I had to look at this panorama all day long. I had it in my room, when I woke up in the morning with my cup of tea – I tried to memorise it. What we had to do was to take a glider over there.

On D-Day we had to fly somewhere up to Newcastle to start with, because that take-off was between two and three minutes, and you had 40 to do, so it's quite a long time. We had to go up north for about 50 minutes, come back over the airfield and by then the rest of the gliders were airborne to go across together.

When we got there there was nothing happening. We saw the area and we had a wire through the tow rope to talk telephonically to the glider pilot without going through the air. We circled over the area and asked the glider pilot if he could recognise his landing zone and he said he could. So we asked him to let us know when we should release them. He said, 'It's OK, you can release us right now.' This was at about 2.00 or 3.00 in the morning that the drop took place, some eight or nine miles inland.

There was a battery three or four miles up the coast, of heavy German 'Atlantic Wall' stuff, and that was being bombed very heavily by about 80 Wellingtons.

It wasn't until three or four in the morning, when you saw the dawn, that you could see the fantastic sight. It was like a tail-back on the M25! The air was full of aircraft going in every direction. I've never seen so many aeroplanes in all my life. Of course at night, when you were flying, you never thought of that. You just took your course and went ahead. I wasn't aware of anything at sea until the return journey, when dawn broke, and the pilot said, 'Come up and look at this,' and you saw all these ships coming in, the bombing and the fighting.

I have to say the operation didn't worry me at all – you get used to it, don't you? It's like driving a new car you've never driven before but after you've had it for about six months it becomes second nature. I went to the Loire so many times, looking for these three islands, that I knew what was going to happen. The only thing that would have been frightening would have been if we had lost an engine – then we'd have problems. There again, I planned for all exigencies. I used to pack everything up in my room in case I didn't come back, and I used to take with me all sorts of things. Just before I left the mess, I used to tear the front page off the Daily Mail and stuff it in my back pocket. This was because if I had to land in France, the Germans were setting up decoys to pretend they were British airmen trying to escape, to try to find out the French families who were helping them, then rounding them up and shooting them. So to let anybody know I am a British airman, I would have that day's date on a newspaper.

I thought of everything for survival – I carried yards of string and had razor blades stitched into my trousers. They gave us one or two pieces of survival equipment – a handkerchief with a map of France on it, some French money. I had a pipe which had a compass built into the bowl, and that sort of thing, and I also took a pair of shoes, because if you baled out, I'd heard people say that they lost their flying boots. Most of this was my idea. But on D-Day I didn't do anything at all. I felt it was a mass organisation and we'd all be back in five minutes. It didn't worry me one little bit."

Lieutenant Sumpter Blackmon was leader of First Platoon, Company A, First Battalion, 501st Parachute Infantry Regiment. He recalls his part in the 101st Airborne's D-Day drop into France. Their aim was to seize bridges and main road junctions to prevent the Germans from flooding the estuary area behind the beaches and to nip any counter attack in the bud.

"It was 10 o'clock in the evening of June 5, and it was nearly time to go. The officers and men of our First Platoon joined hands and prayed that God guide us. I took my 'stick' of 18 men on to the aircraft. Our equipment was so abundant and binding that we could scarcely move.

We took off just after 10.30 pm that night, and all the planes circled above the airfield and waited, then began forming up in Vs. It took us an hour to get into formation. The V was so perfect that I could have pitched a grenade at the plane just outside the open cargo door of the C-47. Then our formation turned inland and the sky erupted in fireworks – flak.

All around my plane the others were jinking and diving, but my pilot – I never did learn his name – flew the course without a tremor. He flew directly into a fogbank, and all the other planes disappeared. When we came out of the fog, we were all alone.

I stood at the cargo door with the equipment bundle of machine gun and ammunition, ready to kick it out when the jump light came on. I saw the proper landmarks come up, but felt no tap from the No. 2 jumper, Private Thurman Day, or from Sergeant Adams. Then I saw the ground disappear and then whitecaps – we were back over the sea.

Private Day pulled me back from the door and shouted that the pilot wanted to see me. He looked worried. 'Lieutenant', he said, 'we missed the drop zone and are over the Channel, headed back to England. What shall we do?'. I told him to take us to land and we'd get out.

The pilot dived, came around and headed for the French shore again. He took us down just above the waves to evade the flak, and as the plane reached the shoreline, he put it into a climb so steep that it threw several men off their feet.

I decided it was now or never. I pushed out the equipment bundle, hooked up my chute ring and followed. I was jerked by the ring and my parachute opened automatically just before I hit the ground.

After I landed hard, I cut myself loose from the parachute. I found the equipment chute in a low tree, a part of one of the Normandy hedgerows – thick, nearly impenetrable lines of trees and bushes. I pulled the red light attached to the pack, which was showing clearly, and pulled it down and turned it off. Then I pulled out my carbine. I crawled into a hedgerow and waited and listened. Finally Private Day came up.

We had no idea where we were. I pulled out my flashlight and map. I studied the map but could not find any points of terrain that matched – we'd obviously jumped off the map. We waited some time, but no-one else showed up and we decided we'd better take the machine gun and two boxes of ammunition out of the bundle and head south. After about half a mile, we were exhausted, and had to stash the gun and ammo.

Finally we met up with some other troopers and I really felt as if I had an army, with the 34 men I collected. Soon we approached a village and saw a light in a house on the outskirts. The others surrounded the house while I went to the door and knocked.

A woman came to the door and as she opened it, I could see another woman sitting at a table in the kitchen, three empty chairs, bread on the table and two bottles of wine.

The woman was not very friendly and she seemed monstrously stupid, but she told me we were in Foucarville, near the fourth causeway that led the beach road – about three miles from Utah beach and about ten miles northwest of St Come-du-Mont, where I thought I could find some of my battalion. I asked the woman the way and she didn't understand, or said she didn't. I repeated my question. She became sullen, and when I told her I was an American paratrooper, her eyes widened, and she shouted something and tried to run out the door. I stuck my carbine in her belly and she stopped.

I didn't know if she was a German collaborator, or just frightened. I told her to sit down at the table, and when she did not, I went out, closed the door firmly and motioned to the men to come with me, back to the road. We had just rounded the bend when we ran into our first enemy fire. Had there been men in the farmhouse, and had they run off to warn the Germans? A burst from a German light machine gun swept over the road. It sounded like someone tearing paper. We dropped and crawled off the road to the left and moved into a field of grain. The noise started up again.

I got up and started to run. I saw a ditch ahead and got ready to jump it. Just then, a German soldier stood up in the ditch and raised his hands. I could not understand what he was saying. Private Nick Denovchik came up and said the German was speaking Polish, which he understood. They began to talk, and the firing suddenly stopped. They must have decided that we had moved on.

The Polish German told Denovchik that he and his buddy were manning an aircraft listening station. He shouted and his buddy stood up about 50 yards away. After some more talk, they led us to a pillbox buried underground in a grove of trees, in which was a big radio set and enough ammo to withstand a minor siege.

The two prisoners helped us destroy the listening device, four large instruments perfectly camouflaged in the trees. We blew up the ammo dump and wrecked the radio. We accepted these two soldiers as our allies, and they showed us the way to the causeway. We were still a long way from our assigned objective, the locks of the

Douves. It was nearly time for the troops to be landing on Utah Beach, I could only hope and pray that someone else had taken the locks at La Barquette.

They had, and a vast armada of ships were in the English Channel – the invasion of Normandy was on."

Corporal Hans-Rudolf Thiel, in the German Regimental platoon of 6th Paratroop Regiment, recalls how it was left to him to sound the alarm for the airborne invasion of the Allies over Cherbourg, on 6 June 1944.

"The invasion alarm of the previous day and last night has been lifted. The storm has abated and it has stopped raining. The sun is even shining today, as if it wants to compensate us for the unbearable tension of the last 24 hours. The rumour is going round that the Allies have ordered their invasion fleet to turn back because of the poor weather. This can only help us – a stay of execution.

Today no *Rommelspargel* ['Rommel's asparagus' – anti-glider obstacles] are planted, instead of this we have machine-gun exercises in the field. We march out to the surrounding meadows and move into cover positions. Sergeant Major Geiss, our platoon commander, allows us to catch up on the sleep we missed last night. As well as we can, we all seek out a place with good cover in the hedges, or sunbathe.

At high altitude above us one enemy bomber squadron after another flies into the hinterland, and from there we can hear a terrible thundering. The daily reconnaissance plane does his rounds and now and then a few fighter-bombers buzz by like hornets. Our morale is good, but the old front veterans have 'something in their water'. They don't trust the overall aura of peace.

Arthur Volker, my bunker comrade, has indigestion. He says he always feels like this when something's afoot. Even I can't conceal a sense of unease. After the relative calm of the last few weeks I turn my thoughts to the massive bombardments of the hinterland. Something is going to come down on us.

The food today was wretched once again – a lot of groats and no meat – a lot of jam and no sausage. Hopefully it will remain quiet tonight, and we're all hoping that there won't be another 'false alarm'.

Arthur and I are assigned the task of 'high-chair watch'. This is a very exposed and windy job. There's a stiff breeze coming in from the sea, the moon shines brightly now and again through the gaps in the clouds. It is not cold – just chilly – and up on the high-chair in the poplars you get a real shaking.

At midnight I have to take over from Arthur, and until then I try to get a few winks of sleep. No chance. I just can't get to sleep. I'm getting more restless with every hour that passes. I try to read with only the Hindenburg light, but I can't concentrate. What the devil is going on? The night is so quiet, no sound of engines. Only the wind rustling through the poplars. I have to take over from Arthur soon.

Since I can't get any sleep anyway, I take over from him earlier. I get dressed, fasten my belt, check my machine pistol and magazine and crawl out of the bunker. The fresh air suddenly makes me shudder and I look around in the darkness. Strange – this peace is just not normal. I have the feeling that there's something lying in wait for us.

I go up to the high-chair tree and call out, 'Arthur, come down. I can't sleep, I'm going to take over now'. Arthur climbs down the ladder and says, 'Bloody wind. It's damned cold, and there's absolutely nothing to report,' and he disappears into the night.

I climb up to the high chair and look at my watch. Still 10 minutes before midnight. I hang my binoculars round my neck, load my machine pistol and put the catch on, then I sit down and make myself comfortable. A few minutes later I can hear the familiar but distant sound of aircraft engines. 'Bloody hell', I think to myself, 'there's more than a few – I hope they're not going to drop their bombs on us.' I look at my watch again, and take a look through the binoculars.

It was seven minutes after midnight when I saw masses of red and bright white lights in a north-westerly direction. To every soldier with any experience at all this could mean only one thing – ENEMY ATTACK! ! !

My common sense told me 'this is the invasion'. After the first shock I grabbed the telephone connecting the high-chair position with the regimental command post and turned the handle like a madman. At the regimental command post: 'Duty clerk here, Corporal?' I told him what I had seen. In the meantime the sound of the engines could be heard over our position.

Duty clerk: 'One moment, I'll get the adjutant'. Regimental command post: 'Lieutenant Peiser! What's going on? Report!'. I give the report: 'Corporal Thiel here, platoon, direction north-west, Cherbourg, red and white lights sighted, loud aircraft noise. The enemy is attacking!'.

As the receiver was not put down at the command post I could hear Lieutenant Peiser give the duty clerk the order to fetch the Major straight away. Then I could hear the major rushing up and could pick out a few scraps of the conversation – 'this afternoon' – Frenchmen' – 'damn' – 'why no alarm?' – (a word I couldn't understand). Major: 'Platoon, report!'. Me: 'Corporal Thiel here, platoon. Mass of lights direction of the coast and Cherbourg. Enemy attacking. This is the invasion, Herr Major, should I sound the alarm?'. I look at my watch – it's 11 minutes after midnight.

Major: 'Sound the alarm! Sergeant Major Geiss to me immediately.' The receiver is put down.

I put down the receiver and shout out as loud as I can: 'Alarm, alarm!'. Again and again I shout 'Invasion! Invasion!' and fire off two machine-pistol magazines..."

D-Day – Struggling Ashore

The invasion force was composed of 4,000 ships carrying 176,000 troops and their equipment, escorted by a fleet of 600 warships. The defences along the coast had been softened up by 2,500 heavy bombers, which dropped 10,000 tons of bombs, while 7,000 fighters and fighter bombers swept the skies. After a rough and nauseous Channel crossing British and American troops landed on the Normandy coast. At Utah the US Fourth Division had surprisingly few casualties and by 13.00 was in contact with the advance paratroops; by the end of the day it had secured a beachhead 4 miles (6.5 km) wide and 9 miles (14.5 km) deep. Meanwhile, on Omaha, the US First and 29th Divisions suffered over 3,000 casualties and had penetrated only 1½ miles (2.5 km) inland by the end of the day. On the British and Canadian beaches, longer naval bombardments and specially developed tanks and armoured vehicles for breaching the coastal defences kept casualty levels lower. At Gold Beach, the 50th Division captured Arromanches and by midnight had reached the outskirts of Bayeux, which fell the following day. The Canadian Third Division, which landed at Juno pushed 7 miles (11.25 km) inland. On Sword, the British Third Division linked up with the Sixth Airborne and advanced to within sight of Caen. Though the German High Command was slow to react, individual units such as the 21st Panzer Division were quick to counter-attack the invaders. Nevertheless, the end of D-Day saw 57,500 American and 75,000 British and

Canadian forces ashore. They had suffered losses of 2,500 killed and 8,500 wounded: but, with a bridgehead established in Europe, the Allies were at last in a position to begin to push the Germans back.

Richard Todd, possibly better known for his acting role in *The Longest Day* than for his real-life action on D-Day, went through officer training at Sandhurst and after a varied career in the Army joined the 6th Airborne Division. His battalion was to be the first in on D-Day.

"I was to be in aircraft 33. We had very carefully worked out our load tables for the aircraft in terms of who should be in there first, who would have such and such weapons and who would have other things with them. On that particular night, first of all we were in a *laager* on Salisbury Plain, wired in for about a week, even our supplies and food were just dumped outside the wire gates, and our own chaps went out and brought it in, because we weren't allowed to talk to anybody. We were being briefed, a week or so before D-Day, we knew where, when, how and everything about it. We had no communication at all with the outside world, except me one day, because I was Assistant Adjutant, and I was sent to Southern Command Headquarters. I was terrified. I thought, 'Oh, my God, I hope I don't open my mouth'.

We knew the whole thing, all the planning. We knew our own particular thing – we had sand-table models of the area we were dropping in and we knew every tree and every house intimately. We had maps galore and every day we had a fresh batch of aerial photographs for our intelligence officer to interpret.

We were getting worried because we saw a lot of little holes being dug and we found out that it was posts being put in with wire between them as anti-glider defences. We also saw large areas flooded – we wondered if the whole thing had been blown.

That night of D-Day, or the night before, at about 11 o'clock, we drove round the airfield perimeter, each stick of paratroopers in a three-ton truck, and each truck stopped by its numbered aircraft. Mine stopped at aircraft number 33, as that was the one I was to be in – and I was going out first from the aircraft.

The pilot and crew were lined up beside the aircraft – they shook hands and wished us luck and all the rest of it. The pilot was a very senior officer, an Air Commodore or something. He said to me, quite blithely, 'As I'm the senior officer going in tonight, I'm going in first, because we've got the gem crew'.

I thought, 'Oh Christ – I'm going to be the first out of the first aircraft,' but I couldn't argue with them because he was senior to me, and I couldn't say, 'Look, this will upset our load tables.' It wasn't the time.

So I got in – and that actually saved my life. I'll tell you why in a minute. I think people thought I was very cool because I fell asleep on the way – but that's a thing of mine. If I'm very worried or really down about something, my tendency is to be like an old ostrich, and put my head in the sand and go to sleep – and I was very worried and had lots of stress on me that night.

I was wakened up – we lined up and hooked up. The old green light came on and out we went, with me in the lead. Incidentally, it was a very big hole in the bottom of the Stirling, with enough room for two men to straddle it, and on the word 'go' pull their legs together and drop out through the hole. The man behind me had to hang on to me because the aircraft was jinking a bit. I could easily have fallen out – in fact a few people did fall out over the sea – because I hadn't a hand to hold on with as I had kit bags on each of my legs. One kit bag was full of a rubber dinghy, and the other had picks and shovels for digging in. They were fixed to your legs – you pulled the rip-cord when you were out of the aircraft and they dropped 20 feet below you and then dangled below on a rope. I was having to hold these things to my leg. Out I went.

We dropped from 400 feet, which didn't give you much time in the air – about seven seconds. In the flurry of all this, I let the bloody kitbag on my right side slip instead of letting it out hand over hand. That gave me a very nasty burn all down my right hand. Then I thumped down.

We had got in with the element of surprise. A certain amount of light flak came up and we could see tracer, floating by us. But nothing hit us – the big stuff hadn't really started, and as I was getting out of my 'chute on the ground, looking up at the other aircraft, they started getting shot down. By that time, the ground defences had wakened up to what was happening and the ack-ack guns had gone into action. The aircraft round about the numbers 30 were the ones that all got shot down, and it was just my luck that I went in first."

John Leopard commanded a troop of four 95 mm howitzers, mounted in Centaur tanks – part of a 100-strong tank unit, formed specially to give close support for the assaulting infantry. The Royal Artillery and tank boys had bowed out – this job fell to the Royal Marine Armoured Support Group.

"I was woken before dawn on what was to be one of the most significant days of my life. After having slept fitfully with violent motions of the boat adding to my inner strain, I went through all the automatic preparations for any ordinary day. I tidied myself up, checking my few possessions, and stowed away my supply of just two ounces of tobacco. It was an absurdly small amount, but I felt I might be tempting fate if I took a sensible supply!

I stepped out on to the spray-blown, wind-swept tank deck. In the half light of near dawn, the tanks stood up in the dark silhouette, straining against their rasping chains. One of my lads was lying on the water-swept deck, being too sick to care. I hoisted him to his feet and bundled him into the mess deck. I then climbed up to the wheel house and, circling round it to the narrow after deck, I paused to look at the vague shapes of the vessels which were following us. Our wake carried a quite brilliant display of multicoloured phosphorescent lights which seemed singularly inappropriate in a setting, and on a day when beauty was the last thing one might expect. It was there, completely alone, that I found I had to fight down a feeling of near panic which made me want to dive overboard and swim home. I just could not accept the situation I had made for myself.

I made my way into the Mess Deck where the Colour Sergeant had already assembled the men, washed, dressed and in all respects ready to face the day. We lined them up and the Sergeant issued the grog. It is a strange thing that when troops are facing a particularly perilous situation, they become noisy, tell outrageous jokes – at which they roar with laughter, and generally behave as if life was one big party. On this occasion, when we could not even guess our chances of survival, everyone – including me – was unbelievably cheerful.

We were now close enough for those fearsome rocket-launching craft which operated from not far astern of us to send their warheads over our heads towards the beach. Each of these vessels carried 1,000 rockets which were released in a series of volleys. To have released them all at one time would have threatened the fabric of the vessel itself. We had always disliked these rockets, they passed all too close above our heads in an erratic cloud. We feared a mid-air collision over our heads, or a drop-out in our direction. On this, the only 'for real' occasion, a swarm of these things was flying towards an area also the target of one of our diving aircraft. I foresaw the tragedy ten seconds before it happened. The aircraft exploded in a ball of fire.

Before we too went into the water, the tank jarred violently. I knew we had been hit. I checked that nothing untoward had happened in the driver's compartment, so assumed that nothing too serious had happened. Later I found a scar on the turret about a foot long and one inch deep in the middle. Had the anti-tank solid shot which had bitten so deeply into the steel of the turret struck us at a slightly less acute angle, it would have been curtains for us.

The plan had been for the first wave to land below the first of the obstacles so that the Royal Engineers could tackle their clearance problems before the rising tide put later arrivals at risk from obstacles which would then be underwater and capable of doing considerable damage. It occurred to me that had there been an experienced yachtsman on the planning committee, he would have recognised that with the heavy westerly winds which had been storming up the Channel for some days, tides would have been earlier than stated in the tide tables and have brought H-Hour forward.

Still dodging these obstructions, I was concerned to hear some erratic noises from our engines. At the same time, the driver reported that he was up to his ankles in water – but somehow we made the waterline to join the two Centaurs and I ordered the drain cocks to be opened. A glance back showed me what I suspected. Our air and exhaust extensions were pitted with bullet holes.

We were now in our required position and were joined by the other two Centaurs which landed only shortly after we did. We could now settle down to keeping as many German heads down as possible to ease the lot of the Queens Own Rifles of Canada, who were now beginning to come ashore. We had no more open sight targets in view. We could only wait for indirect fire instructions from the advancing troops, or await our orders to move off the beach to our first normal gun position. With devastation all about us I could scarcely belive that my five tanks were largely undamaged and we had no casualties.

During the lull, I ordered all tank crews to dismount to clear the bodies which had been washed up against our tracks. I could not move the tanks further up the beach while they were still there, in case any were still alive."

At the age of only 19, Bill Williams joined the RASC, seconded to the 3rd Canadian Division for supplies. Having led, by his own admission, a sheltered life until then, his first foray abroad on D-Day was a voyage of discovery.

"It was around midnight on June 5 when we became aware that we were moving. One could sense tension rising. At last the order came for us to don our equipment and prepare to move down to the vehicle deck. Nothing could be heard except the drone of the ship's engines, and it was 6 am when we sensed that we had stopped.

Once outside, we found we were at least two miles out from the coast, which we could just see from our low position. The sea was full of ships of all shapes and sizes. Naval destroyers were firing over our heads towards the coast. All this time we were plodding forward, so slowly it seemed at times we were not moving. A DUKW's normal speed is about 4 knots in calm water, but loaded and in a heavy swell, our speed was more like 2 knots.

I suppose one could describe the scene on the beach as organised chaos. A boat had been sent out to guide us in and the engineers had done a fantastic job in clearing areas of the beach enforcements, which were all piled in huge heaps. I can't say how many landing craft were on the beach at that time – a number of them were burning and had obviously been struck by shells. But apart from the spasmodic shell coming over on to the beach, there didn't appear at that time to be very much danger. We understood that the Canadians had moved inland some half, three quarters of a mile. One was still conscious of a lot of gunfire – in other words, ships were still firing inland to various points, but basically we were very tensed up about it, and one could say it was organised confusion.

The beach itself was cluttered with debris, a number of landing craft were burning on the water's edge.

My first shock was spotting the first dead body. I'd never seen a dead body in my life before. This particular chap was so immaculate – just as though he had been stood to attention, with his small pack and his webbing all beautifully blancoed. There he was, and we had to stop for a moment right beside him. It was if he had been standing then just gone flat down on his face. It absolutely shattered me – I couldn't take my eyes off him. We saw quite a lot of other bodies lying around, but what the Medical Corps had done was to set about treating the wounded and get them away, and then take care of the bodies afterwards.

There were snipers in the church tower and we had to wait for them to be cleared. We passed into the centre of this small town – not even a square – then we turned into an open field. Looking over the fence, the best part of a herd of cows had been slaughtered by the shell fire and were lying around with their feet in the air – which rather upset me, coming as I did from the country.

After that we dismounted and unloaded the ammunition into heaps and were escorted back down through Courseulles, along the causeway, to the outskirts of Bernières-sur-Mer. We turned into a fantastic driveway of a château which had hardly been damaged at all. We drew round the back where orchards were laid out and were told to disperse around the perimeter there. There was a lot of noise going on there, but one felt quite remote from it. We were very delighted to have got there in one piece.

We got together and dug one hell of a big trench then constructed a ledge half way down so we could sit, and covered the top with apple branches which had been knocked down by the shells. We covered over with groundsheets and had a hot meal of stew – we did nothing else but smoke and talk about the events of that day."

As a Tank Commander with the 24th Lancers, Charles Wilmot landed with his men at Arromanches beach. After months of training for the actual landing, they did not expect that their tank would be put out of action so quickly.

"Prior to D-Day we had done lots of training manoeuvres – we knew exactly what we were going to do. We were all formed up, in and around Fordingbridge, waiting to go.

We were crewed up, gunned up and, what's more, sealed up. We had fitted various chutes on the tanks so that they could take what they called a six-foot wave. We had spent weeks and weeks filling each crevice with plastic stuff which was similar to plasticine. Wherever there was a join, it had to be filled and the guns and gun turrets had to be closed and sealed. They called it 'feathering'.

In preparation, we had been issued with Rhinos. They were huge platforms fitted with engines to control them. The idea was that we would come off the LST and then get on to the Rhino. This was in case the LST couldn't get close enough to the beach. We had to practise driving up the ramps and on to the middle of the Rhino and stopping there. It wasn't easy, as you can imagine, because these Rhinos would tip up in the water. None of the tanks fell off them, but they nearly did.

As it happened, we lost the Rhinos on the way over. They broke away from the tow. There they were, floating in the Channel. I've no idea where ours went. Fortunately, we didn't need it, our ship went inshore as far as it could, where the water was just a couple of feet deep.

We were all ready to go on the 5th, but the weather was bad, so it was cancelled. We were completely fed up. Then the message came across 'Advance' – and it was a wonderful sight. There were ships coming up here, ships going up there, all in arrow-head formations, heading towards specific beaches.

As we went over, the Navy were running up and down the beaches with their rocket ships, clearing the beaches for us before the landings. I noticed a hospital ship – she looked lovely at night because of all the Red Cross lights. We were under air attack – they would keep nipping in – but they didn't bomb her at all.

When we got in on the beaches, the Beachmasters shepherded us off the LST and then up the beach. We had a little bit of an explosive charge to unseal the equipment, and after that we could operate the guns. The beaches were all mined and we had to follow the white tapes showing where they had been cleared – but the worst thing was the snipers.

Anyway, I didn't last very long. An 8-pound mortar came over and hit the top of the tank and, of course, we all got blown to the bottom of it. It was all down with sympathetic detonation, which means that the power with which we were hit set the ammunition off around the tank. There was a round up the gun, and the pressure set that off. I was in the way of the recoil which came back and smashed my arm up.

We managed to crawl out and the medical people were soon with us in a half-track. They brought us up forward of the beach where all the medical tents were. They put me in the compound where I was waiting for about a day and a half before they got me on to the hospital ship. There were quite a few young Germans on the ship – two of them refused to be attended to, and died."

Friedrich August Freiherr von der Heydte was CO of Parachute Regiment 6, part of the German 2nd Parachute Division under Commanding General Ramcke, which fought at the French coast from 6 June onwards. In 1941 he secretly conspired against Hitler.

"I was in the north of Périers, just in the middle of the peninsula, the most westward part of Normandy, covering Utah Beach. The funny thing was that the Germans were expecting a landing north of where the landing actually occurred, west of Ste Mére-Eglise. On the first day I received no orders. I was my own boss. Most of the divisional commanders had been called to Rennes for an operational exercise. I tried to get through to the corps commander General Marcks.

The only contact was by the normal French phone network. The Germans were forbidden to use this, officially, because of the spies. But I couldn't get through on our own network, because the French Resistance had prepared well for the invasion, sabotaging the phone lines.

I first saw what was happening when I arrived in St Come du Mont. I had come across an old church tower, had got hold of the key, and went up there to take a look out over the coast. I knew that I had to tell General Marcks what I had seen. I wanted to tell him that in my opinion the forces we had were not in a position to offer vigorous resistance to the invading forces. At every mile along the coastline was a German bunker and, of the three that I could see, only one was actually firing at the Americans. All the bunkers were manned, of course, but only one was firing. In my opinion, they feared for their lives, considering that they would be easily wiped out by the invading Americans. Only one bunker did its duty, forcing the Americans to spread out.

I felt that my troops were very vulnerable with no artillery assistance. We had our heavy company with 12 cm mortars. I gave the order for them to get forward quickly and fire.

When I saw the invading troops, I gave the order by radio to the regiment, but I didn't dare use the same route back to the Command Post. I made a detour, and on this detour I came across a German battery which had been totally deserted. This was the second line of defence, the artillery line, about six guns in the battery, totally unmanned, but all ready to fire, the ammunition boxes open on the left side of each gun. I don't know what had happened to the gunners, but it was my opinion that they had deserted, though it is possible that they had received a new order. But all the Americans had to do was turn the guns round and fire them at our men. I had no artillery men with me, so I could do nothing with the guns. When I finally contacted Marcks I reported what I had seen.

I told him I had to try to defend the line north of St Come du Mont, and he agreed. But then I had to leave the place for two reasons. First, because someone, I don't know who, had given the order to the engineers to blow up all the bridges. So we had no way to fall back from St Come du Mont to Carentan. Then, there was a funny thing. It was on the second or third day, and all the forces who had been north of Carentan, including the Regimental Staff, had been given the order to withdraw to the south, because we were afraid that we would be surrounded. The Americans attacked to the west, and this attack would have led them to the south and behind me, and so I said, no, it's nonsense to stay in St Come du Mont, we should defend Carentan instead, because in my opinion Carentan was more important. But how the hell could we get to Carentan? All the bridges had been blown up. So, nearly all parts of my regiment, a reinforced battalion, had to cross the water. It was up to our chests and we had all our heavy guns with us. But we had to do it. And thank goodness the Americans didn't spot this. They continued to attack St Come du Mont. Two of my soldiers drowned. One of them was a Jew who had signed up for the German Army using a false name. I had two Jews in my regiment. Both had used false names. One was the nephew of Albert Schweitzer, the famous German doctor and the other was the son of a German aristocrat whose mother was Jewish.

At Carentan I had parts of the 2nd and parts of the 3rd Battalion with me, and some regimental units, intelligence troops etc. Then I was given a reinforcement battalion of Russians, Georgians, in fact. These were anti-Communist Russians fighting on the German side. They fought very well, but they couldn't stand the bombing from the air. The American bombers attacked my regiment near Carentan the whole day, and after the attack the Russians deserted.

The heaviest fighting was at the north-west part of the town. The Americans had managed to get over the flooded area by the railway bridge, which my 2nd Battalion had used. The only way of destroying this bridge would have been by bombing it from the air, but the German Luftwaffe was held back by the superiority of the American air force. I did not see one German fighter plane. As we said then: 'We have the ground but the sky belongs to the Americans'. So, in my opinion, the crucial factor was American air superiority – and second, the lack of unity among the German forces."

The Battle for Caen – a Hard Fought Prize

The initial shock of the landing is settling down into an acceptance of an entirely new sort of close-country fighting for Allies and defending Germans alike. The main objective of Caen now looms large. For the men fighting around this French city, which now became a key to the Allied advance, progress was measured in yards as they fought for each field. Men on both sides remember the struggle.

Walter Heritage, a Regimental Sergeant Major with the 20th Anti-Tank Regiment during the battle for Caen, had to witness the effects of continual attrition and heavy casualties on his men.

"Having landed at Sword Beach on D-Day, we pressed on inland. The object was that we would be in support of the 6th Airborne Division, some of whom had landed the previous night. There were a lot of minefields and we suffered very heavy casualties *en route.*

We made our headquarters about four or five hours' march inland. We made contact with the 6th Airborne Division who were established at the bridgehead at the now famous Pegasus Café. In those days it was called Maison Vendre. It was owned by Georges Vendre, his wife and his three daughters. They were very kind to us and were delightful.

I was responsible for discipline and behaviour, as well as for ammunition for the guns and the general administration of the regiment. We had very good equipment and there was no shortage of ammunition. There were four batteries, so it was rather a spread out job as they were all in different places.

Whether you are fighting or not, there is the daily routine to be done, such as the maintenance of guns and vehicles and the supply of ammunition, and it was my job to ensure that the daily tasks were done.

We were there for six or seven weeks, and it was out and out warfare. Morale among the men was very good – very high. There were casualties, of course – people got wounded, some killed – but morale did not waver.

The Germans had their headquarters in a factory on the outskirts of Caen and their observation posts were in the tall chimneys. They were shelling and bombing us. Our bombing of the line which the Germans held was colossal, and a lot of them were killed in their tanks.

When we got through we saw that the German equipment was good, but there is a limit to how much saturation bombing any equipment can stand up to, however good it is.

Everything in Caen was dead – dead horses, dead cattle – everything. We were told that the people of Caen were in the church. They had been suffering wartime conditions for a long, long time.

Caen had been a beautiful old city, but now every building was destroyed. It was so obliterated that you couldn't go through it. It was in ruins, but fortunately we did not have to stay there because our avenue of approach into Europe was open and we were all anxious to get on."

Sergeant Bernard Griffith was a Driver Operator with the Royal Horse Artillery when he landed in Normandy on D-Day. As his regiment saw the total destruction of the city of Caen, he recalls the pitiful sight of shell-shocked civilians fleeing the town.

"We had got quite far inland by the first night. After we got into position, it was decided that we would need the four vehicles that had been lost in the actual landings.

I went back to the beaches, which were only about 2 km away, on my motor bike. It was pitch dark and the British had scattered smoke canisters all over the beaches as camouflage for movement because they were under such heavy air attack. It was very hard to breathe in the smoke.

We found two of the vehicles, and we got them going. When you don't have proper facilities, you learn to make do, using tricks of the trade.

I wasn't in the best of moods on the way back. Suddenly my motor cycle and I parted company. I was sent head first into a hedge, and as I landed, my dispatch-rider's helmet got jammed on to my head, right down to my eyebrows. I couldn't get the bloody thing off. We used everything to try and lever it off. I ended up with black eyes and a broken nose. It was funny afterwards, but not at the time.

We pressed on with the two new vehicles. We were stopped outside Caen for about ten days. It was difficult with heavy fighting – the Germans were very keen to keep it. The town had already been attacked when we got there, by the Canadians. We were bombarding it heavily and the Typhoon bombers did terrible damage.

Most of the civilians that had survived had gone underground, but we saw some that had managed to escape. They came through our lines on horses and carts or on foot. It was terrible – their suffering was often worse than that of the soldiers. After we captured the town, it was a clearing-up operation. The infantry went in to get rid of the rubbish and to winkle out any snipers.

Bayeux had been taken and our next objective was Falaise. The Germans had two armoured divisions in a pocket there and we bombarded them for four or five days amid very heavy fighting.

Most of the Germans who had been killed in the Falaise pocket had been buried by their own people. They buried the British too, if they were in their sector, and we did likewise. If we came across a German who hadn't been buried, we used to dig a 6-foot hole, wrap the body in a blanket which we would sew up with a big needle, and lower it into the grave. Then more often than not you stuck a rifle into the ground and put his tin hat on top of it, with his name written on the hat.

I have never seen so many dead horses. Although the Germans had very modern panzers and equipment superior to ours in many ways, their artillery and some of their supply vehicles were horse drawn. I have never seen anything like those horses. They were bloated up lying there. It was a horrific sight. When everything was over, the horses were burned by the French farmers."

Wilson S Money served as Radio Officer and Signalsman on a coastal oil tanker throughout the war. After the D-Day landing his ship's task was to bring in oil supplies through the mined waters of the Channel as part of a convoy.

"It was interesting work – something was always happening. There were those tremendously thrilling spectacles, our daylight bombing raids, 500 or more planes passing over in perfect formation, the flak vainly reaching towards them. The heavy battleships throwing their broadsides – with that characteristically deep 'woof' the 16-inchers had – into the enemy's lines.

We had loaded as usual at Hamble in Southampton Water, then proceeded via Cowes to the convoy assembly point at Freshwater, joined up with our companion ships and began the long, slow, crocodile crawl between the buoys marking the swept channel.

Those buoys were a headache to the junior mates. They would leave one astern and steer optimistically at a point inside the next in line. The tide would be westerly, sweeping down strongly, driving us to leeward. Time and again the ship's head would have to be brought up. Gradually, inevitably she would be borne to the west, approaching the buoy crabwise. Too often there was a ship off the port column in the same plight, crowding us out, and there were we, sandwiched, while the distance between us decreased yard by yard. The nearer we got to the buoy, the more certain it appeared collision was imminent.

I would watch silently while the nervous young mate weighed things up and tried to decide for the best – should he clear the buoy and risk hitting the ship to port, or take a gamble on there being no mines to strike if he swung out of the swept channel?

I think God must have kept us under His wing, as He had throughout the whole war, for our ship bore a charmed life. We would either miss the buoy by inches on the safe side, or steer outside to fight our way back into line with every pound of steam we could muster, ready for the next marker.

Soon after leaving the English coast, a ship's anti-aircraft balloon was observed floating several feet above the surface, obviously all that remained of an unlucky vessel that had strayed from its charted course and met the fate of so many by striking a mine. Beyond looking about in the vicinity for signs of wreckage or possible survivors, few comments were made, except perhaps for some facetious remark like, 'I suppose there's a ship hanging on the end of that wire.' The loss of one was so commonplace, too frequent to be of any but brief passing interest.

We kept our station as best we could in that collection of small slow craft, when suddenly someone hailed. 'Is that a Mae West right ahead?' It was – a yellow life jacket supporting its owner. As we steamed closer, all hands leaned over the side and looked straight into the face of an RAF boy. Head back, he returned our gaze, eyes wide open, unblinking. He was dead...

He was very young – too young to have died. His hands rose and fell in the swell as if waving to us. His dark, wavy hair, wet with sea water, clung in tight curls to his forehead – his mouth held a faint, sad smile, his face had an expression of absolute peace.

We flashed our information to the rescue launch and continued our convoy duties, but apart from the necessary routine orders, we were silent, each wrapped up in his own thoughts. None of us to my knowledge had, up to that time, seen an actual war casualty, let alone a death as the result of enemy action, and I guessed the others' minds worked on the same lines as my own. I only know that this, our first, affected us deeply.

How long had he been drifting in the Channel? Had he baled out unhurt and spent hours and hours praying to be rescued, been cheered by the sight of a ship or plane, only to know the heart-breaking despair of seeing them pass unaware of his existence, gradually lost hope, sunk into a coma and died of exposure? Were his people still awaiting news of him, starting at every knock on the door, hoping he was at least still alive, even if a prisoner of war? Did he have a girl – a wife, kids?

The sunken ship we passed earlier probably had scores of dead seamen or troops lying within her hull and we hardly gave them a thought, but the sight of that youngster left us isolated, each to himself, locked in his private thoughts for hours afterwards. We pottered about, pretending to be busy, avoiding each others' eyes, and no mention of the dead boy was ever made. Not one word."

Trained under the Empire Training Scheme, Clive Price, a 20-year old Australian, became Flight-Sergeant Bomb Aimer with a British crew in 619 Squadron of Lancasters, based at Dunholme Lodge, Lincolnshire. In the battle for Caen he recalls his crew's bombing missions over France.

"Around late July 1944, there was a great deal of buzz-bomb activity. In fact it had started around D-Day and they were becoming a bit of a menace by July.

We started doing daylight ops on sites around Paris-Beauvais area. It was quite good fun map-reading over north France. It looked as peaceful as England from 15,000 ft, and it was hard to realise that it was alive with Germans. I got a kick out of getting my pinpoints confirmed by the navigator, over strange country, and was feeling pretty bucked.

There was a lot of flak around the target, but it seemed so lovely a day that you couldn't read danger into it. The black smoke puffs of spent flak drifted lazily and harmlessly past. I did a lovely run-up and followed my bombs all the way down till I saw them burst right on the aiming point. I was terribly thrilled and hollered that I had got a direct hit.

Indeed, I was feeling so fine that when, after we left the target, I heard the rear gunner's high-pitched voice tell us in frightened tones that he saw a kite going down in flames, I could have hit him for spoiling it.

It wasn't long, however, before I realised why his voice sounded urgent and tense. I saw three kites go down in flames a couple of ops later, and believe me, there is, I think, no more petrifying sight on ops than to see a kite in daylight, spinning earthwards in flames.

One day I saw three Lancs go down in flames. Everything seemed to go wrong. No-one seemed to be able to find the target until we were nearly on it. I was looking frantically, but it was hazy and I couldn't find a pinpoint. The flak was getting hotter and then I saw a kite go careering down ahead of us. It was a mass of flames from wingtip to wingtip and its tail flew off halfway down and spun down beside it.

I didn't see any chutes open. By that time, being fascinated by watching this, I was hopelessly lost as well as petrified, and we were nearly on top of the target. Then someone dropped his bombs through someone else's wing.

The kite hit went into a spin and hit another aircraft, and the two went down in flames with bits of wing flying off. Everyone seemed to panic after that and the boys were weaving in all directions, trying to bomb or getting out of the way. I had to drop my bombs into a wood. Then, when there were only about a dozen kites who had a chance of bombing, the controller yelled out that the target was 'down there, where that Lanc is burning on the deck!' That cheered us up no end, and we went home disgusted.

We did another op to a road and rail junction target. All went well until we were running up on the target, when (as if they were going to spite us for having the hide to go on) they started shooting at us. It must have been pretty close to us, for no-one saw the shells explode. They must have been right under our bomb doors which were by now open. I think the thick cases of those bombs saved the navigator and wireless-operator from being hit. As it was, we had quite a few holes ripped in the floor between the bombs. We heard the 'whump' three times and we shook violently. They were getting close to us too, but we were on the run-up and couldn't weave. I was able to drop my bombs after the third shell – we rose a bit and we weren't hit any more.

Roy (pilot) and Len (flight engineer) kept an eye on the petrol and although we found out when we landed that we had every petrol tank holed, the leaks soon stopped up. There was a petrol line punctured inside the kite too, so we were quite lucky. There were about 20 holes in her when we landed, so we were quite proud of ourselves. I usen't to believe the old ops tale that the flak was close when you could smell it, but we could smell it that day!

On the night of 7 August 1944 we were put on one of the most interesting ops I've ever done. The target was Secquesville la Campagne, where the battle of the Falaise Gap was raging.

We got to the briefing room and the Intelligence bod explained the scheme. Each of the five Groups in Bomber Command (about 200 Lancasters or Halifaxes in each) was to have a separate aiming point that night. They were bombing at 20-minute intervals starting from 11 pm. Every Group's aiming point was a few hundred yards ahead of the previous one. The army was to advance as the bombers did, so that each group would be bombing just ahead of our troops.

I don't know how emotional the others were, but I felt a distinct thrill that night and, as the plan was unfolded to us. I could feel the hairs on my neck rise with excitement. We were being told about what our highest military leaders had planned just a few hours before. We were doing work where a few hundred yards understoot would mean tragedy to our own men. We were playing a direct part in the advance down France, doing in a few minutes what the army would have taken weeks to do – and the army had called on us to help them!

I studied my maps and photos that night until I looked like them. If there were any of our troops killed, I was going to make certain that they weren't killed by *my* bombs.

We took off on a pitch black night. As we were over the Channel, I saw dead ahead of us the red TI (target indicator) go down. I prayed that it wouldn't be blown out by the time we got there. We seemed to take ages to approach it, but we finally got there and I gave a smart correction and flashed my eyes round the cabin to make sure the bombing equipment was OK. We were running up and the TI was coming unerringly down my line of sight.

'Steady, steady, steady – bombs gone!' And it was all over. Just as I let them go, I saw the red TI blown up by other bombs and after I pressed the tit, I heard the controller give the order to stop bombing as someone had blown the TI out. I was pretty lucky to get them away. So three hours and 55 minutes later we were back on the ground.

The race through France was on, so we (with 999 others) did a good job that night, evidently."

Adolf Mertens, age 24, was commander of the regimental intelligence unit of the German 6 Parachute Regiment, as German forces struggled to break out of the area of Coutances, where US troops encircled them.

"We were constantly on the march, initially in vehicles and on motorbikes until the petrol ran out, and we had to leave the cars and bikes and continue on foot.

I would say that the combat readiness of the troops at this point was more or less unbroken, although the demands on the troops were very high, and we had no chance to sleep, or rest and there was absolutely nothing to eat. But none of this affected our will to do all we could to get out of the pocket.

We had been moving throughout the whole of the night. Sleep you could forget – we did not get a wink. We had to be alert at every moment, as the area was under constant fire from the naval artillery off the coast, and we had to take every opportunity to find room between the falling shells to push forward. It was impossible to set any kind of overview of the area, it was total chaos, and so the troops were dispersed into groups.

You couldn't really talk of specific orders on this day. The regimental commander succeeded merely in gathering together as many of the units as possible and instructing them to wait in a specific place until he came back to take them away. Of course, we discovered that it was impossible to wait very long and so we decided to break up into groups and break out on our own.

Now in a situation like this you live totally on the hope that you will get out in a reasonable state. You'd had no sleep. You thought very little about it, and if you did, these thoughts were quickly washed away by the sight of dead comrades, destroyed tanks, corpses lying all around, men hanging dead out of blown-up trucks, and your only thought was 'how am I going to get out of this?'. I'm not saying that you were not affected by the sight of all this horror, of your dead comrades lying around. You were cut to the bone by this, but this did not change the bald fact that you had to carry out your duty to the men and get them out of this encirclement.

The day had no beginning and no end. It was simply a continuation of the day and the night before. Pushing forward constantly, trying to find cover where you could get it, and where possible trying to find something to eat. We had no provisions with us but we would sometimes come upon destroyed trucks, which had some provisions in them. In a situation like this you run on adrenalin. It is difficult to say what actually drives a man forward in this situation. You have to imagine that we had been involved in uninterrupted heavy fighting since 6 June. We were used to such extreme situations by now. Comradeship is a major factor here. It is very important to you not to bring your comrades into dangerous situations.

I remember particular experiences while retreating. I came upon one of my comrades lying at the side of the road with a badly wounded leg. He had tied a piece of wire around it to try to stop the bleeding. I offered him help, but he said, it's OK, one of the orderlies is on his way to carry me out of here, and he told me to make sure that I got out all right.

There were about 12 of us together, 12 paratroopers, under the command of a lieutenant, and we were trying to get through a path. We could hardly see anything, and had not a clue where the path would take us. We were just trying to make our way north out of the pocket. There were shots ahead of us, and then we heard English voices shouting out: 'Hands up!'. Hand grenades were exploding all around us, and the lieutenant ahead of me was wounded in the arm from a shot. He told me to take his pistol, which he could no longer get hold of, and told me to shoot him. I immediately took the weapon off him, and took it apart so that it couldn't be used. I pushed him up out of the ditch, and he was immediately taken prisoner by the American soldiers. We, in turn, were also taken prisoner by the large group of American soldiers standing before us. We were told to stand against a wood at about 20 or 30 metres from our captors, and just at that moment, a fighter plane dived down and fired a salvo directly at us as we stood with hands over our eyes. Fortunately, the shots went over our heads. Then we were taken away on American jeeps. We were treated reasonably well. I have to say, and we were taken off to an open camp where all the prisoners who had been taken in the pocket were assembled. Quite a high number. We were then taken to the church at Sainte Mère-Eglise, and we spent the night on church pews. We were taken to England, to an interrogation camp in Manchester, and after about ten days there we were shipped to America.

The paratroopers were volunteers. It was clear to us now what sort of scrupulous brutality the enemy would stoop to against us, the bombing of our cities etc., and in this sense, we were fighting the war not for ideological purposes, but to protect our fatherland."

Rudolf Wuester was a German gunner in a Tiger with the Heavy SS-Panzer Battalion 102, in action from 10 to 30 July on Height 112 near Caen. He recalls taking a mysterious 'Englishman' prisoner south of this point.

"Through a gap in the forest I saw an English soldier limping, and we wanted to take him in as a prisoner of war. We fired a warning salvo to bring him to a halt and waved him towards us. He climbed on to our tank and we carried him back with us. I had a reasonable command of English, as between April and August 1939 I had spent some time in Torquay in Devon, and I attempted to start up a conversation with him. He would not answer and remained *stumm.*

Quite a while after this I heard an answer in English, but it was not exactly a good English. After I'd repeated several questions he suddenly replied to me in a broken German, and explained to me that he was not English, he was in fact a German from Dirschau in Poland. I immediately brought the tank to a halt and turned off the engine. I made it clear to him that I knew that he was a member of the Polish army under General Anders, and that I was officially acknowledging him as a combatant. I told him that, should he fall into other hands again, he should on no account say that he was German, because he would be shot dead on the spot.

In spite of his wound, I let him jump down from the tank and told him to sit down in the roadside ditch and wait for his own men, who were not far away, to pick him up. Perhaps he's still alive and can confirm this."

Normandy – The Road to Paris

*A*s the Allies worked hard to expand their beachhead, the Germans rushed reinforcements from the Pas de Calais to try and drive them back to the sea. The terrain of the Norman *bocage* – small fields separated by thick hedges – was ideal for defenders. As the British and Canadians battered away at German forces around Caen, the Americans prepared for a breakout and a drive inland. On 25 July, Operation Cobra was heralded by a heavy air attack on the German positions. General 'Lightning Joe' Collin's VII Corps led the main effort and, after advancing through tough resistance at Coutance, broke the German defences at Avranches. General Patton's Third Army punched through the hole into open country. The final German counterattack, at Avranches, was foiled by Allied air support responding to Ultra signals interception. The way to the French capital of Paris lay open. In a huge sweeping manoeuvre, American forces linked up with British near Falais, trapping or killing 60,000 German troops. On August 23, as Resistance forces rose against the city's German garrison, the US Fifth Corps, headed by the Second Free French Armoured Division, made a drive for the city. It reached it on the 25th, liberating the French capital after four years of German occupation. The men who paved the way to Paris and those in the city recall the liberation.

Dropped into Central France, Gordon Davidson and his stick of eight SAS men were to make strikes against German transport columns retreating from Nantes and other U-boat bases on the west coast. As their Halifax transport turned back towards England, the men prepared for the job in hand.

"For all of us, this was our first experience of the Continent. What would the reception committee be like? Were they FFI or FTP? No idle question. A week or two before half the Squadron had dropped at Châteauroux, to the north west in the same area just south of the Loire. They had been met by FTP (communists), betrayed to the *Milice* and shot out of hand.

The group of figures approached. '*Vous êtes les bienvenus*', called out one taller than the rest, and there was a mutual pumping of hands before we hurried to some cars and along the mysterious darkness of a country road to a farmhouse. Once inside the large warm kitchen, we could take stock of our hosts and load up with omelettes, bread, cheese and wine.

Chief of the reception committee of the local *maquis* was the tall, thin Commandant Duret, whose appearance and manner were strikingly similar to that of de Gaulle. Definitely FFI, so, all things being equal, we shouldn't risk another Châteauroux. There were four or five other *maquisards* besides the farmer, his wife and two daughters. The atmosphere was friendly, even jovial, and we were indeed welcome – perhaps not so much for our military skills, as the assurance we represented of arms and supplies.

With the busy German supply route from Bourges to Nevers only a few kilometres away, we were guided into the adjoining woods for the night. *Milice* patrols were a hazard and the farmer and his family could not be compromised.

Dawn came and went unnoticed, and by midday it was time to take stock of the situation. In any case, no action could be taken until cover of night, and it was a good time to assess resources and tasks now that we were safely in position on the chess board. Arms and ammunition were sufficient for several small strikes until the next supply drop.

What of the men? We were a stick of eight. The sergeant, a cheerful, solid man from Glasgow. Like almost all of us, he was new to the SAS and his approach was that of a regimental soldier. His battalion had recently been dispersed and he was more fortunate than his comrades sent to the Glider Regiment, who had come to grief in Normandy.

There were two corporals. One from Norfolk had been with the SAS in North Africa, where he had earned the MM. He was small, lively, quick-witted and a demolition expert. A natural 'jelly' man, and ideal for this mission. The other, a small, saturnine man from Dorset, who had apparently run donkey rides on the sands at Weymouth. Perhaps he had been a stable-lad in happier times, for he exuded a sort of horsiness and, as he cheerfully carried a Bren gun, it could have been a saddle in Lambourn Yard.

Like him, three others were from the west. Two from Swindon, a butcher and a railwayman. The third, a Swansea lad, was quick to make his mark with the farmer's teenage daughter. All four, Weymouth, Swindon and Swansea, had come from Auxiliary Units, set up earlier in the war for defensive guerrilla operations in south-west England in the event of a German landing. They were trained to live rough and were familiar with the night attack techniques.

The remaining two came from London. A tall, youngish, rather academic-looking man who, it transpired, was an actor who had recently worked at Stratford. I am not sure how he came to the Unit, but he was a good and reliable man. A cockney medical orderly of uncertain background, but certain humour, made up the number.

Like the sergeant, my own experience had been with another Highland regiment and, after working at Airborne Forces HQ as SAS liaison officer, I got a transfer to B Squadron at Fairford.

In August 1944 the military situation was fluid, to say the least. The main Allied forces moved towards Paris and Brussels and the pattern of conflict was reasonably clear. However, in central France, no Allied forces came nearer to us than Orléans, some 100 miles to the north, where Patton and his armoured divisions paused briefly in the drive to the Belfort Gap. Meanwhile, the Germans withdrawing from their naval bases had to pass from Bourges in the central Sologne to Nevers or La Charité – both with bridges over the Loire – and make for the Belfort Gap before Patton could close it.

It is useful to 'paint the picture', as Monty had said, because the odds in our case were 20 SAS to cover an area half the size of Surrey against a constant flow of Germans moving east and culminating in the von Elster column of 20,000 men, halted at Bourges on 5 September.

Our mission, to harass German columns, would have been quite impossible without the wholehearted cooperation of the *maquis* and local population. A typical operation meant leaving at nightfall in a couple of ancient cars, and a drive of 10–15 miles to a point where enemy transport was most vulnerable.

Sten and Bren guns with precious grenades were our weapons against the highly armed Germans, so that our attacks would be met by a hail of Schmeisser automatic fire, and as their bullets whistled all around us, we gave inward thanks for the camouflage of trees and darkness.

In one engagement, the hail of Schmeisser fire was so intense that it claimed an inevitable victim and my corporal (the actor) was shot in the head beside me. Taken to a *maquis* 'hospital', he was given every attention, but lack of supplies meant that he could not be saved.

We carried out eight or nine missions of this kind and, in addition, the blowing up of railway bridges which halted a couple of German armoured trains.

These were small operations compared to what was occurring elsewhere in the campaign at that time, but the pressure on the ordinary soldier in extraordinary conditions was considerable. Apart from the adrenalin of battle, he had to cope with the uncertainty of who was on our side – who gets a bullet in his back from a traitor? How were we going to eat? It is here that regimental discipline, training and a bit of humour show their true value.

The large German column, under General von Elster, halted at Bourges, would not surrender to the *maquis* (half of them communists), but was persuaded to move north to Orléans and surrender to Patton on 10 September. It was good to see Allied troops again. After our meeting, a visit to his Ordnance Park for supplies. A sergeant asked me to choose from one of 15 menus: Chicken Maryland never tasted so good."

Flying Officer Philip Murton was with 183 Squadron of the RAF, based at a makeshift airfield just outside Caen. Flying rocket-armed Typhoons, it was his job to clear obstructions from the Allies' way and hunt down the retreating Germans.

"On any operations there would be, say, a section of four going out looking for anything – anything German. We had the bomb-line marked on our maps that we flew with, so anything beyond that which was moving – guns, artillery, despatch riders – was fair game. Depending on what it was, the leader decided whether to use cannon or rockets, or whether it warranted a second attack.

This was simply freelance stuff, anything you found, you just attacked it. The leader tried to make a note of where it was so he could report the exact position when he got back. But sometimes we'd go to do a rocket attack on a gun somewhere: that was probably the army that had called us up, given us a map reference and said, 'There are guns here which are holding up the advance in one part on the front' – then you would go and knock them out. Very often the army would fire red smoke on to the target which gave us an extra guide – until the Germans learned this and of course, they would fire red smoke in the hope that they would confuse us.

A lot of the time it was cheating in a way because there was nothing firing back at us. It was almost like a practice, though obviously the tanks and troops on the ground *would* fire back. Later on, when the Germans increased their flak everywhere, you could be attacking something and there would be no flak at all. Then, as soon as you got in a dive, they would open up and you would have to go through the lot. Actually, the attacking, once you had gone into echelon and peeled off to go into the attack, you were so busy trying to get the sight on what you were attacking and looking at your turn and slip indicator to try and get the skid out, allowing for wind, that really, unless the flak was quite intense and the balls were whipping past you, you were concentrating only on what you were doing.

We had complete air superiority, so we never had to bother about looking for German aeroplanes. In fact, apart from chasing two Focke-Wulfs over the Channel after they had bombed Brighton, I never saw a German aeroplane in the air through the whole of my tour.

The Falaise Gap was an absolute shambles. There was a pocket of hundreds of tanks, vehicles and goodness knows what, and there was this gap which wasn't closed. Montgomery didn't make the right decision and thousands of troops got away through it. They reckon that if the gap had been closed three or four days earlier, then we would never have had the Ardennes offensive or Bastogne, because all those German troops were seasoned men and they went back and reformed.

Falaise was horrible because it was absolute carnage. There were dead bodies and horses and cows all over the place, and after three or four days, you could actually smell rotting bodies at 2,000 feet. The smell actually came into your cockpit. An awful lot of the local French people (because of the ground battle going on) were down in cellars but at one stage, when our flight was standing down, our army liaison officer said, 'Come on you chaps', and we piled into an army three-tonner to go and look around. There were still bodies lying around and the cows and horses all tended to lie, goodness knows why, with their legs up in the air, and they were all bloated and swollen. There were vehicles everywhere too – everything left behind by a retreating army.

When we went in on an attack I honestly don't think we had any feelings about it. We were young, and you tended to enjoy things. Over the years you tended to forget the horrible things, and shooting up a whole lot of troops on the road was a lot of fun. It was very impersonal. I know you were killing people, but it wasn't like the army who went in hand-to-hand fighting. You were just letting loose at a whole lot of people on the ground and you would see them fall over like nine-pins and not think an awful lot about it.

We were doing it because it was a job to do. We didn't hate the Germans – possibly not as much as I hated them after the war after Belsen and all the atrocities came out. We were fighting to knock out Nazism really, and I think a lot of the army boys who were involved in hand-to-hand fighting and the tank boys who were literally blowing up people 100 yards away, were revolted by it. But eventually you got very hard. You got hard too because you saw one of your chums shot down or crash – and it was no good getting all soppy and sentimental about it, so you built a shell. In fact, about five or so years ago, I started having the most God-awful nightmares about being shot down, shooting up troops, planes, and goodness knows what. I mentioned it to my doctor and he said that it was a natural reaction. All the nasty stuff is stored away in the back of your mind and now it is starting to come out.

We all had the feeling it wasn't going to happen to us."

Jack Clark, an air gunner with an Albemarle crew in 297 Squadron, 38 Group, based at Brize Norton, was not due to be flying on 20 August, 1944 – but a friend approached him to fly with his crew on a trip to drop supplies to the French SAS in Brittany.

"The Albemarle had been designed just before the start of the war as one of the answers to the question, 'What shall we make aeroplanes out of when there is no more aluminium?'.

The Mosquito, built from balsa wood, had been the correct answer. The Albemarle, constructed from mild steel, was the other solution. It had been passed on to 38 Group to replace the Whitley after being turned down by Bomber Command, and even those sent to the Russian Air Force had been melted down, and only the engines were used by our hard-up allies.

Apart from being very heavy for its size (because, of course, mild steel is heavier than aluminium) it had also been designed with the tail wheel at the front of the aeroplane, so that the landings were usually bumpier because the drivers had been trained on aeroplanes that had the tail wheel under the tail. This meant that the electrical system wiring was constantly affected by the shocks and vibration, and until the landing had been made, we were often not sure that the undercarriage would actually lock as we hit the deck, or whether we would be coming in on a belly landing. Actually those were not the problems that were worrying my friend Bert Moss. After all, we had learned to live with those little bits of excitement.

When the Albemarle was first produced, the Air Gunner used to strut around a small open platform in the centre of the fuselage, waving a couple of Vickers K guns that ran on a ball race around the rim of a hole in the top of the fuselage, hopefully in the direction of the enemy. By this stage in the war, the gun ring had been replaced by a power-operated Boulton Paul gun turret, fitted with four Browning 303 MGs – which brings us to my friend Bert's problem.

Neither the Air Gunner, the Pilot, the Navigator, the Bomb Aimer (we didn't carry bombs but to ensure the pinpoint accuracy that was needed of crews dropping supplies to the resistance groups, the pilot was directed for the final stages of the drop by a Bomb Aimer – an expert map-reader), nor the Wireless Operator could see if anything approached from behind and below.

Because of this blind spot, one of the *Luftwaffe*'s fighter techniques was to attack from below and behind any unfortunate Albemarle they were lucky enough to find. They were also much faster, better armed and infinitely more manoeuvrable.

However, there was a little window at the bottom rear end of the fuselage and just sufficient room for one intrepid, not-too-tall airman to lie down and peer through this window to observe if indeed an enemy was approaching from below and behind. Yes, you've guessed, Bert wanted me to come with him and his 'sprog' crew, and look out of the window.

Some hours later I had tidied my kit, cleaned my boots, written my last letters, envelopes addressed and sealed, but not stamped. We had just flown over the French coast through a welcoming barrage of flak from some trigger-happy Americans – we always blamed them. They probably blamed our ack-ack gunners too.

I say light flak now, but a few years ago I was looking through some papers in the Public Records Office where the combat reports are now held, and the descriptions of the flak varied from 'light' (Bert) to 'heavy' (guess who). Anyway, as we weaved through this red hot hostile metal, I realised we were being pursued.

In the best traditional cool British manner, I switched on the intercom and spoke in cool, calm, modulated soft tones to the pilot. 'Tail to pilot. Stand by corkscrew starboard – corkscrew starboard. GO.' And nothing happened.

The pilot should immediately have slung the several tons of mild steel, Browning machine guns and assorted air crew down into a right-hand dive, maintained that for several seconds, climbed up to the left for a few seconds, dived again to the right, climbed again to the left, thus maintaining the same direction.

Nothing happened for several moments. In a slightly authoritative, but still cool and gentle tone. I repeated, 'Corkscrew starboard. GO!'

Nothing happened … Then, with all the authority and command I could summon to my voice, shouted down the intercom. 'Corkscrew starboard. GO!'

The voices of Bert, plus the navigator, the bomb aimer and the wireless operator joined in. This heavenly choir awoke the pilot from his reverie. He threw his quivering Albemarle into violent evasive action.

Both engines cut out … then the starboard engine picked up and the port began to purr and roar again. The same pursuer was still in the same relative position, astern and slightly below. 'No,' I thought, 'it's impossible'. And then I realised, it had to be part of our own aeroplane. It was, of course, the tow bar to which gliders were attached when the Albemarle was used as a tug.

I ordered the pilot to cease these dangerous aerial acrobatics, telling him that we had shaken off our pursuer, and we settled back, bodies and minds alive with adrenalin. I was a little angry with myself, but glad that I had learned the only way to ensure instant urgency in battle with that particular pilot. A lesson some five minutes later I was able to apply, for coming up from below and astern was a Dornier 217.

This time it took only moments to get the pilot into a corkscrew and direct Bert just where to aim his four Brownings. I watched him pour tracer into the Dornier starboard wing and engine at a rate of about 80 bullets a second, and saw it fluttering and spinning down out of sight into the cloud below.

We had been flying just above the cloud so we could use its cover, but soon it was time to descend through this shelter. We were due to drop a load of supplies (petrol and ammunition were part of the normal cargo, although one tried not to think about it), to the French SAS who were fighting for control of Brittany, assisted by a very active and courageous local *maquis*.

We flew over the Dropping Zone. There was a battle going on and it seemed sensible to fly on and return a little later as the DZ party were a bit too busy to be flashing recognition letters and colours and collecting panniers and so on.

As we flashed past, at treetop height over the coast, I could see a priest, cassock flapping in the wind, with his parishioners, beating out a fire in a tiny village. Perhaps they too were involved in the same immediate strife as the SAS soldiers to the north. I don't know.

We flew back to the dropping zone, but everybody on the ground was still 'too busy' – so reluctantly back to Brize Norton, cargo intact, to fly again."

William Spray had served in a Friends' Ambulance Unit in Morocco until the invasion of France, when his unit became attached to a tank column of the USA Third Army.

"We had no idea of the shape of the war. The Falaise Gap got closed and we stopped fighting, then the buzz got round that it was Paris. This was terrific. On August 25th, we went, a mixture of fêting and fighting on the way, into Paris.

It was unbelievable. I don't think I'd ever attached any particular meaning to the word 'liberation' until now. Certainly I can't ever now see or use the word 'liberation' without thinking of the experience of that day, rolling into Paris.

We were bang behind the tanks. People were out on the streets, throwing flowers, hugging every soldier they could see, and suddenly discovering we were English, and transferring their affections to us, quite as much as to the French.

I have pages in my diary about this – most of them concern particular young ladies whom we met and gave a lift to until a German sniper would open up, at which point, tin hats had to go on and we had to go into action in case there were wounded. There weren't really any wounded we met until we got right into Paris itself.

There was this enormous outpouring of joy and relief and everything else fell into what seemed the right perspective – that is as unimportant. I suppose on that day, it was.

So we drove in slowly. I remember going across the Pont du Sèvres, rolling into the Place Victor Hugo, down into the Avenue Raymond Point Calais, and there we stopped and a lovely lady handed out *vin rouge* from her sitting room window.

Snipers opened up. We had wounded in the Church of the Place Victor Hugo, and we had to evacuate them to the nearest hospital. We slept, that night, in the street, in our ambulances, with the local Parisians absolutely marvellous in their welcome and hospitality.

We were the first lot in, apart from British Secret Service. I'm sure there were lots of British in Paris before, but we were the first – and only – ones to make a public entry. So it was the French and these 30 conscientious objectors, rolling into Paris. Indeed, the very next day, in one of the local French papers (one of our chaps was called Marcus Dukes and the other was Raymond Mann) they had conflated the two and the great headline was 'Duke Man first Englishman in Paris'.

There was not a lot of resistance going through. What had happened was, I think, that the hardened Nazis were clearly going to die fighting and they were some of the snipers, I've no doubt...

Paris looked just like any other town. Certain bits of it were obviously damaged, but it was difficult to know when. My memory is mainly of people – great crowds of people cheering. Where the French ladies had got their lovely dresses from on this sunny morning, I don't know, but there they were, looking simply magnificent – the young ones. Then there were the old ones and widows in their black, being motherly. It was a great occasion for the human spirit. It was astonishing, really, that it required a war to produce it."

Herbert Eckelmann was an official in the Reich Ministry of Economic Affairs when he was suddenly drafted into the army as Germany built up her military power before the war. August 1944 found him living in Paris's Hotel Raphael, the *Stadtkommissar*, responsible for the economic running of occupied Paris.

"My new – and last – commanding officer, von Choltitz, received his scorched-earth orders that Paris was to be destroyed – gas, electricity, power stations, Métro, the lot. Choltitz summoned me to hear my opinion, and I answered that on military grounds such destruction was pointless.

On August 17th, Abetz came to Choltitz to explain that he was removing the Vichy regime. With Choltitz I inspected the fortified blockhouses (*Stutzpunkte*) we had built, and saw how they were manned by dear old daddies. As luck would have it, nobody bothered them. On the 20th, we agreed it was too late in the day for any destruction. Had we simply marched out of Paris along with the rest, however, we would certainly have been condemned to death by a military tribunal. So we remained at our post in the Meurice. Jay asked Choltitz what orders he had to give, for the soldiers could not be expected to continue fighting after their senior officers had been captured. Choltitz replied that he had no new orders to give.

Choltitz's bedroom and sitting room were on the fourth floor, and he and Colonel von Unger and Jay and I and a few orderlies had retired up there. Then in came an older man in a German uniform with the insignia of the Resistance on it, and a hammer and sickle on his helmet. He manipulated the bolt of his Sten gun and that was too much for Choltitz, who told him to rip off his badges. At that point there came a French lieutenant who saluted and asked whether he had the honour to be speaking to General von Choltitz. The Frenchman said, 'Will you give the order for a cease-fire?' Choltitz answered. 'Since you are in my bedroom, it's a little late for it.'

We were led off to Leclerc. Out in the street a huge mob had already assembled, and they screamed and spat at us, which was none too good. A French Red Cross van then drove us through Paris to the Préfecture de Police, where I was preparing myself to be sentenced to death. Instead, the behaviour was perfectly correct. About ten of us German officers were driven to the Gare Montparnasse, and on the way the Resistance men were polite. De Gaulle had arrived, and was with other officers, when Leclerc and Choltitz turned up. They agreed that fighting at the *Stutzpunkte* should be broken off. It fell to me and an escorting French officer to make the arrangements.

We drove out towards Vincennes, which was where I knew there were German troops. I told the Frenchman that he might be shot at and should therefore wave a white handkerchief. We crossed into the

German lines and there my French officer was held prisoner, though really he had come under a flag of truce. My conscience still bothers me a little about this. But I was free. I had been in the hands of the French only one day. And I'd lived through the occupation of Paris from the first day to the last."

Summer 1944 – Joy and Reflection

By the late summer of 1944, Hitler's dominance in Europe is growing shaky. As his armies withdraw under pressure from the Allied invasions in both the north and south of France, the Führer's popularity even among his staunchest erstwhile supporters is not what it was. On the Allied side, however, morale is high and still rising as more and more seized territory is reclaimed and France is carried away by the euphoria of liberation.

Friedrich August Freiherr von der Heydte, commander of Parachute Regiment 6, was one of the original circle of conspirators against Hitler. He describes the make-up of this circle and his feelings after hearing of the assassination attempt of 20 July 1944.

"I was not exactly in the best of moods at the time. I had just heard a number of reports that friends of mine had been arrested, because they had allegedly, or had in fact, been involved in the conspiracy against Hitler. I had been initiated into the plans drawn up by the conspirators around the beginning of 1942, and after the assassination attempt on 20 July 1944 I was under suspicion. I escaped arrest because they mixed me up with another man whose name was von der Heyde (without a 't'), and he was arrested instead of me. I felt very bad about this, but I did find out later that he escaped any serious consequences.

Having been in loose contact with this resistance circle from 1942 onwards. I feel able to give a reasonable assessment of the men who made their first serious coup attempt on 20 July 1944. The common conviction that Hitler was leading the German people down a fatal path brought me together with a number of other officers, who were of the same opinion. This circle of people included General Olbricht, Count Claus Stauffenberg, the former Chief of General Staff, General Beck, Colonels Hans Oster and Wessel von Freytag-Loringhoven, First Lieutenant Friedrich Wilhelm Heinz, Christoph von Gersdorff, Albrecht Merz von Quernheim, Werner von Häften and Alexis von Rönne. I was once assigned to take part in capturing the SS headquarters in Kochstrasse in Berlin from a base in Doeberitz, but was side-tracked from this by my engagement at the front. It is almost impossible that the Anglo-Saxon spy network knew nothing about the hastily arranged get-togethers between diplomats, politicians and army officers, who would meet on the way from one front to another, in Berlin or in some office or other on a side-street off the Lützowufer or the Wilhelmstrasse, to take advantage of the few hours before a new posting against the Russian enemy to discuss tactics and forge new plans...

Any plan would always run up against new difficulties. Hitler was getting more and more suspicious. Certain individuals who were vital to the success of the plans hesitated fatally, or the troops who they depended upon to carry out the operation were torn apart. They did not want a civil war, they wanted a trouble-free *coup d'état*. They felt a profound inner sense of responsibility, and were fully aware that a failed *coup* would bring untold new misery to the German people. Whoever resolves, from a deep sense of responsibility for the destiny of his people, to carry out a violent coup against a despotic state leadership, cannot afford the prospect of defeat. An absolute resolve, which takes the prospect of defeat into account, and nevertheless risks a *coup* while at war with an external enemy, this is the conviction of a political gambler, an adventurer, who only fights for himself, not for higher ideals. Hitler was one of those people who saw only the absolute choice between victory and defeat, and once it became clear that 'total victory' would not come his way, instead of seeking some kind of negotiated settlement for Germany he chose 'total defeat'.

One worrying question plagued all the plans for toppling Hitler right from the start – how would the German worker, the ordinary German soldier, who under the influence of Goebbels' propaganda, still believed in Hitler's qualities as a leader, react to a *putsch* by officers? The conspirators were robbed by the Nazi régime of all means of influencing the masses. The masses still – in 1942 – believed in Hitler, though no longer in 'Hitler as God', but certainly still in 'Hitler as demon'. We hear today that the conspirators against Hitler 'could not break out of their social class.' I have to say that whoever considers himself a Christian and who has had death as his constant companion in every kind of form at the front or at home, and who was prepared to lay down his life – for him social class is, at most, a sociological fact, but in no sense a fixed value which he was unable to shake off.

The men of 20 July did not want a return to old forms, the assassination attempt of 20 July was a monarchist *putsch* only in the imagination of Goebbels and Ley. The men of 20 July were not so concerned about what form of state they were fighting for, they were fighting for the German people and were prepared to die in the fight against the external enemy."

Colonel William Quinn in the Office of the Assistant Chief of Staff at the Headquarters of the US Seventh Army, documented the action between the liberating American forces and the occupying Germans.

"By the time the German Nineteenth Army recovered from the surprise of the Allied landings on 15 August, it was too late. Although the German High Command had every reason to expect such an Allied operation, and knew in advance, from aerial reconnaissance, that the invasion fleet was under way, it failed to deduce the target area of attack.

There are conflicting versions of just what the enemy did expect. Some prisoners, including General-Major Pieringer, Feldkommandant of the Var Department, stated that the Germans were alert for an attack in the Genoa area – others say the landings were expected west of Toulon, although this area was unsuitable. In any case, the enemy was not prepared in the right area.

The shock and surprise of the assault, and the resulting speed of the advance inland, so disorganised the Nineteenth Army that its commander, General Friedrich Wiese, never succeeded in assembling the bulk of his forces to attempt to contain the beachhead. By the end of August, he had lost four of the nine divisions that had been available to him, in whole or in part, on the 15th; all of the rest had suffered heavy losses in both men and equipment; he had lost

Toulon and Marseille; he had given up nearly 60,000 prisoners, and, faced with the threat of being outflanked and cut off by the simultaneous successes of the United States Seventh and Third Armies, he was withdrawing northward and had abandoned all of France south and south-west of Lyon.

It would not be correct to say that surprise was the only factor entering into the Nineteenth Army's failure to put up appreciable resistance to the Seventh Army's northward drive. The weakness of the Riviera garrison, which made possible the accomplishment of a decisive breakthrough as early as D plus Two, was a result of two factors: the enemy's conviction that the attack would come somewhere else, and the fact that his overall strength in southern France was on the deadline.

In early June 1944, prior to the Overlord assault on Normandy, the enemy had disposed 16 divisions in southern France (south of the Loire) for the defence of the Mediterranean and Bay of Biscay coasts.

However, the Overlord operation, and the subsequent breakthrough into Brittany, led to a reshuffling of these forces. The Nineteenth Army lost the 9th Panzer Division and the 271st, 272nd and 277th Infantry Divisions – it gained the 11th Panzer (transferred from First Army), the 198th Infantry (from Russia, reinforced by Bohemian units) and the 716th Infantry, which had been badly mauled in Normandy and sent south for a refit. These, together with the divisions it had retained through the shuffle, gave the Nineteenth Army nine divisions at the time of the Dragoon landing.

In summary, after the operation, prisoners taken on the last day of the month brought the total to 57,068 since D-Day. The enemy had also lost an unestimated number of dead and wounded and large quantities of equipment; he had abandoned two divisions to their fate in Toulon and Marseille, and had lost two others to guard duty on the Italian border.

But by deciding on evacuation early in the battle (the disengagement order had been issued on D plus Four), then carrying it out boldly despite our efforts to block the route, Nineteenth Army had salvaged a considerable portion of its strength for renewal of the fight on the approaches to the Fatherland. In particular the 11th Panzer Division had escaped and was to be met again in subsequent weeks."

Aimé Fallère, age 26, was one of the first inhabitants of Cannes La Bocca to see US troops arriving. After being captured in 1940, while fighting in the French Army, he escaped to work as a member of the Comité de Liberation.

"We all knew that the Americans were on their way, but it always seemed a dream because we had no way of knowing when. We had no means of communication and everything we heard was based on rumour, though a few people sometimes managed to listen to the English radio. We all knew about the Allied landing in June in Normandy, and we were all waiting and praying for our freedom to come.

Cannes wasn't a heavily occupied town in comparison with the North – it was a bit like a holiday resort for the Germans. But the Gestapo headquarters was based in the Montfleury Hotel and the small islands opposite the town were crawling with German troops. A huge wooden wall was built along the seafront and no civilians were allowed on the sea road.

We knew from 14 August that our liberation would soon come. On that day, two French warships, the *Emil Bertin* and the *Georges Leygues*, appeared in the Bay of Cannes. The next day we heard that American bombers were destroying the major bridges and viaducts in the Alpes Maritimes and the Var – the main rail line for German convoys.

The Germans knew the Americans were coming before we did. It was all so unreal. They just packed up and left on the evening of 23 August. They were in flight, but it was all very ordered. There was no panic – but before going, the German troops blew up Cannes Harbour.

It was on 24 August at about 11 o'clock in the morning, when I saw two American soldiers standing in the street in Cannes La Bocca. When I saw them I started shivering all over and I still shiver when I think about it now. It was a feeling of unforgettable joy – but fear at the same time. Deliverance had come in the shape of these two Americans.

There weren't many people about at the time and nobody spoke any English. The soldiers gave out some chewing gum and then walked away. A couple of hours later, a force of about 100 Americans walked through the town, giving out chewing gum, chocolate and cigarettes. The women kissed them and we all danced and sang. It was complete euphoria. The joy and the look on people's faces was unforgettable.

After that the main army came through with the tanks and we knew our liberation had finally come. The look on the face of every man, woman and child was the same – an explosion of joy. It's a day I shall never forget."

Monique Acerbo was just six years old when the Allies arrived in her home town of Marseille, but she clearly recalls the dramatic events that occurred in the weeks leading up to the German surrender.

"During the war my family lived in the Quartier St Gabrielle to the north of Marseille. When the bombing started in May we were evacuated for safety with some friends and relations to a small hamlet further inland called Le Grande Prêtre, a short way from the village of Destrousse. At that time my mother was pregnant with my sister Danielle. Destrousse was occupied by German soldiers, and by August the Americans had reached the neighbouring village of Peypin. The Germans installed their cannons in readiness, and when the fighting began we were in the middle of it all. On 15 August, my mother gave birth to my sister, while the fighting was going on all around. The adults were terrified, but being so young I thought nothing of it.

Then we were evacuated to Destrousse. My parents thought it was the Germans coming for us, but it was a group of American soldiers. They took us to an old *château*, owned by three sisters, all spinsters. We stayed there about three hours. Then the Americans came back for us and took us to my grandmother's house in Destrousse. They were very kind. They gave us tins of condensed milk, biscuits, corned beef and chewing gum, and made us shelter from the fire in the cellar. We stayed there, about 20 of us, for 21 days. The rest of the village had been evacuated and there was no way for us to get out.

The house was next to the main road running through the village, and there was a small peep-hole through which the adults could see what was going on. We had taken the food that the Americans had given us down into the cellar, along with some fruit and whatever we could find, but it didn't last long. My mother had no milk to give my sister. Her own had dried up and we didn't understand how to use the tins of condensed milk, so she was fed for weeks just on herbal tea. We had no radio and no cooking facilities.

I was with some cousins of my own age, and to us it was an adventure. We weren't scared, but the adults wouldn't let us look out of the peep-hole. I remember there was a German soldier who one day stole a ring from a dead woman by cutting off her finger. The Americans caught him and rounded up 15 young Germans to kill as a reprisal. I saw them marched at gunpoint into the cemetery. Then I heard gunfire as they shot each one.

Both the Germans and Americans had loudhailers, which kept us informed of what was going on. But I remember the great celebrations when it was all over. We adored the Americans – they gave us chocolate and chewing gum. When we finally returned to Marseille, it was quite a shock. Half the town had been demolished."

Eastern Front –
Soviet Revenge

As exhausted German tank crews and Panzer grenadiers licked their wounds during the night of 12/13 July 1943, Kursk no longer an attainable objective, few of them had the energy to think beyond the needs of the moment – a drink, a smoke, something to eat and the merciful respite of sleep. What even fewer can have realised was that this would be the tenor of their existence for the remainder of the war, the basic needs of survival overriding any thoughts of renewing the offensive. From this point onwards, despite many brilliant local successes to prove that the Wehrmacht was still a formidable fighting force, the initiative had passed inexorably to the Russians who were now poised to reclaim their homeland from the German intruders.

Léon Degrelle was Commander of the Belgian *Legion Wallonie* fighting with the SS-Division *Wiking* and witnessed the horrific human suffering from the cold and hunger in the Cherkassy pocket around the middle of February 1944.

"From our makeshift position in Nowo-Buda we had been expecting the breakthrough to come on Monday. By Tuesday it had still not come. When would it happen? What were we to live on in the meantime – that is if we managed to escape the bullets? I brought in some horses which had been used to pull the carts carrying the wounded to Sanderowka. I picked out the most resourceful of the Walloons under my command and put them on the horses, 'Get going! See what you can find. Go into the *isbas* (peasant huts), the ones furthest out, under the noses of the Russians if need be. Get some stuff to bake bread with. Go on, and make it snappy!'

I had turned up a few bakers among our men. There was a half-destroyed oven in my *isba*. They soon got it to work again. A few hours later the riders came back with sacks of flour flung over their saddles. We still needed yeast. There wasn't an ounce to be had. Our riders set off again, searched everything and found a small sack of sugar. With flour and sugar you could get something together.

By the end of the afternoon I was sending round strange-tasting plate-shaped pieces of bread to the positions. Each man got a quarter of one of these strange loaves. Some other men had brought back cattle. We slaughtered them immediately and cut them up into several hundred pieces. We couldn't rustle up any stoves, so we made some clay ovens outside the doors and the men who were unfit for fighting roasted blood-soaked pieces of meat over the fire using pokers and bayonets. We had no salt or pepper, but at least everyone got their twice-daily ration of more or less roasted beef, which they tore into like savages...

There was a field kitchen two kilometres north of Sanderowka where several hundred trucks stood sunk into the mud. Our cooks managed to rustle up a fantastic stew out of the most bizarre ingredients...

Wherever we found ourselves, we soon came under enemy fire. Sanderowka was under fire day and night from 'Stalin's organs'. Wherever we went we came upon dead horses, smashed-up vehicles and corpses, which we no longer had time to bury. We had turned the *kolkhoz* (Russian collective farm) into a field hospital, which was open on all sides, but at least provided a roof for our wounded soldiers. We had completely run out of medicaments, and there was no more material for bandages to be found in the whole of the pocket. To get hold of bandaging our medical orderlies had to wrestle the peasant girls to the floor and pull down their long military underpants – presents from German Don Juans. They screamed and ran off, holding on tight to their skirts. We just let them scream. Two or three seriously wounded men were provided with some kind of emergency bandaging by this method... The war had its grotesque side as well.

The Stalin's organs bombarded the *kolkhoz*. The roof caved in. Dozens of wounded men were killed in the bloody confusion. Others went crazy, letting out terrifying screams. The barracks had to be evacuated. Even our wounded men now had to stay out in the open. For several days and nights more than 1,200 wounded men from other units lay out in the open on hundreds of farm carts on a bed of straw. The rain had soaked them to the skin and now they were at the mercy of the biting frost.

Since Tuesday morning it had been 20 degrees below freezing, and lying outside in their hundreds were wounded men whose faces were nothing more than a hideous violet mass, men with amputated arms and legs, dying men, their eyes rolling convulsively.

Snow fell endlessly in the evening. It was soon a foot high. Twenty or thirty thousand people waited in our village for some kind of military end to the drama, with no sort of accommodation. It was reminiscent of Napoleon's army retreating across the Beresina. Oblivious to the danger, the people stood out in the open in groups around the fires they had lit in the snow. Sleep was impossible. Lying out in this biting cold would have meant certain death. The flames from burning *isbas* could be seen from far away. In the valley hundreds of little fires burned, around which disconsolate shadows huddled, soldiers with reddened eyes and ten-day-old beards, warming their yellow fingers. They waited. Nothing happened.

They were still there in the morning – they didn't even bother trying to get some food. Their eyes looked to the south-west. Wild rumours were flying round. Hardly anyone listened to them any more. The silence was suddenly broken by the Stalin's organs. Everyone threw themselves down into the snow and then got to their feet again wearily. Wounded men screamed out. The doctors saw to them, to salve their consciences...

Twelve hundred wounded men still lay on the carts. Many of them had given up asking for help. They lay crushed together under a miserable cover, all their efforts geared to the task of staying alive. Hundreds of vehicles stood in a confused huddle. Horses reduced to skeletons chewed on the wooden slats of the carts in front of them. Here and there you could hear isolated groans and cries of wounded men. Crazed men raised themselves up, bleeding and with snow in their hair. What was the point of driving yourself crazy thinking of how you might feed these unfortunate men? They hid their heads under the covers. Every now and then the drivers would brush off the snow from these lifeless bodies with their hands. Many had been lying on these carts for ten days. They could feel themselves rotting alive. No injection could ease their most unbearable pains. There was nothing to be had. Nothing! Nothing! All they could do was wait – wait for death or a miracle. The number of yellowing bodies beside the carts kept increasing. Nothing could surprise us any more, nothing could stir our feelings. When you've witnessed such horrors your senses are numb."

Lieutenant Erich Jainek, age 23, was serving with the German Panzer Grenadier Division *Feldherrnhalle* during the bloody battles around Vitebsk, Bobruisk and Mogilev in December and January 1943–44 during which the German Army Group Centre was finally destroyed.

"A total of 2.5 million soldiers in 185 Soviet divisions were deployed against Army Group Centre, which comprised around 600,000 German soldiers.

The Forty-Ninth Soviet Army under Lieutenant-General Grischin was given the task of advancing to Mogilev across Height 103. The 4th Air Arm under General Werschin was ordered to bombard the German positions at Mogilev and destroy the German artillery positions. The Russian bombers and their infantry regiments attacked.

This same evening, Major-General von Steinkeller was given the order by the Army High Command to take his division (the 60th Panzer Grenadier Division *Feldherrnhalle*), to which I belonged, and plug the 'huge holes' in the main combat line. Five T-34s appeared out of the dust. Two storm guns followed, one on each flank of the wedge. They pulled up and fired. The shells whizzed towards our anti-tank guns at the edge of the wood. We opened fire and shot up 17 T-34s with our 7.5 cm guns.

The Russian shells blew up the ammunition post serving our own anti-tank guns. As the tanks came closer, T-mines (flat anti-tank mines) and explosives were used. This is where the Niemann group showed its mettle. Our losses were increased by the minute. My comrades were dead and so I put another ammunition belt in the 42 machine gun and fired at the Russians running towards me. The tank shells of the Russians lashed down over my cover and over 40 T-34s rolled on in the direction of our artillery and collection point.

They moved on in wedge formation towards Minsk. In this bloody battle, two German armies went under and few men survived. The few groups of German soldiers who got out of this only did so thanks to the divisions who held their ground right up to the last moment – the *Feldherrnhalle* Division, the 102nd Infantry Division, the 296th Division, the 36th Infantry Division and a few other units, who fought on against superior numbers. The 110th, 197th, 45th and 206th

Infantry Divisions also continued to fight, or at least the parts of them which had not been wiped out.

In the course of a terrible, grinding, deadly odyssey, my company was ground down to only eight men. Ten minutes later I headed off. We waded through the deep snow at a fierce 40 degrees below, on field compass reading 277 – directly west. By using our *Do-Werfer* I managed to get through with eight men under the cover of the woods. We finally reached the advance division of the 18th Panzer Division, drained, hungry and cold, at the end of a three-day march, during which we had to fight the partisans. I described to the Tank Commander what had happened and compiled a report showing where the Russian artillery and units were.

During a counterattack with the 18th Panzer Division, under cover of darkness, I was seriously wounded. I was taken to the main field hospital on the back of a storm gun. There they discovered that I had second or third degree frostbite on both feet. It was only when I was at the hospital that I realised that I had marched about 130 km to escape being taken prisoner by the Russians. This Russian break-through could only have succeeded due to an act of betrayal."

Trofim Yaskin was a canal boat mechanic when he was called up in 1942. By 1944 he was battalion staff officer in the Russian 42nd Rifle Division and, in June, was one of the first over the Dnieper.

"Emerging from the Dnieper, we saw on the right bank, about 400–500 metres away, the settlement of Dobreika lying at the foot of the steep slope. Several one-horse and two-horse enemy carts were hurriedly making off…

To our dismay, it turned out that only two or three men in our company could swim. There had been no order from the regimental commander about the battalion crossing the river, but there was no time to waste. We had to force the crossing before the enemy had time to organise its defence.

At first I thought of dismantling part of a house that was about 60 metres downstream, but there were some beams nearby and I ordered them to be rolled down to the river to make a raft. When this was built, one of our soldiers, a Tartar, swam across the river with a doubled telephone wire that was attached to it as a towrope. We rapidly crossed to the other side, taking with us a heavy machine gun, anti-tank rifles and anti-tank grenades. The enemy detachment in

Dobreika did not put up much opposition to the incisive action of our troops, and fled in panic.

Thus, literally under the enemy's nose, we had seized an important line without loss, and were able to hold the height until the whole company came up, followed by the rest of the battalion which made possible a strengthening of the bridgehead and the crossing of the regiment.

Literally within half an hour, before we had time to dig in properly, six 'Ferdinands' came at us out of the wood on our left. Our gunners immediately knocked out two of these with several shots. Two of the others, having attached themselves to the stricken tanks, pulled them back into the wood and the others also went into cover...

Some time later I was with the machine gun and did not notice a car which drove up from somewhere. I saw it only when it was close to us. We ceased fire, and the Germans also stopped shooting. But then, when they had evidently realised what had happened, they started again, very powerfully, but by then it was too late. The car, rushing past us from the right, rolled down the hill and our intelligence officer Pinuzhnyi jumped out, pulling behind him a Fritz signals warrant officer. There was a transmitter in the car, and also a rocket pistol, with a variety of signal rockets as well as staff documents, maps and even films.

Intelligence personnel had boldly infiltrated into the enemy's rear and carried out important and timely reconnaissance. That is what had happened on this occasion. First Lieutenant Pinuzhnyi and his men had penetrated into the enemy rear. The Germans, not suspecting this activity, were calmly moving along in their car. Pinuzhnyi had recklessly stopped the car, captured the warrant officer and shot two soldiers who resisted."

Elena Chukhnyuk was one of a number of female locomotive drivers in Russia. Rail workers had a vital role in bringing supplies up to advanced military depots, and civilians worked in close cooperation with the military to keep the supply lines open. She recalls transporting munitions in a zone close to the front line.

"Three of our fighters dived in. The enemy planes now scattered, and one immediately crashed in close to us. The explosion was so powerful that it seemed as though the locomotive had jumped off the rails. We all cheered up, having got rid of the German vermin.

As he flew off, one pilot twice dipped his wings, as if to wish us a good trip.

We passed two stations, then enemy planes appeared again. Now the train endured attacks every 20 or 30 minutes. At one station two freight cars caught fire, but the crew put the fire out without uncoupling them. In a new attack the flat-car with the guns was blown to pieces. Two machine gunners were killed by fragments. No efforts were spared to get the flat-car off the line. The Hitlerites were chattering away with their machine guns while we, not paying any attention to the enemy, fixed up cables and rails so that the flat-car was thrown to one side and the train coupled up again.

There were four more attacks while we waited for the track to be put right. So long as the train was going and there was work to be done, we did not think of danger. Being caught in an air attack is not very pleasant. There was nowhere to hide – like being in a trap.

A locomotive came towards us from the other direction. 'But where's your train?' we asked. The driver waved his arms hopelessly. A fitter was lying on the floor of the cab with his leg torn off at the hip."

Ivan Varzalov was a technician with the rank of Junior Lieutenant, serving in the vehicle platoon of a Russian signals battalion. He recalls the ferocious Ukraine offensive in 1944 to reclaim their lost territory.

"Before the start of the Carpathian campaign, the offensive of our 11th Rifle Corps was so powerful and victorious in the Chernovtsy and Kolomy areas that the fascist warriors got confused.

Some of their detachments, left behind by other troops fleeing in disorder, hid in the woods, hoping somehow to make their way through to their own side across the front. Those left behind lay in wait for our detachments.

As it turned out, their plan was to beat off our fighting vehicles to enable them to catch up with their retreating units. A fierce exchange of fire developed, but the soldiers of my detachment kept calm. Orientating themselves perfectly in the complex night situation, they took up defensive positions and then closed with the enemy and destroyed him.

I can remember another incident. There was a big battle, so hard-fought on both sides that a small settlement changed hands several times. It suddenly became apparent that one of my detachment's radio vehicles had been left in the area between the two sides. The Germans kept it under constant bombardment, trying to drag it over to their side. In the depth of the night, illuminated by the flaring of enemy parachute rockets, under a hail of bullets and exploding mortar bombs, we pulled the vehicle back to our own people, literally from under the noses of the enemy."

Nadezhda Mozharova, age 27, had been called up as an army nurse in 1941, and by 1944 was a medical orderly. In the Russian Army, the women's nursing role was not necessarily a non-combatant one, as she recalls.

"In this battle I was with the soldiers in the trenches. As soon as there was a moment of quiet, you fell asleep so soundly that you didn't wake up when the cannonade started up again. It was at a moment like this that a soldier shook me and said, 'You're wanted at the observation post'.

Colonel Demchenko, commanding the Guards regiment, had been injured in the head by shrapnel. The telephone rang, with the commander of the division calling Demchenko. I wanted to take the receiver and say that he was wounded, but he shouted, 'Don't you dare report that I'm wounded!' and he took it himself. The division commander ordered us to hold on at any cost – the battalion was advancing far ahead and we had to hold the ground that had been won.

A rumour floated around the trenches that we were surrounded. The regiment commander jumped out of the trench, shouting, 'Communists! Follow me! We're going forward!' He was the first to go into the attack. Pulling my revolver from its holster, I rushed after him, and at that moment felt a lashing at my legs, and I crashed down on to the snow.

Apparently an explosive bullet had gone through one leg and lodged in the other. Spreading out a groundsheet, some soldiers dragged me in a snowstorm from the front line to the immediate rear – first the regimental dressing station, then the divisional medical post. Still in my sheepskin, they put me straight on to the operating table. I don't remember anything until I woke up.

The chief surgeon of the division soon came along and said bitterly, 'There was nothing else we could do. We've amputated your right leg'."

The Marianas – Turkey Shoot

The islands of the Marianas chain point like an arrow at the heart of Japan. When the Americans landed on Saipan on 15 June 1944, the stage was set for a major sea battle in the Philippine Sea. In a two-day action, Admiral Marc Mitscher's fast-carrier strike-force, Task Force 58, tangled with Admiral Jisaburo Ozawa's First Mobile Fleet. By the end of the 15th, 240 Japanese planes had been shot down, and two carriers sunk, including Ozawa's flagship Taiho. *American tactics and intelligence, combined with numerical superiority and the poor training of new Japanese pilots, made the exercise so straightforward that it became known as 'The Great Marianas Turkey Shoot'. At around 16.00 the following afternoon, Mitscher's planes discovered the position of the Japanese fleet. Taking a calculated risk – the fleets were 300 miles (483 km) apart and the US planes would not return before dark – he launched a 216-plane attack, which sank the carrier* Hiyo, *damaged* Zuikaku *and* Chiyoda *and the battleship* Haruna, *and sank two oilers. Although it would make the ships vulnerable to attack, Mitscher ordered his carriers to switch on their landing lights to assist his returning pilots. The gamble worked: although 80 aircraft were lost in crashes, most of the pilots and crew were recovered. Ozawa's force was decisively beaten and defeat left the Japanese Combined Fleet ill-equipped to stop the invasion of the Philippines four months later. June 1944 would prove unforgettable for the land and carrier-based pilots of America and Japan. Two accounts by pilots, one from each side, illustrate this.*

Commander David McCampbell was Commander of Air Group 15, the three fighting squadrons of the US carrier *Essex* which took part in the battle against the Japanese Combined Fleet. He later became the most celebrated of US naval airmen and was awarded the Medal of Honor.

"June 12, 1944, Admiral Raymond Spruance had led the 5th US Fleet to the Philippine Sea, preparing to invade Saipan and the other major islands of the Marianas chain, which were needed as air bases for the B-29 bombers to strike Japan. My carrier, the USS *Essex*, was part of the fleet's Task Group 58.4, which comprised three carriers, three cruisers and twelve destroyers. The other carriers were the *Langley* and the *Cowpens*. Rear Admiral W K Harrill was the officer in command. Altogether there were 15 carriers now with the 5th Fleet.

Our first task was to soften up the air defences of Saipan, and the smaller island of Pagan which was important because it housed an airfield with one small runway, and a number of barracks and shops. Saipan was the first objective. The job – destroy enemy aircraft.

Just before one o'clock on the afternoon of 11 June, we had the order to launch the planes. I led the air strike, which consisted of 15 fighters from the *Essex* and two dive-bombers along with a dozen fighters from the *Cowpens* and a dozen from the *Langley*. The two dive-bombers were rescue planes, equipped with extra life-rafts and other survival gear to drop to downed pilots. Later an amphibian or a submarine or a destroyer would pick the pilots up.

Seven of our F6F fighters carried 350-pound demolition bombs, and they dived from 12,000 feet and bombed at 2,500 feet, and then formed a strafing line and strafed the island from east to west. The other eight fighters stayed above flying cover until the bombing runs ended, and then they went down to strafe. For an hour and a half they concentrated on strafing runs on Saipan's airfields and sea-plane bases.

The Japanese drew first blood. On the way in over Tanapag Harbour, Lieutenant Kenney's fighter was hit by flak. He was diving but he just continued to dive straight down to the water and splashed. Lieutenant-Commander Brewer led the fighter attack on the harbour seaplane ramp. I saw his bomb strike in the middle of three seaplanes parked neatly on the ramp, and destroy all three.

Brewer then strafed, came around and headed out to sea. Five miles out at sea, northwest of Marpi Point, Brewer and Ensign R E Fowler Junior spotted a dark green Kawanishi flying boat called an Emily, with the dull red circles. They attacked. As they came up, several other fighters were shooting at the Emily. Brewer attacked from above on the side of the plane – he said he saw his bullets hit the Emily's number two engine and the port wing. Ensign Fowler reported that he attacked the cockpit and noticed that the plane was smoking. Twenty seconds later the flying boat turned over on one wing, dropped with engine aflame and smoke coming from the fuselage, and struck the water. It exploded in a geyser of smoke, water and flame.

Lieutenant-Commander Brewer turned west of the town of Garapan and saw three Zero fighters, but by the time he arrived on the scene, they had all been shot down by other American fighters.

This was our first encounter as an air group with enemy aircraft. We had heard a great deal about the Zero fighter. I was pleased to note that the F6F could stay with the Zero in turns, climbs and dives – particularly at altitudes above 12,000 feet, where most of the air action took place. I noted two deficiencies of the Zero – its lack of armour and its unprotected gas tanks. All but one of the Zeros I saw shot down that day went down in flames.

At about 2.30 pm I was flying 'mattress' (low air cover) and observing the attack. Suddenly a Zero came down from above our fighters and pulled up in a high wingover on my port beam. I turned into the Zero and gave it a short burst from close up – not more than 250 yards. The Zero turned over on its left wing. I followed and got in another short burst, got on the tail and gave the Zero another burst. The pilot made another wingover, but he was already going down. The plane fell off on the right wing and spiralled toward the sea. Another F6F followed the Zero down, firing. I remained in position. The Zero hit the water without burning and sank. No head appeared.

On 19 June Admiral Ozawa launched his first strike against the American fleet, beginning from Guam. At 10 o'clock our radar picked up a large force of 'bogies' approaching, distance 150 miles.

At that point Commander Brewer was already in the air, in command of the combat air patrol, and he was ordered to take his planes up to 24,000 feet. We heard Brewer shout 'Tallyho! 24 rats, 16 hawks, no fish at 18,000' (24 fighters, 16 dive-bombers and no torpedo planes at 18,000 feet).

He then spotted 15 Judys (Aichi dive-bombers) at 18,000 feet in tight formation with four Zeros on each flank – and 1,000 feet above and behind, 16 more Zeros. Brewer selected the leading dive-bomber and came up to 800 feet from the plane. The Judy exploded so quickly it was unbelievable. He flew through the debris and attacked another. This one blew up too, half the wing fell off and the plane cartwheeled into the sea.

Two minutes after Brewer's 'Tallyho', my fighter was launched, and I led 12 fighters to join in fighting off the attackers – but by the time my fighters were organised, the fighter controller announced that another raid was coming in – 50 planes travelling 150 knots, 45 miles to the east. I was to intercept and stop them.

I took them up to 25,000 feet. Two were affected by the altitude and their engines began to cut out, so I ordered them to orbit over the carrier. We had altitude and speed and when we reached the enemy formation, were able to make a high-speed run, leaving four planes above for protection.

My first target was a Judy (dive-bomber) on the left flank and approximately halfway back in the formation. It was my intention after completing the run on the plane, to pass under it, retire across the formation and take under fire a plane on the right flank with a low side attack. The plans became upset when the first plane I fired at blew up practically in my face, and caused a pullout above the entire formation. I remember being unable to get to the other side fast enough, feeling as though every rear gunner had his fire directed at me.

My second attack was made on a Judy on the right flank of the formation, which burned favourably on one pass and fell away from the formation out of control – a rather long burst from above rear to tail position. Retirement was made below and ahead.

My efforts were directed to retaining as much speed as possible and working myself ahead into position for an attack on the leader. A third pass was made from below rear on a Judy which was hit and smoking as he pulled out and down from the formation.

After my first pass on the leader with no visible damage observed, pullout was made below and to the left. Deciding that it would be easier to concentrate on the port wingman than on the leader, my next pass was an above-rear from seven o'clock, causing the wingman to explode in an envelope of flames. Breaking away down and to the left placed me in a position for a below rear run on the leader from six o'clock, after which I worked on his tail and continued to fire until he burned furiously and spiralled down out of control. During the last bursts on the leader, gun stoppages occurred. Both port and starboard guns were charged in an attempt to clear before firing again. I decided I must be out of ammunition and started back for the carrier."

Yoshida Katsuyoshi was a naval warrant officer in the Japanese 202 Air Group when the Americans showed signs of moving against Biak Island. The Group transferred to the Island of Yap and then to the Solong base to make preliminary arrangements for operations.

"On 3 June, we were ordered to attack the enemy landing points on Biak. Apart from us, there were Army Hayabusa fighters, and Suisei (Comet) carrier-borne aircraft of 503 Air Group. We set off in high spirits.

When the carrier-borne planes had finished their attack, we dived down and strafed the enemy positions, firing at will. The skies over Biak were not the clear skies of the south – they were leaden and overcast, and I took off my tinted flying goggles during the attack. It was more important to improve, however slightly, my field of vision, though it added to the dangers. Ahead of me, and below, the carrier-borne bombers waggled their stubby wings and went into a dive, showing their bellies as they went down. Brave chaps. I watched them, but I also kept my eyes peeled for enemy aircraft coming suddenly in to the attack, but no enemy planes showed up – and, oddly enough, there didn't seem to be much flak either.

Then four planes of Sakaguchi's section, in front and to our left, went into a dive and disappeared from view. A short pause while I checked above and behind, then I signalled to my wing planes and we too went into a dive. So far, we had concentrated on what was happening in the sky, but as we went into our dive, I noticed the angle to the objective was pretty steep. Still, I could see a fair amount of supplies, tanks and ammunition had accumulated along the sandy beaches of the shoreline. I had the prize in front of my eyes and I could hardly change my goal now.

As I approached, the ack-ack fire was more intense than I had bargained for – the enemy was putting up a determined defence. I wasn't too clear about where the carrier-borne units were, or the section which had dived before, but I pounded the shore at close range. I could see enemy troops running away into the sea, as I strafed the stores, but I did not aim at them. I mean, from my experience so far, it was difficult to hit a running man.

The diving angle was poor, so I pulled out sooner than usual, but perhaps because I'd gone over the terminal velocity, my plane gave a protesting scream. When I looked round, I saw my wing plane climbing and almost at a stroke we had climbed to 10,000 feet. I drew breath, a sigh of relief, and looked around. My wing man was keeping tight close behind me. I could not make out what was happening on the ground, apart from a few glimpses snatched here and there between the clouds. I wondered whether to dive again, and put her nose down, then, as I looked in the direction of New Guinea, I could see, far ahead in front, a dog-fight in progress. I flew straight towards it, and saw our planes were latching on to a four-engined PB2Y flying boat. I joined in. As our aircraft closed in for the attack, a door opened in the enemy plane and a W/T set and some heavy objects were thrust out. This was to enable him to increase speed a little – he was doing his best to escape. He was too low for me to fire at him from below, his weak spot, so I attacked right in front, and as he did a slow right turn and came within range, my shells passed by him on the left. I had already used up a fair amount of ammunition in the land strafing, and in this frontal attack I ran out of 20 mm ammunition.

Surely I must have scored some hits? I looked for some time, I felt sure he was going to go down – but he kept hanging on. I wanted to try one more attack, but I was out of ammunition, so there was no point. I turned towards Babo Base without being able to check the outcome.

On the west of New Guinea, Babo was in a marshy zone, which, seen from above, looked like solid earth. In fact it was only like that near the airfield. Further out there was jungle and swamp up to your waist, a place of oil gushers. When I looked down from above on the L-shaped runway. I had the feeling something was wrong, and when I landed, I heard that Captain Takao and WO Furuya of 603 Air

Group had gone up to meet an attack by P38s some time before, and had been killed.

On 9 June, army reinforcements were being sent to Biak where the situation had gone against us. They were being taken in six destroyers and close escort was being provided by army and navy planes, taking it in turns. I Section, Captain Kagami, CPO Okano, PO Miyagaki, and II Section, myself and CPO Mishimoto and CPO Omori, made for Manokwari. We found the six destroyers steaming eastward full speed ahead and, judging from their wake, they must have been doing something like 40 knots.

About 6,000 feet above them, as they zig-zagged, flew several B-24 bombers, carrying out horizontal bombing attacks. Our six Zeros instantly flew into the midst of the enemy bombers. Unfortunately, the ack-ack fire from our destroyers kept coming up to us, uncomfortably close. In such a situation, all we could do was put our fate in Heaven's hands. Accurate aiming was not necessary, and we pressed the enemy close from the side, with one attack after the other. Then, when I took a glance in front and above, I saw those hated P38s sneaking up on us. There must have been more than 20 or 30 planes. We were too low to challenge them to aerial combat and there was no time to take up a position of advantage. We sailed right into the middle of them, a confused *mêlée*, and blazed away. Accurate aiming was out of the question, and all we could do was dodge their fire. I spotted my chance, I came out of the *mêlée*. I'd been hit two or three times, and with my wing tanks shot through I was likely to turn into a ball of flame at any minute. But I got back to Ekman Island base. PO Miyagaki failed to return.

On 17 June, I was transferred from Kau to Peleliu. It was the night before what was called afterwards 'The Battle of the Marianas' (the Battle of the Philippine Sea). In discussions, it was decided that 202 Air Group was to fill up the bomber gap. All our planes were to be fitted out with 60 kg bombs. We would become a fighter-bomber unit, and attack enemy forces landing on Saipan.

The next day, 18 June, reveille was at 3.30 am, and we set off, breathing in great lungfuls of the bracing air of Peleliu. After one and a half hours, we landed at the airfield on Yap. The ground crews bustled to and fro, filling us up with ammunition, bombs and fuel. At the control station, the Z-flag flew, as it had traditionally since the Battle of the Japan Sea, as if to stress the crucial importance of this battle for our country. I squatted down beside the runway to smoke a cigarette, and Furumura came up. He had been in the same reserve training unit as me. He was just as I remembered him, quite unchanged, the same thick black bushy eyebrows. We hadn't seen each other for a long time and there was a lot to talk about. From what he said, we were to set off together, as decoy planes, with the Suisei carrier-borne bombers. We slapped each other on the back and said we'd see who was the more skilful pilot of the two. I don't know whether it was a joke, or whether he was being serious, but he said 'I'll show you a good place to die'. That's how it ended.

We set out at 12 noon, a large formation of about 200 aircraft, and made a big detour east of Guam. The plan was to attack enemy ships at sea south-east of Saipan. When you fly for three hours with a load of two 60 kg bombs, the hand grasping the joystick gets tired. I felt tense just after setting off, but after an hour had gone by, then two hours, I felt pains in my legs and bottom in the narrow seat, and dull-spirited.

We were flying in a bomber role, so other fighter units were in formation in front of us and behind, and below and above us, acting as escort. Soon the southern shore of Guam came up on our left, and we came out over the eastern sea. About 30 minutes later, we were in enemy skies. I had been wounded two years before, and my neck was still not in good shape, so in order to be able to keep a lookout to the rear, I unfastened my shoulder seat belt. Flying upside down had to be done with one lap-belt.

I turned my head left, then right, then tried to move so that I could see to my rear. I worked the 7.7 mm gun and, as a precaution, went through the loading procedure again. The foremost interceptor unit was a fair way ahead, with its accompanying escort flying above it. I noticed they were flying ahead of our bombing unit, but perhaps because of the clouds I could not make out where they were making for.

After a while the bomber unit command plane began to lose altitude. Finally it seemed to be dodging between the clouds to go into a bombing run. I changed over the fuel cock on the wing tanks and took off my glasses. In an emergency I had the habit of removing my glasses, since I felt them to be a nuisance.

High overhead, our escort unit and the enemy fighters were already engaged in dog-fights. Today, whatever happened, we were going to introduce the enemy to our 60 kg bombs, but below the clouds our field of vision was not too good, and apart from ten transport ships up ahead, no warships could be seen.

Suddenly a bunch of fighters, ours and the enemy's, came falling down through the sky ahead, to my right. At the same time there was an uproar on all sides, and little time to take aim at a target. Even for objectives close to, the distance was too great for the height. The instant I became aware of this, the ack-ack fire from below became more intense than anything I'd experienced so far. A pillar of flame, as if from a dozen heavy ack-ack machine guns, roared past like an express train.

I felt a long time had elapsed up to the time I burst through, and I took a quick glance above and below, but whether or not our bombing unit had spread out, what entered my field of vision was about 20 or 30 aircraft, apparently suspended over a 5,000-ton transport, but the angle was too narrow for horizontal bombing. Partly from impatience to return to my true role as a fighter, I dropped my bombs from both wings.

An enemy fighter came in to attack me from the right as I tried to confirm what had happened below me, and I switched to the right to dodge him. The joystick had stiffened, and I put some force into it and finally came out on top of the clouds, where both sides were engaged in dog-fights.

Some distance off, a number of aircraft were locked in combat and tracer shells flew to and fro. My wing plane was no longer behind me. I must have come out in the opposite direction of the cloud after dropping my bombs.

Then I tangled with a Grumman flying in the opposite direction. I made as if to climb and just an instant before colliding with him, I pulled the trigger from about 400 yards away. I'd meant to aim in front, but it shot past him to the right and behind. The cloud was thin, and I came out at once below it. The instant I was out, I could see I was somewhere off Saipan, I didn't know where, but I could see what looked like a military position and an enormous number of landing-craft.

I decided to dive straight down and strafe them. Aiming at a spot on the shoreline, I suddenly put her nose down. Once again, intense ack-ack fire came up at me. What ship was aiming at my plane? It seemed to be even fiercer than the ack-ack fire on shore. After glancing behind and above, I took aim at the enemy position which had come into my sights and squeezed the trigger. I felt terrific and let out a roar as if my 20 mm and 7.7 mm guns were bursting through at the landing craft which were touching down on the sandy strip of shore. The aircraft's nose juddered as I aimed and fired.

No flames burst out, so it wasn't very satisfactory, and I thought, let's put the finishing touches to it, but then I realised all my 20 mm ammunition had gone, so I climbed out through the middle of the dog-fight and turned the plane's nose towards Guam. As I looked around, I could see several streamers of black smoke on the surface of the sea, and in the sky, far off, distant aircraft looking like rubber balls.

A great many aircraft had returned to Guam by the time I came down. PO Kawada's big body was shaking and alive with gestures as he explained how he had shot down a Grumman. Below my flying cap, I was soaked in sweat.

Night came – 202 Air Group confirmed all its aircraft had returned, and gradually our spirits rose. But we had no quarters, and the evening meal was eaten sitting near our aircraft. We slept beneath the wings, using our life-jackets for pillows.

The next day, 19 June, we were attacked in the course of the morning by enemy fighter-bombers. Fierce encounter battles took place in the skies above the airfield, and we suffered casualities – a total of four pilots killed. In the evening the carrier-borne planes of 2 Air Flotilla were attacked by Grummans in the sky over the base, just as they came in to land. Half of them were shot to pieces before they even knew what was happening.

On 20 June, reinforcements for 202 Air Group flew in from Yap and went up to meet the Grummans as they came in again for the attack. They shot down a fair number, but CPO Saito of 301 Flying Unit was hit – his engine conked out and he had to make a forced landing just outside the town. He was injured by the impact, but even so he returned ahead of us in good spirits.

Day by day, the situation on Saipan grew steadily worse and here on Guam, we fighter units lost nearly all our usable machines from combat actions and the ceaseless night and day bombing by the enemy.

I was selected to go and see the situation on Saipan on 22 June, because no news had come through. We had had no spare time for repairs on Guam, and by this time there were only two Zeros left. They were guarded the way a tiger guards its cubs. It was considered a great honour for me to be picked out of so many scores of aircrew, and I set off with PO Yamashita of 603 Flying Unit at 3 am, coming out west of Rota Island. The sea was so covered with huge numbers of enemy ships that it was hard to know where you were. There were also dozens of scout planes above them, but they did not come near us. Down below were two or three large carriers.

On the way back, we flew at a height of around 21,000 feet and came into Guam from the north-east. We recced the situation on land for some time, and after confirming there was no danger, we landed.

We were attacked again, many times, on 23 June, but by this time we had no planes at all to send up against the enemy. When night came, reinforcements came in from 202 Air Group, making a marvellous landing in the darkness.

With the worst possible timing, my fever – malaria – broke out again on the 24th. Guam seemed to be done for, if the naval bombardment was anything to go by. Enemy landings couldn't be far off, I thought, but what could we do? We hadn't a single aircraft to send up against them. Nonetheless, I had a stroke of luck the following night. I think it was about 11 pm, a Type-1 Army Attack plane from Yokohama Air Group was on its way from Iwo Jima to make a night attack on Saipan. Its left engine conked out, and it had to make a forced landing. There were only a few people at the airfield, and after the engine was repaired, we asked the young aircraft commander, a captain, to take us with him. He agreed.

I don't recall clearly, I'm afraid, but I think that around seven of our eight men succeeded in escaping from Guam before the surrender. Early next morning, we set foot on Peleliu. For the first time, I became aware how hungry I was."

Burma – Jungle Nightmare

*F*ollowing the fall of Malaya and Singapore in early
1942, the Japanese enjoyed a reputation among
British, Australian and Indian troops as invincible jungle
fighters. By the spring, they had managed to push British
and Chinese troops back to the western borders of Burma
and into India. There, following the tough but indecisive
Arakan campaign, the British and Indian forces were to
win decisive battles at Kohima and Imphal in April 1944
and pave the way for the liberation of Burma. Between
April and July 1944, the Japanese 15th Army at Kohima
and Imphal surrounded 50,000 British and Indian troops
of IV Corps. During an 88-day siege, they failed to dislodge
the defenders, until, starved of supplies and suffering from
the monsoon, the Japanese were themselves defeated when
the XXXIII Corps fought through to relieve Kohima and
Imphal. Of the 65,000 Japanese dead, around half had
died from starvation and disease. The Burma campaign
was unlike most other theatres of war, in which it was clear
where your own territory ended and the enemy's began. This
is clear from the accounts of either side or trapped in the
middle as civilians.

**Martin McLane was Company Sergeant-Major of C Company,
2nd Battalion of the Durham Light Infantry. His story begins as
his men are on a tropical island, training before the Arakan
offensive. They have just received new guns.**

"As CSM, I was scheduled to have one of these new Thompson sub-machine guns. We had received them without any instructions whatever. The Company Commander came over to me and said, 'Bring my Thompson sub-machine gun – I want to shoot it'. Everybody wanted to shoot them – they were such an outstanding weapon.

The CC went on to the beach with me. He picks up the gun and fires one round. I said, 'Stop, sir. Wait. Wait'. He says, 'What's the matter?' 'I don't like the sound of that shot'. I was watching to see if I could see the streak of the round on the water.

'You're over-cautious. I'm going to fire'. He fired, and BANG. I looked round at this explosion, and I grabbed him – he was falling to the ground. I looked for wounds – but I couldn't find anything.

I was blaming myself – but it was not my fault really. The first round he'd fired hadn't cleared the barrel – so I would never have seen it on the sea. The second shot hadn't had a clear passage through the barrel, jammed and blew the gun to bits. Now that's just an example for what follows on later.

Eventually they decided to put us in by land, and we took over the positions from the Indian battalion which had been there for a few days. They had been having really jitter shoots-up. Now, jitters means that the Japanese, when they found anyone on defence, would fire crackers or spring grenades at you, hoping you would start firing and shooting them up. Or they would shout at you, trying to get you to fire, so they could pinpoint your positions. We were told on no account to fire until we saw the whites of their eyes and, being English lads, we all obeyed.

It was decided, after a few days, to put in an attack on their four strong positions. Now, we were near the sea on the right, but there was flat land where we were. We were in the jungle and partially out in the open. The water, when the monsoons came, used to sweep down from the ridge and gouge out rivers in the soft soil on the seaward side.

There were three dried river beds and we had to attack over them. My company was to attack two points where the Japanese had been for some time. They used slave labour to dig a deep hole in the ground. They'd criss cross it with tree trunks to get a two-tiered bunker, solid against all sorts of shooting up.

Before we were due to attack, someone in a high observation post had seen a carrying party of Japs coming up with ammunition for these bunkers of a night-time.

They decided to send our guerrilla platoon, a group of our own men, trained like commandos, to do special stunts. Lieutenant Wilson was to take them across the *chung* (a water or tidal river), down by the beach and keeping them under cover, down to Fall Point, with an intent to ambush the Japanese carrying party. They all had Thompson sub-machine guns, rifles and grenades. They were dressed up commando-style, with blackened faces.

When they were due to put the attack in, I was on stand-by at our observation post, listening for the Thompson sub-machine guns firing – and I never heard them. But I heard grenades bumping. All of a sudden, up come running these lads, the guerrilla platoon, cursing and blinding – their Thompson sub-machine guns had blown up, the same as ours.

They should have had an enquiry on mine to find out the cause of the thing blowing up – but they didn't. Being wartime, they just accepted it as maybe a dirty barrel – but I had just cleaned the thing. They decided that the American ammunition mustn't be waterproof. The propellant charge had got damp and wasn't driving the round out with sufficient force to send it out of the barrel. The second round followed on because it was an automatic action, and blew the gun up.

Fortunately no-one was hurt. They withdrew my company out of the line altogether and decided to change all our ammunition. The next day we went back down to our positions for the attack. We set off very early in the morning, in the dark, and filed our way down to a dried river bed. We lined up there for the attack. The artillery pounded the area in front with three-inch shells. They made quite a din.

It was just breaking daylight and over the top we went, with two platoons, 10 and 11, and Company Headquarters. Another platoon was detached to attack the other positions. My orders were to move the men from the first dried-up river bed and into the second – then wait. The other two platoons were to push on and go into the attack from there. Now they had to go to the third river bed, so I halted my men.

The CC didn't come up, and I decided to move up to the next river bed. As I went up to the next one, I saw a Japanese in a fox-hole. I didn't know how many were in there. I got my Thompson sub-machine gun up – and it wouldn't fire. You've got grenades, but if you fling them in close proximity you'd kill your own men.

Anyway, we came back to where we were supposed to meet the CC – I wouldn't commit them to get injured if I could help it. The attack went in – you could hear the shooting. The CO came on the set and asked what was happening. 'I've been on attacks before, sir, but this is a strange one to me. I can't hear any of our weapons firing, and they should be full blast as they went in – grenades and bren guns as they charged the bunkers. There were no rifle shots coming from the front'.

He told me to get the men moving, so I went out and found the CC. He was wounded, and I dragged him back. Then I went to the officer commanding A Company. Again I was told to get the men moving, so I run forward. The other river bed was insurmountable. The rain had gouged the earth out and it was like a steep cliff. We were carrying 76 lb of kit and couldn't get up there.

I looked for the platoon I was supposed to follow – but they had gone round to the right and come in at a lower part – so I ran round there. I was determined to get the men running and the attack moving.

I ran around a corner and there's the platoon commander, lying on a stretcher with 20 pieces of shrapnel in him. He said the attack had gone in and he'd lost a lot of men. I run round the next corner and there's a pile of dead men. The remainder of them were lying on the ground.

I said, 'Right, come on lads. We're going in to the attack'. One of the corporals shouted, 'Wait a minute, Sergeant. Wait! The guns won't fire.'. I tried a Bren gun and a rifle – all the weapons we had. 'Hold it', I said, 'We're not going on the attack'. I run back to the set and tell the CO that the guns won't fire. Well, there's no man in his right mind would believe you!

The sergeant said, 'Let's go in with grenades' – a very brave man. They didn't have a lot of grenades, so I was to go to 9 Platoon and get all of theirs. These six men went in with grenades. They all got killed.

I ran round again through Japanese territory to where the other platoon was, and when I saw them, I nearly cried. Young National Servicemen who were brought up from Dunkirk, taught and made good soldiers – and they were lying on this river bed, devastated. They'd got in this steep trench and the Japs had just poured grenades on them.

I knew they couldn't do an attack because the body of the men had gone. The men couldn't get up the side, so I put two Bren gunners up (they didn't know their guns wouldn't fire because they'd never had a chance to use them). I put both these men in for a gallantry award and both got immediate MMs.

A terrific bang went off just above my head – it must have been a Japanese shell or one of our own dropped short – and it left me semi-conscious. When I recovered. I went on the set and explained to the CO that there were no men to go in and that it was foolhardy to go in with Bren guns and rifles that wouldn't fire. I didn't know at the time that both of my eyes had turned brick red. The pupils were all right, but the irises were bleeding. I had a fuzzy head too, and the major sent me to the dressing station.

All the lads who were National Servicemen were a great credit to this country – great young men, great soldiers – and with hardly any training. They fought like heroes.

In a later attack, the CC says, 'We're in a serious state – have a look up there'. All this hill, right the way round, was covered with positions where the Japs could fire on to us. On a barren place at the front, the Japanese were digging in. You could see them and tied in the middle there was a person in white and another one about five or six yards further down, tied to another tree. We assumed they were tied. It was only our brigadier, Cavendish, and the brigade major.

Now there's no way you can fire at them unless you're hitting the brigade commander and brigade major. They sited them right in the middle of this area where they were digging in. They were standing up, the Japs, and you would have loved to get a Bren gun or a three-inch mortar – but we couldn't because we'd kill our own officers. They had to make a decision. If the Japs got dug in there, they would completely stop any evacuation we were going to try along the beach later. Eventually the Lieutenant-Colonel said. 'We've got to knock that position out'.

He let me look through his binoculars. They started firing, knocking the Japs out, and of course, the lumps of shrapnel killed the brigadier and the brigade major. Now according to the Japan-ese story, the brigadier wasn't tied to a tree – he was found dead way behind the positions, dead with a piece of British shrapnel in him, and and also the Japanese escort was dead with British shrap-nel. That was a plant. I saw them and I'd swear on any Bible that I saw these two men slump. They were tied to trees and in a position where we had to fire on them. They were killed by our own 99

Field Battery. Contrary to all the history books you read, Arakan was a shambles."

Private Ernest Faulkner was 23 when he was drafted out to the Far East. Although in the same regiment as Jim Howard (the following witness to war), his reminiscences are from the men's, not the officers', point of view.

"We went through all the proper training for jungle warfare – marching and walking, sleeping out in the wild. We used to go on tea and rubber plantations, and of a night you could hear the beaters keeping the animals away. There were quite a lot of wild animals around – elephants and leopards.

We had scorpions and centipedes too. The chaps used to dig a pit and take a scorpion and a centipede and let them fight it out, taking a bet on it. Then they'd get a little snake and put it in too. The centipedes were five or six inches long.

We relied a lot on air drops of food and we used to look forward to them. A couple of times we ran out of rations. Once, one of our officers said to a chap, after we'd left one area, 'Go back and get the potato peelings'. We'd buried them in paper (we used to bury things like that). This chap had a tin of jam, so we dipped the peelings in it.

We were on half rations sometimes in Burma. Once I put these white panels out so that the aircraft could see where we were so food could be dropped. As it happened, we had to move on, and we went off so fast, I don't know what the result was – but I did hear a story that they dropped rubber dinghies instead of food!

We were mainly on the defensive. In Burma they were building these roads right down to the Chindwin and as the roads progressed, we moved down to the Chindwin itself. While they were building these roads, the army was preparing all these defences on the hills – trenches, so that when we did withdraw, it was already dug and all we had to do was wait for the Japs.

It was good thinking. It must have been about 50 miles we withdrew, from the Chindwin up into these hills. We went into prepared positions all the time, so we had an advantage on the hills. You only dug trenches when you were advancing. On the Ukhrul road, when we went round to the back of the Japs, we built our own trenches then.

We would just lie in wait for them in these trenches and they'd arrive – swarms of them. We were really outnumbered and on each

hill we had a small number of men. Sometimes on a hill you'd just
have a section of chaps – another might have a platoon, another one
a company. The Japanese would capture one hill, then bypass the
next one.

I wasn't actually on Nippon Hill, but I was on the next one. The
Japs would attack Nippon Hill, but at the same time bypass it, working round, then capture another small hill. We were on Crete Hill,
and they went around that one and captured this little pimple –
Lynch's Pimple, we had only a section of men there and they overran them.

They did manage to cut us off by this tactic eventually, but the
Gurkhas went in on the last night and put in a counterattack. They
didn't completely get rid of the Japs – they had so many men – but
somehow we got ourselves and the wounded down.

The Japs' main attacks were by night – daytimes there was just
shelling with mortars. They had these 105s and 75s, and you could
tell what they were by the noise. With a 105 you knew you had a few
more seconds – you got used to it. They had a 72, and when they used
to come over you had to get down quick. They were nearer – didn't
fire so far away. The worst ones were these whizzbangs – little things
on wheels – cannons deadly at about 500 yards. You never heard
them – it was just SHOOSH...

When we got off that hill one night – we were just running across
the road as they opened up their machine guns. You know we only
lost one bloke. We were running through them and they were firing
in the dark. We got just round a bend then, and saw the wounded
Gurkhas, all bandaged up after they'd put in their counterattack
during the night.

The Japs were really vicious – they'd fight to the end. They were
so good at camouflage and getting underground, they couldn't be
seen by aircraft. The artillery would bombard them, but they were
still there.

We, on the other hand, would attack during the day. We never
got any peace or sleep at night. Half the night they'd shell you,
then half an hour would go by – and then another attack. They'd
do the same thing again, the Japs. On Nippon Hill they had barbed
wire and left a gap, and you could see them there – they'd be shot
down and a little while later another mob would come in. In the
morning they had 60 to 70 bodies lying by the wire. They had no
brains to alter their tactics. The Company Commander used to

shoot the Very light, so you could see and just sling the grenades at them. They seemed doped!

It was a job to get hold of any prisoners, but we started getting more on the Ukhrul road. They all had their hair shaved off. They were only kids, a lot of them. Maybe it was shock – or it could be they were brain-washed. They knew their officers would mow them down with their swords if they failed them.

On several occasions we found these Japs, not a mark on them, with skin like a new-born baby. They must have been killed by the blast. We found bodies stone dead without a mark on them. They couldn't have known a thing about it. They used to have these Jap flags tied around their waists – when they captured a hill, they'd put the flag up. A lot of them had flags – it was an honour to get there first.

On another hill at Tamu there was an outbreak of scrub typhus – we lost a lot of blokes through that. We were on this hill and, one night when I was on guard, there was a sort of earth-tremor. I sort of went up in the air and the ground shook. We heard it was an earthquake along the Brahmaputra. After that, everyone was going down with typhus. The order came that we had to scrape all the green vegetation off the hill and burn it. They reckoned these ticks were living on it.

We did this patrol for six or seven weeks and no-one was allowed to shave – in fact, our CSM did shave, and they busted him down to a sergeant. It was in case they cut themselves and got an infection. We ended up like a load of tramps.

Fleas – don't talk to me of fleas. We went up on this hill and there were head-hunters' huts. When you came out of them, you were running alive – scratching.

In the monsoons you were never dry. You got used to it and plonked down where you were in the mud. The gas cape was your only protection. We were on the move and it would take all day to get up one hill, slipping and sliding in the mud with these mules – they went through hell. We had elephants too, on some hills. We fed them on special rations which came on the air drops and they ate grass and bamboo too. Boys would give them biscuits – mouldy stuff from their rations. The corned beef was really corned mutton and when it was hot you'd open the tin and it would come out liquid. Horrible. It was rotten, but we'd boil it up as a stew. I think it was the First War rations – some of them had 1918 on the bottom. We had some Canadian rations too – Quaker Oats – and they were full of weevils. You just put them in the pot too.

Eventually we knew the Japs were taking hell of a beating and withdrawing all the time. The men were pushing the Japs back on to us. It was a nightmare for them. You should have seen the graves. Bones and arms sticking out – they couldn't bury them. We knew we were winning."

Jim Howard was Second Lieutenant with the 1st Battalion of the Devonshire Regiment – otherwise known as 'the 11th of Foot' or 'the Bloody Eleventh'. The name was coined by the Duke of Wellington in 1812 due to the frequency of their getting decimated...

"We got put on a ship – no-one knows why – and sailed up to Karachi. Nobody knew what the hell we'd come for, so we spent six or seven weeks there, until someone said we were expected in Ceylon.

There was me with these bright little gold pips and 20 years of age. I don't think that any of my men had served less than six months in jail, but they looked after me like a child. They were in command – I wasn't. We joined the battalion in May 1942 then did some really first-class 100 per cent training. It was good – awful but absolutely first-class.

One thing that was a great comfort – and was always true – is that the Japs are a lousy shot. If he gets a machine gun, he'll tear hell out of the trees above your head, and with reasonable luck he'll get nowhere near you at all. But he's absolutely deadly with a mortar – and the first thing you know about a mortar is that you've got a bomb among you.

We developed an attitude of crawling about the jungle – we stalking them and them stalking us. We had a Gurkha battalion with us and a Sikh battalion and we all learned from each other. We got acclimatised to the jungle. You'd get people in high command saying, 'It's only seven miles – ought to be able to do that in a couple of hours'. Seven miles in thorn jungle in Ceylon takes you *five days*. You learned that sort of thing. More important, the officers and commanders learned too. The generals knew what to expect. If some idiot from Corps HQ said, 'It's only seven miles – do it in a couple of days', a general would say, 'Don't be silly, it's going to take them a fortnight.'

In Ceylon we picked up about seven to ten casualties a week with malaria. It was recognised that you couldn't expect to operate in that sort of country without doing something about it – so they got top scientists from the UK and they brought out malarial suppressants. It took a month to get anywhere, and by that time 40 per cent were down with malaria. In action, if someone came down with malaria, they'd be taken off. Later in '44, the Americans were there with these tiny light aircraft and they'd take you away.

We would wander around in the jungle singing, in the most unmelodious sense – *You are my Sunshine* – in the pitch dark. Wherever the Devons went you'd hear this converging through the jungle. We always had scouts out in front making a single track through the jungle. If you've got mules with you you've got to cut it twice as wide and it takes you twice as long. Something happens – and you can hear it. Everybody just scatters – the whole column disappears, because you're all mobile. You've got nothing – everything you've got is with you, on your mule or on your back.

It was a very relaxed war for the Devons. I said to my sergeant one day, 'Look, somebody reckons there are some Japs down there'. He replied, 'Ooh ar. I should leave them alone, sir. They ain't doing you no harm'. That's what we did.

In Ceylon there's either a Russell's viper or a yellow-banded krait – deadly little bootlace snakes. They were so miserable in the monsoon that they snuggled up inside our monsoon capes with us to keep warm. I remember a chap came in and asked 'What's this?' with a deadly krait in his hand.

In battle you knew what would happen if you were captured – so you didn't surrender. *They* didn't surrender. There was no heroism involved – it just wasn't one of the options open to you. We lost one officer as a prisoner – we were pretty sure he was killed, and I'm sure we didn't lose anybody as prisoners. Nobody thought of surrendering any more than the Jap did.

Surrender wasn't an option, which makes it a lot easier for a young officer. When you fought a reasonably civilised enemy like the Germans (not including Buchenwald) you've got a chance of being treated decently as a prisoner – but not with the Japs.

A young officer was never under pressure to surrender to save unnecessary casualties. It takes a load off your mind. The troops never wanted that either – it was a different fighting ethic from any other circumstances. You just fight on to the logical conclusion. It reduces your options – it was win or die, and that was it."

Toshio Hamachi was a section commander in the Japanese No. 3 Platoon, Sakazawa Company of Takemura Battalion. After months in Burma, the battalion commander, Takemura, assembled all his companies to plan an attack on the Chindits (the British 77th Brigade) towards Katha.

"I got the job of recceing the enemy situation. I was to give a burst of rapid fire if I met the enemy, then leave at once. With a feeling, 'This is it', we gripped our bayonets and felt the hot blood coursing through our veins. 'Fix bayonets!' I gave the order. The men whipped their bayonets from their scabbards and fixed them firmly on the end of their rifles. The yellow gold sun began to glow on the horizon. Suddenly, through a gap in the clouds, a US Mustang hurled itself on us. Someone screamed, 'They've spotted us! Scatter!'. Then there was the metallic scream of the aircraft diving low, raking the ground with machine-gun bullets.

I heard someone panting up behind me. It was Lance Corporal Toshio Hakobe. 'Section leader, it's the enemy!'. He pointed, 'That house there – they're coming this way!'.

Lance Corporal Iwama, Corporal Moriyama, PFCs Fujii, Kato and Inaba vanished into the trees, keeping an eye open for the enemy. As they moved off – can it have been about 800 metres away? – eight enemy soldiers carrying rifles came into view. 'Kato, watch out for enemy on our flank, now!' I warned him. 'Yes, sergeant. I can see three more men'.

Moriyama stood beside him, tense, and hissed to Hakobe, 'You've got the LMG – shoot them down!'. I controlled them, 'Wait! It's too soon to fire'. Meanwhile, the enemy, quite unawares, came along the path towards us. Moriyama said to me, 'Let's do something'. As he urged me on, I watched the enemy come up, step by step, then gave the order. 'Right, let the bastards have it. Kill the lot!'.

They were about 500–600 metres away. Hakobe had quite a reputation as a marksman with the LMG: 100 shots, 100 bull's-eyes. I was confident he would deal with the enemy, and left it to him. I saw the khaki uniforms coming closer, '300 metres, FIRE!'.

Their rifles spat fire, the bullets tore into the enemy soldiers. They were obviously taken completely by surprise, but at once they began to return our fire. Four of them were hit as they ran forward. Brave chaps, even though they're the enemy. On the edge of the group one of them was hit by a burst from the LMG and fell to the ground, soaked in blood and moaning in pain.

'Corporal Hakobe, you're firing high! 250 metres, fire lower!' I yelled. He gripped the LMG and cut a swath with it from left to right. Three of the enemy dropped. They were down on the ground now, crawling forward – but when they saw one of their men fall in front of their very eyes, they panicked. 'Cease fire! Take the enemy alive'. I searched the blood-soaked corpse of one of them. Cigarettes, chewing-gum, tins – and distributed it round the section.

We continued to sweep north in pursuit of the disappearing phantom enemy airborne troops, cutting our way through the thorny creepers. The men moved slowly forward further and further into the interior, 2 km, 3 km. A mood of disquiet and unease began to come over the men. The path was a series of hills covered in deep forest – it was simply an endless track, covered in weeds.

We broke off the search and returned to our unit. At the time, the enemy force was reputed to have increased to 10,000 men. The main body of the company kept recceing the area, but the airborne troops were forever changing their ground and never showed up.

Two days before Sakazawa Unit arrived at Katha, a British airborne unit tried to cross the Irrawaddy in broad daylight. They were seen by one man of the Japanese garrison unit who was bewildered and paralysed with fear when he saw them. The garrison put together two sections in charge of an NCO and hid behind the embankment to observe the enemy on the opposite bank. The marksman of the group, LMG already aimed at the enemy, nervously fingered the grip as he waited impatiently for the command.

The enemy was crowded on to wooden rafts, their weapons and ammunition piled up, with mules to complete the load. It looked to be only 80 metres across at this point, as the raft left the river bank. The LMG chattered and spat flame, breaking the peace and calm of the river. The enemy troops, crowded and bunched together on the raft, were mown down with no chance of returning our fire.

In the smoke, the screams of the British troops in their agony were drowned by the din of the rifles and the LMG. You could hear the mules whinnying as the bullets found their mark. It was as if the enemy were so many blood-sacrifices. The bullets sang in the midst of the scattering spray of water. 'Got you! Die, you hairy bastards!' our men shouted.

Those British troops who were still alive dived into the water, only to sink into the weeds at the river bottom. In the eddies you could see the profuse bright blood of the British troops. It was the work of a moment, and we had knocked the heart out of the astounded airborne troops."

Trooper Brian Yates finally succeeded in getting himself into the front-line action. As an air-minded schoolboy he had wanted to be in Air Crew – but lacking the necessary 20/20 vision, he finally found himself in the 3rd Carabiniers (Prince of Wales' Dragoon Guards) on the Imphal front in Burma.

"I was called up and posted to the Royal Army Pay Corps – a clerk in uniform, unbearable. I refused to work and at each weekly pay parade submitted an application for transfer. I went through many pay offices – but it was at Leicester where I went as spectator to a darts match at the Cherry Tree Pub, that I found a permanent way out.

Our section was playing an artillery team. Someone was late and in his usual style, the RSM said 'You'll play' – the army practice of detailing a volunteer. I barely scored anything. At the end, both teams having won the same number of games, this last game was the decider. They told me what to throw for, and I hardly believed it, but each went in – treble 15, 20 and double 20 – sheer luck. We won – and it led to my transfer.

The RSM said, 'Name it, name it. Anything you like' – meaning any drink. I said, 'What I want is my transfer to the Royal Tank Regiment'. I didn't know, but before the war he had been in the RTR. He asked what I meant and, laughing, he promised he would do what he could. In two months I was out.

After training at Bovington, we sailed in the P&O liner *Stratheden* from Greenock. We were on that boat two and a half months before disembarking at Bombay. We were to undertake training for Grant tanks – seven-man tanks with a commander, a 37 gunner and a loader in the turret, and a driver, wireless operator, 75 gunner and loader in the lower compartment. We didn't have tanks but still had to train – so seven people walked together, the driver holding a white flag – and as such we used to go and do training schemes.

One day I remember, during the siege of Imphal, 8 May 1944, we attacked a village, Potsangbam. Our 16 Grants moved off at 4.15 am and we were in position by first light.

We were put on flank guard, high above the village. Our Grants, the Indian Honeys and the infantry went in under smoke we laid down and we attacked across a very deep *nullah*, which the tanks couldn't cross. They brought up Valentine bridging tanks which unfolded their bridges across the *nullah*, but they either didn't reach, or tipped up as our tanks crossed them. Some did get across, but were quickly knocked out. Almost half our tanks were lost and the infantry and the crews pinned down. They made a strongpoint of the *nullah*, but had to stay there for five days until we took the village.

It got dark and nothing seemed to be happening. Our sergeant broke wireless silence and was told to return to box. It was a very dark night – hard for the driver to see. The sergeant told me to get outside and I sat by the driver's hatch to direct him. It was easier when we got to the small hamlet we'd used as a supply base, as it was quite bright and still burning, set on fire by shelling from the hills, but it was very dark along the road amid the trees.

The large bridge over the river was still there, and we rattled on to our box. A drunken major came and started swearing at the sergeant. 'You should have been back with the rest of us. Where's the Honey?'. The Sergeant said, 'I didn't see a Honey'. The major, 'You were told to bring it back. Their box has been taken by the Japs'. There had been no such order at all. This we knew because we could hear the radio in our headsets, and there had been no such order.

I was still on the front of the tank and he thrust his torch at me and said, 'You. Go and fetch it'. Well, I was very vulnerable sitting on the tank, and relieved to get into our box, having been in or on the tank for 15 hours. I had wanted to see if there was anything left to eat and get in a hole somewhere.

However, I took my six grenades, took the butt off my Tommy gun and left everything that might rattle. The guards on the wire said, 'Tell us what flowers you want – we'll come and find you in the morning'. Nice of them.

I slipped very quietly through the village below our box – I had put on soft PT shoes. Near the road I lay down to listen – I wanted to avoid any Jap patrols. They used to raid intermittently, causing the whole box to stand to, so that we missed a lot of sleep every night.

Eight or ten men could keep most of a division awake.

I slid into the ditch and moved, Red-Indian fashion, quietly through the undergrowth, listening all the time and lying still if I heard anything. I heard a group coming and crawled away from the road and lay still. I could hear they were Japs as they passed by, although they were talking quietly. Back in the ditch, I wondered what I would do when I got to the big bridge 200 yards across – a long dash fully exposed.

I thought I'd better go down one bank and up the other, although the Honey might come by while I was down there. I had to stop it going back to its own box full of Japs. Tanks were very valuable – we couldn't fly new ones in, and we had already lost seven that day. I decided not to cross the bridge, and lay low.

Another group came by me on the other side. It was still very dark – no moon. I had to stop a closed-down tank. They would only speak Urdu and me English – it didn't seem easy.

Anyway, then I could hear the unmistakable sound of a Honey, far off. How do you stop a tank in the middle of the night, when they are going to assume you are the enemy? I thought the only thing to do was to stand in the middle of the road, hold my hand up like a police-man and shine a torch on myself.

I got into the middle of the road and did this. They came up, training the Besa on me. The Havildar said to me, '*Japani wallah?*' I said, 'No', and showed him my discs and paybook. All this in the middle of the road, with his torch and mine and all the noise in great contrast with my careful creep to meet them. '*Kya chàhte?* (what do you want?)

It seemed best to ask for a lift – they would assume I was a lost British trooper. Then I had to talk them out of going back to their own box and back to our own. He said, 'Yes, get on'. There's not room for a fourth person in the Honey, so I had my second ride out-side. We moved, clattering off.

I remembered the name of their CO. I said there were '*Japani wallah*' at their box, and their officer *sahib* had sent me to fetch them. Although on the face of it, it wasn't very likely, they agreed to come and see. There was no firing around the box and they let us in at the wire. I found an Urdu-speaking officer, left him with them, then found my hole and went to bed hungry – pathetic."

Jim Howard, Second Lieutenant with the 1st Battalion of the Devonshire Regiment, had been only 20 when he sailed from Britain in 1942. After rigorous training in Ceylon his men are put into the fight in the jungles of Burma.

"Sometimes when we really achieved something, we'd just tear right through a Japanese position – and we didn't stop but went straight on and disappeared. This was rather fun – guerrilla warfare. That's when we did our best work. That's what we were trained for.

In '44 they set us on top of a hill and said that no Jap must pass. This was in March. By July we'd lost about 500 yards and about 2,000 men – but we were still there.

Infantry battle must necessarily always be the same – someone throwing shells at you or throwing mortar bombs at you; someone shoots at you with a machine gun; if you were unlucky, the air force joins in and gives you a clobbering. It depends very largely on what you've got and what he's got, and the good position you've chosen, who succeeds. With the Jap, of course, it was a great advantage that he *wanted* to die – and it was out business to see that he did. So we and he had the same object. There were two schools of thought among the Japanese Army – there were the militarists who were completely stupid, and there were those who were just good soldiers, who valued their soldiers' lives and military principles above all the suicidal nonsense.

One of the things that makes me smile was that the Japs used to come up – and we'd sit there in amazement in the same place, night after night after night – and get clobbered. They'd never get to the top of this hill where we were sitting. It sounds so daft, doesn't it? Their general would be told to go take a hill – he'd get there, plant his flag and in doing so get all his men killed – and that's seeing the Japanese fighting from the other side. It's no pleasure having to kill people.

We were lucky in another way too. As we went in, we moved ever so cautiously from Imphal, and did patrols as we'd learned in Ceylon. One of our patrols hit some Japs. You were expecting something knee-high to a grasshopper with ruddy great pebble glasses – not on your Nellie. They were six foot three – it was a lie about these small chaps!

Even though they were a lousy shot, they were lethal with mortars – and nobody likes mortars. They don't make a noise as they come, then suddenly BANG! I never personally had any individual thoughts about them at all. As far as I was concerned, we always had a task to perform, and we did it. In infantry battle it's the survivor who wins: if there's only one man left, he's the winner. But you're there to perform a task, so individuals trying to stop you don't matter. It's *all* terrifying – then that's what you expect it to be. It's just as bad, but infinitely worse than anything you'd ever dreamed of – and yet it is something set totally apart. You can't have experiences like that and not be affected by it.

It's odd, sometimes a unit runs out of steam. They deliberately put us through that, to see how far they could go and to see how the troops would put up with it. In the defence of that hill after March, April, May, they reckoned we'd had enough. We'd been knocked about something rotten, and they were honest, our generals. They didn't relieve us – they said we were due for a change of air, so instead of sitting on a hill and being shot at by the Japs, we went in right behind the Jap and attacked him! It was literally trackless jungle – and we only had mules at this time. Much of the time we were carrying the loads and pulling the mules through the mud with ropes, it was that bad. Down in the valleys it was warm and steamy and wet – it was on top that the Nagas and Manapuris used to build their villages. One of our patrols found a deserted village and said they'd have a nice rest there. They went into the hut and the whole floor was alive with fleas and bugs – bed bugs. They were crawling!

It was raining, raining, raining. And the first thing that happens is that all your blankets get wet. Ever tried carrying a wet blanket? You just have to throw them away.

We all expected to get arthritis, but we don't seem to have done too badly really. Wet for six weeks on end – literally never dry. The medical authorities were more worried about us than we were. We were winning, we were happy to go on – but we found we couldn't digest food. They never understood why, but it just passed straight through, undigested. We weren't getting enough food anyway, but we just lost the ability to digest it. Some were all right – the army found it odd, though, that morale was high. We were tickled to death that we were winning and clobbering the Japs something terrible.

In those days, you buried a bloke and didn't give a twopenny damn whether he was a Roman Catholic, a Presbyterian or what. You'd say some prayers over your mate, and that was it. They were all people who believed in God somehow – and that would do. We had a Roman

Catholic padre for a long time, and he was just a padre as far as we were concerned – he did his best to please all denominations.

There was one chap, late in the campaign, who got a bullet which entered the top of his head on one side and came out at the front. Well, we didn't waste too much time making deep holes for burial, you understand, but they wanted to cover him up decently. So they did a couple of dog scratches around him and, as is the way (some people may take it badly), if anybody had a good pair of boots and you didn't, you had 'em. Someone said, 'That's a good pair of boots there'. So they took his boots off – they weren't even buried, and as they took them off, his toes twitched. 'He isn't dead! Dig him up again!' He became consciously aware a year and a half later – became himself again – if they hadn't pinched his boots he'd probably still be there. He had a sort of free leucotomy – but he doesn't want to talk about it, though…"

Eveline Broughton-Smart, née Gaudoin, was reading English at the University of Rangoon when war broke out. She returned to the Japanese-occupied Shan State of Hsenwi, where her family were the local rulers, living in an old palace off the Burma Road.

"The palace was in huge grounds and even had a Japanese sentry at the gate – which we didn't notice really, because he was so far away. They used to send cavalry charges and tanks through our grounds, just to show us, I suppose. We'd suddenly see tanks in the garden – but otherwise we hardly saw them.

In the big towns the people had food shortages, but we had plenty – and meat too. We had a very disciplined life. Servants always served our food and we followed all the little rules and protocols – it helps you to keep your dignity and self-respect, I think.

We were very cut off. We had no news from elsewhere because we were not allowed to have radios – but at one time someone had got hold of one and they asked my father, as the best educated, to go and listen to summarise it for them. However, after a while it was noticed that a Japanese was hovering about every time he went – so they decided it was a bit dangerous. Since he was not a Shan but an Anglo-Indian, and a government official at that, he was naturally always suspect.

At one time they wanted us to learn Japanese, but it didn't last long – though they made all the school children learn it. They sent the

Japanese who taught at the school to the place to teach us, but it fizzled out after a while.

My father went to pieces. His favourite son, Edgar, was in the RAMC as a 14-year-old but he bluffed his age and the British Army took him, even though they knew he wasn't 18. He went to India and my father went to pieces. From then I couldn't talk to my father. It was a lonely life. Also, living with my uncle, there was a very strict protocol about who you spoke to. We were not allowed to speak unless we were spoken to first! Even before the war we used to go backwards out of my uncle's presence. It was very medieval – there was no middle class at all, just the peasants. There was no-one you could be friendly with – everyone was either your relative or one of the servants.

It was very boring. We supervised the servants and did a bit of gardening – but there wasn't really anything to do. We sat around, all living in different wings of the palace, and did formal visits to the other wings. I used to make clothes for children from old dresses. I had a complete Shakespeare and the Oxford Book of English Verse and the Indian doctor had Dickens – but I got fed up with that after a while.

Around 1944 the bombing was getting worse. There is one point where the Burma Road crosses the river, and they were always aiming for that bridge. One day they actually bombed the town and my uncle said we ought to move out. We went to various villages, divided off so that we wouldn't be too much of a strain on one village. From then we didn't see much of each other.

At that time, the American 101 forces parachuted in and got in touch with the various chiefs to get them to co-operate and to give arms to the villagers. They didn't come to us because my father would be immediately suspect, so the first we heard was a message from my uncle – 'Please come at once'. We discovered the Americans were flying them out in their little Piper Cubs.

By the time my uncle sent the message, the Japanese knew what was happening and about 600 of them surrounded the airstrip. When we got the message we couldn't join him, and were just wondering what to do when the Japanese turned up and arrested all my family.

They asked my Chinese cousin if she had been communicating with her father, who was a general in Chiang Kai-shek's army – they even asked me if I was a British spy. I must say, they didn't ill-treat us. We expected it, though, and were terrified.

We had to sit on a mattress and they sat at a table and shouted at us. My sister who had been at a convent boarding school, though they were going to rape us. You can imagine the sort of person she was! My father had said 'When the Japanese come, they might rape all the women – you'd better go and hide in the jungle'. My sister asked why they wouldn't rape daddy! Those were the kind of people we were, though!

They didn't lay a finger on us and one secret police chap was quite nice to us. He might have been doing it to get information, but they found we hadn't been in touch with any Americans. They searched everything we had – every bit of my father's legal stuff to find some excuse – they didn't have to find one if they didn't want to! They could do what they wanted. Eventually they returned every bit of paper – even my knitting patterns!

I remember once, we were cooking in a little open place after our arrest. A sergeant came along – he was drunk – and he was rattling away in Japanese. We didn't know what he was saying, but our brother Alec said he was just making a political speech. The next day the captain apologised to us – 'we're so sorry he came and bothered you'.

After the war, one of my uncles who was arrested with us, tried to get in touch with this captain, Horita, to thank him – after all, they could have done anything. We were all young girls, children, old men – helpless. He managed to trace him in Japan, but sadly the letter arrived on the day of his funeral. His widow wrote back. I often wondered why they didn't ill-treat us. Maybe they thought we were more influential than we were.

One day they just told us we could go. Being the sort of family we were, we were known by the other princes in the other states. A Japanese secret police chap asked how we would earn a living and how we would manage. 'Don't worry', I said, 'We have been brought up in these states – the people will always help us'. Wherever we went they always fed us and we never had to worry. He said, 'Three pretty girls like you won't starve.'. When I look back, we really were very lucky."

Flying Officer Kenneth Holliday had completed a tour of duty as a flying instructor in light aircraft in Canada and was keen to get onto operations with some action. The call came to go to Burma to fly the 'Flying Jeep', doing casualty evacuations.

"There was a cryptic note on the Sergeants' Mess notice board that said, 'Flying Officer Jones and Flight Sergeant Holliday will each take an aircraft and fly south into Burma and join the 82nd West African Division. They should expect to remain with the army division for several months and they must be prepared to sleep in foxholes and travel light'.

An unholy marriage of army and air force took place. The army, for all they were in a battle situation in jungle, still persisted in army disciplines and routines – and it took some little time for them to understand that I was a Flight Sergeant and not some heaven-sent god from higher ranks!

On the first night, I was asked to dine with the colonel in a tent, at a table laid with parachute bottoms. The menu was very limited – dehydrated mutton and peanuts – and when he saw my rank was three stripes and a crown, the colonel immediately insisted on a Regimental Sergeant Major joining us, so I was not alone – and I dare say so that he was not alone either! That was typical of the way the army and air force looked at each other.

We'd been sent in answer to an obvious development of what was going on. In the retreat from Burma earlier, many men were lost simply because they happened to be left. You see the films where they say, 'I'm going to leave you this revolver and this one bullet – you know what to do with it'. There's an element of truth in it, though not perhaps as dramatic as that. People could not be evacuated. There was tremendous heroism shown where people were carried out, but regrettably, people were left.

Now the Stinson Sentinel was one of the L range of American aircraft and the L5A, as it was called, was a simple army co-operation aircraft with two seats in tandem. The L5B had a stretcher behind the pilot and was extremely good at short landings and quick take-offs.

We moved forward with the army – this meant moving virtually every other day. As casualties occurred, we evacuated them to a casualty clearing station. The procedure would normally be that the local medical officer would ask the people who knew if they needed immediate first aid or surgery, then we would fly them out. Within half an hour they'd be in a comfortable hospital on an island off Burma, where they could get proper treatment. It would not be too ridiculous to say that you could get shot on Friday, be in hospital that day, and be back with a gun in your hand next Friday.

The only time you flew high was when you knew very well there was nobody down there who was liable to take a shot at you or tell someone else to come and take a shot at you. When you are low down, you can have passed them before they could train anything on to you.

The Japs did a lot of funny things which I've never heard reported. They stretched wires from one side of a river to the other. I don't know if their main purpose was to bring down low-flying aircraft, but certainly you had to look out for that.

We lived, the two of us, with the army unit, doing whatever they said, and in three or four months I had flown 350 hours – but in terms of what we called operational sorties, I had flown 457. A Bomber Command tour of operations would be 30 sorties – so you can see that it was a matter of take-off and land. If there was a serious battle, the chances were that we'd be employed from dawn to dusk. I have never, ever derided the Americans' work in co-operation with us.

I remember one particular day, at an airstrip called Grey Hen, actually on the side of a small mountain. If you can imagine, it was crescent-shaped and went round the shape of the mountain. There wasn't a lot of room for manoeuvre. That day there was a very heavy battle with heavy casualties. The Americans came in with us and worked all day. It was a matter of taking a casualty out, coming back and taking another out. You didn't stop to ask – there was only one purpose that day, and that was to fly between the hospital and the airstrip. One American collapsed at the end of the day and had to be lifted from his aircraft. It was found that he had been wounded very early on, but had never got out of his aircraft. I don't know what his name was, but his friends called him Tex – he was a very brave man."

Lance Corporal Muragishi, serving with II/60 Battalion, Japanese 15th Division, was involved as two sections of his company were under British artillery barrage on a steep hill on the Imphal front. To his disbelief, four British tanks climbed the hill.

"Four tanks came towards us, but Kagawa platoon hadn't a single anti-tank gun to confront them with. Not only Kagawa platoon – there wasn't a single anti-tank gun in the whole of II Battalion.

The men held their breath and went rigid with fear as the tank caterpillars grated towards them – ready to trample down the trench sides. At that moment, one of our men heaved himself up out of the trench and seemed to prance in front of us. It was Lance Corporal Uehara of 6 Company. Just before leaping out of the trench, he said in a low urgent voice, 'I'm going to get that tank. Just watch me!' He dashed forward, just as the men in the trench understood what he said. He was clutching in his right hand a globe the size of a fist. He closed up to the tank and, from about ten yards, hurled the globe.

Immediately, for some reason, the British tank was enveloped in white smoke, like steam. It wasn't a hand-grenade nor an armour-piercing mine, nor a mine of any sort. When the ball struck against the front of the tank and splintered, the white smoke poured straight-away inside the tank which was covered in it.

A few seconds later, the lid of the tank's gun-turret was thrust open and the tank crew, giving queer screams, jumped out and down from the tank. Down the slope they tumbled, rolling over and over as if to escape something. From the turret of the now empty tank a terrific amount of black smoke gushed. Uehara had climbed up the side of the tank, slipped the pin of a handgrenade and flung it inside.

In no time at all, the black smoke turned into a red pillar of flame, while the echo of explosions reverberated among the hills. The tank began to blaze. The bursting grenade had induced an explosion of the ammunition inside."

Lieutenant-General Nobuo Tanaka succeeded Yanagida as commander of Japanese 33rd Division. This excerpt comes from his diary at the point where he and his men reached Three-Pimple Hill, west of Bishenpur.

"Both officers and men look dreadful. They've let their hair and beards grow until they look exactly like wild men of the mountains. Over a hundred days have passed since this two-month operation began. In that time the men have had almost nothing to eat – they're undernourished and pale.

The weather's been clear for two or three days, but last night it began to pour, which adds to the men's hardships. Last night some comforts and a few rations came up from the rear. Up to now we've been short of candles and have had no light except when absolutely necessary.

I was particularly pleased to get some pickled plums. Jungle greens have a bitter taste and a grassy smell, but we eat them because there's no alternative. But even one plum each makes the food taste better.

Since 15th June I've not used a watch. Watches aren't much use on the battlefield. The rain pours down endlessly, but enemy aircraft are still flying. They're at it 24 hours a day, almost as if the skies were clear."

Arnhem – No Garden Party

*A*s *the Allies in Europe turned their attention to the German homeland, Field Marshal Montgomery proposed operation Market Garden, a plan intended to outflank German defences on the River Rhine. In Market, US airborne divisions would capture vital bridges across the Wilhelmina Canal and the Maas, and the British First Airborne Division the bridge at Arnhem on the Neder Rhine. In Garden, meanwhile, the British XXX Corps would drive north from Belgium to link up the bridgeheads. The initial landings took place on 17 September 1944, and by the evening of the next day the XXX Corps had linked up with the 101st at their bridges at Zon and Veghel. The British reached the 82nd Airborne at Grave by 08.20 am and in a joint operation captured the bridge at Nijmegen on the 20th. At Arnhem, however, the British paratroops landed in an area in which the Second Waffen-SS Panzer Corps was refitting: the Germans reacted quickly. Signals equipment did not work correctly and bad weather prevented the Allied air forces flying in close support. Despite the setbacks, the Second Battalion Parachute Regiment reached the northern bank of the road bridge and, under heavy attack, held it for several days. The rest of First Airborne meanwhile were trapped in the suburb of Oosterbeek. On 21 September the Polish First Airborne Brigade was dropped at Driel on the south bank of the Neder Rhine in an attempt to reinforce the British survivors. They were joined by 43rd Wessex Division, which had fought its way overland,*

> but on 25 September Montgomery decided that the First
> Airborne would have to be evacuated. The failed operation
> had cost 1,130 dead and 6,000 captured.

Brigadier J W Hackett DSO, MBE, MC (later General Sir John, GCB) was commander of the 4th Parachute Brigade. Injured after six days' furious fighting, he discovered the extraordinary compassion and determination of the Dutch Resistance workers as he made his recovery.

"It was really a major error not to open the port of Antwerp before this operation. I'd add to this, that it was really very important to get the 1st British Airborne Division into action.

This Division was really the cream of the British Army at the time. These were very highly motivated, highly trained men, who had been much mucked about. They had something like 15 abortive operations, on three of which we were already in aeroplanes with our parachutes on ready for take-off, all our letters to our loved ones posted. Then somebody would come round, open the aircraft door and say, 'It's all cancelled, everybody gets three days' leave.' You can't go on doing that without irreparably damaging the morale of a first-rate, highly strung, wonderfully trained, admirably chosen and officer-manned division – without its going very badly downhill. Even though the omens were not good, it was important to go.

The best commander of an airborne formation in the whole war. Jim Gavin of the 82nd American Airborne Division, said: 'If you are going to put down an airborne force some way away from the objective, you ought to reconsider the plan – and perhaps even cancel it – because unless you put them down close on it, even with casualties which you have got to be prepared to take, you would probably fail.'. You see, what they did to us was put us down six to eight miles from the objective. They feared the flak defences of Deelen Airfield which, when we got up to them, proved to be far less formidable than expected.

There is the added complication that airborne operations depend very largely on surprise. The 17th September was the day on which Market Garden opened, and when the first lift of the 1st Airborne Division went in. I commanded the second lift the next day, when surprise had gone, and instead of brandy and bonhomie, we met a whole lot of angry Germans.

The loss of surprise was really very painful, and this distance from the object was of critical importance. You see, my orders were to take the 4th Parachute Brigade in and defend the northern outskirts of Arnhem town, which would be the bridgehead around the crossing, seized by the 1st Parachute Brigade under Gerald Lathbury – Johnny Frost commanding the 2nd Parachute Battalion and putting up that magnificent performance at the bridge.

People who hadn't fought the Germans enough generally thought everything was a piece of cake, but the thing about the Germans was that they were the finest professional army fighting in World War II, and whatever there was on the ground that was weak, as soon as you threatened something vital, the German response would be swift and violent. We were told, on the intelligence available, that there were only a few Mark I tanks on the Corps front, and units of trainee cadets with a battalion of broken-down old men they called the 'stomach battalion' (men who were unfit for much more than garrison guard duties) were all we would find. That is what XXX Corps and 21st Army Group told us.

I was asked, 30 years after the war, 'When did you first realise that this operation was, if not doomed to failure, at least, not very likely to succeed?' I said, 'Before it began,' and recounted my own experience.

I had a final briefing with all the officers of the Brigade and key personnel – about 100 people. I went through, in meticulous detail, what we were to do, down to platoons, in the occupation of the northern defences of Arnhem town, to form the bridgehead around 1st Brigade's seizure of the bridge. When it was all over, I dismissed everyone but the three Battalion Commanders and key personnel and said, 'Now, you can forget all that. Your hardest fighting and worst casualties will not be in the defence of the northern perimeter of Arnhem town, but in trying to get there.' We never did.

We now come to Ultra. We didn't have Ultra – it didn't come down to divisional level. It only came down cooked in the form of coded interpolations in intelligence summaries. It certainly didn't come down to Corps, let alone Division – and as for Brigade, that would have been laughable.

Brian Urquhart – not Roy – was G2 Intelligence in Boy Browning's Corps HQ, 1st British Airborne Corps, and had some inkling that there might be German armour in the area. He might have had some sort of spill-over from Ultra, but Brian had tacked on to a fighter sweep going over the area two days before some oblique reconnaissance photography. There was clearly some armour there, and it wasn't old Mark Is at all – in fact, as we knew later, and as the outcome says, they were the 9th and 10th SS Panzer Divisions, going to refit in Germany. They were not fit to go into battle as armoured divisions, but they did have a few tanks and some SP guns, and it wasn't difficult to rustle up some more along the railway line within 24 hours.

On the 18th they were too much for us. I did what I was intended to – I tried to move in, but it was quite impossible because of the tanks. What can lightly armed airbornes do against even a trace of heavy armour?

The tragic thing – and this relates to the whole battle – was that General Urquhart, who was a splendid battlefield commander – the best battle-fighting general I ever served under, a great, imperturbable, courageous fighting Scot, and a marvellous man – went forward to see for himself what was happening at the bridge, owing to the fact that signals communication was not of the best and, indeed, failed on the very first day. He got pinned by the enemy there and couldn't get out.

There he was, incommunicado, for about 36 hours at a really crucial stage of the battle. Had he been back in command and in touch, he would have called off the 4th Parachute Brigade from this abortive attempt against hopeless opposition to the northern end of the town, and put it into the reinforcement of Frost and the perimeter the Division had established around Oosterbeek.

Pip Hicks, the brigadier commanding the 1st Airlanding Brigade of glider-borne infantry, had been designated by Roy to take command of the division in the event that he, Roy, was a casualty, and his chosen successor, Gerald Lathbury, was also a casualty. Then the only brigadier who was a dyed-in-the-wool infantry soldier, Pip Hicks (Roy used to refer to me as 'my broken-down cavalryman'), was going to take over. But nobody told me of this, so when I got into the Division on the night of the 18th, having had some pretty stiffish fighting that day and prepared for much worse on the day to come, I found that Pip Hicks was in charge, and they really were in a state of confusion. It was a monstrously tangled situation. The idea was that I should go on doing what I had originally been intended to do, but I said, 'I want some orders about this.' Nobody was in a position to give any orders, so I said, 'This is a simple, staff duties exercise – let's treat it as such.

I need to know my objectives. I need to agree with you phase lines – a central thrust line. I want to know who is on my right, who is on my left – what the boundaries are, and inclusive to whom, what support I am going to have.' But nobody had thought these things out.

Finally I had a bit of a showdown with Pip Hicks and said, 'Look, you're senior to me in the army, but I'm senior to you as a Brigadier commanding brigades in this division. I have it in mind to exert the authority this gives me to take command of this division, and give myself the orders I need. I will then go back to the 4th Para Brigade, hand the division back to you, and carry out the orders I have just received.' So I did – it was simply a very tidy way to resolve it. I wrote my own orders and took them away – but they were impossible because of the opposition which was building up in front of us.

Why did the Guards Armoured Division never arrive to relieve the 2nd Para Battalion? There were some good reasons for this. One was, I believe, XXX Corps planning. There was a euphoria that hovered over everyone after this dash from Normandy to Holland – a wonderful, thunderous advance of a victorious army against an enemy defeated, but not destroyed and still formidable.

They were so cockahoop they thought it was all a bit easy. Then there was the choice of the single road from Nijmegen to Arnhem – that really was a great mistake. This road is about 60 km long, and built on an embankment running across low-level fields. You couldn't everywhere get tanks off the road because very often the fields on either side were too wet and boggy – and it was very easily interrupted by well-placed anti-tank guns. As I later discovered, when the Dutch Staff College used to do exercises on an approach to Arnhem from Nijmegen, anybody who moved straight up that single road got no marks!

Urquhart withdrew into the perimeter around Oosterbeek about the 20th, and I was brought in, my brigade very ragged, but splendid – this lot were absolutely first-class. They'd had a terrible time, and suffered a reduction from about 1,000 to 300, and that didn't do their morale any good, but they were absolutely on top of the world. Urquhart divided the last bridgehead of the 1st Airborne Division into two halves, one commanded by Brigadier Hicks, the other right-hand half commanded by me.

I was wounded on the 23rd and was carted off to St Elisabeth's Hospital in Arnhem. I got a splinter in the stomach and spent four and a half months in Holland, hiding.

My dear wife knew that I was alive, but in poor shape – this thing inside had carved ten perforations and two sections in the lower intestine – and one perforation is lethal! A miraculous operation was done on me by a British airborne surgeon.

I had made myself a Lance Corporal – I didn't want them to know they had a parachute brigadier because they might want to add me to their butterfly collection, and it was my intention that they shouldn't do that. Then, because the last of my three Battalion Commanders was dying there, and I wanted to get from him accounts of recommendations for honours and awards, I promoted myself to Major, so I could share his room until he died.

I was helped out of the hospital by the Dutch underground and spent the next four months, hidden, nursed, cherished, fed, loved, by a Dutch family – four elderly ladies and the son and daughter of one of them. That's why my book is called, as it is, *I was a Stranger* – it's a thinly disguised sermon on a text in St Matthew – but it's interesting stuff.

In the house where I was hidden, I was put up in the loft or down in the cellar when the house was searched. I read – one of the aunts had trained as an English teacher and she had a bunch of books in the house – the authorised version of *The Bible* (I must be one of few people who has read the whole of *The Bible*, straight through). That was how I occupied myself – I read the *Complete Shakespeare* too. I would read a tragedy in the morning and two comedies in the afternoon. I had a Greek testament as well, and one or two other books – *A Thousand and One Gems of English Poetry* – but what I really pined for was Thackeray and *Paradise Lost*.

I learned some Dutch and I was our military correspondent for a Dutch underground newspaper. We used to have a little wireless under the floor and we'd listen to the odd broadcast. Then I would write a column called *Notes on the War in the West* by our military correspondent, in English. It only went to three editions because the *Gestapo* got on to it, and they had to move me somewhere else less dangerous.

It is remarkable, the degree of adaptability in the human constitution. You live a life which you consider to be normal, and suddenly you are thrust into something quite different. It's astonishing how soon that becomes the norm, and you live that life as if you had always lived it. It is when you come back that it's difficult to adjust.

When I got better I'd be allowed to come downstairs. My presence was a very closely guarded secret – and of course, friends used to come and call. It would be December and dark early and I'd be coming down to the *Huiskamer* (parlour) and, before coming in, the door would be just ajar and I would touch it with my foot so it swung slightly as it would from a draught. One of the old ladies would get up and excuse herself to come out. If there was nobody there, or if there was nobody it would be dangerous to have see me, they'd invite me in. Otherwise I'd be told to wait upstairs.

When I got home, I couldn't, for weeks and weeks, go down to my own drawing room without just touching the door first. That was the norm – how I lived."

Lieutenant Joseph Hardy of the Border Regiment landed outside Arnhem. His actions under fire and, as the recommendation for his MC stated, 'his vigour and contempt for danger', were largely responsible for the successful withdrawal of B Company to the main Battalion position.

"My unit had been cut about in the Sicily and Italy affairs, so that a lot of our men were very young, and quite new to this fighting business. I thought that I had seen it all before, until I reached a point possibly half way towards the area where we were to congregate. Here I found two young lads, so delighted to be back on to *terra firma*, that they decided to get their gear off and brew up a cup of tea. I screamed at them so long and loud that I might have been heard five miles away, reminding them that this was war, not some sort of bloody picnic – but it was extremely hard to keep a straight face. Within seconds I had them back into their gear and travelling towards the forming up area at a very healthy pace, probably muttering to themselves that Joe Hardy was a rotten old b...

Our duty was to hold the landing strips until the second lift came in, but the weather broke down in England and things started to go wrong. We eventually took up our positions to cover the western side of a defence circle, and found that it was much more heavily wooded country than we had expected it to be. At the time, all our communications were by wireless, and in the wooded country, reception of signal was very, very, poor. We were able to make contact with A, C and D Companies, but B Company, who had been sent right out to the western edge of the defence perimeter, were completely out of touch. It was considered that they would be the first to be hit by any enemy force advancing from the west, so it became imperative that, as their wireless link was screened out, the next best thing was to run a telephone line out to them.

The only two persons who had no specific duty other than to supervise, were myself and Signals Sergeant Jock McClusky. Off the pair of us went, hell for leather, down the Utrecht Road to the village of Renkum. We arrived there just on dark, tested the line and it worked like a dream. No problems at all.

I had expected that B Company would be sitting astride the Utrecht/Arnhem road, so that when the enemy came along, they would be able to surprise them then, as enemy weight increased, they would be able to disengage and move back to the outer perimeter of the battalion position. However, the company had reached the village of Renkum then turned left down a lane towards the river. It did not strike me as being a good position – but I had them back in touch with the telephone.

Jock and I jumped into the jeep, me in the passenger seat with a Sten automatic laid across my knee, and we made our way up the lane to the main road. Just before the lane joined the main road, there was a fairly steep rise in the ground and as we neared the road junction, I saw the outline of two soldiers heading towards Arnhem. The Company Commander had not told me that he had any men this far up the lane – they were not B Company men at all – they were Germans.

Jock slammed the brakes on, and I half leapt and was half thrown over the bonnet of the jeep. I landed at the feet of the two German boys with my automatic pointed at their guts and the only stupid thing that I could think of to say was 'How's about it chum'. I honestly believe that they were just the slightest little bit more frightened than I was. They dropped their Schmeissers, we picked them up, bundled the two Germans into the jeep and turned back into B Company lines.

Two Dutch interpreters questioned the Germans, and they told us that they were part of a unit that was marching along the Utrecht/Arnhem road, that they had been the connecting file between the companies in front of and behind them. This meant, of course, that there was at least one company – perhaps two or three – of enemy troops on the road that I had been going to take back to my HQ. The B Company Commander told me that his second-in-command's glider had gone astray and suggested that I take over as second-in-command. I reported the situation to HQ. There was little we could do until dawn, and then the instruction came that we were to fight our way out.

So, we discussed how we might do a break-out job, and while we were doing so, it became obvious that the enemy had decided to make their HQ straight opposite the edge of the lane, about 200 yards directly in front of us – and they still didn't know that we were there.

Soon after dawn, a German motor cycle and sidecar drove into the HQ and all the soldiers rushed over, no doubt to ask what was going on. It is hard to estimate how many there were – but there were a lot, and I had them covered with about three Bren guns at about 200 yards' range.

I had no thought of them being exactly the same sort of lads as my own fellows – no thought that they had parents, wives or children – no thought of the fact that some of the same sort of people had killed my brother before Dunkirk. They represented a target, and I gave the order to open fire. War is a dreadful, disgusting, horrible waste!

It took the enemy some time to recover from what we had inflicted on them, during which time I had a look round the area. The water level in the Rhine was about 10–12 feet below the ground level and it appeared that, with a bit of luck, it might be possible to get our troops, obscured from the enemy by the house that was the Company HQ, down to the water's edge. From here they could advance in single file perhaps half a mile towards Arnhem, and then break out into the open to deal with anything between us and the Battalion position. I suggested to the CC that he led the company out, and I would do a rearguard job with one platoon.

The enemy now started to throw everything they had at us, and proved our theory that there were an awful lot of them. Our position quickly became a very unhealthy sort of place to be. A sergeant lying next to me was hit and killed instantly, but it became clear that all the enemy fire was directed at us, the rearguard, and that the men dropping down the riverbank were getting away with it.

I gave them time to travel a couple of hundred yards, then had my own fellows sneak away a few at a time. The scheme worked to an almost unbelievable degree. We had to leave our dead there, of course, and the two German prisoners were killed by their own fire.

The Germans continued to lay a tremendous amount of fire on the place – they must have had an odd sort of feeling when they put their attack in to take the position, only to find that we had gone.

We were greeted back at HQ as conquering heroes. We had killed a great number of the enemy and had virtually walked through an enemy that was perhaps five or six times stronger than we were. The citation for gallantry paints a rosy picture of what went on that day – it makes no mention at all of Lady Luck – *she* had been gallant in the extreme.

Jock and I went back to HQ. The enemy, presumably having taken Renkum, closed in on the battalion position and started to make life quite difficult for us. The enemy were in the open ground to the west. There was plenty of cover for them and they came in quite close – bayonet-close on a number of occasions – but they were beaten back time after time.

On the third or fourth day, I had a message over the wireless from one of my Signals Corporals, attached to D Company. I shall never forget it. He said, with not the slightest quiver in his voice. 'There is a flame-thrower coming in to our HQ now sir. Goodbye and good luck.' Corporal Larry Cowan must have been killed within seconds of sending the message. D Company as a fighting unit had ceased to exist – a few may have been taken prisoner, but most of them were killed.

I had taken two homing pigeons with me. I had not very much faith in them, but taking them was a way of ensuring that I was carrying as heavy a load as any of my men, and there was always a chance that they could be useful. I released the first one with a message from a senior airforce officer to Air Defence Great Britain. A couple of days later I ran out of pigeon food and realised that if the bird was weakened through being starved, it would stand no chance of getting home at all. I requested permission to release it. I sent the following message – which amounted to a load of nonsense:

'From Lieut JSD Hardy: Have to release birds owing to shortage of food and water. About eight tanks laying about in sub unit areas, very untidy but not causing us any trouble. Now using as many German weapons as we have British. MGs most effective when aiming towards Germany. Dutch people grand, but Dutch tobacco rather stringy. Great beard-growing competition on in our unit, but no time to check up on the winner.'

The bird miraculously arrived back at Corps HQ and the newsmen got hold of the message. It made headlines in the English papers the next day and was given such a degree of importance that it ended up in the War Museum, classified as one of the epic messages from a field of battle.

Come the fourth, fifth and sixth days, the men were becoming terribly tired. There was no sleep, they were down to their last scraps of food, they were haggard, weary almost to the point of collapse. There were continual rumours of disaster, but through it all, the men were steadfast, confident and could still raise a smile.

A patrol was sent out at one time, and they had no sooner left, than the NCO returned with the news that they had been hit by shellfire. I went out to see what could be done, and found a young lad, just barely 18, with a gaping hole in his back. He was beyond help, but still conscious, with only seconds to live. Try as I might, I shall never forget the look in the lad's eyes. Try as I might, I could never explain it.

I think it was somewhere around the sixth day that our Artillery Officer was killed, and that left me, as Signals Officer, to take over his job. I asked for shellfire on a few occasions, but the best they could do was a few rounds. On the eight or ninth day, I again had to ask for shellfire, and was answered by a very, very American voice that told me he represented a regiment of 'Long Toms', and asked how much do I need. I asked him what the danger area was from his type of shellfire. He explained and I told him that I wanted him to plaster an area so that the inner edge of his danger area was within a few yards of our troops. I took it that he was firing from 10 to 12 miles away. It was very effective.

As each day came along, we were all quite sure that this would be the day that the Second Army would reach us. We had become used to the hunger, but the shortage of water was punishment indeed. We were short of ammunition – the men had to make every shot count.

Finally the message came through that we were to pull out. We had to observe absolute silence, and to add to our misery, it was pouring with rain. It was a journey through hell, but finally we made it."

Willi Renner was a sergeant in the 2nd Battalion of the German 6th Parachute Regiment and was involved in fierce house-to-house fighting in the town of Reusel, south of Eindhoven, as Operation Market Garden began.

"Hand-grenades were thrown up or down, and our raiding group, which consisted of about 15 men, was given the task of fighting clear one street's worth of houses. That meant clearing the enemy out using whatever means possible. The best method, of course, is to make them run away, to avoid having to shoot them. Of course, if they don't run away, you have to use force – and to use force, in a war context, means to shoot them. So we had to shoot at them or throw hand-grenades, and there were, of course, losses on both sides.

On the way back, while clearing the houses, we came upon an Englishman who had been shot in the stomach. I assumed that the man had been hit by someone from the street or something like that, and that his own men had left him lying there in the house – they couldn't take him with them.

I came towards the house and, while we ran, shots came out of the cellar window. A few metres to the left of me, one of our men was hit in the throat. Blood came pouring from his throat – it was terrible. Another comrade of mine was hit in the chest. In his wallet he had a picture of his girlfriend, and the bullet went straight through the photo.

Another comrade of ours was shot through the thigh. These were the three casualties that we could see at this stage, and of course, we now knew that there were people still in the house, shooting at us from the cellar. We took cover to the right and ran round to the other side of the house.

We moved so that we couldn't be seen by the English soldiers in the house, and kicked in one of the cellar windows. We threw in a hand-grenade – whether it was one or a few, I can't remember exactly. There was a terrible explosion. It's a terrible thing when a grenade explodes in such a small space – I had experienced this myself. The English emerged – a few of them were wounded and some inside must have been dead. Four of them came out and I took them back with me.

Just before this, we shot at some English who had tried to run away across a turnip field. They had been trained how to run in this situation – lie down, jump up, run, throw yourself down again, and so on.

So, the direct fighting was now over, and we searched the house to check whether anyone else was there – and now we had to take care of the wounded and dead men. We took from the dead men all their papers, all their valuables, their watch and identity tag and packed this all away. Then the dead were buried and the wounded taken to the main field hospital. I was given the job of taking the four prisoners back.

Everything was going smoothly until at one point I could see that the prisoners had become afraid. The first thing that came to mind was that these men were afraid that they were going to be shot. Then things relaxed a little. We exchanged cigarettes. These were only young men and they were suffering from the psychological effects of the house fighting – the guilt that they might have killed someone; the shock from the exploding grenades."

Battle of the Bulge – Cold Christmas

Although the Germans had suffered heavy losses on both the Eastern and Western Fronts, new units called Volksgrenadiers were raised and equipped under the forceful leadership of Goebbels and Production Minister Albert Speer. On 16 December 1944, using these units, Hitler launched a counter-attack in the west to split the British and American armies with a drive from the Ardennes to Antwerp. Despite considerable German success, however, their fuel supplies were running very low and they had been blocked at Bastogne, where the 101st Airborne Division was surrounded but fighting hard. The weather improved, allowing the Allied air forces into the attack, and General Patton's Third Army swung north to relieve Bastogne on 26 December. On 3 January 1945, the Allies went on the offensive and eliminated the German salient in what became known as the Battle of the Bulge. Both sides lost about 800 tanks, the US Army suffered 81,000 casualties, the British 1,400 and the Germans 100,000. Overall, the attack had achieved only a six-week respite for Germany and squandered its last tank and air resources. Combatants of the Bulge recall the desperate days of Christmas 1944.

Flight Lieutenant Maurice Garton of 103 Squadron flew on bombing missions over Germany as part of the Allied softening up process of the enemy's homeland. One such mission ended in an extraordinary close squeak – others were lessons in pinpointed mass destruction.

"October 30, 1944. On returning from a night raid on Cologne, we were over England, flying north for Elsham and looking for the three Sandra lights coned over the aerodrome. The Wireless Op came up with a message saying that German night fighters were about and so all lights on aerodromes had been extinguished – so also must be our navigation lights. We continued to travel north on a compass bearing, waiting for the all-clear to come through from the Wireless Op.

'All clear'. We started looking for Elsham again. Suddenly, Jock Kinnear, my Engineer, staring out of the starboard window, shouted, 'There is an aerodrome – and the red light on the control tower', when suddenly there was a terrific roar as another aircraft passed very close underneath. The red light the Engineer saw was no control tower – it was the red port navigation light on the wing tip of another aircraft! After the shock, we settled down again, thinking that a near miss was as good as a mile. We proceeded to land safely.

The next day, when we went out to the aircraft for another raid on Cologne, the flight sergeant in charge of the ground crew came over and asked what had happened the previous night, and asked us to come and have a look at the state of our starboard tail fin. Lo and behold, there was a big dent about 18 inches long where the aerial of the other aircraft had caught us.

In the first heavy bomber raid on the *Reich* in daylight, a Lanc of 103 Squadron was hit in the fuel tank on the way home. On fire and in a steep glide, all seven of the crew bailed out. As the pilot came out last man, the plane exploded and then the German ack-ack opened up at the parachutes, killing the men as they plummeted down.

On another raid, however, on Emmerich am Rhein, 340 Lancasters and 10 Mosquitoes dropped 4,000 lb bombs and incendiaries. In a very accurate attack, the total damage was 2,424 buildings destroyed, 689 buildings damaged, 680,000 cubic metres of rubble, 641 civilians and 96 soldiers killed."

Private Alfred Jenkins of A Company of the 2nd Battalion of the Argyll and Sutherland Highlanders, was training in Holland for the forthcoming Reichswald offensive, when the Germans launched their all-out attack in the Ardennes.

"When the Germans broke through, all the available troops were rushed south and as I remember it for the first few days, we seemed to be going all over the place in Belgium.

We finally wound up at a place near Maastricht, near the German border, and that was just before Christmas. It looked as if we were going to be there for a few days, so they had a sit-down Christmas dinner planned for us. Well, what happened was, on Christmas morning we were put on a half hour stand-by which meant we had to be ready to move at a moment's notice. That meant that we had our Christmas dinner out of mess tins and standing up in the open. We finally moved at 8 o'clock that night.

From there we went to a suburb of Liège. When we went into the house where we were billetted, the owners of the house were a middle-aged couple with a young daughter, and it was obvious that the daughter had been suffering from the food shortages, but they had this banner across the living room 'Welcome to our liberators – welcome to brave British soldiers'. We were there a few days, then we moved over to the other side of Liège, where we actually did guard a bridge at Amay.

It was while we were there that we captured what we thought was a German spy. One of our section came in one day with a chap he had met, dressed in American uniform. He shook hands all round – which made us a bit suspicious, because this is a Continental, not a British or American habit. So we had difficulty understanding him and asked him if he spoke English. He said no, but he said he spoke American. We noticed that he was only wearing the liner of his steel helmet, which we knew had been forbidden by the US command. Then when he told us he had come from Paris that day, we thought 'Aha, what have we got here?', because we knew that all movement between Paris and the front had been stopped, because it was at that time they had the scare that there was an assassination team out looking for Eisenhower. We handed him over to the American Military Police. Whether he was a spy or not, I don't know.

We were there over the New Year, and it was about this time that it really started snowing. Up until then it had been fairly cold, but not the sort of snow you usually associate with the Ardennes. I always remember, we were billetted a section to a house, and we had been there for about a week, and the lady of the house had formed a sort of attachment for us. She had baked a special cake for us on the day when we had to move. She couldn't see why we had to go, only to be replaced by more British troops. The last we saw of her, she was standing in the doorway of her house, barring the Seaforths.

On the 7th January we spent the night travelling in an absolute blizzard and arrived the next day at Bertogne and then they decided the roads were unfit for vehicles and we had to take to our feet. We went on to a place where the East Lancs had had a battle – we found several of their bodies lying around there.

We got a warning that there were some German tanks and infantry approaching, so we stood to, but all that happened was we captured one prisoner, who said he was a Polish deserter. It was funny, you usually found in the German Army that there were no Germans – they were all Poles or Russians. When we got into Germany, we never found anybody who supported Hitler. They were all members of the 20th July bomb plot! You had to wonder where he got all his troops from!

We had to march back to Bertogne. I remember that march. It wasn't exactly cross-country, but the roads were fairly indistinguishable, and the shelling had brought down a lot of branches of trees – and they are nearly all fir trees down there. There must have been a slight thaw, then it had refrozen, and each individual needle on these trees was coated in ice, so trying to march over that in hob-nailed boots was rather like walking over ball bearings.

We had as many layers of clothes as we could, Balaclava helmets, greatcoats, leather jerkins – at that point we didn't have snow suits. They didn't think of issuing them until it was all over. It was so cold there that we had to wipe all the oil off our weapons. Usually you had to keep the moving parts of your weapon slightly oiled, but we had to wipe it off because it was freezing.

Each section had a Bren gun – I had the Bren gun in our section. The rest were armed with rifles, apart from the corporal who had either a Sten gun, or, if he was lucky, he looted a Schmeisser machine pistol – this was preferable to a Sten gun because they were notedly very unreliable weapons. At one point earlier in the year after a couple of accidents, anyone who had Sten guns in their battalion was told to remove the magazines from them when travelling in transport, because more than one had been dropped and gone off. Bren guns were different – they were using them in the British Army up until the 1960s, because they said it was so accurate that you could shoot through its bullet-holes.

Next day the Black Watch were going to take Laroche, and we had to move through them. We were travelling in transport and we got held up because the Black Watch were delayed. It was night time, and the three-tonner that we were in skidded off the road and landed on its side. There was an entire platoon in there – about 30 men – and how none of us got injured with all the equipment flying all over the place, I don't know.

En route from Lavaux we stopped at a sort of barn at a crossroads. We could see the road ahead of us went down into a valley and up again – and just at the bottom of this valley was some sort of small hut. The leading section started off and it just reached this hut. There was this burst of machine-gun and shell fire from the ridge ahead of us. It caught them all in the open – there was no cover there, and it took several hours for them to get back.

There was one chap in that section, he had his younger brother with him, and he saw him killed right in front of his eyes. They told us afterwards that they had to hold him back because he wanted to take off after these Germans by himself. Then another section had a go. The same thing happened. We could see what was going to happen. They would just get down to this hut, and the Germans were waiting for them. Then it was our turn to go. As you can imagine, everyone was trying to be last out of this barn where we were sheltering.

It was at that point that Major Samwell, the Company Commander, decided that he'd come down with us. He called up a troop of Sherman tanks we had there, and we started off down. He walked behind one of the tanks to use the phone on the back of it – it was for communications with the infantry. He just walked behind this, and the tank was hit by either an armour-piercing shell or a shell – but my main memory of that was a cloud of shrapnel and dust flying everywhere. I saw Major Samwell fall there. We beat it back to the barn.

They decided, after all this, that it really was a waste of time trying to get round that road. According to the records, there were something like 28 casualties. Fighting there had come to a stop and the Americans were just sweeping up. What happened was that we were at the tip of our movement forward, and we were pinched out by the Americans coming in from each side of us."

Lieutenant Virgil Lary was with Battery B of the US 7th Armored Division's 285th Field Artillery Observation Battalion. On 17 December, he was ordered to move up to reinforce the slender American line at St Vith.

"The battery was on the road that morning, and by noon had reached a point three miles south of Malmédy on the St Vith road. Some 300 yards behind the crossroads of the cutoff for St Vith, the column was suddenly stopped by German machine-gun and mortar fire. We jumped down from our vehicles and took cover in the ditches on the sides of the road.

The German unit was an element of Colonel Peiper's 1st SS Panzer Division. They had stopped at the crossroads, surprised the MP who was directing traffic there (and who had escaped behind a house), turned the signs around to confuse us and then opened fire on the convoy.

I jumped down from my truck and crawled to a small stream 40 feet from the road. I covered myself with grass and mud and headed for that house. A captain from my battery followed – but a tank came up the road and I put up my hands. A German officer stuck his head out of the turret of the tank and aimed his pistol at me. I ducked and the shot missed. The German then aimed at the captain and fired again. He missed and I jumped into a ditch.

By this time, three more tanks had come up the road. They were all Tiger tanks of the newest German design. They moved along the road, spewing fire at the ditches. One German tank shot up an American ambulance. Other German tanks knocked out 24 American vehicles of the convoy. Colonel Peiper then beckoned his task force onwards, and left the mopping up to the parachute infantry troops accompanying them.

The German infantrymen came down the road, examining the ditches. I surrendered again and soon found myself in a field with about 150 other POWs, guarded by the paratroops. The Germans searched the Americans and took wallets, gloves, rings, cigarettes – and all weapons. They ordered us into a field south of the crossroads, and I noticed that they had set up machine guns surrounding the field. We were told to raise our hands above our heads. Tanks at the two ends of the field along the road covered them. A German command car drew up and run on. An officer spoke. 'You will go across the Siegfried Line, will you, you dirty swine'?

The officer took aim at an American doctor and fired his pistol. The medical officer fell. The German fired again, and another American dropped. Then the two tanks and the machine guns in the field began firing.

I dropped. I was hit in the arm and the foot. I lay, bleeding – as if dead. German soldiers came along the line of bodies and shot some of the wounded and bayonetted some and bashed the heads of others with rifle butts. (When the bodies were found later, the eyes of some of the soldiers had been gouged out.)

The Germans came up to me. 'Is he dead?' asked one. Something diverted his attention and he moved away. I lay perfectly still, my eyes closed, but I could hear the sound of pistols firing and the noise of rifle butts against skulls.

After about an hour, the German column formed up and moved off, leaving the field silent. Several survivors decided to make a break for it and got up and ran for the house on the road – including me. The Germans opened fire. Several men dropped, but I made it to the house and lay doggo. A German officer came along, saw us, but did not fire at us – then went away. The German armoured column began to pass and for two hours, tanks and half-tracks ran down the road to St Vith. When they seemed to be gone, two of us ran down the road towards Malmédy. From the crossroads the Germans began to fire at us, but they didn't hit us and we ran on for two miles. Then a jeep came along and picked us up, and took us into Malmédy and safety. A few days later, I learned that of the 150 Americans in the field, only 43 survived, and three quarters of *them* were wounded."

Lieutenant-Colonel A W Brown (later Brigadier, CBE, DSO, MC) with the 3rd Royal Tank Regiment, was at Dinant, northwest of Bastogne as Christmas approached in the Ardennes.

"During the morning A Squadron made contact with a Belgian officer who had led the *maquis* throughout the war. This officer is now the Baron de Sorinne. He stayed with the regiment throughout the action and was invaluable because of his local knowledge of the country.

The Regimental Group remained in these positions for the whole of the 22nd and the night 22nd/23rd, but at night, the forward squadrons closed up into a tight leaguer mounting only guard tanks around them. Except in Dinant, there were no infantry with the tank squadrons.

During the night 22nd/23rd December, C Squadron Commander and his SSM (Signals Sergeant-Major) did a further reconnaissance through Marche, where they found an American Infantry Division, whose commander said that he was proposing to hold on there, and that the US 2nd Armored Division was due to come down from the north-east on the left flank of the 3rd Royal Tank regimental group.

This clarified the position somewhat, but at the same time, raised further complications, because the Germans were using American equipment and uniforms and consequently the task of telling friend from foe was extremely tricky.

The situation now was that there were endless good positions to the south, north, south-east and north-east of the main Dinant-Sorinne road, from which any attack could be dealt with – but for such a small force, it was impossible to go too far east, otherwise the enemy could have outflanked the group either to the south or to the north, and reached the bridge without making contact.

The most dangerous flank was the south-east, in the direction of Celles and, as I did not wish to become engaged too far out in this direction, the reconnaissance troop was sent to this area and ordered to take up a position of observation. This was done and as a result, it was found that there were some enemy in Celles – but this was not known until the evening of 22 December.

The morning of the 23rd December dawned foggy and visibility was almost nil. Regimental Tactical Headquarters established itself in the château of Sorinne with A Squadron. Apart from the arrival of a British Air Liaison officer and an American officer from US 2nd Armored Division, very little occurred on this day.

Acting on information received from the American Officer, I sent a liaison officer from 3 RTR up to Celles to try and contact Headquarters of the 2nd US Armored Division. After some delay, he succeeded in doing this and remained there as a liaison officer throughout the period of the action.

It was on this day also that an apparently American jeep drove through one of the road blocks approaching the bridge at Dinant on the east side of the river. This road block, as were all the others, was manned by the 8 RBs, who had established a movable barrier and arranged for mines to be pulled across the road should any vehicle break through the barrier without stopping. As we were by now in contact with the Americans, this jeep was not fired on, but as it refused to stop, the mines were drawn across the road and it was blown up. It was found to contain three German SS – two were killed and one taken prisoner.

On the evening of the 23rd, it was confirmed from local information that German infantry and some tanks or half-tracked vehicles had got into the village of Conneux. In fact, their vehicles could be heard moving about just as light was failing. As there was still no infantry with the tank squadron east of the river, it was not deemed possible to take any action that night. Therefore the squadrons went into leaguer in their respective positions, but gun tanks were posted to cover the road approaches.

In the case of the main road leading through Sorinne, an RAC officer was placed out with a wireless set 400 yards forward of the edge of the village. This officer established himself in the upper storey of a cottage, from which he obtained a good field of view down the road. The mist had lifted by this time, and it was a clear, moonlight night, so that he would be able to give warning of enemy vehicles approaching.

He had only been there for a short while when he found that German infantry had, undetected by him, moved into the ground floor of the same house. The enemy were not aware of his presence.

He was able to give warning of their presence, and also escape on foot back to Regimental Headquarters at Sorinne. As the enemy infantry were now only some 400 yards from Regimental Headquarters and A Squadron were 'stood to' for the remainder of the night, no attack was made."

Sergeant Willi Renner of the German 6th Parachute Regiment was at Obermarbach, near the Belgian border with Germany, at Christmas. His story begins as he makes a check on the company's foxholes and emplacements.

"I heard a noise. I turned to the right and there I saw a black soldier right in front of me, and from where I was standing, about 30 or 40 metres away, he had a very warlike look. He had wrapped himself up against the cold – it was freezing in the Eifel at that time. He had a long scarf around his neck and there he stood in front of me, this huge guy, a lot taller than me, a spade in his hand.

If I remember correctly he laughed when he spotted me, but in a situation like this, you remember your training – he who shoots first lives longer. I had a machine pistol and I was about to shoot – but because of the cold and the poor conditions of the last few days, I was only able to get one shot out of it. It was jammed. Anyway, I was more or less sure that I'd dismissed him, and he appeared to be in the hedge.

I got back to my duties and hardly even thought about the incident. It was only later that it occurred to me that it was a mistake to leave the man there – not to run back and report him – to tell the commander that the enemy had got so far.

Eventually I got to the last position, which was a machine-gun position, the guns pointed at the valley where the Americans were on the other side. I was a bit puzzled, everything was so quiet, then suddenly someone shouted out to me, 'What the hell are you doing? Take cover. You'll be blasted out of sight.'. Anyway, shots rang out and I dived for cover, but I didn't do this properly. My legs should have lain flat along the ground, but I had dived behind the mound of earth behind which the machine-guns were, and my legs were sticking over the top.

I felt a sudden thump. It's a really strange feeling – a dull thud as if someone has just hit you with a heavy club. I'd been shot in the leg, in the left calf. I scrambled in panic into the machine-gun hole and my comrades tore up some pieces of bed sheets which they had picked up from the houses they had been holed up in. They wrapped them round my leg as an emergency dressing. I lay there for an hour, just waiting, but after a while the pain was too much, and I told my comrades that I couldn't wait around any longer – I'd bleed to death. But if I tried to run out, I'd probably get blasted again.

We discussed it among ourselves. One of them thought I should stay there – others said they would leave it up to me. Anyway, I decided I should make a run for it. I took a piece of the white rag that they had used to bandage my leg, tied it to the end of my machine pistol and held that out above the mound.

Nothing happened for a while. All quiet. Eventually I popped my head out. There was nothing heroic – I had no choice but to chance it.

I managed to scramble out up to my stomach, and eventually the whole of me was out, lying flat on my stomach. A few seconds passed, then there was a noise in the bushes and I heard one of the Americans – it must have been one who spoke German. He shouted over to me, '*komm 'rüber*' (come over). I'll never forget those two words as long as I live. I remember then, what I did. Just to gain some time, I shouted back, 'I cannot walk'. Then the other thought came over me all of a sudden. I could have given myself up, and of course, there's always the possibility that you are accused of deserting to the other side. It can happen that way. I thought there was no way I could let that happen – my family might suffer as a result. The only other thought that came into my head at that moment was that I should try to save myself by throwing myself behind the hedge, but of course, they could have come along the hedge with a machine gun and I'd be hit somehow.

Of course, I didn't really have the time to think these thoughts through. I just threw myself aside. I crawled on my elbows for a while, then flung myself into the bush. Anyway, there was a lot of firing, but they had lost sight of which direction I was heading in, and I managed to scramble away and get back to my comrades. One of them got hold of me and wanted to start carrying me off, like a sack of coal, back to the company combat post. He began to run, hauling me along across a turnip field. I don't think he realised how heavy I was, and he stumbled while he was running and did his knee in. Now we both had one leg out of action, but we carried on and eventually reached the company combat post."

Poland – The People's Uprising

*L*ate in the afternoon of 1 August 1944, Warsaw suddenly erupted. The Polish underground had risen up
against their German occupiers in an attempt to liberate the
city before the arrival of the Red Army. Soviet artillery fire
could be heard in the distance from the streets of Warsaw,
and the Poles thought it would be only a matter of days before
the Germans would be forced to retreat from the Polish capital. In this they were to be cruelly mistaken. But the uprising
in Warsaw was political operation as much as a military,
designed to show the world that Poland intended to re-emerge
as an independent state once the war was over.

Herbert Brunnegger was a platoon leader in the German SS
Totenkopf **Division when, in autumn 1943, he was posted to**
Warsaw – into the tense atmosphere which prevailed as the
Polish resistance built up to their ultimate counterstrike.

"Warsaw was a dangerous place. Poland's capital was like a pot of bub-
bling lava whose lid was about to blow. My orders were to report to
the Replacement Battalion III at the Marbuta Barracks. On the way
from the station to my new unit, I witnessed a shoot-out as men from
the Polish Resistance were chased through the streets.

I soon discovered that scenes like this had become routine. It was
strictly forbidden to go out alone or even in twos. If you wanted to
go into the city, you had to be armed. We were told quite clearly
which bars we were allowed to visit, and were told to stay clear of
the others. Nevertheless, soldiers kept disappearing without trace.

Their uniforms and weapons turned up again on men from the Polish underground.

One SS *Unterscharführer*, awarded the Iron Cross First Class, was suddenly arrested because the Security Service had found out that he had been seeing a very pretty Polish girl, and through her had latched on to the Polish underground. He jumped from the first floor of a house on to the street and was gunned down by a sentry. Yesterday he was a brave soldier in Russia – today a traitor to his people. Yesterday a comrade – today an enemy. Was it only the Polish girl who changed his mind?

In Warsaw I couldn't find any volunteers from the 'class of '38'. The place was swarming with foreigners in SS uniform. What had happened to our once so-proud elite troop? Croatians, Galicians, Lithuanians, Estonians, Hungarians, Russians and French were now members of the SS. We'd soon be having Tartars, Turks, Serbs, Rumanians, Bulgarians, Indians and Italians with us! Alongside the volunteers from Holland, the men from Denmark and Norway in the *Wiking* and *Norland* divisions had already proved their worth. The *Freikorps Denmark*, who fought with us in the Demyansk pocket, had shown fantastic bravery. The continuing deployment of new SS divisions could not disguise the fact that the original fighting strength had been whittled away.

One day I was awarded the Iron Cross II Class. My company commander had sent on the decoration certificate. As platoon leader, I would have been delighted and very proud, but now, having been through three field hospitals, where I'd seen medals dished out like they were going out of fashion, I saw this differently."

Marzenna Karczewska was 19 when the uprising began. Since her home was important as an Underground base, she and her sister were not to take any overtly active part in the preparations – but as the uprising went on, her role necessarily became a military one.

"During the German occupation I was simply involved in preparing cigarettes for our soldiers who were in the hospitals. We'd make up parcels for them, or take them soup cooked in special field kitchens.

We, the insurgents, knew what was going on, and when the time came we went to the jewellers in a main street in Warsaw. We had rings, and we took them to the jeweller who engraved the date of the start of the uprising on them.

It was afternoon when I went there with my sister and another friend. When we left the shop, the fighting started on the street. I was a long way away from my home, so we just went from house to house and stayed during the night wherever we were. Where there was fighting we helped, carried wounded, made bandages and did whatever was needed to help.

We finally got back to my house on 6 August. Only my mother was at home – father was out somewhere fighting. We couldn't stay at home, so we had a quick wash and went to the street to join some people there. We knew that many people didn't reach their destinations to get to their local organised units – so everyone just went to the nearest unit.

We joined this group. We were sworn in, then we were ready to do anything. We carried wounded – I collected medicines and bandages and medical equipment wherever I heard a place had been blown open or burned. I went to see if I could recover anything which I could bring back to the unit. I also went as a messenger between units – and this went on until the end of August.

On the night of the 1st and 2nd of September, the old part of the city was falling. A few days before we had transferred some wounded people through the sewers from the old part of the city to the centre. I wasn't involved in this, but my sister was wounded and she was taken away.

I was to go with my group – 39 of us – and we were almost the last group to leave through the sewer. It was very narrow – 78 × 80 cm. We had no idea what it would be like – but we tried to do it because we knew some people before us had gone through sewage channels before to another part of the town.

My mother was with me in the queue to go into the scuttle, and unfortunately, because we didn't know what to expect, the person about three ahead of me didn't realise that there were steps, so she jumped from the top – on to the head of someone who had not yet moved along into the tunnel. He was injured and fainted, and we didn't know if perhaps she had killed him. So there was a delay until we explained to her that there were steps, and she went back. Then we had to try and get him out. Somebody had to be left behind to look after him and the rest had to go – as many as possible. But because of the delay, my mother didn't get into the sewer – she was left behind. When the Germans caught her they realised that she must have been fighting in the uprising, so they took her straight to a concentration camp.

We didn't realise that the sewer would be so small. They told us the journey would take about two and a half hours – but it took us 24 hours. The problem was that the person who was supposed to direct us lost his way. Also we learned that on a previous occasion the Germans had heard some movement from above the scuttle and thrown petrol into the entrance and set fire to it to kill the people below. So we had to be so careful – so silent. We couldn't talk, nothing. We had to pull each other towards the way out. Suddenly we couldn't move and we started to talk quietly to each other. 'What's happening? Why aren't we moving?' Somebody had died in the tunnel in front of us, and the body had swollen up and filled the whole tunnel. We couldn't move – so we had to push this body – whatever it was (we didn't have light to see what it was). We only thought it was a body at the time, and found out later. We had to push it to another scuttle with a bigger opening.

When we started the journey it was arranged that we'd go alternatively, boy, girl, boy all the way down the line – but unfortunately the men were very weak. They were the worst, and they didn't have the guts to keep going. They got claustrophobia. They panicked and started shouting that they wanted to kill themselves – they said they would be better off going and being taken by the Germans. We had to cover their mouths – we wanted to survive!

We had a bit of a fight as we had to calm them down and get moving again. We had to get together enough energy to push the obstacle that was stopping us. Eventually we knew we were nearing the end of the sewage tunnel because the cover of the scuttle was removed – they were expecting us. We saw a light – it was a miracle for us. We knew then we could just crawl on slowly – that we would survive. The energy came back to us and we were keen to get out.

The first person who reached the scuttle couldn't go out. They collapsed from the fresh air after being in the sewer for so long. I remember it was a sunny day – there were plenty of people walking around. It was like a completely new world!

They took us to the public bath – we were dirty – filthy, from the sewers – and I had scratches on my forehead and the tops of my arms from the hours of pushing through the tunnel. I didn't know, but I'd got an infection in the scratches and had a very high temperature.

The warm water suddenly stopped, so I went to find the water barrel to wash myself – and I just passed out. I don't know what happened to me. The next thing I remember was my colleagues searching for me. I vaguely heard my name – they were saying, 'She was here somewhere, with us'. I just couldn't speak – but luckily they found me.

My doctor who was with us in the sewer, gave me dressings for my infected wounds, and I was all right after a few days. I was full of energy and ready to fight again.

For the rest of the time, until the end of the uprising, we searched for food. Whenever we learned that there was anything available, we went to get bread or buckwheat or whatever we could find for our wounded and helpless.

On 2 October we were in the centre of the city and we learned that we had been recognised as army by the Germans, and they called an armistice. We had two days of freedom for people to go where they wanted. We had to decide if we wanted to stay in the town or go as POWs with the Germans. I knew then, that since my mother didn't come through the sewer – nor my father – they would still be in the old part of the city. Subconsciously I decided, without having to think and without hesitation. I told my sister we would go as POWs – I wouldn't stay. I couldn't believe that we would be liberated by the Russians.

In one prison camp they tried to persuade us to give up our POW status and go as farm or factory workers in Germany. We refused. We said that under the Geneva Convention we were not allowed to work, and they had to treat us as POWs like the others. They couldn't persuade us and wanted to punish us, so they sent us to a special camp for hard labour – Oberlangen, 9 km from the Dutch border. There we stayed until the end of the war.

They didn't treat us very badly, but we were very hungry – it was a hard time for them as well, because it was near to the end of the war. We had to clean our camp – we had to clean out latrines, dig up potatoes from the fields and cut turf for burning in our stove. This was very little and we were very cold.

You wouldn't believe it – we were liberated by the Polish Army from Scotland, under the command of General Maczek – the 1st Armoured Division. The soldiers were surprised – they didn't expect there to be all these 1,728 Polish girls (and nine infants) in the camp.

By the end of the war, when we were liberated, we were hungry – but within hours we had everything. The Polish Army fed us and brought us food and clothes. Everybody came to visit us – even General Alexander. It was so well known, this camp, and the liberation of such a big number of Polish girls. It was the first time in history that there had been a women's POW camp. There had never been a camp for women soldiers. We wanted to be recognised as soldiers and have POW status."

Lucjan Kindlein was 21 when he left his law studies to train with the military, so when called upon to fight with the Polish Home Army, he was already part-trained – part of a great national movement who would use all their resources to reclaim their homeland and re-assert their independence against Russia too.

"To a certain extent, we all enjoyed it, because it was the first time that we could really stop running from the Germans – and make them run.

We had a very limited amount of arms and ammunition. My unit was lucky – we had quite a lot of automatic weapons and ammunition. Therefore we were used on many occasions for action where there was a bit of trouble. We were very busy in the first few days of the uprising. We had a few losses, of course, but after a few days, we adjusted ourselves to this different way of fighting.

Street fighting is something you have to be specially trained for. We found that we could even cope with the tanks – and we didn't have to be afraid of them. In the town they were very vulnerable, and we threw grenades and burned them with petrol. We learned as we went along.

On many occasions we were asked to attack particular objectives and we had to suffer some losses, but we had a number of wins, and one of these was the police headquarters. At night we dug holes through the buildings to get nearer to the German positions. This was supposed to be a surprise attack during the night, but to a certain extent it wasn't, because they were waiting for us. We met with heavy fire and were stopped, so we had to find some way to go round. That cost us some lives, but we had our ways to do this – mainly by burning them out. We had flame throwers and we managed to penetrate their line, and after about 12 hours, we succeeded. They had to surrender. We managed to capture quite a lot of arms there, and it was a great victory.

I remember on the telephone exchange, the second big attack, there were a number of units involved. We were facing quite a lot of heavy machine-gun fire and grenades from the building coming down on us, because it was occupied by the SS. They knew that eventually we would attack them because the telephone exchange was very important. This operation cost us quite a number of lives, but somehow I survived and got only one bit of metal in my forehead – I'm still carrying it somewhere here – but again, we managed to get in only by burning the heavy front door.

Once we got in, it was all in darkness, and we could hear only the bells ringing – they had an alarm system and it had been switched on by the short circuit at the door. There was a lot of noise and you didn't know which your friends or enemies were. Some Germans shouted, in German, '*Kamarad, Kamarad! Nicht schiessen!*' and we took it that they had had enough, but unfortunately we were not very experienced – they just wanted to find out where we were. When one of our boys called, '*Komm her. Waffen abwerfen!*' that was what they were waiting for – they threw a couple of grenades on us and that was the end of our operation. We knew then, that in the darkness, when they shouted, it was better not to reply to them.

We were fighting for 63 days – it went on and on, and the suffering of the civilian population was even greater. Where we were, we only had the army against us. Sometimes they were drunk; sometimes they were not Germans really – they were just Ukrainians and people they had employed.

We didn't have their heavy artillery or the Stukas against us, because they were afraid of bombing their own positions. Sometimes we would be facing each other over the other side of the same building! So we were better off to a certain extent than the civilian population because the civilians suffered from the bombardment of artillery and the Stukas, and shortages of water, food and medicines.

We got quite a lot of our ammunition from the Germans, and quite a bit of food, too – and German uniforms. In the end we were all dressed differently. Some of the units in the old town were dressed as German parachutists, but with the Polish emblem on their helmets.

With the town so much under German control, we had our headquarters in strong buildings, in the basements. We had to have some rest and food, and in the first month, the arrangements were quite reasonable. In the second month, we were hungry and short of water – but we were still better off than civilians. Each unit had their own ladies who tried to find food for us. In the last weeks of the uprising there was no water and practically no food.

There are some people who find it too upsetting to talk about it, but I myself find it was the most interesting 60 days of my life. I have no doubt about that. There was great comradeship – great elation. We found we were doing something that had to be done, and we were taking part in, as we found out later, one of the biggest battles in the last war. It looked, in the beginning, just to be a skirmish, but in the end it was a very important battle.

You must remember this was after nearly five years of occupation. We had to do something. We had had enough of this treatment from the Germans. Enough is enough. We were preparing ourselves for this during the four years of the occupation. We were building, training, collecting arms. Life was near normal before the uprising. You could buy anything you could think of because Warsaw was on the way to Russia, and there was very heavy movement of troops and supplies from the German war apparatus – and some of it got 'lost' in Warsaw on the black market.

The Germans terrorised the people. They were trying to find out about our Home Army and the underground organisation. They were killing people without any proper trial – taking in the intelligentsia, arresting them for no reason but reprisals.

At the beginning, some elderly people who wanted to have peace, were apprehensive about the violence the uprising would bring. But most of we young people were not afraid – so it was the sacrifice and the effort of young people. Even kids were fighting.

The Polish Home Army was part of the overall operation of Polish forces. It was all geared to that final act – we wanted to show the Germans that we were in power in our country, and were taking revenge for what they were doing to us. It was also to protect our young people from being taken to labour camps.

But the third and most important reason was that Warsaw, as a city, in the centre of Poland, had to be taken – not by Russians, but by the Polish Home Army. That was why we had to do it."

K A Nazarov was a battery commander in an anti-tank regiment of the Red Army. His men had been sent over the River Narowa to defend a Russian bridgehead which the German command was determined to liquidate, some 20 miles (32 km) from Warsaw.

"Immediately in front of our battery it was relatively quiet. But then, somewhere on the other side of the ridge, could be heard a sound that was instantly recognisable – the low howl of a heavy tank's engine. It was still invisible to us as it crawled up the steep western slope of the height toward the ridge.

'Aim at the tank. Armour-piercing!' I ordered. The breech-blocks clanged as armour-piercing shells were loaded into the barrels. This was a tense minute, as all eyes focused on the ridge where just 200 metres away the roar of the tank engine was growing louder. The tank was climbing steeply upward and therefore the first part to appear above the ridge was the gun-barrel with its knobbly shock-absorbing muzzle. Then came the turret and part of the hull and, finally, its armoured belly. It was a T-VI Tiger tank, and was moving directly on to Sergeant Ivanilov's gun.

I saw Ivanilov, tall, dark-haired and habitually cool, rush to the gun-layer and say something to him. A shot thundered out and I clearly saw a black hole in the bottom of the tank. I was all tense inside ... then another hole appeared in the bottom of the machine. So before it could cross the ridge, the tank began to withdraw backwards. The hull, turret and gun-barrel disappeared from view – but it did not go far. From behind the ridge we could see some smoke, then a burst of smoky flame.

Evidently the German submachine gunners had been advancing under the cover of this tank. Within a few minutes they jumped on to the ridge and hurled themselves at the battery. There was a battle of grenades and point-blank firing. The fascist soldiers lay down 30–40 metres from us and for a time we exchanged short-range fire and grenades. We still had anti-personnel shells. The guns went into rapid fire with these, showering thousands of round bullets right up to the ridge. The few surviving enemy retreated."

Petr Alekseevich Uvarov was a history lecturer at Irkutsk University in Russia when he was called up at the outbreak of the war. By summer 1944 he was an artillery officer, taking part in the drive to cross the Bug to reach the Vistula and Warsaw. By the end of July he was on Polish soil.

"I well remember one battle on a sultry day near Siedlce, when we had to repel continual attacks by drunken German soldiers sup-ported by tanks. We hurriedly dug in (the battle was head-on) in an irrigation ditch in front of a wide field of tall, thick, wheat. The Germans stuck ears of wheat in their helmets and came into the attack in columns. They crawled as though they were demented, firing their automatic grenades at us as they came. They kept an intensive mortar fire on our position, and on our right flank, a Ferdinand tank hit at us from an open firing position. The Germans came so close, it was difficult to bring our fire down on them, but all our firing positions were hitting the crowds of fascists with every available weapon. The situation became so bad that our neighbours on the flanks withdrew.

But in these difficult moments, nobody wavered. Everyone was fearless and self-controlled. The bearers continually brought up cartridges and grenades. The lightly wounded either stayed where they were or helped the seriously wounded to get back into the rear. The battalion nurse and her medical girls, paying no attention to the whistle of bullets and explosions of mortar-bombs, did what was necessary for the wounded, complaining only of the shortage of bandages and tearing their tunics and blouses to make more.

The commander of the intelligence section, the much-loved Sergeant Kostrov died in this battle. Many others died, including the commander of my own howitzer battery, a young competent officer, who had just come from college. They were all given posthumous awards and buried near Siedlce."

Leyte Gulf – Last-ditch Attack

When it was clear that the Americans would land on Leyte in the Philippine islands, the Japanese launched on 17 October 1944 a complex naval operation codenamed Sho, or Victory. A decoy force would draw the US fleet to the north and so allow two forces from the west and south to attack the US Seventh Fleet Fleet near Leyte. The ensuing battle fell into four main actions. The first came in the Sibuyan Sea between 23 and 24 October, when a US submarine sank the cruiser Atago, *and the battleship* Musashi *was sunk by carrier aircraft. The Japanese sank the light carrier USS* Princeton *and damaged the cruiser USS* Birmingham. *Then, in Surigao Strait between 24 and 25 October, the Japanese lost the battleship* Fuso *and two destroyers to PT boats; the Japanese then ran into six US battleships which wrecked the battleship* Yamashiro. *On the 25th off Samar the Japanese plan nearly succeeded. In a fast-moving gun battle the Japanese lost two destroyers, with two more crippled by air attack. Japanese gunfire badly damaged the carrier USS* Gambier Bay *and the destroyers USS* Johnston *and* Roberts *were sunk, with the USS* Dennis *seriously damaged;* Gambier Bay *sank at at 09.07 am. But although the Japanese could now have gone on to destroy the US escort carrier group, the aggressive American tactics convinced Admiral Kurita he was fighting a superior force and he withdrew. To the north off Cape Engano on the same day the decoy force of Japanese battleships came under aggressive air attack from US Task Force 38. By the end of the day the Japanese force had lost all its carriers, a cruiser and three destroyers. The Battle of Leyte Gulf's significance was that it finished the Japanese Imperial Fleet – it lost three battleships, four carriers, ten cruisers, 11 destroyers and a submarine. In addition 500 aircraft were lost and personnel casualties were 10,500 seamen and pilots.*

Lieutenant B D Morris, known popularly in the late 30s and early 40s as Wayne Morris, a Hollywood actor, was manning one of the F6Fs of the *Essex*'s Air Group 15 as the Americans tried to intercept the Japanese attack.

"I took off at 10.15 am in the morning with eight other planes, when the fighting was getting hot. One fighter's engine began to miss and that pilot went back to the carrier, but the rest of us went in. We circled over the Task Force, giving special attention to the damaged *Princeton* which was already pouring out smoke, having been hit on the flight deck by a 550 lb bomb from one of the Japanese bombers in the clouds.

There were about 30 Japanese planes. When they saw us, the dive bombers and torpedo bombers broke off and ducked away while the 'rats' [the fighters] formed a Lufberry circle above and went around, nose to tail. I noted they were all Zeroes this time. They stayed high and the bombers were breaking off to go it alone. I decided to go after the lead of one Zero section. I made a high run and saw four bursts strike him. It flamed up and crashed. My wingman broke off just then to chase one of the four bombers that slipped out of the Lufberry circle, shot it down and then rejoined us.

I then made a pass at a pair of Zeroes coming at me. I missed on the first pass and turned to find the Zeroes turning with me and firing shots that were hitting my plane. I tried to run with the Zeroes for a few seconds but then I saw I was not going to win that way so I ducked into a cloud. Once inside the cloud I made a 360 degree turn and came back out where I had gone in. The two Zeroes were circling out towards the other side where they expected me to come out. I got on the tail of one and, in a few seconds, shot it down. But I knew my plane had been hit plenty. The engine began to cough and the cockpit was filling up with hydraulic fluid. I broke off the action and headed back to the carrier."

Lieutenant L Odum, the Aerology Officer of the American 'baby flattop' carrier, *Gambier Bay,* **was on the starboard catwalk as, his devastated ship's decks covered with dead and wounded, the order came to abandon the stricken ship.**

"I didn't relish the idea of going off the high side, so I started walking to the passageway in the centre of the ship, down the stairs by my room, heading for the port side. Near my room there was an explosion and I was thrown against the bulkhead. Shell fragments were ricocheting around me but I wasn't hit. I reached my stateroom and found my bunkmate collecting survival gear. I picked up a palm-sized mirror and stuffed it and an unopened pack of cigarettes in my shirt pocket.

I got to the port side, unlaced my shoes, dropped my helmet and sidearm and holster and slid down a heavy rope. First I was dragged under by the weight of my shoes but I kicked them off and started swimming away from the ship. I spotted a raft and swam to it. About 30 men were aboard. Suddenly I found I was in charge. The leader of the group had sunk into a stupor. I got the uninjured men off the raft and had them cling to the ropes on the sides.

We were so close still that we could see the American fighters and bombers attacking the Japanese cruisers and destroyers as they were heading north. We could only wait until someone came to find us. That night in the water we all had one biscuit the size of a Ritz cracker with a piece of Spam. There was no fresh water. One by one some of the men just drifted away from the raft and were not seen again.

Somehow we got through the night. In the morning we had another bite of biscuit and a malted milk tablet. Sharks began to appear round the raft. Some of the men began drinking sea water and they became delirious.

The second day the sun was hot and the men were dispirited as they saw planes flying overhead which didn't see us. I swam over to the raft next to ours. The men here were in as bad shape as we were, without food and water. The night was full of terrors. Men who had drunk the sea water began hallucinating. Some of them thought they could swim to Samar, and went into the water and had to be dragged back. Some did not come back.

Most of the men had given up hope. I was sure that we would be rescued if we waited. Flares were sent up every hour in hope. At one o'clock the next morning, hope arrived.

A crew member on *PC 623* called out to us 'What ship are you from?' None of us would answer. What if these were Japanese rescuers? Then the patrol boat snapped on its searchlights and began probing us. Suddenly, as with one voice we all yelled, 'Yes, yes, we are Americans. *Gambier Bay*.' By now we could see the big number 623 on the patrol craft. It slowed down and sailors began lowering nets over the side for our men to climb. I started swimming over and was overrun and nearly drowned by some men as the boat pulled in towards the rafts. Men were crawling over me to get to the boat. I shook myself free and climbed to the deck, lay down on that cold steel and wept and thanked God for His deliverance."

Torao Suematsu had climbed through the ranks of the Japanese Imperial Navy since 1939 and, by late 1944 was Staff Officer, Number 1 Special Attack Forces. He recalls the events in the Sibuyan Sea, 24 October.

"At about 2 pm, *Musashi*, battered on all sides, and already the victim of at least ten torpedoes and countless bombs, was ordered to make for Manila, and we sailed on leaving her behind. She had her escort vessels, of course – however, air attacks by enemy ship-borne aircraft increased in ferocity as time went on, and as the damage we had sustained was not insignificant, we needed to turn back and take stock. At about 3.30 pm, C-in-C Kurita changed fleet course westward.

He judged that if we continued to advance as we were, we would sustain far greater damage (besides, *Musashi*, and the flagship of No. 5 Squadron, *Myoko*, had been torpedoed and had fallen out of line, and both *Yamato* and *Nagato* had been damaged by bombing), since the enemy assault planes had increased in number. He decided to wait for the results of the attack on the enemy's mobile force by our aircraft, avoiding for a while bearing the brunt of the attack – also, I think there was the chance that he would mislead the enemy.

So there's not the slightest justification for thinking he was going to abandon the breakthrough into Leyte. I think this was sufficiently clarified by the second reverse course after 5 pm, because of the receipt of the signal from Combined Fleet C-in-C Toyota, 'Heaven is on our side. Attack with all forces', was made about 7 pm.

Kurita realised that the breakthrough into Leyte Gulf would be delayed – he wouldn't reach it until dawn on the 25th. I remember we were anxious about adjusting with Nishimura Force how we should go about it.

But there was a more urgent problem – the passage through San Bernardino Strait. I mean, we were worried that we might be ambushed at the exit from the strait. At any rate, because we'd taken a fair hiding from the submarines the day before, we would be in a real fix if we became a target at the exit from the strait, when we would have no freedom of manoeuvre. However, the enemy seems to have judged our previous reverse course to be a withdrawal, and made no provision.

Our getting out of the strait safely didn't depend on the enemy or ourselves – of course we didn't know it at the time, but the enemy had finally become aware of Ozawa Force. The enemy had no reason to think that Ozawa Force was a decoy, and the fact that it was, unlike us, an air fleet must have meant they felt it to be a threat. So there seemed to be no need to pay attention to Kurita Force, which had changed course.

At any rate, that night we were able to pass uneventfully through San Bernardino Strait. Even if there were no submarines, we expected to find the enemy fleet lying in wait for us. We had to pass through the strait in a single column. At the exit, if it had come to a gunnery engagement, the enemy in line abreast, we wouldn't have stood a chance.

The loss due to the reverse course alone was about three hours, but besides that there was considerable delay due to the air attacks by enemy aircraft, so that when we came out of the strait, it was just past midnight – deep night. And at exactly that time, Nishimura Force was approaching Surigao Strait. They came down on the 25th, and when our force reformed into a ring for night sailing, the enemy aircraft carrier units suddenly came into view. I was on the bridge at the time, and I was astounded – it was something we had not considered.

For an instant we had a bit of a scene on the bridge – of shock, surprise, quite unheard of. Ordinarily you'd never consider such an encounter. Clearly the enemy had not properly interpreted our movements. In this situation, the advantage was with us. It is the Chief of Staff who issues a fleet movement order in such a case – after, of course, obtaining the consent of the C-in-C. But if the Chief of Staff says to the C-in-C, 'We'll do it!' the C-in-C replies yes or no. If he differs from the Chief of Staff's opinion, he can say, 'No, let's do something else', but I don't think the Chief of Staff was on the bridge at this time. For what seemed a long interval, although it can't have been more than a minute, no-one said a word. But I was impatient, being afraid we might let slip a thousand-to-one chance, and in the end I couldn't stand it any longer. I said, 'C-in-C, we must move towards the enemy.'. 'Yes,' he answered, and then gave the order, 'Column unit turn, let's go!' looking at the compass. We raised the flag, 'column unit turn', on a bearing to contain the enemy – it must have been 110. (The order means the fleet changes direction completely as one unit, not just as individual ships.)

Because the enemy were a force of aircraft carriers and destroyers, they could not open fire on us at once with their guns. So as soon as we had completed 'column unit turn', *Yamato* began to fire. However, when she'd fired four or five rounds, enemy destroyers advanced at speed and spread a smoke screen.

This was the first time *Yamato* had opened fire with her main guns on an enemy fleet. She had only fired her AA guns before that. So everybody shouted, 'We've sunk her!' – but in fact it wasn't possible to confirm whether we'd sunk a ship or not, because of the smoke screen. Passing close by later, we saw an enemy aircraft carrier up to the deck in water, so we can only have sunk one ship for certain. Nearby, half-naked crew members were drifting on rafts.

As far as the sunk aircraft carrier is concerned, it's anyone's guess whether she was hit by a torpedo or by gunfire. She was an escort carrier, so the enemy was not a large force. At the time we thought they were standard carriers. At any rate, we made an all-out attack. Then, unluckily, when we were getting a thorough pasting from enemy bombers, a squall came up between us and the enemy. How can I describe it? When we were going into the attack, a squall comes up – how about that?

We spent about two hours searching for them, but we too had been the victims of torpedo attacks from the enemy's destroyers. In order to dodge these torpedoes, *Yamato* had to run in the opposite direction from the enemy. We ran for about ten minutes, but that was a lot of time to lose. But because visibility was poor due to the squall, it was impossible to estimate what our situation was in relation to one another. Fleet high command was possibly no better off.

Estimating was out of the question, so we had to consider our fuel situation. To control the battle line, we ordered the fleet to concentrate. The basic course in this case was north, and that was a problem. On that course, we were increasing our distance from Leyte. Moreover, all units were pretty scattered – it took a fair amount of time to concentrate them, but then we made course once more for Leyte and ran for about two hours.

The enemy bombed us the entire time. They bombed us for three days during this sea battle, without a break, and it felt as if your head was being pressed down into your shoulders – but when we ourselves went into the attack, it was exhilarating.

What kind of psychology is that, eh? The air might have been hot and humid, but we felt as if we were under blue skies. When we pursued the enemy, even when they were bombing us, we weren't worried. There's a big difference between defence and attack.

Kurita Force ended up not charging into Leyte Gulf – in fact, we withdrew northwards – and I bear some responsibility for it. I've had misgivings about it, even in post-war days. Was I the cause of an appalling failure? That's been my worry. Because I was the one who brought about the occasion by which Kurita Force reversed course. I was on the bridge, but I had no idea what was happening in Leyte Gulf.

Yamato was carrying her ship-borne aircraft, so I said to the C-in-C, since I wanted to know what was going on at Leyte, 'I'm sending off an aircraft to find out the situation at Leyte'. He agreed readily, and the aircraft took off – but it was a float-plane, and the enemy had complete air supremacy, so we couldn't carry out the recce as wished. All we could do was use cloud as much as possible and catch glimpses through breaks in the cloud, and we did not, as I recall, get any useful information. We sent off two aircraft from *Yamato* but they were ordered to go to their seaplane base once their duty was finished.

But we needed to find out what was happening at Leyte, at all costs. We couldn't discover a thing. At about 3 am, the signal came in that Nishimura Force had been annihilated in Surigao Strait.

A signal came in, based on aircraft intelligence, to the effect that an enemy mobile task force was in a position comparatively close to our force. And just at that time, on the northern horizon, several enemy aircraft appeared, looking as if they were about to land on a deck. Aboard *Yamato*, we discussed this and judged that there must be an aircraft carrier over there. Taking what we had seen and the fact of that signal, we felt that the enemy mobile task force was really there.

Nishimura Force must have had it! Even if we charged ahead into Leyte Gulf, it was already 2 pm. We wondered whether to have a go at the aircraft carrier instead, but we felt we couldn't be sure of taking her. Battlefield psychology, you could say.

Yamamoto heard what I had to say, and assembled everyone to pass on my opinion. I went back to the bridge, and after about ten minutes, the order was issued, 'Reverse course to annihilate enemy mobile task force', but in the end we never managed to catch the enemy aircraft carriers.

Although we didn't break into Leyte Gulf, and reversed course, we did not catch the mobile task force we aimed at – the whole thing was a flop. That happened as a result of my expressing an opinion.

I suppose a fair amount of time had passed since the enemy group had gone into Leyte Gulf, and we probably thought the enemy transports were empty, and indeed, might already have gone. At any rate, we knew nothing of what was going on at Leyte. Nishimura Force had already ceased to exist, and to go into the attack in the middle of the day, under conditions of enemy air supremacy, was not how we had planned it. We wanted to have a go at this new mobile task force.

But we couldn't catch them. I felt terribly depressed. I can remember worrying about this, even when the war was over. I learned later that the enemy thought the situation at that juncture was serious, that Japanese aircraft carriers were present to the north in great strength, and were moving south. So if we *had* gone into Leyte Gulf, we might certainly have put paid to the transport ships, but I don't think we'd have come out of it alive ourselves. However, since then, I've seen the question asked in a number of books, 'Why did Admiral Kurita reverse course at that time? Didn't he miss the opportunity he was hoping for?'. When I read these things, I wonder if I was wrong.

I'm afraid, from start to finish, we had no luck at all. In particular, there was that squall. If that hadn't happened, perhaps the whole course of battle might have been different. Moreover, I wonder whether the effect of the enemy's smoke screen would have been so great if there had been a squall *then*. If there'd been no squall, we might have destroyed the enemy at that moment. Again, might we not have been able to go smoothly into Leyte Gulf without spending time concentrating the force?

As evening began to draw in, and as we'd not been able to catch the enemy carriers, we withdrew through San Bernardino Strait. The next day, during the morning, we took a pretty fair bashing from enemy aircraft. Finally, the enemy's base air units joined in.

We weren't in despair, however. By this time we had already had some experience of being knocked about. I don't think there was any feeling that things were desperate. We felt worse after Saipan.

You could say this was the last decisive fleet battle. We needed total air back-up – and we would have preferred the opposition to be warships, not aircraft."

The Philippines – 'I Shall Return'

After General Douglas MacArthur had been chased out by the Japanese from the Philippine Islands in March 1942, he provided one of World War II's famous quotes: 'I shall return'. On 20 October 1944, the US Sixth Army landed in Leyte Gulf, thus throwing combatants into a battle of attrition, where the immense superiority in arms and continuity of supply would finally swing the balance in America's favour. As the starving Japanese were driven back into the inland hills of the Philippines, the Americans grimly pressed home their advantage to the now inevitable end.

James Fahey enlisted in the US Navy in October 1942 and was assigned as a seaman to the light cruiser USS *Montpelier*. After leave late in 1944, after the US invasion of Leyte, his ship left to join and give support to the Seventh Fleet.

"On Saturday November 5, 1944 we pulled into Leyte Gulf in the Philippines at noon. This is a very big place, they say it is 60 miles long and 30 miles wide. We also passed the spot where our navy and the Jap navy slugged it out at 3 am.

We will now be under the Supreme Command of General MacArthur. Our job is to patrol near the spot of the sea battle and destroy any Jap warships that try to attack our merchant ships and our troops on Leyte.

November 27. At 10.50 this morning, General Quarters sounded. All hands went to their battle stations. At the same time, a battleship and a destroyer were alongside the tanker getting fuel. Out of the clouds I saw a big Jap bomber come crashing down into the water. It was not smoking and looked in good condition. I felt like I was in it as it hit the water not too far from the tanker, and the two ships that were refuelling.

One of our P-38 fighters hit it. He must have got the pilot. At first I thought it was one of our bombers that had engine trouble. It was not long after that when a force of about 30 Jap planes attacked us – dive-bombers and torpedo planes. Our two ships were busy getting away from the tanker because one bomb-hit on the tanker and it would be all over for the three ships.

Jap planes were coming at us from all directions. Before the attack started we did not know that they were suicide planes, with no intention of returning to their base. They had one thing in mind – and that was to crash into our ships, bombs and all. You have to blow them up – to damage them doesn't mean much.

Right off the bat a Jap plane made a suicide dive at the cruiser *St Louis*. There was a big explosion and flames were seen shortly from the stern. Another one tried to do the same thing but he was shot away. A Jap plane came in on a battleship with his guns blazing away. Other Jap planes came in strafing one ship, dropping their bombs on another, and crashing into another. Jap planes were falling all around us – the air was full of Jap machine-gun bullets.

We knocked our share of Jap planes down, but we also got hit by three suicide planes – but lucky for us they dropped their bombs before they crashed into us. It looked like it was raining plane parts. Quite a few of the men were hit by pieces of planes. We were supposed to have air coverage, but all we had was four P-38 fighters, and when we opened up on the Japanese they got out of the way of our exploding shells.

The men on my mount were also showered with parts from Japanese planes. One suicide bomber was headed right for us while we were firing at another attacking plane, and if the 40 mm mount behind us on the port side hadn't blown the Jap wing off, it would have killed all of us. When the wing was blown off, the plane turned some and it bounced off into the water. The bombs blew part of the plane on to our ship.

Another suicide plane crashed into one of the five-inch mounts, pushing the side of the mount in and injuring some of the men inside. A lot of five-inch shells were damaged – it was a miracle that they did not explode. If that happened, the powder and the shells would have blown up the ship.

A Jap dive-bomber crashed into one of the 40 mm mounts, but lucky for them it dropped its bombs on another ship before crashing. Part of the motor hit Tomlinson. He had chunks of it all over him – his stomach, back, legs and so on. The rest of the crew were wounded, most of them sprayed with gasoline from the plane. Tomlinson was thrown a great distance and at first they thought he was knocked over the side. They finally found him in a corner in bad shape.

The explosions were terrific as the suicide planes entered the water not far from our ship. The water was covered with black smoke that rose high in the air. The water looked like it was on fire."

Chester W Driest was with the 1st Fighter Control Squadron of the US Fifth Army Air Force, operating from Australia. His squadron was sent to Leyte to control air traffic then, after a few weeks, was ordered to take part in the landing on Mindoro, set up a base to cover later landings at Lingayen Gulf and go in with the landing forces.

"We loaded in LST 1036 and 1025 and sat off Leyte. D-Day was postponed for 12 days.

Twelve days aboard an LST can be a very long time. Since few men had prepared for more than a few days aboard ship and the facilities of an LST are not designed to accommodate a large number of men comfortably, baths and changes of clothing were few during this period. Beards often remained unshaven, clothes became very dirty and grease-streaked, and a miasma of body-odour came up from down below through the open doorways and vents of the landing craft.

Bunks were assigned to the enlisted men on a ratio of eight bunks to 32 men. Consequently, most of the men slept above deck. The sleeping quarters in the hold were, for the most part, unventilated, and after a few days the air became foul and foetid. Water faucets were turned on for only a few minutes each morning to permit hasty ablutions.

The convoy set sail on 12 December. On the voyage to Mindoro the convoy was attacked by Japanese aircraft a number of times. The anti-aircraft guns boomed and the Allied fighters overhead moved in to hit the enemy planes. Planes of Marine Air Group 12, Fifth Air Force fighters, and Navy aircraft from Admiral Felix Stump's escort carriers protected the invasion force.

But on the second day out of Leyte, a Japanese reconnaissance plane discovered our invasion convoy at about nine in the morning. That afternoon the *kamikazes* came. They arrived at 3 o'clock in the afternoon as the convoy was about to turn around the southern cape of Negros island, into the Sulu Sea. An Aichi dive-bomber zoomed down to crash into the cruiser *Nashville*, near the cabin of Rear Admiral A D Struble. The flag bridge was wrecked and 133 men were killed, including Struble's chief of staff and several high-ranking officers. Colonel John T Mutha, commander of the 310th Bombardment Wing, was one of them. Another 190 men were wounded, and the *Nashville* was out of the battle.

Two hours later, we aboard the LSTs watched another *kamikaze* attack. Three fighters escorted seven *kamikazes*. The combat air patrol intercepted the Japanese a dozen miles out, but three *kamikazes* broke through the screen. One was shot down by a destroyer, another was shot down by a cruiser, but the third ploughed into the destroyer *Harden*, doing great damage and killing 14 men and wounding 24, putting that destroyer out of the action.

On 13 December the Japanese planned to destroy the convoy and sent 186 planes to find it – but the planes missed the convoy and their attacks were diluted elsewhere. The convoy steamed on to Mindoro. The landings began early on the morning of 15 December. First the destroyers and landing craft equipped with rockets hit the beaches. The mission was to establish a perimeter around the village of San Jose and begin airstrip construction at the four Japanese airstrips in the area.

I was in LST 1025, under Captain M Bonfoey, and this was the forward detachment of the 1st Fighter Control Squadron. We landed at Blue Beach near Agustin, virtually on the bank of the Bugsanga river. The LST pulled right up to the sandy beach and the men landed with dry feet. We began unloading – it was very quiet and there was no enemy opposition."

Tai Kubota was 19 and fresh from training with the Japanese Red Cross when she was posted to the Philippines. There she experienced at first-hand the harsh conditions of life familiar to the combatants of both sides.

"We were all conscripted – it didn't seem unnatural then. Almost everybody was called up for something. We were ordered to an undefined destination – although it seemed likely to be the Phillippines.

When the ship first came into Manila Bay after passing through the straits, the first building we saw was most impressive. It was the Manila Hotel – that was where General MacArthur, when he retreated, left behind his wife's crocodile-skin handbag.

There were several warships in Manila Bay, absolutely crammed with troops. On the dockside, US POWs and Filipinos were working as labourers. So, here we are at the battlefield, I thought. I was in a carefree mood, and it struck me as a beautiful country. The next day, we went to Cabanatuan.

There was no bombing at the time – the hospital was properly run. There were clinical reports, we wore white uniforms, everything neat and tidy – the patients wore hospital uniforms and had proper beds, and we were well treated and cared for. They also had regular meals, morning, noon and night.

This lasted for about five and a half months after we got there. Later, conditions grew worse. Formations of US planes began to fill the skies with their noise. Then the guerrillas became active. We were forbidden to go outside, and at night we had emergency assemblies when the bells rang. It was weird. That was when we dyed our white coats green.

When the bombers came over Cabanatuan in formation, without dropping bombs, we thought they were ours, but by that time, the enemy had already landed on Leyte.

The wounded came in steadily, but where they came from and where they went when they left us, I hadn't the faintest idea. Everything in the main hospital was soon in terrible confusion. The advance units had already left for the detachment hospital at Munoz. Afterwards, by November, those patients who were to be sent back to Japan were unable to leave because it was too dangerous, and the roads and bridges were bombed. In January 1945 the hospital closed down and we all moved into the mountains.

The most numerous sicknesses in the Philippines were amoebic dysentery, typhus – then tuberculosis, malaria, and dengue fever. As a Line of Communication Hospital we got those who needed surgical treatment as well as the sick. In time, soldiers who received treatment went back to their units, but after we went into the mountains it was just like a field hospital for us. We could only give simple treatment to the soldiers who came in, in blood-soaked uniforms – a steady stream of them.

At the time of our first move, the trucks loaded with our kit were bombed, and all we had left was what we stood up in. Then the soldiers gave us khaki-coloured uniforms, for tropical use. We were given a set each and we wore that. We carried out our duties wearing the same outfits as the soldiers.

Conditions were hard – no toilet articles were to be had. We couldn't even get pins to hold up our hair, so we just pulled it back and tied it with string. I caught malaria and three-day fever (a high fever that lasted three days), but that's all.

I wasn't wounded, but I had one or two close shaves. Life in the mountains became most dreadful from about May 1945. Food had run out and there were only 40 of our patients left in the jungle. We were bombed every day, and all the time, sick and wounded kept coming in to us from the army. After we retreated from Cabanatuan, we never spent more than a month in one place. Even so, the bombing went on. It was terrible. In the end we moved further into the mountains and the patients came with us.

Supplies from Japan had been cut off, almost completely, so it was a question of self-supply, do-it-yourself. When our bellies were empty, we experimented with things to eat, like the little wild tomatoes the size of quails' eggs that we found in the mountains. We used to dig them up and eat them, and *kalamansi* (a Filipino term for a small, sour, citrus fruit) – we'd eat the seeds. There were mountain potatoes, like Japanese potatoes, and something called *kamotekahoi*, but they seemed to be poisonous and some people died after eating them. There were plenty of black beans, and some people gave in to the temptation to eat them – even some medics – and they died as a result. They must have been poisonous too. However hungry I was myself, I would never risk eating anything unless I was sure it was edible.

There was an appalling shortage of drugs and medical equipment. We had absolutely no supplies, so there was little we could do for wounds, and little adequate medical treatment. It wasn't the case that those with severe wounds had priority over the sick. Indeed, for those who were in a really bad way, spiritual treatment was indicated. This was spiritual comfort or some form of encouragement – that was all we could do.

You gave priority to those who could fight again in the front line if they were cured. If they were all right, or reasonably so, they were sent back there. I still can't get out of my mind the sight of those soldiers, sent off from our jungle sick-bay, with a dressing on the wrist or shoulder, taking with them a bandage and a small 5 cc bottle of mercurochrome.

The order came to us, 'You are not to use medicines for casualties with no expectation of life. They are to be given spiritual nursing.' That was the order we got, as relief personnel. By that time there wasn't much we could do. It's difficult to imagine the details of such cases, but that's what happens in war.

When we went round the main sick bay, some of the casualties would be screaming, 'Please kill me!'. I say 'sick-bay', but it was nothing more than a little hut in the jungle with a bamboo roof and floor. They just lay there in their blood-soaked uniforms, all over the place. Many of them drew their last breaths as we went our rounds. We might think, 'This one doesn't look too good', and bend down to take his pulse – and you'd find he'd just stopped breathing.

Those who died, we stripped naked and kept all their things that could be used for the next casualties. If *they* got well, we'd hand them on to those going to the front line. We took nail clippings and locks of hair, in the proper way, but I expect these got lost in the bombing and during our moves. Sometimes we would bury five men together.

While we were examining those who looked as if they wouldn't make it, some of the others who weren't dying would make claims on them – 'Nurse, if so-and-so dies, please let me have his uniform!'

Discipline and fighting spirit were really on their way out, and there were more shocks to come. Up to about May 1945, we could bury the dead in the earth, but after that we had to leave them just as they were. It was really sad. People died as they lay, in rice-fields, face turned upwards, staring at the sky. Terrible.

There was nothing we could do. The sound of guns was everywhere, the bombing went on and on, as we escaped further into the mountains, striding over the bodies of the dead. It was desperate. Tragic.

We had boots – we put them into bags, but when they wore out, we didn't carry them, we just went barefoot. We walked barefoot into the hills. I was just turned 19. I left Women's College then graduated from the Japanese Red Cross Training. It was just after that.

General Yamashita was in the mountains too. Our unit was living in a village in the depths of the mountains, called 4RH. We were scattered among the huts there. And 3RH was Yamamoto Base. At the beginning of July, General Yamashita, who was due to pass by the mountain called 'Hakozaki Village', asked to see our medical section. So, we looked for a suitable spot in which to receive him and swept clean a very grassy area. We found a place where he could sit on a tree stump, and mashed some potatoes in a soldier's helmet to make a dish called *kinton,* with sweetened chestnuts. There was no food to be had at 4RH, and not a single grain of rice in the paddy fields. Everything was used up. We had to go some distance away to find the potatoes.

The general had an orderly with him. They had walked from Fundoan. He was a really big man, very stout, and he chatted about all sorts of things to the village headman. We were all thin and emaciated by then – and he ate our *kinton.* I was involved in work behind the scenes and I took a big banana leaf and stood behind the general to serve him.

We thought we might hear some news, so the conversation became lively, and we were all trying to be at our best. I did speak to the general – I said something about why the medical section had not been sent back to Japan. It was a thoughtless question, really. There was no question of anyone returning.

There was sickness, but we did see mental cases too – nervous breakdowns. I think they were quite common among the soldiers of the intellectual type – soldiers who had been university graduates. They were queer in the head at times – and there were soldiers who had been in prison...

At the time, in a diary, I wrote: 'We live only in order to prolong life, yet if the enemy were to come, we would commit suicide. We get thinner and thinner, and our reason for living comes to an end. Men keep collapsing from malnutrition – medics and nurses too. I San, who is senior to me, said, 'Oh, I'd simply love to eat some bean-paste soup made from bean curd', and that was the last thing she said before she died... About the middle of September, everyone seems to have reached the limits of exhaustion – then we learn the war is over. My stomach was so empty I didn't even have the strength to weep. I was too deadbeat to shed tears for our defeat.'.

If the enemy had come, we were going to use mercuric chloride to commit suicide. Diluted a thousand times, it's for disinfecting your hands – but it's a virulent poison and the lethal dose is 0.2 to 0.4 grams. In fact, I heard about it after we went to the surrender camps.

The day before we went there, we burned everything that might have been used by the US Army – Japanese yen, swords, rifles and so on. When we went into the US base, we were separated from the soldiers of our unit. The women were assembled by themselves in rows and we were body-searched. It was all part of disarming us and it was all very gentlemanly.

We must have looked absolutely filthy, and the US soldiers kept snapping pictures of us. We felt humiliated. Although we were dressed like soldiers, they seemed to acknowledge that we were nurses. Some of the healthy ones put on uniforms and were given nursing duties. When we first went into the camp, everything we had – all our belongings – was filthy. The things we were wearing were verminous, so they had all that burned and made us wear a khaki-coloured blouse sort of thing, with POW on the back.

Before we entered the camp, we were driven in an open-top vehicle, and name tags were fixed on our chests. I kept a peso note – the Philippine currency we were paid in when I was in the army. We had lots of money, but after we went into the mountains, these things ceased to have any value, so we used the notes to roll cigarettes or as toilet paper.

Looking back now, on the 'Field Service Instructions', I think of the order, 'Never permit yourself to be humiliated by being taken prisoner alive. Do not leave behind you a name sullied by dishonour – kill yourself first'. If that phrase had never existed, how many tens of thousands of men's lives would have been saved? Many men would have now been safe at home. Many men died in battle in the Philippines, many died from disease or starvation, but there were also those who were so sick they could not even move, and I think they must have received medical treatment when they were taken prisoner."

Rhine Crossing – Operation Varsity

*T*he psychological and physical barrier of the Rhine stretching 825 miles (1,328 km) from Switzerland to the North Sea, had been a source of concern to Allied planners since before the D-Day landings in June 1944. The river was the major obstacle to the defeat of Germany, a natural defensive line behind which Hitler could reorganise his forces. Crossing the Rhine was vital for the Allies' progress. General Eisenhower's 'broad-front' approach involved all three Allied Army Groups advancing in unison. In the north, British and Canadian troops under Field Marshal Montgomery overcame fierce German resistance and heavy rain to combine with the US Ninth Army and establish control over the Rhine's west bank; further south the American troops unexpectedly captured an intact bridge across the river at Remagen during Operation Lumberjack, which drove back the overstretched German Seventh Army. Now the river was all that stood in the way of an Allied advance. In a supporting operation codenamed Varsity, the British Sixth and US 17th Airborne Divisions landed by parachute and glider near Wesel on 24 March 1945 to reinforce the ground units in establishing a 40-mile (64.5-km-) long bridgehead from which to push eastwards to the Rhur, the industrial heart of Germany. Beyond the way lay open into the heart of the Reich.

John Leopard, formerly Staff Captain with the artillery of 6th Airborne Division, was transferred to the 10th City of Glasgow Field Regiment, Royal Artillery, and witnessed what was, reportedly, the heaviest artillery bombardment in military history, covering the Rhine crossing.

"The plan was to so damage the opposing forces that our assault troops could gain the enemy shore with the minimum casualties. The main crossings were to be made by the 15th and 51st Divisions, just north of Xanten. We in the 52nd were among those in close support.

For days before the attack, shells and masses of equipment for the crossing were brought well forward under the cloak of continuous smoke screens. On the night before the action, all the field guns were deployed in positions as close to the river as possible. Artificial moonlight to provide reasonable visibility was produced by a long line of searchlights, with their beams reflected from the clouds into the area of activity. The reason for bringing the guns so far forward was that they would still be in range of more distant targets without the need for time-wasting redeployment during the early stages of the advance beyond the Rhine. When our move was completed. I went forward with my signaller to a pre-planned observation post on top of a flood barrier, some 50 yards back from the river bank. Here we dug a slit trench from which I would have a clear view of the German-held side of the river. Cunningly, we were very close to a forward aid post. We'd be assured of endless hot sweet tea during the coming battle.

I had a map showing the scores of target areas and the artillery units responsible for each of them. It was my unenviable task to assess the accuracy of the fall of shot and to signal back such corrections as I deemed proper. How I was supposed to accomplish this during the night, lit only by the light of thousands of exploding shells. I had not the least idea. In the event, the light from the many fires started helped a bit.

Our guns in their vulnerable positions remained silent all day. There was quite a lot of random fire from the Germans, no doubt in the hope of an informative response. At night, there was a cautious movement of men and equipment between my dam and the river. Came the hour, and the world exploded. The noise was ear-splitting and got worse as the German guns hit our side of the river. Terrified stampeding cattle, some of whom thundered along the top of my dam, presented a far greater danger to us in our slit trench than enemy shells.

Some of our shells just fell in the river – this I knew was incorrect, so I went through the motions of making adjustments. To be honest, it would have been pure, blind chance had any of them been accurate, but at least it kept us busy. At one point, out of the corner of my eye, I saw the signaller duck. Like any old soldier, I followed him a split second later.

Eventually the devastating shelling ended and our advance troops made a triumphant crossing and established a bridgehead from which the advance proceeded. The dawn came up and everything was relatively peaceful. I questioned my signaller about his ducking during the night. He indicated a shell hole a few yards from our trench. He saw the shell burst – I did not.

Our questionable night's work concluded, I looked with admiration at the long tank-carrying Bailey bridge the Royal Engineers had built. At a forward aid post. I saw a well-bandaged German officer inside. At the same time, the 6th Airborne Division, with its scores of aircraft and gliders, was passing overhead to stiffen our forward troops. I pointed upwards. The German looked pretty glum, but said in passable English, 'Zee var ees ofer'."

Flying Officer Rosemary Britten, unbeknown to her uncle, Ian Toler (see next account), had bartered and bluffed her way into a place on the Rhine landings operation. The only woman on the flight, her story is a unique one.

"All the night before, my conscience pricked me horribly, and I was like a cat on hot bricks, knowing I should have let one of the men go. However, too many people knew I was going, although I had been very careful not to tell a soul, so I couldn't back out, even had I wanted to!

Having got Ops to ring me in the Waafery at 03.45 am, I was at breakfast at 04.15 am, having emptied my pockets in the approved manner. Contents were now comb, £2, escape kit and powder and lipstick (which I didn't use the whole time – at first, because I wanted to look like a German girl in case of baling out, and afterwards because I was too dirty to make any difference!).

A bad moment was when Uncle Ian [Ian Toler] came up to say

goodbye and asked me to come and see take-off. An even worse one was when I found myself getting into the crew bus alongside a Canadian war correspondent. He started to interrogate me about being the only woman on ops, and being in quite a panic anyway, I told him my name. Afterwards I appealed to his better nature and, I think, persuaded him to leave it out until after the war.

Holland was a shattering sight – some of the fields were flooded, others had been and were now dryer – a bit black and quite dead. I don't think I saw a single sign of life in the part of Holland that we crossed, every little village was gutted.

I was surprised to find I could recognise the country from the briefing photographs, and saw the wood near Hamminkeln, although the actual LZ was out of sight in a very effective smoke screen. We wished our glider good luck and he was gone – down into the smoke with the hundreds of others.

We did a violent turn to port, miraculously avoiding other aircraft, for there were black puffs of flak coming up ahead, and a Halifax went down in flames with only three parachutes, one of which went into the crash, and a Hamilcar disintegrated, spitting out its tank and crew.

The flak seemed to be singling out our aircraft, and Ron took some pretty violent evasive action – but not violent enough, as there was suddenly an almighty crack, and D-Dog shook all over, and various parts of the controls began quite obviously not to connect.

We crossed back over the Rhine, which was one great comfort anyway, as at least we should not have to bale out into the battle – but it became very apparent that we should have to bale out somewhere, as more and more things became conspicuous by their absence. Ron was holding the stick with his knees and couldn't take his hands off for a moment.

Then the intercom went u/s [unserviceable], but the wireless operator did something to Ron's helmet which improved matters spasmodically – though it was difficult getting it back on his head, as he couldn't spare his hands. I did a small amount of shouting messages, but it's hopeless when you can hardly hear yourself speak.

The control column was hanging together by a quarter inch of metal, so, of course, everything depended on whether it snapped or whether it didn't. Fred tied a hammer on to it as a kind of splint, which saved the situation – luckily, I didn't see it, but only knew from the frantic activity that things were NOT WORKING.

I then remembered the crew had said, on getting into the aircraft, that they didn't bother to do their parachutes up properly, so, not wanting to be a sissy, I didn't either. That took me a few minutes fumbling and so I got hot and bothered and oily. Mac opened the escape hatch and told me what to do. I was afraid they would not trust me to jump of my own free will and give me a push when I wasn't expecting it. Holland looked even more dead and desolate than on the outward journey. By that time I knew I was going to be either killed or court-martialled, and was amazed to find I didn't really mind either. I remember thinking that now I wouldn't have to live to a dreary old age, which was a good thing. But I could do with another year or two, now it had come to the point. It all seemed too extraordinary to be true – but very interesting.

Harry worked out the distance home and, as it still seemed to be getting on for 200 miles, and a stretch of sea, it was decided we couldn't make it, as any minute the column might break altogether.

The compasses were u/s, so we didn't really know where we were. The hydraulics were u/s, so there was the problem of whether to bale out or crash land – I had a slight leaning to baling out, myself, as I hate being chopped about by metal and I had visions of the Caterpillar Club.

Ron decided to land, having found a suitable looking airfield. He asked me what would happen if I turned up on the Continent, which I thought very considerate of him. Quite immaterial, though, as I had no hope of being in a state to try and explain when we did reach the ground, as I thought we'd all be mixed up with bits of aircraft.

George, Harry and I sat on the floor in the rear bay in crash positions, with the escape hatches open above and below, and the wind blowing through what had been the door. I couldn't help thinking what a horrible mess we three would make.

George went back to the turret to get his hat, so I got mine too, just in case we survived, in which event, one might as well put up as good a show as possible. Then a fountain of evil-smelling hydraulic oil came up all over us. We had the option of moving from our crash positions, or sitting in the spray – so we sat in it.

Then Fred performed some amazing technical feat with the hydraulics and got the undercarriage down. We landed perfectly, but I felt rather sick when I saw what had been the control column – a direct hit had burst inside the fuselage, blowing the door away and pepperating the aircraft all round, cutting a lot of vital parts – but it missed the petrol tanks and the crew.

There wasn't a door, but there were so many jagged edges that one couldn't get through it, so we had to jump through the escape hatch. We found ourselves on Strip B53, Merville, near Lille – an American LG for lame ducks. A circle of Yanks and gaping French surrounded us.

After a good deal of waiting and questioning, we were finally flown back to our base. I would have done anything to have gone to bed as I had a ghastly headache, but rather than it should be thought I couldn't take it, I took a few aspirins and went up to the mess with Ron, where we were greeted as if returned from the dead. Apparently four crews had reported D-Dog shot down.

I felt rather bad about turning up after all, and decided to acquire an operational twitch at least!"

Ian Toler, a member of the Army's Glider Pilot Regiment, trained by the RAF, was part of the airborne armada which reinforced the ground troops' crossing of the Rhine. A survivor of the Arnhem landing, he was well prepared for events.

"As we approached the Rhine, a great pall of smoke appeared on the far side, covering our objective. There were several crashed Dakotas on our side of the Rhine and my tug pilot told me later, 'I saw a lot of very frightened Daks streaking out of the smoke like bats out of hell, and I said to the crew, "This is it, chaps".'.

On my landing zone there was a very prominent feature – a small wood, codenamed Bunty. This was completely obscured, but luckily our run-in release point was clear. Over the release point I released the tow rope and flew towards the railway, which I could just see. We were then flying completely blind in the smoke. I followed my planned flight path from the release point. At about 200 feet I saw the tops of some high-tension power lines, and knew I was going in the right direction. However, just as I was preparing to land, I saw some low-tension cables or telephone wires on posts below me. There was no time to avoid them, so I ploughed straight into them, hoping they would break – which they did, but in so doing, caused me to stall about 20 feet up, so that we landed heavily and the front of the glider was damaged – but no-one was injured. As the smoke cleared, I was able to identify Bunty, which was only 100 yards away, and I found I was within 50 yards of where I should have been.

We now had to unload the glider, and as the nose had been damaged, we were not able to use the new method of nose unloading, so had to remove the tail. We were lucky not to be under fire – if we had landed further forward, I should probably not be telling this story.

Having unloaded the jeep and stores, the gunners moved to their headquarters. I moved to a farm-house which I had selected as our HQ at the briefing, and we found that we had about 200 prisoners to deal with. We put the farmhouse in a state of defence and collected food and water – remembering how important this was at Arnhem. We put the occupants in one room and set up a guard, as they didn't seem very cooperative. One of my pilots came to me and said there were a number of pigeons in the farm, and he thought they might be carriers to take information to the enemy. I went to have a look, and a small boy, with tears in his eyes, indicated, as he had no English, that we must not shoot them – they were his pets. I thought he was right, and we didn't.

The Division had taken all objectives within four hours of landing. Next day, looking around the landing zone, it appeared to be a mass of crashed and broken gliders. Many had been attacked on the ground as soon as they landed. I tried to assess my casualties, which seemed to be pretty high. Captain Rex Norton had been killed – the only officer of the squadron apart from myself to return from the Arnhem battle. I went to where he had been killed by a mortar burst, and saw him buried in a temporary grave. I reckoned my casualties were about 20 per cent.

The following morning, we heard the thunder of approaching tanks and shortly a whole regiment of the Guards Armoured Division with their Sherman tanks drove through our positions on their way into Germany. What a lovely sight – and one I shall never forget. This was the third day after landing and, as far as we were concerned, the party was over. I have recollections of going back through the woods with hundreds of German prisoners shepherded by an American (surely a cowboy) riding bareback on a commandeered horse.

So ended the last airborne operation of the war. Historians will argue whether it was necessary to use such a large and expensive force to take ground which would probably have been taken by the ground forces, or if it was right to send highly vulnerable gliders and parachute aircraft into an area where the anti-aircraft guns were still active. Casualties were heavy – but perhaps not as heavy as would have been those of the ground forces, had we not been there. Objectives were achieved, and that is what counts."

Glider Pilot David Brook's Dakota-towed Horsa made a hurried landing amid heavy fire, close to the Rhine village of Haminkeln. He then faced a hostile reception from the German forces on the ground.

"The Horsa came to a halt in soft soil, warm with the early spring morning. Suddenly a rather persistent MG34 turned its undivided attention on our Horsa. Its much faster rate of fire than our Bren was unmistakable, and I recall the captain of the small group of Ox and Bucks Light Infantry that we were carrying, who had recently won the MC at Arnhem, saying, as they struggled to open an uncooperative door, 'This is f****** terrible'. Realising I was still wearing my flying helmet, I dived back into the cockpit to dress properly for the occasion by fastening on my round pudding basin of an airborne helmet. As I made back for the doorway, a steady stream of bullets banged through it. I dropped down behind large crates of stew which were stored under the troop seats and watched, fascinated, as the machine gunner slowly raked the glider back and forth from stem to stern.

The noise of battle outside my plywood coffin was overwhelming in its intensity and I barely heard a voice shouting my name and urging me to get out if I was still there, as German tanks were coming. There was a pause in the machine-gun fire and I made a headlong dive, landing on the soft soil some four and a half feet below. I lay behind the portside main wheel in the furrow it had made and watched the first of several German anti-airborne troops roaring down the road on the half-tracks which they had designed specially for the opposition of unwelcome visitors.

My role when I reached the ground safely, which I had at last now achieved, was as PIAT man. This weapon was still with the rest of the gear in the Horsa, and all I had on me was my personal 9 mm automatic which I proceeded to fire in earnest at the men seated on the half track and the motor cyclist following them, all of whom had the unmistakable mien of people who were no more wishing to find themselves just at that moment where they were, than we did. At any rate, they did not stop and mop us up, but disappeared down the road. Then I noticed that noise was coming from another battery of light anti-aircraft guns to my right on the side of the railway track. Evidently they had temporarily tired of knocking our gliders out of the sky. I could see dead men lying everywhere, each a pathetic little heap, and only two live ones some distance off firing back from behind the wheel of their glider. I then found that the captain and the rest of the men were sheltering in a small weapon pit recently vacated by the first Germans I had seen.

Meanwhile, the battery had turned its three guns down low angle and were firing at my Horsa. I felt a blow as if a hammer hit me on the right shoulder. The shells were bursting just above me and unknown to me, in the heat of the moment, I now had a piece of one in my shoulder.

The captain was obviously feeling much better since he had got out of the Horsa and, unrestricted, proceeded to lead an attack on the gun position. We had to run directly at it, and as I ran I had what proved to be my last look at the Horsa which had carried us here so well. A shell hit the glazed nose of the machine, which was also the closed cockpit, and from a nice shining office, it instantly collapsed in drooping pieces. Had I been able to maintain my glance, I would have seen her go up in flames, destroying everything in her, including the three bodies in the back, one of which, I was told days later by a seasoned veteran, was one of the worst he had seen on any battlefield. Apparently his charred remains stuck in the ground upside down with the iron tips on his boots being all that remained of his uniform, stuck to his heels.

We had landed close by a small farmhouse and I and another man ran up to it. A large barn-like door was closed and I fired some bullets through it before bursting it open. We ran in to find a room at the side with a large pile of turnips and hay on the floor. The Ox and Bucks captain, his face red and perspiring with nervous and physical effort, ran up, pushing a tough-looking young German paratrooper ahead of him. 'Here, glider pilot, you've been wounded – stay here and guard this prisoner until we come back'. I pushed my prisoner back into the house and sat him down on the heap of turnips, telling him to keep his hands over his head.

Later the Ox and Bucks captain returned and told me to take the prisoner up to join the others at the railway station. He assured me that the station was ours, so I left the house and set off with my charge up the railway line. The chaos was indescribable. Trucks were overturned and the huge broken remains of a couple of Horsas lay across the tracks. Men were lying alongside the rails as if to shelter from the small-arms fire which was still banging about my ears.

I handed my prisoner over and went into the station house. Shattered bodies lay everywhere on the floors, their camouflage

smocks torn and blasted by shot, grenade or mortar and stained with
the mixture of earth and blood. I recognised a fellow pilot who was
in great pain, having received a bullet through the bottom of his foot,
which had continued up into his leg.

A medic poured sulphonamide powder in my wound and applied
a field dressing. It was to be a week later in England before the piece
of shrapnel was removed.

The walking wounded were told to get themselves to a large country house about half a mile away, where, exhausted, I lay down on the
floorboards of a large downstairs room. I dozed fitfully and later was
aware of a trooper in an adjoining small room which had the door
open, gasping in a terrible way at about 120 to the minute. He had
fearful chest injuries, and had been injected with morphine. They
had turned him over on what remained of his chest and left him.

For some time now the heavy rumble of Monty's artillery on the
other side of the Rhine had been growing in intensity and the house
was beginning to vibrate. 'A creeping barrage', I thought. I wondered
if they knew where we were and where to stop.

Outside, the machine guns started up again as the promised
counter-attack developed. Close fighting was taking place in the
orchard around the house and the woods beyond. Our Ox and Bucks,
Devons and RURs were defending our position while the barrage
lifted again so that it must only be half a mile away – or so it seemed.
The noise increased until it filled everything. The building was now
shaking and I could not believe that we were going to live through it.
Suddenly it stopped. The silence that followed for a minute or so was
uncanny, and I realised that something was missing. As the barrage
had stopped, so had the struggle for life of the wounded trooper."

**Jack Taylor, a Driver with 227 Company RASC, VIII Corps,
Second Army, had landed with the invasion force in June 1944.
Having fought through the Netherlands, his Company faced the
Rhine crossing. The following are excerpts from a closely
guarded secret diary he kept at the time.**

"Wednesday March 28. Arrived back with my Company in Geldern
after being on a course for training as a Driver/Wireless Operator in
a Tank Crew, using Morse Code. White flags are hanging outside all
the houses and we are not allowed to speak to civvies. Moving to
Wesel over the Rhine tomorrow, so went on the scrounge in civvy

houses and found hundreds of notes in German Marks in the rafters of a roof of a house, but they were 50s, 100s and 1,000s and of no use.

March 29. Moving to Reesfeld across the Rhine, moved off early and arrived at Wesel. The Rhine is some river, and we crossed on a pontoon bridge built by the 7th Armoured Division. It was a fantastic job – I will never forget it. The roads are choked with vehicles and troops. On the left side of the road I could see scores of dead paras hanging from trees and in the fields, dead horses still in their harnesses, dead cows and a lot of dead Germans.

It was utter confusion. All kinds of nationalities were here – Poles, French, Dutch Resistance – all giving themselves up, and also quite a few SS who had been betrayed by the people they had forced to fight for them – the tattoo mark under their left arm gave them away.

We commandeered a house for a guard room and prison and that night it was hell on earth. The confusion was endless – no-one slept a wink and wholesale looting went on all night by the freed labour force, and we didn't stop it. Quite a few of us spent the night burying the dead British Paras in our sector.

March 30. Set off for Borkan, arrived and billeted in a German factory. The town is a terrible wreck and wholesale looting is still going on – by both sides.

Thursday April 5. Moved again to Bissendorf, some 20 miles northeast of Münster, and billeted on a farm. It was a bad journey through seas of mud, the vehicles bogged down.

April 6. Moved again to Utche at 18.00 hours – it's about 25 miles. What a life. Arrived at 20.00 hours and billeted in a grand German house. We were the first troops in the town – the main body had passed it by for some reason. I and a pal of mine – a Driver Howells – went into the main Post Office. The staff were still working – all middle-aged women, so we cleared them out.

We opened a very large safe and there were stacks of paper money in it. We helped ourselves and, of course, took large notes – but remembered in time to change them for smaller-value notes.

We stayed one night in the large house, and found large packing cases in the cellar full of clothes – all women's clothes, including fur coats which had been taken from the inmates of the death camps. (Up to that point we had not come across these camps, but were to do so in the next few days). There were also a lot of bottles of fruit and sides of bacon, legs of pork – and plenty of eggs. There were no men in the town, only women and children.

During the night we heard sounds of gunfire and a lot of screaming going on in the town, but we still had a good sleep on the first real bed for a very long time. The next morning we were told that a lot of raping and murders had taken place by the Russian slave workers who had been released. During the night we were bombed by aircraft and a lot of anti-personnel bombs were dropped. A boy picked one up and lost his hand."

Heinz Deutsch (24) was a lieutenant (later 1st Lieutenant) with the German 12th Paratrooper Storm Gun battalions. He recounts the events of 9/10 March 1945 in the vicinity of Wesel, when his unit was attempting to cross the Rhine.

"German troops had withdrawn, and we were on the left side of the Rhine about to cross by a railway bridge leading to Wesel. The German engineers, however, had blown this up earlier to prevent the Allies crossing there. So there we were with all our heavy weaponry. Some of our men had already crossed. I had been given the order to oversee the crossing of the bridge, so I had to wait until last. The bridge had been blown so that it was still possible for infantry to cross, but no vehicles. The engineers had to build a makeshift ferry to carry the guns.

The engineers put this together on the night of 8/9 March, with steel supports and wooden planks laid over these. It floated by means of empty air canisters. On 9 March this ferry managed to carry across most of the guns.

When we reached Wesel, it had been completely destroyed. We were then told to withdraw to the north-east with our guns. But we had no reason to use them. The enemy troops were staying back. We didn't know exactly why. Perhaps they thought it was a trap.

Later there was an enemy landing from the air, partly with gliders. I shot down two of these gliders with the storm gun. The other two I could see had already landed, and it wasn't usual to fire at them when they were on the ground. We would point the storm guns at them and the infantry would take them prisoner.

Looking back at this time, morale among our men was surprisingly good. Our battalion were all volunteers, and frankly, we wanted a bit of action. We thought the war could still be rescued. Of course, most of the time in action, you only have enough time to think of your own situation, not to be shot yourself. We were defending our Fatherland,

and we thought we still had a good chance. I would say that politics never really entered into it for us. You never spoke about it, whether someone was in the party or had been in the Hitler Youth. We had a bit of doubt about the conduct of the war, but we were confident. There were no deserters.

I was awarded the *Ritterkreuz* (Knight's Cross) in April for knocking out 44 enemy tanks with my own gun in the space of eight weeks, and I was mentioned by name in the *Wehrmacht* Command Report.

About 10 or 15 years ago I went back to Wesel. I drove through this area, and I have a little story about something I saw. When we were withdrawing to build a position, there was a house standing behind us – it must have been one of the only ones still standing. Now I couldn't see this and so I ploughed into the back wall with my gun. When I looked to see what had happened, there were German soldiers in there roasting potatoes. When I went back, the house was still there and the wall newly built. We spoke to the people in the house, but I didn't tell them about the wall."

Battle of Berlin – Brothers in Arms

Berlin, the capital of Hitler's Third Reich, had suffered badly from 16 massive RAF raids between November 1943 and March 1944. Now it was the prestige objective for the Russian advance from the east. On 16 April 1945, General Zhukov's First Belorussian Front and Ivan Konev's First Ukrainian Front began the final offensive, having linked up to isolate the city and begin its final agony. On 25 April, men of the US First Army met with the Soviet Fifth Guards Army at Torgau on the River Elbe north-east of Leipzig. The Western and Eastern fronts had joined. In a series of concentric attacks, the Russians used artillery and tanks at close range to fight their way through the suburbs into the central area. Among their opponents in the Reich's death throes were boys from the Hitler Youth and men from Occupied Europe who had volunteered for the Waffen-SS and now had no future. The Reichstag building was captured on May 1, although Soviet troops had raised the Hammer and Sickle *above the building in the half light of the previous evening. On 2 May General Karl Weidling, the recently appointed commander of the city, surrendered unconditionally. The Russians took 136,000 prisoners. Hitler and Goebbels, meanwhile, had committed suicide in their bunker on 30 April: the Reich they had created perished without them. Both sides recall the pressures of the Battle of Berlin and the personal tragedies.*

Vladimir Shatilov was commander of the Russian 150th Rifle Division, which, on the evening of 28 April, fought through to the banks of the Spree – behind which lay the *Reichstag*, Hitler's last resistance.

"I went to the observation post of the 756th Regiment, commanded by Zinchenko. This regiment was to cross by the Moltke-the-Younger Bridge, seize the Foreign Ministry (we called this 'the white house') then, with Plekhodanov's regiment, was to be ready to attack the Ministry of the Interior – 'Himmler's House'.

Covered by artillery and mortar fire, our infantry rushed to the bridge. At first, small groups of soldiers under Sergeant Petr Pyatnitskii and Petr Shcherbina leaped through. Behind them came Lieutenant Ponkratov's company and finally the entire battalion of Captain Neustroev, with the Captain running in front and Political Adviser Berest and Chief of Staff Gusev running beside him.

The first to break into 'Himmler's House' were Davydov's and Neustroev's battalions. The fight inside the building lasted all night, and only at dawn on April 30 did our division's battalions completely clean out the buildings of the Interior Ministry. Then the fascists held only the *Reichstag* and the Kroll Opera House.

The Hitlerites brought new reinforcements into battle. We found facing us sea cadets from the Rostock naval college. They were ordered to stop, at any price, our troops' advance against the government buildings. It was Plekhodanov's troops who dealt with these cadets – the *Führer*'s last hope.

The Third Reich was living out its last days. There were very many prisoners, but I especially remember two Hitlerite generals, Major-General Schreiber and Lieutenant-General Wilhelm Brenckenfeldt. They were brought to me at the observation post, which at that time was close to the Spree. Seeing me, the two Germans fell on their knees, saying. 'We German generals bend our knees before the Soviet general...' The words sounded pathetic. It was revolting."

Lieutenant-General Telegin was a member of the war council of the 1st Belorussian Front which, under Marshal Zhukov shared the Berlin operation with the 1st Ukrainian Front under Marshal Koniev.

"Captain Archangelsk's tank company was halted by gun and rocket fire near a massive obstacle at a crossroads near the *Reichstag*. The leading tank, trying to ram the obstacle, was set on fire and fell out of action in the centre of a square.

The tank commander and the turret gunner, badly wounded, just managed to pull themselves out on to the paving stones through the lower hatch, and then sheltered behind the armour of the tank from enemy machine-gun fire. In the burning tank remained only the driver-mechanic, the Young Communist, Anatoli Ivanov – but after a few moments, the commander's hatch cover opened and Anatoli's head appeared, accompanied by his loud boyish voice, 'Forward, for motherland and victory!'

The burning tank, gathering speed, hurled itself at the obstruction – but another missile penetrated the tank's armour. The ammunition exploded and the tank was destroyed Anatoli Ivanov likewise perished. The gap that Ivanov had succeeded in making was too small to allow tanks through.

Only a few minutes after the destruction of the tank, a fair-haired soldier jumped out from the window of a nearby house with a box of explosives on his back. He hurried to the place where Anatoli had met his end. Who was this hero? Most probably a soldier from the neighbouring assault group. The tank men covered this daring fellow with their cannon and machine guns. Wounded by an enemy bullet, he laboriously pulled himself along on his hands, crawling forward and dragging his box behind him. The tanks gave all the gun and machine-gun fire they could, and the hero crawled to the gap made by Anatoli Ivanov. He placed his explosives, lit the fuse, then collapsed. There was an explosion that threw the obstacle aside. The road to the *Reichstag* was clear – but the unknown hero had perished."

Lieutenant-General Nikolai Popel had served as a professional soldier for 40 years by the time of the battle for Berlin. By this time he was a member of the Russian war council – the highest political/military group of the First Guards Tank Army. He remembers events towards the end of the battle for Berlin.

"Red flags had been put out on the roofs – signs that our men had passed this way. Without such indications in urban warfare, it would have been impossible to know which parts were one's own.

'And do you remember how we knew where the Germans were in 1941,' Mikhail Efimovich suddenly asked, 'especially towards evening?'. 'Of course I remember. Wherever we saw flames, that's where the Germans were.'.

We stopped our armoured personnel carrier near the entrance arch of a multistorey house, where a field-kitchen had been placed. It was the centre of a lively scene. Soldiers, NCOs and officers were getting food, waiting their turn, or already eating with healthy appetites. Among them, I spotted several German children. These little Berliners went up to our people and stretched out skinny little hands that tightly grasped cups and saucers. Beside the cook stood a curly-haired boy in ragged trousers. 'Eat!' he said. This was the first bit of Russian he had learned. The cook neatly poured him a full cup, and the boy, in a thin, grateful voice, said thank-you in German. The cook suddenly slid his wide palm affectionately over the curls. But, catching sight of us and not knowing how we would look on his behaviour, he blushed and immediately began to defend himself. 'I gave something to the child. Comrade General. I've seen all kinds of things in this war, but you know, my heart can't take hungry children.'.

A boy of about seven, to whom a junior sergeant had poured some sweet tea out of his flask, gazed fixedly with hungry eyes at this delicacy, but overcame himself and, explaining that it was for his mother, carried the tea inside.

We watched anxiously some planes that were leaving a narrow white trail in the sky. 'Terrific speed!' said Kanukov, as he watched them with a calculating eye, 'It's all right if Hitler doesn't have many of them, but if there are a lot of them, things will get hot.'.

This day, for the first time, we had encountered jet aircraft. Coming down like lightning on the column, a flight of them shot it up with machine guns. The sergeant who had poured tea for the German boy, was killed."

Untersturmführer Heinz Landau, a Transylvanian Saxon fighting with the German Army against their mutual enemy – the Russians – had arrived on the outskirts of Berlin after fierce fighting.

"Nearing an open square, we could see a high-ranking *Feldgendarmerie* officer and half a dozen or so *gendarmes* with the unmistakable plaque around their necks. We immediately made towards them, welcoming their company, when to our horror, they opened fire on us with automatic weapons, instantly killing Willy and grazing Wolfgang and myself.

'Hey, you bastards, we're Germans! Are you short-sighted?' The next instant, firing broke out again, and we thought the Russians had caught up with us. It was one Schmeisser only – and I spotted the man firing it from another corner of the square into the *Feldgendarmes*.

We approached the sprawling bodies of the berserk gendarmes with caution. One was only just alive, cursing and moaning in Russian. We tore open their tunics – no shirt, no identification disc. Their facial structure and, above all, their smell, was unmistakably Russian. The first bullets started to ricochet off the houses and the asphalt all around us, and there was not time to do anything about Willy.

That evening, to our surprise, we actually made contact with a large force of our regular army troops, just receiving their rations. To our delight, we were provided with some unexpected food, cigarettes and tobacco, a small bottle of schnapps each, and tablets to keep us awake.

We sat in complete darkness on the damp floor of the cellar of an otherwise completely destroyed building, eating, drinking and smoking and trying to snatch some sleep, while the Russian artillery started their night-shift. The shells and bombs rocked the ground like a ceaseless earthquake, when an unseen body fell in amongst us, muttering a curse in Russian. All three of us had our bayonets or hunting knives out, groping in the dark. There was a short but violent tussle to my left, and, 'I've got him', from Wolfgang. A heavy body fell over me and a knife slashed a long tear in my sleeve and arm. I was frantically slashing and stabbing with my knife, and the body went limp. Out we scrambled as fast as we could – and not too soon. A couple of hand grenades exploded in the cellar and we lay crouched in silence. Sure enough, half a dozen figures hove into dim sight and we emptied our Schmeissers with feeling.

As far as I could see, the sky was a gold-red, fires of assorted sizes were burning everywhere, the sound of several thousand Russian artillery and *Katyushas* was one endless clap and roll of terrifying thunder and lightning and, believe it or not, the well-known sound of German flak was adding its furious rapid bark to this infernal crescendo. Overhead, enemy aircraft were droning like endless swarms of mad bumble bees and bombs kept raining down on the tortured, but still defiant city.

We trooped out cautiously into the night. I peered carefully up and down the rubble-laden street. It was now getting quite light and nothing moved in the immediate vicinity. After waiting another ten minutes or so, we proceeded, leap-frogging in the usual manner, towards the west.

Ivan tanks were rumbling towards us in the distance – we immediately deployed. Wolfgang and I, with a scratch unit of experienced *Panzerjäger*, ran towards the Russians under cover of the trees, carrying as many *Panzerfaust* as possible with us, our boots and belts bristling with hand grenades.

We took up our positions and waited. I noticed to my dismay, that I was shaking all over, and my poor loose teeth were making a noise like castanets. Also, once again, my stomach hurt, and I kept thinking. 'Oh God, don't let me be sick now'. I bit my jaws together, fought down the trembling and fused my hand grenades. The first T34 was now about 40 or 50 metres away. I set my sights at 25 metres and took aim, noticing Wolfgang going through the motions with me, as if on an exercise ground.

Then 35 metres, 30 metres, 25 metres – and I squeezed the trigger. As I was flattening myself against the ground, I caught a glimpse of the spinning-top-like projectile racing towards the tank. In a split second, the tank veered to one side, flattening one of the trees, burst into flames and stopped. The hatch flew open and the crew, their uniforms already ablaze, jumped out as fast as they could. The lads behind us mowed them down.

The next in line turned off the road, crossing the ditch, then rattled into the field, hit a mine and lost one of its tracks. Wolfgang blew this one up with his *Panzerfaust*. I caught the third at a distance of 30 metres and, glory be, it must have been carrying ammunition or fuel, for it literally disintegrated, the huge wheels and tracks – even the long barrel of its gun – whirling through the air in slow motion.

To my horror, one of the tracks was hurtling towards me, and by thunder, it sure wasn't in slow motion any more. I was trying to dig myself in deeper to the rather shallow ditch with my fingernails, when this monstrosity hit the ground with a thump and crunch – and I blacked out. I was only out for a second, as quite obviously Wolfgang had not even noticed the close shave I had had, but was busily preparing for the next target.

The Russians now stepped on the gas and thundered past us at speed, firing with everything they had. Someone managed to knock out the last but one. This stopped the last one with a bang, and

Wolfgang and I put a *Panzerfaust* in it. Further down the road, more tanks hove into sight and, watching them through my field glasses, I could see the massed Russian infantry behind them. Time to start moving back.

We held this square for the rest of that day and night, repulsing countless assaults and weathering furious artillery and aerial bombardments. We booby-trapped the buildings we were in and then retreated under the cover of a small, tough rear-guard.

By 27 April, the fighting was so confused that Wolfgang and I were not too surprised to come across a complete company of Russians, standing about in a huge open square, eating, drinking and talking. Many of them died on their feet as we opened fire with everything at our disposal. The whole thing was over in a matter of seconds. We were about 40 strong, and emerged completely unscathed from this encounter, which must have cost the Ivans more than 200 lives.

A day later, at 10 am, we knew the end, for us at any rate, was very near indeed. We realised we were encircled and that to expect outside help was ridiculous. Wolfgang and I, with two others in tow, had just managed once again to shake off the enemy after a particularly nasty bit of house-to-house, room-to-room fighting, and were leap-frogging down a main road. I crouched in a doorway to give covering fire, when I saw a shell explode in the midst of my friends. About half a dozen of us ran back into the hail of Russian bullets, but all of them were either dead or terribly wounded – and we did not even have our usual first-aid kits.

I found what I dreaded most – Wolfgang minus his legs. I thought he was dead. I grabbed hold of my last friend's head and yelled in agony, 'Wolfgang, Wolfgang!' He opened his eyes and smiled – then realised what had happened. His lips moved, but his voice was so weak in all that din, I could not hear anything. I bent close with my ear to his lips: 'Shoot me, *Kamerad*, for God's sake, shoot me'. His hand squeezed mine, then let go. '*Lebe wohl, Heinz*'. A quick burst through the head, and Wolfgang was at peace.

About three hours later, after almost ceaseless fighting, approximately 25 Germans, surrounded by an army of the brave, heroic Soviet Union, with tanks and artillery, fought their last battle. There was an unexpectedly long lull in the fighting, giving me the opportunity to collect my wits – and this rather depressed me. The few lads and men around me were complete strangers, and we obviously weren't going to have the chance to get acquainted. The end was just around the corner.

What worried me most was the fact that in this situation, one was dying like a dog – a stray dog – for who was there to report to whom? 'Sorry to inform you that your son has given his life on the field of honour'?

I knew only too well that, by the time it would be possible for the surviving Germans to come and sort out our mangled bodies, there would be no papers in our pockets, no boots on our feet, no rings on our fingers, no watches – nothing.

I took out my diary and fountain pen and wrote, 'Anyone finding this wallet, containing all my documents, photographs, money etc, please keep the money if it's any good. Send the rest to …' and the address of my parents. 'Please attach a few notes of your own, explaining that I hid these things in my last hours. The end for me came on 28 April 1945, here in Berlin, Köpenick.'

In one corner stood the huge terracotta oven. I wrapped my wallet in a piece of cloth and pushed it well behind the oven. Would anyone ever find it? Would the building even survive? Suddenly the safety of this building became very important.

We occupied the building across the road and waited for the curtain to go up on the last act. We did not have long to wait. Tanks and infantry started pouring towards us from every direction. It would have been senseless to try to meet them in the street with our *Panzerfaust*. I took up a position on the ground floor in a corner room from which I could cover two major roads, and as the T34s started rolling past, I started firing *Panzerfausts*.

Two T34s were burning, their crews scattered all over the place. The roads were literally choked with dead and wounded infantry. One following tank veered off and burried itself in the wall of a building and got stuck. The others managed to reverse and open fire. I knocked out the one stuck in the wall, then grabbed an MG42 and joined the others in concentrating on the infantry. Several of our chaps were now dead, many wounded, and for these there was no choice but to carry on fighting or just lie still – or shoot themselves, which some of them did.

Some Ivans forced the entry, killing several of the men in their way, and the few of us still on our feet rushed to meet them – amongst others, a boy of 13 in his Hitler Youth uniform. We got them out of the building, but there were only five of us left. I left three at the

entry, and took the boy down to the cellar, hoping to hide him somewhere. Ivan gave us no time, and I rushed to the narrow concrete
window, firing my MG. Shrapnel whizzed past my head and went
through the boy's face. Another rush by the infantry and my MG42
burst into ear-splitting cacophony in the confined space. There was a
crash on my helmet – and my lights went out."

**Jean Porter was 22 when she was sent from her home town of
Antwerp in Belgium to work in a restaurant in Berlin in 1943.
She stayed there until the end of the war and witnessed the final
days when the Russians entered Berlin.**

"I was sent to Germany in 1943. I got a letter, saying I had to go and
work there. You had to report to a certain place; you were given
money and coupons to buy some extra clothes. They asked you
whether you wanted to work in a factory or privately, like in a restaurant or something, and I said I'd work in a restaurant, because I
thought, you know, I don't want to go hungry. If you didn't go, they
would find you and put you in prison. To tell the truth I was glad to
go to Germany, because things were never that good at home. I had
a stepmother, you see, and she didn't want me, so I went to live with
an aunt, and she didn't really want me either. So when the chance
came to go to Germany, where I would at least have an occupation. I
was secretly pleased.

So, they sent us on this train to Berlin. We didn't know where we
were going at first. I worked in a café in the Anhalterstrasse near the
Anhalter Bahnhof. Workers from the railway used to come in, lorry
drivers, that sort of thing – there were a lot of people working you
know, they weren't all in the war. They would all come in for a plate
of stew, because you didn't need to use your coupons for it, as there
was no meat in it. We stayed in a private house just round the corner.
The boss rented this room. Me and this other girl from Belgium,
Marie, stayed there. They were very good to us at the restaurant and
in the house.

Life was very much the same from day to day. It was only at the
end that the real action started for us. We knew there was something in the air. Nobody knew what was happening, but there were
rumours going around that Russia was invading. The following day
we went home to get some stuff. There were German soldiers on
the corner of the streets with guns, lying dead. And when we got

home, we just took what we could carry and went again to the shelter. And we could see on the bridge over the canal they'd piled up furniture ever so high, as a sort of barricade. I don't know how they could have built it so high. The next day we had to be evacuated, because the Russians were almost on the doorstep, so to speak. We walked all the way alongside the rails in the underground from one station to the other through the tunnels. We have to be very quiet, everybody was saying 'shsssh' … In the meantime they had tried to flood the underground to stop the Russians coming in. We were up to our knees in water, and if you fell over the rails that was your lot. You couldn't get up. You were so weak by then. In the underground there's like a ledge, and people were all trying to get up on there, but the people who couldn't get up were walking in the water. It was very hard to get up on the ledge, because it was every man for himself. We had to walk in the water, and there was one couple with a new-born baby, and it must have been dead, because I saw them laying it down in the water. They had no food, and we had no food – we had no food for five days. We lived on a little bit of butter and sugar. The next day the Russians came into the underground and told us, 'All out, all out, the war is over'. So we all came out, and there was this girl there, and she said to me, 'I'm going to my boss, do you want to come with me?'. So I said, 'All right, I'll come'. Well, we went home, and, of course, there was nothing standing. There were bodies everywhere, half-burned bodies and horses as well. It was terrible. Anyway, we went to this girl's boss's house, and we stayed there the night. The Russians were knocking on the doors, and they said, 'Any Fraüleins here?' And the boss said, 'Oh no, no Fraüleins here, upstairs.'. And so he sent them upstairs. The next day he told us we'd better go.

We walked all the way from Berlin to Potsdam, and that was 40 km. There were thousands of us, and when we got to Potsdam, there were loads of people there staying in a farm. The Russians there were burning down all the houses. I think they were mostly pretty uneducated people, they were just doing it for the hell of it. We had to sleep in the hayloft, and the lady there gave us food. I just followed this Dutch chap. He seemed to know where he was going, and we thought, well, if we get to Potsdam, we must be on our way home. There were loads of Dutch people there at the farm, and the next day the lady from the farm gave us a horse and cart and we set off. There were streams of people along the roads, moving out like us. Well, after a while, the horse would get tired, and so, what we did, we just let it go and took another one from the fields. The horses didn't mind, of course. At that time, nobody bothered, you see, everything was still a shambles."

Iwo Jima and Okinawa – Last-ditch Bushido

*D*espite being only 8 miles square (20.75 km square), and suffering from a massive air and sea bombardment, the volcanic island of Iwo Jima exacted a heavy toll from the US Marines of V Amphibious Corps. But, lying only two hours' flying time from Japan, the island's small air-fields were strategically essential both as a base for short-range fighters defending B-29 bombers attacking the main Japanese islands, and as a bolt hole for damaged bombers which had to divert. The month taken for its capture early in 1945 cost 6,891 Americans killed and 18,700 wounded. The defending Japanese garrison suffered even more: of 22,000 men, only 212 chose to surrender. The island's dominant feature, the volcano of Mount Suribachi, was captured on 23 February; Marines raising the 'Stars and Stripes' on its summit was to provide one of the most memorable photographs of the war. Okinawa, a Japanese island 67 miles (108 km) long and 8 miles (13 km) wide was attacked on 1 April 4 1945, by the US Tenth Army, a force of about 170,000 troops, following an air and sea bombardment which began on 25 March. On 3 and 4 May, the Japanese launched a suicidal counter-attack, which cost the Americans 12,513 dead and 36,600 wounded, before the island was declared secure on 21 June. The Japanese losses were ten times as heavy, with 110,000 dead and only

7,400 surrendering as prisoners. Many Japanese civilians chose to jump to their deaths from the island's steep cliffs rather than face the indignity of surrender to the Americans.

Vice-Admiral Richmond Kelly Turner, commander of US amphibious troops, was notified after a military conference in San Francisco in late September 1944 that the next objectives of the US Pacific campaign would be Iwo Jima and Okinawa – and that he would lead the assaults.

"We estimated that there were 13,000 Japanese troops on Iwo Jima (we were wrong, actually there were about 20,000). The scheme of manoeuvre called for landing two divisions abreast on the south-eastern beaches – the 4th Marine Division on the right and the 5th Marine Division on the left. The 5th Marine Division was to drive across the island, and then swing to the northeast. One Combat Team was to swing left and take Mount Suribachi. The right flank of the 4th Division was to wheel to the right and head for the East Boat Basin, while the rest of the division was to push to the centre of the island, overrun the main airfield, and then head for Motoyama Plateau. The 3rd Marine Division, in reserve, would land on the same beaches, either to assist the attack, or to occupy defensive positions.

Some 900 ships and craft were assigned to this operation and they began to move toward Iwo at the end of January. They were observed by Japanese submarines, so there was no surprise, either tactical or strategic. I had secured a generous amount of air bombardment, most of it high-level bombardment by B-24s and B-29s, flying out of the Marianas. But as we progressed, I found that the effect of the heavy bombardment did not appear to have caused appreciable destruction of specific installations or to have reduced the morale of the enemy. Once the Japanese had started moving their gun and mortar installations into concrete-lined caves, narrow ravines, tortuous gullies and cement-covered emplacements, the actual damage done was very little.

The pre-invasion naval bombardment started off on the wrong foot on D minus 3 because of rain squalls and poor visibility. Only about half the contemplated bombardment was actually delivered. On the second day the weather cleared and the heavy ships worked their way inshore during the morning. The Japanese were enticed to open up from a few well concealed batteries. At 11 o'clock in the morning the LCI gunboats moved in close to provide close support for the underwater demolition teams. Three unnoticed Japanese guns overlooking the beach from Mount Suribachi started firing just after the gunboats let go their rockets. The LCIs were hit hard, 11 of 12 were damaged, one was sunk, and they suffered 170 casualties. The battleship *Nevada* fired on the shore guns until they were silenced.

The landing plan called for putting 9,000 men ashore in the first 45 minutes. At 08.05 am naval gunfire was lifted and 120 aircraft shot rockets and machine gunned and bombed the beach area – some used napalm. At 08.30 am the first wave landed and hit the beach along the 3,000-yard front at nine o'clock. The troops moved forward for the first 350 yards under a rolling barrage of naval gunfire. Japanese fire was relatively light at first, but picked up so that at 09.20 am heavy fire was reported against the right flank beaches. Progress was rapid across the southern belt of the island but progress on the right flank was much slower.

Principal problems were the heavy swell, which swamped landing craft, and the volcanic sand on the beaches. The depth of the beach at water's edge varied from five to 90 feet, and the volcanic sand was treacherous. Troops struggled up the slopes ankle-deep in sand. Wheeled vehicles bogged down to their frames and a few tanks stalled in the surf and were swamped. As vehicles left the ramps, they sank down and their spinning treads banked the sand back under the ramps.

On D plus 1, the weather deteriorated, making the beach landings harder. Japanese suicide planes came in one coordinated attack on February 21. The escort carrier *Bismarck Sea* was sunk, the escort carrier *Lunga Point* was damaged and so were the net tender *Keokuk Point* and LST-477. The fleet carrier *Saratoga* was hit by five suicide planes and damaged so badly she had to retire to an American Navy yard.

The Marines of the 28th Regiment of the 5th Marine Division raised the American flag on the summit of Mount Suribachi at 10.35 am on February 23.

The fighting was 'unto death' for the Japanese. On this day, Domei news agency in Tokyo said, 'This man Turner shall not return home alive. He must not and he won't. This is one of the many things we can do to rest at ease the many souls of those who have paid the supreme sacrifice.'

After Mount Suribachi there was no question as to the outcome. On March 9 I turned over command to Rear Admiral Hill and departed for Guam to concentrate on preparations for the landings on Okinawa. The landings were made on the Hagushi coral sand beaches, 11 miles north of the city of Naha. It was estimated that there were 65,000 Japanese troops on the island. This operation was under command of the US Tenth Army with 185,000 assault troops.

The scheme called for the Marines to capture Ishikawa Isthmus, and Yontan airfield north of Hagushi. The XXIV Corps would establish an east-west line across Okinawa and take Kadena airfield, then capture the southern part of the island. The small island of Ie Shima would be captured simultaneously, and then Northern Okinawa.

The Japanese did not seriously oppose the assault landings. Before dark on the second day, the XXIV Corps had reached the eastern shore of the island and the Marines were on their way to the Ishikawa Isthmus, which they occupied on April 3. But from the outset, the fleet was bedevilled by Japanese *kamikaze* attacks. On the first day's shore bombardment, eight ships were damaged.

One of the most effective weapons that the Japanese developed, in my opinion, was the use of the suicide bombers. The suiciders hurt the Navy badly at Okinawa. Our chief method of defence was to spread out around the ships of the Amphibious Force, at a considerable distance, pickets composed of one to five ships, destroyers, destroyer escorts and small amphibious craft.

The cost, 368 ships damaged and 36 (including 15 amphibious ships and 12 destroyers) sunk during the Okinawa campaign. The carnage among naval personnel was equally heavy – 4,907 officers and men killed by the *kamikazes* and 600 more personnel killed than army soldiers fighting on the land, and 2,000 more killed than marines fighting on the island."

Captain Kōichi Itō, Commanding Officer of the Japanese 1st Battalion, 32nd Infantry Regiment, witnessed the 'fight to the death' by many Japanese soldiers throughout the Pacific campaigns. Proudly he could say that his own battalion never surrendered at Okinawa.

"Early on 4th June, I took a roll-call. My battalion had been in the fighting since April, and our strength had dropped from a total of

700 to 120 men. That day, we arrived at the village of Zaawa from the Shuri Line. From 11th June onwards we fought off the enemy's over-all offensive.

According to the US war history, the US forces sustained 1,500 casualties, killed or wounded, and lost 21 tanks in the fighting for Kuniyoshi, and the fierce Japanese counter-attacks made them rely on aircraft and tanks.

The Army's right and centre collapsed, and soon the extreme left collapsed also. Our battalion continued to resist stubbornly, but was cut off from battalion headquarters, so that the state of units under command was totally unknown.

One night at the beginning of July, I went on a tour of inspection with Kashiki, my adjutant, at the eastern end of Kuniyoshi Village on the south side of the plateau. We met two men who said they had escaped from Mabuni. It was through them we learned that the GOC, Lt-General Ushijima, had committed suicide on 23rd June. I felt a huge shudder pass right through my body.

Now the Army's organised resistance was at an end, we moved over to guerrilla warfare, to be fought by each unit in the place where it had survived. In the case of my battalion, the headquarters was at Kuniyoshi, and we made up units of 20 men each, from about 100 men who were still alive. In all, we could only muster ten rifles between us, but we did what we could to interfere with the enemy's mopping-up operations – but nine-tenths of the men were wounded or fell sick. I myself was suffering from a recurrence of amoebic dysentery, and for a long time I could not walk. If we put together all our arms and ammunition, we could seek a chance to die in one last attack on a nearby airfield, but although we put together a suicide unit, our physical condition was simply not up to it.

Then our food supplies began to run out. Our food supplies had come to us through the efforts of village girls who were attached to us. During the daytime they hid in trenches, but at night, they came down from the mountains and dug potatoes for us. I was amazed how much fitter and more cheerful these women were than the soldiers.

So to the night of August 14th. From time to time a cloud would pass over the moon, which was nearly at its full. As usual, enemy AA began to fire tracer then, as we watched, it seemed to spread over the whole island of Okinawa. I don't know how many thousands – tens of thousands – of star shells they fired. A red light criss-crossed with shafts of light from the searchlights, a stupendous barrage which went on until dawn. I heard that night my first and last noise of bombing by special attack planes. Everywhere the word for VICTORY was spelled out in V-shaped lights.

About August 22nd, I heard someone call out, 'Battalion Commander!' A Japanese Army corporal stood there, guiding a US Army officer. He said he had spent 17 years in Japan and spoke fluent Japanese – he told me Japan had surrendered.

No *kamikaze* planes had flown since August 14th – I knew that – and enemy leaflets had been dropped on us on the 18th, telling us that Japan had surrendered. I put these things together in my head – the premonition I had had became reality.

I waited for sunset that evening and went to see the regimental commander. We were to resist, whatever happened, I knew that – but I forced myself to recount the day's events to him. He seemed to be unconvinced, but in the end, ordered me to act as a peace envoy.

Two days later, I met the American, Morse, again, and asked for certain proof that Japan had surrendered. 'I'll bet you listened to the recording of the Emperor's Rescript ending the war,' he said, 'and the news from Japan. Captain Ito, please accept what has happened.'

'No, that's not proof enough,' I answered. 'Please have me meet our Chief-of-Staff at Army GHQ, who has already been taken into camp.' Lieutenant Morse kept his temper, but refused. 'Well, the parley's broken down. Let's take up our rifles again,' I said. The adjutant and the rest of the men were holding their breath. It was the work of a second. The enemy officer changed tack and granted my demand.

Straight away, I climbed into the jeep with Lieutenant Morse, and we turned towards Kadena, 30 km away to the north, where the US Army GHQ was. I had to get him to stop the jeep from time to time, for calls of nature, because of my dysentery – apart from that, the jeep sped on, through the shattered trees by the roadside. The mountains looked naked, as if they had been stripped bare, with a white, grainy texture like a coral reef.

Let me go back to the fate of the 10,000 officers and men who survived, and who were weaponless. They ended up in all sorts of ways – some were eventually killed in the fighting, some continued to resist, some escaped, and some surrendered. Some 3,000 men surrendered before the news of our defeat, and became POWs – thousands more ended up in US camps. So, even though organised combat by the army on Okinawa came to an end, it may be said there was no *gyokusai*, no fighting until annihilation. It was impossible to crush the Japanese soldier, however brave he was, even if he was weaponless.

Soon we reached US Army Intelligence HQ, and I listened hard to the recording of the Emperor's broadcast, which was very difficult to make out. I listened again and again. I asked for it to be repeated three times. 'Bear the unbearable... for the peace of the whole world...' the phrases stayed in my heart for ever.

Then north again, in the jeep. I met a colonel in a straw-thatched village house. He showed me the *New York Times* and explained the situation, from the Soviet invasion of Manchuria to the end of the war. 'I have no proof, but I do believe Japan has surrendered. Please make your own decision, so that your men do not become casualties wantonly and pointlessly.'. Tears welled in his eyes as he said this.

On the evening of August 25th, all 13 of our officers, with the regimental commander in the centre, assembled and sat in a circle. I reported, to the effect that I had verified that Japan had surrendered. The silence went on, and on... Then the regimental commander, silent, his face full of anguish, said simply, 'We will obey. We will give up our weapons.'

I had one more duty to perform. I had to negotiate our conditions for disarming the 32nd Infantry:

1 The disarming would be on 29 August.
2 Between 27th and 29th, in an area of two square kilometres round our positions, our freedom of movement would be permitted.
3 All round the free-movement zone, the US Army would place sentries, and would prohibit the entry of US troops.

The US Army showed its respect for our unit and its fighting spirit by granting all these requests.

That is how the battle came to an end for us. Each unit, reduced to ten or twelve men, was placed under the command of the senior soldier present, and we assembled, in ranks, in Kuniyoshi village. The soldiers' uniforms were faded and torn, and they could not conceal the pallor of fatigue. The US troops drove forward their vehicles to take up our casualties, and the severely wounded were taken to hospital. Next, a hundred local people from the area were removed to a camp for civilians. The girls who had helped our HQ wept in the trucks which were taking them away. They had helped so much, and now we could do nothing for them.

On the night of August 28th, we carried out the ceremony of burning the regimental flag, which had been the symbol of our tradition and honour ever since 1899. The officers gave a final salute to the flag as it went up in flames.

Next came the day of our disarming. The US Army, through me, demanded that the regimental commander read the surrender rescript. The road through Kuniyoshi village ran from east to west, and by that roadside, we laid down 30 rifles. Next, the 300 officers and men formed up in ranks.

Colonel Hongo Kakuro stood facing Major Train, who was in command of a ten-truck unit, led by one jeep. Both commanding officers walked towards each other and shook hands. 'We give ourselves up to the US Army, by the command of His Majesty the Emperor,' said Colonel Hongo, choosing his words with great care. I had asked that we could say it this way, because to use the word 'surrender' was shameful.

And that is how Japan's 32nd Infantry Regiment never, right to the end, employed the word *kofuku* – surrender."

Admiral Sir Michael Denny was captain of the British carrier HMS *Victorious*, which was part of the British Pacific Fleet. He recalls the fierce *kamikaze* attacks, which seemed to come at the most vulnerable moments.

"Our anti-aircraft fire was pretty effective, and the *Victorious* was an immensely handy ship to handle, with a big rudder. I could spin her around quite rapidly and so I ruined both my *kamikaze* attacks.

They aimed originally for between the lifts – with American ships they could open up the flight deck and go right through into the hangar space below – but eventually they found that this didn't work on the British carriers' armoured decks.

Two *kamikazes* successfully striking an American carrier could put her out of action with regard to operating aircraft, but this did not work with the British carriers. This was possibly the reason why, later on, they seemed to go for the bridges of British ships, with a view to killing our command personnel. But this was a silly thing to do – they could do far more harm to us by going for the hull of the ship. Damage to the actual lifts, while less spectacular, was a far more effective way of putting a carrier out of action.

Our first *kamikaze* started from almost astern of us, and my turn put him on my beam. He tried to pull up and start again, but he was not quick enough. I crossed ahead of him pretty close, and his wheels touched the flight deck at right angles. The undercarriage sheared right off and his plane broke up, sliding 80 feet across the flight deck to crash over the side and on to the 4.5 inch guns.

From the first moment I started to swing the ship, he had been trying to adjust and steer up the flight deck – which would have given him the length of the ship in which to drop his stick and hit – but he missed.

It is interesting to recall that each pilot would react differently – there appeared to be no set formula for an attack, other than the aiming point and the run-in. One could never tell whether one was up against a first-class pilot or not, until the moment one swung the ship and watched the pilot's reactions. If one's timing was good, and the pilot was forced to rethink his attack, the majority of them would veer in at a lower angle, which at once reduced their effectiveness if they did hit. If one could lead an enemy pilot to make a large alteration in his course, or if he failed to make an alteration at all, one felt secure that he would not score a hit. The fatal thing to do was for a carrier to steer a straight course, for in that case he would always get you.

In the cases where more than one aircraft approached, in all cases they would make separate attacks. One could watch them pick their targets, through a good pair of glasses, and as soon as the leading aircraft went into his dive, his wing-men would open up on either side of him, hoping to hit you, no matter how you turned."

Marine Robert Porter, after spending the early years of the war in the Mediterranean, was posted to the Pacific in 1945, to join the flagship of the Task Force 57, *King George V*, in Operation Iceberg.

"The Okinawa campaign was the first of the Pacific campaigns that the British Fleet was involved in. We were directly under the Americans and had to learn their signals and codes before the operation. Every ship in the Force – we were the 57th Task Force – had Americans on board teaching them signals and so on.

The job of the 57th Task Force was to bomb and annihilate the Sakishima group of islands. There were two particular airfields there called Ishigaki and Miyako. The enemy planes would take off from them to bomb us and the American Fleet.

By April we had already been sailing around the islands for about a month, waiting for the campaign to commence. Operation Iceberg, as it was known, commenced on April 1st 1945, when we attacked the islands and the Americans invaded Okinawa.

Our aeroplanes flew off the aircraft-carriers while we bombarded the islands from the battleships. We were about 8 miles from the shore, firing with the 14 inch guns. Those guns had a range of about 20 miles and did a lot of damage. I was on the anti-aircraft guns – the 5.25s. We brought down quite a few planes as they took off from the islands. They would come over in groups of two or three – you were very aware of them most of the time.

The Japanese aircraft were suicide squads and very determined. They would never give way. The planes would come straight at you, flying straight through the flak. If they dropped the bombs and got a hit, they would go away, but if the bombs missed the ship they were after, they would go straight for it. They actually crashed on some of the carriers, causing serious damage.

You would often see the Japanese pilots in the water afterwards, if the plane had dived into the sea. Sometimes they were taken on board and sometimes they were left swimming in the water – it depended. Really, they wanted to sacrifice their lives for their Emperor, so probably didn't want to be rescued.

We used to be at sea for three months at a time during the Pacific campaigns. It was the first time we were allowed beer in the British Navy. We were given one bottle a day, which was on top of the rum ration. It was a privilege allowed to us because we were at sea for so long. The Americans had dry ships and weren't allowed anything.

We used to get the beer at about 6 o'clock. It worked out very well because everyone was given a ticket for the beer and a lot of people didn't drink, so we got all their beer as well. When we were away from the danger zones, a gang of us used to go right to the top of the ship with about 20 bottles of beer between us. We used to sit under the stars, smoking. It was lovely, sailing through the Pacific – I used to feel very contented then.

We were regarded as heroes when we got back to Australia. They were very excited about having the Pacific Fleet with them, and we were fêted everywhere. You could, perhaps, sense a little resentment because some people felt that the Americans had done all the work, and the British had come in at the last minute. However, when we went into Melbourne, so many people came on board to congratulate us that the ship actually sank to the bottom of the harbour and rested in the sand."

Bombing of Japan

Now that America's bombers had acquired the vital bases in the Pacific from which to carry out bombing raids on Japan, it was only a matter of time before all the logistical problems were solved and aircraft could be directed to turn the full force of an all-out fire-bombing campaign on the cities of Japan. The mighty B-29 Superfortresses finally arrived over the home islands of Japan, and the unimagined scenes of destruction and death which ensued left a lasting scar on the memories of an astonished Japanese population.

Mr Isemitsu Kozakai miraculously survived the air raid on Tokyo on 9/10 March 1945. The tragedy is so firmly etched on his memory that, having been a keen artist, he was only able to illustrate his impressions of the raid and its after effects for years after that terrible event.

"I used to run a shoe-shop business and had a wife and three daughters. Since Tokyo was really a dangerous place to be in, I had my family evacuated. They went to my elder brother's place in the country, in Niigata. That was in December 1944. Only my second daughter was evacuated, with her school, to Yamagata.

My brother agreed to our going to him, but considering it thoroughly, I came to the conclusion I was imposing on him too much – it was a burden for him. So I decided to come back to Tokyo with only my eldest daughter, Mieko. It took five days to get back.

Mieko was 15, and if you wanted to work, that's the age at which you could start. The morning we were leaving, she turned to my wife and said, 'Let me see your face, just once more,' and gazed at her for some time. I wonder if she had a premonition that she was going to die. After that, at the Tokyo house, there was just Mieko and me.

On March 10, the day of the air raid, my younger brother, Sakuji, was staying with us. He'd been in the army, at the front, and had caught malaria. He was back for a short time on sick leave, and had been helping round the house in all sorts of ways.

Apart from my job, I was also the local section chief of the National Health Movement on behalf of the town council. This involved taking evacuation drills, or calling people out for their preventative injections. When the air-raid warning sounded, it was my job to be first to go out.

That morning, the air-raid warning sounded as usual. However, it seemed to go on for an awfully long time. I was surprised at this and thought it must be something serious, so I called my younger brother, but whether or not he'd got used to it, I don't know, but he wouldn't get up. I had to shake him awake, forcibly. Both of us took the household treasures outside.

Incendiary bombs started falling straight away. Flames began to spread as we watched. 'We've left something important behind,' my brother said, and he went inside to get it. He was gone for a long time. I couldn't go and look for him because there were enormous sheets of flame everywhere.

When I went to look at the air-raid shelter, the fire seemed to have gone right through it – there was nothing but flames and smoke. I tried to go in first, with Mieko and a neighbour, but we could not get inside, and outside the fires were spreading. It became difficult to breathe in my air-raid hood, and fires were blazing in various places, but there was nothing we could do – so we came away. After we had gone some distance, I fell into a sewerage ditch. The water was stagnant and the silt had accumulated, so I was covered with mud from head to foot.

An old lady appeared ahead of us. 'What dreadful things! It's better to be dead. Please, kill me!'. Her voice trembled and she clung to me. I said, 'Don't worry', and scraped the mud from my back. I wondered where we could go, and looked here, there and everywhere, before I caught sight of some school buildings ablaze. It was Oshima No 2 People's School, and I suddenly remembered – there was a pool in that school garden, and I crawled under the flames and plunged into the pool. There were already people in it before me, competing for their share of the water. The flames began to lick at my air-raid hood. I didn't feel I was burning, but rather I had the impression the flames were on the move – and fast.

At the time, my whole attention was concentrated on the fires. 'If only dawn would come soon – if only it could be soon…' That's what I kept thinking, because apart from that, there was no hope at all. Finally dawn came and I went back to look at the air-raid shelter. The earth on top of it had fallen in, and it had collapsed. Next, I went towards the house. My brother was lying flat on his face. His body was burned black. He was dead. I wondered if perhaps Mieko had managed to escape, and I walked across the smouldering ground, calling out her name.

I retraced my steps to the air-raid shelter. Five or six of my neighbours had gathered there, and we dug up the ground with shovels. As we did so, the backs of two or three bodies came into sight in the dug-up earth. There didn't seem any point in going on. We tried to dig a little more, but our eyes had been damaged. What with the smoke and dust, we could hardly see. We decided it was pointless to go on, and agreed to meet again in three day's time.

I went back to my wife's parents' house in Gumma Prefecture. I had some medical treatment for my eyes, then came back to Tokyo. My younger brother and my daughter were lying on corrugated zinc sheeting. My daughter had on my wife's *mompe* [woman's baggy work trousers]. There were burns all over her body – it looked like the body of a burned fish. I collected firewood from all over and heaped great piles of it on top of the bodies. I set fire to it, but they wouldn't burn. However long the wood burned, it seemed as if they were half-roasting. It was only later I realised that the firewood should not have been piled on top of the corpses, they should have been put on top of the firewood.

So, for two whole days, we kept on burning. I looked for two unglazed jars, washed out the insides throughout, put the bones in them and went to Gumma Prefecture. Later, still carrying the bones, I went to Niigata, where the rest of the family were. When I got there, my wife clung to the bones, weeping almost without a sound. She would not be separated from them – I could not make her let go. When I said 'What is burned does not return,' she was furious with me.

My feelings – well, such things as 'how sad, how pitiful' – there was absolutely none of that. That was true when we burned the corpses too. It was so terribly practical, business-like, you see. There was nothing sad about it, however odd that may seem. Perhaps I did not really think about it at all.

My elder brother said, 'We must have a double funeral ceremony – for them both together.' We had a joint ceremony, a month after. The priest came and read a *sutra*. When he'd done that, I thought for the first time, 'How unbearably sad.'. I remembered many things about them, and I could not stop myself from crying, crying and crying, on and on. I could not bear to lift my face up. I was so ashamed, you see. Tears poured down my face, on to my trousers. They were wringing wet. I think I had come back to myself.

The day after the raid the newspapers announced, 'The Prime Minister has proclaimed a resolution in the Diet. We will not allow the enemy to break his way into our divine country. We have accumulated reserves of strength for thousands of years. If the enemy lands, he will be annihilated.'.

I came on ahead, back to Tokyo, and arranged to stay with a friend, at this house. In the mornings, I used to sell fermented soy beans, and in the lunch hour I used to shine shoes. A man who had run a shoe shop introduced me to a basement store in Aeaji-cho. I now have a shoe shop repair business there.

I am still keen on painting – but now I paint horses flying through the skies – pictures of horses flying away, into the distance. That's what I think of now."

Takeo Ikuma was a schoolboy who lived with his father and two younger sisters in the Fukiai district of western Kobe. From their house on the side of a hill, and especially from the second floor verandah, the Ikumas had a good view of the effects of the American air raids on their city.

"I remember the big raid of 5 June particularly. The bombers came over in broad daylight, big silver aircraft floating through the sky. It was a hot summer day and first the smoke from the bombings hung in the air, rising slowly. But then the wind came up and the fires began to spread. I saw one brave Japanese fighter plane crash into a B-29 and then I saw the parachutes stringing out in the sky behind the plane as it went down.

After half an hour my father and the girls said they were going to the refuge behind the hill. I wanted to stay and watch and anyhow it was my duty to stay and fight the fire if our house was bombed. Somehow I knew that this was the day we would be bombed. We had always escaped before but this time. I watched as the bombers came nearer and nearer to our neighbourhood, as if they were looking for us. After one hour of raiding, the black smoke was moving swiftly toward our district of Fukiai. Yes, the bombers were coming our way.

Most of the people had already left the area even though it was illegal to do so. Every house was supposed to have its *rusuban* (caretaker). But in the past two months there bad been so many raids that the Home Ministry's orders were being: disobeyed every day. As everyone knew, once the firebombers came and hit your house, there was nothing that could be done to save it. The material in the bombs burned everything. As the bombers came closer I could see the tiny bombs dropping from the big silver birds. They were the little incendiaries – the worst kind.

Soon the bombs were falling ever closer and then several bombs struck our roof. Dozens of four-pound bombs hit us and immediately began to burn. I tried a bucket of water, but it just seemed to make the fire burn brighter, and there were twenty places on fire now. There was nothing to do but try and escape. I had waited a long time. Fires were burning all round the house. I decided the best way to go was to follow the electric rail line because the embankment was free of houses. But to get to the line I had to walk through the neighbourhood and all the houses were burning. I met many people moving toward the mountains, carrying their belongings or their children on their backs – suitcases, boxes, bags, and even futons. As I went along I saw all sorts of things abandoned. Down in the valley the sky was no longer visible, the air was full of smoke and I could hear people crying out all around me.

I looked at my left hand. It had turned a strange white colour, and it began to throb. I had been burned somehow by a fire-bomb. I came to a large barrel of water put on the side of the road for the firefighters, and wanted a drink. But the surface was covered with black scum. So I kicked the barrel and then went on.

I reached the edge of the hills at Noda Michinaga. The whole area was abandoned. I walked down the hill to the plain and all around me I saw people walking, stumbling, and many of them were now abandoning their goods and luggage. The place to go was the upland ahead, where the houses were so few the bombers would not bother with them.

Finally I reached the hills. Below I could see Katano Kijo landing, once a beautiful green grassy area, but now scorched and seared. It had been a shelter area, and it had burned like an inferno, trapping thousands of the people who came into the boxlike place seeking shelter. From the hill I could see the Kobe had burned, from Fukiai to Kuta. Everything was burned up.

Then I suddenly remembered my father and sisters. Where had they gone? I walked down into the shelter area and began to search for them. I became very tired and sat down with my back against a concrete wall. I fell asleep. When I awakened I saw more people streaming out of the city toward the hills. I went to look for an aid station to have my burns treated, and finally came to a school that had been turned into a hospital. A doctor looked at my face and immediately gave me some sugar. He looked at my back and told me to lie down. I had a deep wound in my back. A firebomb had exploded right next to me, and I had been burned and wounded by shrapnel at the same time. The doctor had seen scores of such wounds that day.

I rested a while and then began to search again for my family. I found them finally. We went back to the house. There was nothing left but ashes and junk. The authorities gave us food, as well as futons and a canvas tarpaulin to keep the rain off. We stayed near our house for five days, then we knew we must do something.

We decided we would have to leave Kobe and go to stay with my father's family. So on the fifth day after the great air raid, we went down to Kobe central railroad station and bought tickets that would take as to a new life. Then we got on the train – and headed for Hiroshima."

Major-General Curtis LeMay, commanding officer of the XXI Bomber Command of the Twentieth US Air Force, decided to destroy Japan's cities by fire and bring the country to its knees. The following is taken from his report on Raid No. 5.

"Primary target: Nagoya urban area. Continuing the plan of attacking targets on Honshu on alternate days for five consecutive missions, it was decided to return to Nagoya inasmuch as the results from the first attack had not been as good as desired.

Important Japanese aircraft targets lie within the city itself, while others lie to the north of Kamigahara. It is estimated that the above-mentioned units produce between 40 and 50 per cent of the total output of combat aircraft and engines.

Five hundred-pound clusters of M-69 bombs, AN-M17A1 clusters of M-76 incendiary bombs, E-46 clusters fused to open 2,500 feet above target, AN-M17A1 clusters fused to open 3,000 feet above target, AN-M472A instant, M-76 instant. Two general-purpose bombs were included in each third aircraft to disrupt organised fire-fighting and assist incendiary attack in harassing blast effects. Possible severance of electrical lines and blocking of streets was considered highly desirable. On the basis of reports on the first low-level night attack on Tokyo, it was decided that the altitude of attack would remain unchanged at 5,000–7,500 feet. The 290 aircraft dropped a total of 1,858 tons of incendiary bombs. Damage assessment revealed 148,610,000 square feet destroyed in target area. Six aircraft landed at Iwo Jima and returned late. One aircraft of the 313th Wing ditched as the result of damage from anti-aircraft fire. All ten crew members were rescued. As a result of smoke, the majority of the bombing was accomplished exclusively by radar.

The Field Order stipulated that the 313th and 314th Wings were to load tail turrets only. The 73rd was to load lower aft and lower forward turrets with 200 rounds of ammunition per turret. Bombardiers were ordered not to use turrets, control being by side gunners who were authorised to fire on ground targets for the purpose of knocking out searchlights and disrupting anti-aircraft batteries. Tail-turret gunners were to fire only when fired upon.

The Japs are making an effort to light the area over the target. They use parachute flares and they are improving their use of searchlights. Enemy aircraft are using landing lights when pressing attacks, and in one case, a searchlight was mounted on a fighter for searching purposes.

Air opposition was weak, with 192 enemy aircraft being sighted and 37 making 44 attacks. Only one attacking fighter was identified as to name – an Irvine. The others were made by unidentified fighters, 23 twin-engined and four single-engined and 112 wholly unidentified. One enemy fighter was reported to have appeared between five and eight o'clock, passing in back of the plane, and to have fired two bursts out of range. A second enemy aircraft made a pass from three o'clock high, but did not fire, approaching within 500 yards of the reporting aircraft. A third enemy aircraft was reported as firing from 700 to 800 yards – not pointed as in an attack, but firing at random. A fourth aircraft made a pass at seven o'clock, turned off its lights and did not press closely or open fire. No aircraft were lost due to enemy aircraft, and only one B-29 was damaged. Only ten of the attacks were from the tail... Interpretation of photographs obtained on 24 March 1945, assessed visible damage from this attack to 82,000,000 sq ft, which included barracks and buildings in Nagoya Castle, the Toyo Cotton Mill and the Yamada Engineering Works."

Staff Sergeant John Mahan was tail-gunner on a B-25J, flying combat with the 47th Bombardment Squadron of the 41st Bombardment Group of the United States Seventh Air Force, flying conventional bombing and torpedo missions out of Okinawa to Kyushu.

"The B-25s we had were modified to carry a special torpedo. Maybe I should clarify this and say we were equipped to carry a glide torpedo. This was a standard torpedo with a wing and tail assembly and, when dropped at a given air speed, the torpedo would glide one mile for every one thousand feet of altitude. The gyros in the torpedoes were preset on the ground to perform various manoeuvres once they entered the water.

Some zig-zagged, some moved in helixing circles, some performed figure eights. The purpose was to seek targets in a harbour or bay that held a concentration of ships, and the torpedoes would continue these manoeuvres until they ran out of fuel and sank or struck a target. Now this is a good theory, and we did hit a couple of ships, one aircraft carrier and some smaller vessels.

This day, our assigned target was a cove in Sasebo Bay on the northwest end of Kyushu Island. As we approached Kyushu, we ran into strong headwinds and we knew that would affect our torpedo drop – the headwinds would increase the air speed and the torpedo would glide further. So, our pilot throttled back to decrease the air speed, and watched the lead plane of our formation, for it carried the squadron bombardier. When he dropped his torpedo, we would drop ours too. Someone shouted, 'There it goes!' Our pilot hit the tit button and our flying fish fell away from the aircraft.

I should add here that the pilot controlled the button that released the shackles on the torpedo, and he also controlled 12 forward-firing 50-calibre machine guns, the bomb-bay doors, and he also dropped the bombs when we carried them. In the Pacific, the bombardier had been largely dispensed with during the campaign for New Guinea, when it was discovered that the B-25 made an excellent low-level attack plane by removing the bombardier's compartment and installing multiple forward-firing machine guns.

These tit buttons are located on the yoke. Every bombardier was now dual-rated so his classification was bombardier/navigator. So we had a bombardier, but no place for him to bomb from. Would you believe, some of the bombardiers in our squadron had never dropped a bomb in combat?

After the torpedo fell away, we began watching for enemy fighters. The flak came up, but it was not too bad. This cove was sheltered by mountains, and we watched them closely as the fish glided away. We could see some of the other torpedoes entering the water – their wings would fly off and then they were armed (a device that trailed below the torpedo would first strike the water, and that would release the wing and tail assembly). These other torpedoes were on their search mission, looking for something to hit – but our torpedo was still flying. We could see it streaking across the cove, as all the other torpedoes went straight into the water. Still ours flew. It got caught in an updraught and just kept flying – then it ran out of water and was over the land. We lost sight of it, and then we saw an enormous explosion. Our fish, with its 2,000-lb warhead, made history. We torpedoed a mountain!"

A Bombs – Under the Cloud

*A*ware that the Germans had the physicists and knowledge to develop an atomic bomb, European physicists including Niels Bohr, Enrico Fermi and Leo Szilard proposed in 1939 that the United States should start work on an atomic weapon. A British committee was already working in the same field and in 1942 both countries combined their work under the cover name Manhattan Engineer District. Under the leadership of General Leslie Groves the project, with a budget of $500 million a year and a staff of 125,000, flourished in a large plant at Oak Ridge, Tennessee, and in another in Washington State. In December 1942, Enrico Fermi set the first sustaining atomic pile in operation and on July 16, 1945, awed physicists watched as the first atomic bomb exploded at Alamagordo, New Mexico. The first atomic bomb, codenamed 'Little Boy' was dropped from the B-29 Enola Gay at 09.15 am on 6 August 1945, over the Japanese city of Hiroshima. It detonated at a height of 800 ft (244 m) with the force equivalent to 29,000 tons of TNT, destroying about 5 square miles (13 square km) of the city and killing an estimated 70,000 people. The second bomb, 'Fat Man', was dropped on Nagasaki, a substitute for its main target, Kokura, which was cloud covered. The hills surrounding the city sheltered many people from the blast, keeping the death toll down to a relatively low 24,000. The shock of these attacks led the Japanese to accept surrender. If an invasion of the Japanese mainland had taken place the human cost for military and civilians alike would most likely have been far greater.

Colonel Paul Tibbets was the man charged with piloting the *Enola Gay* to drop the bomb on Hiroshima. After intensive work with the Manhattan Project, the time had come for him to perform the real mission.

"I named the crews that were going to make these flights in each aeroplane and I said afterwards that there would be a further briefing at a certain time that evening to allow us to go in a little bit more detail into what these other crews – or more specifically what we wanted each one of them – to do; things we wanted them to look for and be prepared for.

Again, this intensified the atmosphere, so that when we got around to the point that we had all of the briefings over with and we had had a midnight supper (which was commonplace – whenever they were going out on an early morning run, they'd have a midnight supper), I found that it wasn't just the flight crews and the operations people that were there, but everybody was there – the whole organisation. Nobody was sleeping that night. They didn't know *why* they weren't, but they weren't sleeping.

So, when we finally got down to the aircraft and loaded on board (now they all knew that we had loaded the weapon, 'cos you can't hide the fact that an aeroplane has been loaded – they didn't see what was loaded, but everybody knew that that afternoon a bomb had been loaded in the aeroplane) and got to the time of take-off, this word has spread throughout the island.

I think the take-off possibly created a lot of interest on other people's parts – more so than on my own – because it had been decided earlier that there was a possibility that an accident could occur on take-off, so therefore we would not arm this weapon until we had left the runway and were out to sea. This, of course, meant that had there been an accident, there would have been an explosion from normal powder charges, but there would not have been a nuclear explosion. As I said, this worried people more than it worried me, because I had plenty of faith in my aeroplane. I knew my engines were good – I thought I was good. I wasn't anticipating any great problem that evening.

We started our take-off on time, which was somewhere about 2.45 am, I think, and the aeroplane went on down the runway. It was loaded quite heavily, but it responded exactly like I had anticipated it would. I had flown this aeroplane the same way before and there was no problem.

About 3.30 am we had completed the loading of the nuclear portion of the bomb, and we had it armed. This had been done at an altitude of approximately 4,000 feet, to allow the people to be back in the aircraft unpressurised and working in conditions that wouldn't be too uncomfortable because of the chill of the higher altitude. Once the weapon had been armed, we had a radio contact or codes that we were using back to base to let them know the progress of things on the flight. We even had a prearranged code that we would refer to when we dropped the bomb, and this would indicate the results back to these people.

At the time the bomb was armed, we must have been somewhere close to five hours away from the target. Our next point was a rendezvous 600 miles away from Tinian. We had this rendezvous with Chuck Sweeney and George M... because they were going to fly aircraft that would escort me. These aircraft would contain scientific-type instruments that would be dropped from those aeroplanes at the same time my bomb dropped from my aeroplane.

We made the rendezvous quite successfully, then we had about an hour and a half or a little over that to go along in a lazy formation on a beautiful night out on the Pacific, with moon and clouds that looked like powderpuffs. It was quite peaceful, believe me, and nothing much went on – there was a bit of talk in the aeroplane, but that's always normal on a mission. But then you get a quiet period, and while we were going along there, I guess everybody had been dreaming or something, because it was quiet. But we had to start thinking about climbing up to the altitude, pressurising and getting ready to get on this bomb-run before we got to the coastline of Japan, and if my memory serves me correctly, it was something like 6.40 am in the morning when we prepared a climb to altitude in order that we would be in our bombing altitude before reaching the coastline of Japan.

We arrived over the 'initial point' and started in on the bomb-run, which had about 11 minutes to go – rather long for a bomb-run, but on the other hand, we felt that we needed this extra time in straight and level flight to stabilise the airspeed of the aeroplane, to get everything right down to the last detail.

After about three minutes on the bomb-run, I made the last-minute corrections. Now, when I did this, I was also required to advise the crew that they must put on these dark glasses – we had been given dark glasses to shield our eyes from the glare that the blast was expected to produce.

The last three minutes of a bomb-run are quite important because of certain things that have to be performed in the cockpit of the aeroplane, and in this particular case, I wanted Sweeney and M… to know exactly what I was doing because they had things to do in their aircraft. As we came down to the last minute of the bomb-run, a tone was activated on the radio. It was a high-pitched tone that they were receiving in those other two aeroplanes to let them know we were only one minute away from the bomb-drop. At this particular time they had certain actions that they had to perform, which was to get their instruments ready to be released out of the bomb-bay. When the tone stopped in my aeroplane, this meant that the bomb had left the bomb-bay of the aeroplane. It was a cut-off. They automatically opened their bomb-bay to release these instruments.

The problem after the release of the bomb is not to proceed forward, but to turn away, so I immediately went into this steep turn, as did Sweeney and M… behind me, and we tried then to place distance between ourselves and the point of impact. In this particular case, that bomb took 53 seconds from the time it left the aeroplane until it exploded. That's how long it took to fall from the bombing altitude. This gave us adequate time, of course, to make the turn. Now we had just made the turn and rolled out in level flight, when it seemed like somebody had grabbed a hold of my aeroplane and gave it a real hard shaking, because this was the shock-wave that had come up.

This was something I was glad to feel – it gave me a moment of relief, after all, having worked on that bomb for well over a year. You know, that 53 seconds when I'm turning the aeroplane, I'm wondering, 'Is it, or is it not going to work?' and of course the shock-wave hitting us was an indication it had worked.

Now, after we had been hit by a second shock wave, not quite so strong as the first one, I decided we'd turn around and go back and take a look, because each of us in the three aircraft had hand-held cameras. We were looking through the front of the aircraft to take pictures as rapidly as we could of what was transpiring in front of us.

The day was clear when we dropped that bomb – it was a clear, sunshiny day. Visibility was unrestricted, so as we came back round again, facing the direction of Hiroshima, we saw this cloud coming up. The cloud by this time, in two minutes, was up at our altitude (we were at 33,000 feet at this time) and was continuing to go right on up in a boiling fashion. The surface was nothing but a black, boiling – the only thing I could say is a barrel of tar. That's probably the best description I can give. Where before there had been a city – distinctive houses, buildings and everything, that you could see from our altitude – now you couldn't see anything except black, boiling debris down below. It was terrible to look at really – a rather horrifying sight because you knew there were people underneath and you could speculate (but you didn't want to see) what the result was.

I didn't want to delay too long in this air – I don't think that I could have stayed in the Hiroshima area more than about six minutes. It took me about two minutes to make the first turn to come back and take a look at it, then about four more minutes of slow flight, just kind of looking around so we could take these pictures. Then I wanted to get away, because I felt that if I were Japanese and had seen anything like this happen, if it were humanly possible by any means of communication, and I had some fighters to get up into the air, I'd get them up after the aeroplane as fast as I could and make any sacrifice to get it.

Pretty soon it became a rather routine flight back home. As a matter of fact, it was routine enough that I let Bob Lewis and all the pilots fly that aeroplane, and went back and got some sleep for about the first time in 30 hours – and I was ready for it.

I've often been asked how I felt, and I think I have what you might call a rather straightforward stock answer to the question. I had been assigned a military mission to perform. I was most anxious to do the best that I could possibly do in the accomplishment of that mission. I'd been trained for that. As far as my personal feelings are concerned, I never let my personal feelings enter into it. I learned this back in the days when I was flying out of England and bombing targets in Europe. I knew there were people down below, getting hurt by this, and I felt that if I let my emotions get carried away and I got to worrying about who's going to get hurt by something like this, that I wouldn't be effective at all – so I had to school myself not to think about it.

Now, from this point of view, I was not affected emotionally. I haven't been up to this day, because it was something that had to be done. I was convinced that it had to be done, and I was convinced it was the right thing to do at that particular time. I've also been asked, would I do it again? My answer is, if you turn the clock backwards and get the same conditions existing today that you had in 1945, I'd probably do the same thing again with basically the same attitude.

You can't turn the clock backwards – you can't erase it. It has been done. Let's hope we've learned a lesson from it and that we don't have to do it in the future."

Major Charles Sweeney flew the B-29 which escorted *Enola Gay* on the Hiroshima mission and was responsible for the scientific side of the operation. He was to drop instruments in canisters to record the results of the blast for scientific study.

"We made our approach at 30,000 feet, as I recall. It was very close to 30,000 feet and the photographic aeroplane dropped back. I stayed in rather close formation with Colonel Tibbets.

The bomb-bay doors opened and we received a ten-second warning signal by tone, just before the release. Now I must describe the reason for our being there. We were carrying scientific instruments in canisters which were dropped by parachute and they were released by us at the moment that the bomb was released from Colonel Tibbets' aeroplane. Now, at a certain altitude, parachutes dropped those canisters gradually so that they could make recordings of blasts and radioactivity, and other things, and they were telemetered so that three scientists in our aeroplane could make the readings necessary to determine what this thing had done in scientific terms.

Immediately the tone signal stopped, the bomb left Colonel Tibbets' aeroplane and we saw it start to plummet to earth. Our briefing was to turn as quickly as possible in the opposite direction – not quite the opposite direction, but a specified angle to put the greatest distance between the bomb and us on a slant-range that would be mathematically possible, because we had no idea what it would do to the aeroplane.

It takes 52 seconds for an object to drop approximately from 30,000 feet to 1,500 feet, and in that length of time, we were able to get 12 slant-range miles away from the explosion. Very shortly after the explosion, came a white light that just obliterated the very pale blue sky (which is so pale at that altitude). A white light just obliterated the whole sky. I'll never forget it. My back was to the explosion, of course. However, there was a man in the tail, a crew member, and shortly afterwards I heard him say something unintelligible. This was very unusual, because he was a very highly trained man – and he said it again. This was somewhat in opposition to training regulations because once a thing was reported, it wasn't to be reported again, so we could keep track of what things were being reported.

Again he said something that to me was unintelligible and shortly thereafter the aeroplane was smacked on the bottom and my bombardier turned to me, then Captain Clement Behan and he said, 'Flak'. There was a little bit of panic in his eyes, and he thought we'd been hit by flak – but the aeroplane was still steady.

I could still feel the aeroplane flying well – and we were hit again and again, each time with a diminished force and in as much as Behan had been shot down four times in Europe, I had some confidence in his description of flak: it wasn't. The man in the tail was describing something that I guess human eyes hadn't seen before.

These were concentric rings of hot air coming up toward the aeroplane, or coming up radiating from the explosion. These were the things that hit the aeroplane and caused the smacking on the bottom. These diminished, of course, and went away. Afterwards we turned back and flew alongside back toward home base 1,500 miles away. We saw off our right wing, the cloud coming up from Hiroshima. This was a cloud that, as it boiled up, had every colour in the rainbow and at about 25,000 feet the mushroom portion broke off and turned white – and of course we've all seen photographs of that.

We couldn't see the city – it was covered with smoke and, as I recall, even reconnaissance aeroplanes that flew over there almost constantly for the next two days, couldn't photograph the city for – I've forgotten how long it was – 24 or 36 hours or whatever, because it was covered with smoke.

At that moment I felt that the mission had been executed properly and that this just might cause the Japanese government to say 'We're willing to end the war.'. This was what it was all about."

Seiichi Nagai was just ten years old when the bomb exploded over his home town of Nagasaki. He remembers his father, a professor at the town's Medical University, who had previously been studying the use of radium and X-rays and already had leukaemia – and the funeral of his mother killed in the bombing.

"Our house was about 50 metres from the epicentre – but at that time I was at my granny's at Kiba in Miyamacho, about 7 km away. My mother was killed in the blast. I don't know when I first found out, really. I just knew she was no longer alive. When granny went to meet her the day afterwards, she must have gone to our house in Urakami. Granny came back, but she didn't tell us straight away.

Father came back with the relief squad people on August 12. He had a triangular bandage tied around his leg and one on his head. I felt bad about that, but he was alive and he had come back – that was enough. At the time the loss of my mother was the same for the whole family, but the sheer joy that father was still alive was stronger than my grief.

From the book I wrote with my sister, I remember my mother's funeral. 'All four of us walked, bunched close up together, thinking simply that the four of us must keep together, whatever happened – that was what we promised Mummy. The gravestone had been blown down and the stone cross was bent. We unwrapped the white cloth, and stared a long time at Mummy. Those eight eyes stared at her, at that shape which had changed for ever. Our Mummy carried about in a bucket – however many times Kayano and I cried out for her, she would never come back again, would she? Our mother had been burned and reduced to fragments, the rays of sun shone into the bucket and were reflected by those white bones.

A hole was dug on top of where my sisters Ikuko and Sasano were buried, and Mummy's bones were placed in it. With a rustle and a clatter, our mother's bones were poured into that hole where her children were sleeping. We drew in our breaths, as if in greeting. The tears poured down my cheeks. Bending his face down towards his stick, Daddy was crying too. We each poured a little earth on top of Mummy's bones. A big pine tree inclined over the grave, and it was enveloped, as if by a perfume, with the fragrance of pine resin. On a new white cross were written the words: 'MARINA NAGAI MIDORI. DIED IN THE BOMBING, 9 AUGUST 1945. AGED 38 YEARS.'"

Sidney Lawrence, a leading-aircraftsman, had been in the RAFVR in 1938, then was sent to Singapore in 1940 with 36 Torpedo Bomber Squadron. He was finally taken POW by the Japanese in Java in March 1942. 'Officially' dead, he eked out the war in POW camps, finally arriving at a camp in Nagasaki, where he was in August 1945.

"It was a camp called Seisumashi, and there were quite a few other mixed POWs – Japanese, Aussies, a few Americans, and some

British. At that camp we did all sorts of jobs – I've been in coal mines, I've been stevedoring, road-making, all sorts of things – we were slave labour.

When it came to the very last, to Nagasaki, the Japanese said quite definitely, that if they were invaded, under no circumstances would they do other than kill every prisoner. They made that quite plain. In Nagasaki itself, they were going to put us into caves, which we dug out ourselves, and they were just going to blow it in. But we were all to be killed. No prisoner was to be left alive once they were invaded. Everybody knows that the Japanese treatment of us was vile. They hadn't the same standards as us at all. They were quite a different culture. Of course you were just beaten up and knocked about – in certain cases you were tortured. They had all sorts of forms of cruelty, which they didn't consider cruelty, actually. In actuality, I've seen them knock about their own soldiers the same as they knocked us about.

On 9 August, I was working at the camp, near the Mitsubishi Works – it was about 11 o'clock in the morning when they dropped the bomb, and I actually saw it coming down. It came down on a parachute.

I was working in the open, and I was fortunate enough to get away with not being rubbed out with the bomb or being very badly burned. The amazing thing is the effects on me afterwards. I came out in all sorts of strange boils with green pus. I had various different skin complaints. I still suffer from some problems. I still have my hands splitting between the fingers. All my extremities were affected, and it used to look as if my fingers were dropping off. Fortunately that has gradually gone, but only in the last few years. My feet are still the same – every now and again, my skin splits between the toes and it looks as if my toes will drop off. I have to use a certain ointment and deal with it myself.

Right from the beginning here, all the doctors said they didn't know what to do with me – they knew nothing about how to treat the effects of nuclear bombs. They suggested I go back to Japan to get them to treat me. This was how we were treated – appalling really. Some of the fellows went into mental asylums, purely because of their bad treatment when they came home. Nobody cared. They thought at one time that I had radiation sickness, but I didn't, fortunately.

I saw the plane fly over, then the bomb dropping. Then a blinding flash. There were other people around me who were burned to a cinder – and I was saved by a pile of rubble. Prior to their dropping the bomb, the Americans came over and just bombed us and there was a lot of devastation caused. Of course we were the ones who had to clear it up. We used to hope they wouldn't come over as we were still trying to clear the place up.

The horrifying thing was to see that people were just shadows. You didn't find the body, but you found their shadow, emblazoned in the concrete. The person wasn't there – they had gone up in smoke. That was alright. They were dead, gone. The horrible part was to see the torn limbs and flesh hanging on so many of the Japanese. I ended up helping the Japanese, and trying to do everything we could, those of us who were still alive and able to. They couldn't understand that we were trying to treat them.

The Americans came over and dropped food to us on parachutes – and it was food galore, like we hadn't seen in years. It was K rations, and we shared them with the Japanese. They couldn't understand why the few of us that were left didn't turn on the Japanese and kill them. We were British; we couldn't. We helped them and they were grateful – but it was a horrifying sight to see the horrible burns and the way the flesh hung off them.

Buildings were actually destroyed altogether. Things were on fire and just went up in flames. There was one building with its steel girders all twisted, and it looked as if it was still intact. You hit a girder with a stick, and the stick went right through it. It was like brick dust. The girder just looked twisted. It was frightening.

It was quite a little while before I came to my senses after the blast. I was with one particular guard, who also escaped being killed. He was in such a state that he just put his rifle down and ran for it. The biggest horror in the after-effects was the utter silence. I had been used to bombing of all kinds and after it you heard cries for help and noise – things happening. The eerie thing was the silence.

The movement of the Japanese around, who could move – well, they were just scurrying about like mice. We were all in a particular kind of daze. Around me there were 35,000 dead – and I was still alive. That's the time when something horrifying happens to you. You ask yourself, 'Why me?'. You feel terribly guilty – guilty for being alive when thousands around you are dead. I feel guilty today.

From the moment that all this happened, I felt at one with the Japanese, and all the misery and starvation, all the three and a half years of what I had been through seemed to vanish. I felt they were the same as me and I was the same as them. That's why I've never had any hatred. I cannot hate them in any way, for all that they did.

The bomb at Nagasaki is the filthiest bomb which has ever been dropped. The one at Hiroshima was a neutron bomb, but this plutonium bomb was filthy – and the authorities like to keep it quiet. The two are set off in a completely different way. Plutonium effects on human beings are disgusting. You've seen raw meat hanging up in a butcher's – Japanese doctors had no idea what to do with the wounds. We had to heap up bodies and set fire to them – the horror of that. We had to do it, or there would have been plague.

When the Americans came to fetch us out, I was in a pretty bad state. When they landed, one of them came over and looked me up and down. He went for his revolver in its holster, and said, 'Who do want me to shoot?'. He was a big, tall fellow with a shaven head, real American style. I said, 'You put that revolver away. You don't shoot anybody. If you shoot one of these Japanese, I'll kill you myself. All I want you to do is GET US OUT OF HERE! But don't you shoot any Japanese in front of us.'. He couldn't understand how deeply these few of us felt about the horror. After the bomb, we were free to come and go – they didn't look on us as prisoners. They used to bow to us. They were grateful for what we were doing. I used to help with the surgeons and doctors, and I would ask if they had anything I could use to help the wounded. They had some odd stuff but we didn't really know what to do. The doctors had never treated anything like it at all.

We had gauze and a dark brown sort of ointment with a ghastly smell, just to soothe. I was cradling dying people or trying to put this stuff on their wounds. Some of these were the very Japanese who, a few days before, had been treating us most cruelly. But that was us, not just me.

Some of the fellows from the camp left and tried to get to Tokyo, but I knew it was too far. I don't know what happened to them to this day, but I don't see how, in the condition they were in, they could have ever reached Tokyo.

The hills around Nagasaki saved a lot of damage. If you looked at certain hills, it was as if someone had taken a whitewash brush and run a line straight down the side. One side was burned and scorched white – on the other the grass was growing, untouched. Trees – if you looked, one side of the tree was burned to a cinder, and the other side still had leaves on.

The mushroom cloud was there for quite a time. We were very fortunate inasmuch as two days later, we had a typhoon, and there were terrific winds and torrential rains. I think that was a godsend, because this terrific wind was blowing the dust away to sea, and the rain was washing down the ground. It was awful at the time, but I really do think it saved us."

The End of War – Winners and Losers

The first large-scale surrender of German forces occurred in northern Italy on 2 May 1945. Twenty-four hours later, at Montgomery's headquarters on Luneburg Heath, a document was signed, covering northern Germany, Denmark and Holland, to come into effect on 5 May. Two days later, a similar document covering all fronts was signed at Eisenhower's headquarters in Rheims, effective from early on 9 May. The Western Allies celebrated 'VE (Victory in Europe) Day' prematurely on 8 May. Although some German units continued to fight in Czechoslovakia for a further 48 hours, the war in Europe was effectively over. Three months in the Pacific and Far East, however, many Japanese soldiers refused to believe their Emperor's surrender, broadcast on 15 August. Thus, it was not until 2 September that formal documents were signed aboard USS Missouri in Tokyo Bay. If given the choice, anyone would choose victory. But the end of World War II left many wondering if, at the end of the day, it was not as hard to win as it was to lose.

Admiral Karl Dönitz had been Commander-in-Chief of the *Kriegsmarine* since 1943, when he succeeded Raeder. It was he who had masterminded the U-boat campaigns against Allied shipping and so nearly cut Britain's supply lines, but now, after Hitler's suicide, it fell to Dönitz to supervise the German surrender.

"When I got the telegram from the headquarters of Hitler on the evening of 30th April, I knew that now I was the chief of the German

State. But I knew too, that Himmler had the opinion that he had the biggest chance to be the successor of Hitler. And that's why I thought it to be necessary that I spoke to Himmler at once because this man was still a powerful man in the country. When he got my demands he should have come to me at once – but he answered by telephone that it was not possible for him to come. And then I let him see that it was necessary that he had to come – and then he came.

I didn't know what would be the end of this discussion, it was for me a big question and that's why I put, under a piece of paper, my revolver on the table. And he was sitting down and I gave him the telegram which I had got, and in which it was said that I am the Chief of State.

When he had read the telegram, he got pale and he stood up and bowed and told me, 'Please let me be the second man in your state.' Then I told him that I have no position at all for him in my state – not one, no… and then he was not content and he spoke against that – but he had no success. I didn't change my opinion and after, from that time of discussion, I stood up and he had to go. He went home and I was very glad that the end of the discussion with Himmler was like that, because I had the feeling that he wouldn't do anything against me."

Doctor David Bradford was a clinical student in his third year of studies at Bart's Hospital in London when his year was asked if they would sacrifice a month of their training to go abroad to do relief work. Expecting to go to Holland to work with the starving children, he learnt his destination was Belsen.

"We were taken down in army lorries to Belsen camp itself. We didn't know what we'd find at all. As we went in, we went through the gates – which were actually open, although there were sentries on the gates to prevent the inmates from leaving, and we went to a room where we had DDT powder sprayed over our hair, into our clothes and so on, because there was a danger of typhus, which is carried by insects and bugs.

When we got there we found a number of huts, like any hutted camp. Here there were about 120 huts and this awful pall of smoke and the smell hanging over the camp. There were terrible skeletal people walking about.

I was allotted a hut with a fellow called Eddy Boyd, who was at

UCH. We just had to go in and start clearing it up. The hut was about the size of a tennis court, but some six to eight feet narrower. There were supposed to be about 450 people in this hut. One end was partitioned off and there were three-tier bunks, about 24, and a table and chairs. The rest of it, the inmates were lying on the floor, their heads to the walls, all down the sides. Down the centre they were lying head-to-head. You had four rows of people, just lying there in rags. There were no blankets, and they had old clothes and overcoasts covering them. Our first job was simply to go round and see who was alive and who wasn't. You couldn't do anything else. There was no question of treating them at this stage.

There was Eddy Boyd and I, and each hut was allotted two Hungarian military personnel who had been left behind by the Germans. I think the Hungarians were not combatants, and they had been orderlies around the place.

We were told these men were to do the heavy work – which simply consisted of moving the dead from the hut. Eddy Boyd and I went round and we found, on the first day, about 20 people just lying there dead. As we carried them out, their clothes were immediately taken by the other inmates, and they just used them to cover themselves to keep warm. They were all so close together – they were lying touching each other all around the hut. Just as you have seen on television, the bodies were just carried out in the most undignified manner – they got a couple of arms, a couple of feet, and they were just dragged out and put in a pile near the door.

Twice a day, a tractor came round with a flat truck, and the bodies were unceremoniously laden on these trucks and taken round to an open pit, which would be about 50–60 yards long and 30 yards wide, and just chucked in unceremoniously. They would then be covered with lime and twice a day this wagon would come round. We used to get up about half past seven, have breakfast. Half past eight we would be taken down to the camp each day, and each day, two or three people were found to be lying dead there.

Our job was mainly to clear out the dead and to try to decide who was likely to go on living and who wasn't, and also to see that whatever food there was was evenly distributed. What one found, of course, was that, although there were 450 in the hut, some were up and about, and there were probably about 600 people who slept there. There were some ambulant people, and it was natural that they were the ones who got the food. Our job was to see that the food went to those who really needed it. The food we had to give to them was pretty pitiful in a way. Of course they couldn't have a proper meal. We used to give them something called Bengal Famine Mixture, which was a high-protein diet with glucose in it and added vitamins. It would come round in great cans, and we would dole it out, trying to see that those who really needed it, had it. Sometimes we were lucky enough to get some biscuits or potatoes in their jackets, which were cooked in a great cauldron in the cookhouse.

As time went by, the hut got gradually emptier and with my hut, hut 14, we had managed, with some of the other students, to clear out huts 16, 18 and 20 – there were odd and even numbers on either side of a track. So these were next door, and as time went by we got these three huts which had been done up into some sort of primitive hospital.

The only medication we had was aspirin tablets, a very primitive M and B type compound, a sulphonamide which was an early antibiotic, called Prontosil, and opium tablets, which were presumably some sort of laudanum. And we just handed these out like that. There were people in pain – they had sores and they were just lying there in pain. We would dispense these tablets simply to give relief. The main thing was to get fluid and vitamins into them.

The first fortnight we were cleaning out Belsen itself, actually in the huts. The first week we didn't have any time off at all – we worked seven days flat-out. After that we were given a morning off a week, and an afternoon on another day. It was insisted that we do this because it was fairly hard work. It was a bit of an ordeal and we were young.

Being as young as we were – I was about 23 years old at the time – one could stand it more. If one had been more mature, if one had to face it now and realise that the people who were in this terrible state, were human beings – somebody's mother, father, son and so on – I don't think one could have borne it. As it was, they were almost unrecognisable as human beings, and of course we were young medical students, and they were all foreign – couldn't speak English, so I had a young Pole as an interpreter.

An area was kept separate for typhus cases, obviously. There was a lot of tuberculosis, and we were able to get their chests X-rayed. It was quite an efficient service. You'd fill in a form and they would be taken down to the X-ray department by orderlies. The next day you would get an X-ray report.

We had to treat a lot of abcesses, bed-sores – and their general condition was poor. There were people who had poor nourishment and they were likely to get secondary infections and pneumonia.

People have asked how I could possibly stand it, but I think it was because we were young. One didn't think of catching anything oneself. Some of us were afflicted with diarrhoea – and in fact, two of the Barts men got typhus and had to be flown home. We were fit people – the worst thing we could get was probably a sort of dysentery.

There was a crematorium there, and at nearby Bergen there was a room full of watches, one full of human hair, because the people were shaved before they were incinerated. There was another room full of trinkets and things which had been taken from the inmates."

Acting Sergeant Jack Durey, with the 2nd Battalion, Hampshire Regiment, had been taken POW at a canal near the Belgian border, and was subsequently held in *Stalag* XXB at Willenberg which stood near a tributary of the Vistula. It was in mid-January that a rumbling noise began and a glow appeared on the horizon.

"A German officer came along the column asking if there was a padre who would volunteer to stay in Marienberg with the POW hospital there. I had been in the *Stalag* some time, as I had been put forward for the next repatriation board with a duodenal ulcer and bronchitis problems. Although, at the time, feeling well, it was the depth of winter and I did not consider my prospects very highly on a forced march across Germany.

It seemed to me that, if I could get to the hospital in Marienberg, I might fare better than with the column. The idea to those around me was ridiculous. Take a chance with the Russians? No way. However, two elected to try with me, and so, as the column moved off, we slipped through the hedgerow out of sight. When all were gone, we emerged and set off for Marienberg.

The hospital was a large old house in its own grounds, with gates at the entrance and a tree either side. Between the trees was stretched a banner made of three sheets pinned together, showing a red cross either side of some Russian wording in between.

There were several doctors – one British, one French, one Belgian and a South African dentist. The medics were carrying the bed patients down to the basement and had barely finished when shells started coming over – but not close. The walking sick, several medics and ourselves had to settle for the two air-raid shelters that ran either side of several huts in the grounds. The shelters, allowing room to only stand side-by-side, had an air vent half way along, and a deep hole dug into the side and down as a latrine, with chlorine disinfectant, that was choking. We supposed that within 12–24 hours we would know if we had a future of not.

The fact was that Marienberg was the last town before Danzig, and so the battle raged above us for seven days. We were trapped there without food, water or exercise. It was an awful experience that I cannot write about, but only one got wounded and one other killed. Eventually, tanks could be heard and firing died down. After a brief deathly silence, we were called out. It was painful to move, but outside the gate stood an enormous tank, a Russian officer conferred with the doctors and sheepskin-clad infantry peered about with submachine guns – but the atmosphere was victorious. The Russians had nothing to offer us, but allowed the medics from the basement to form a foraging party with an escort who eventually returned with a sack of flour, with which we made pancakes of a sort, and with water and our Red Cross food which had been isolated in one of the huts. We made a meal and went to sleep until the following morning, when we cleaned ourselves up as best we could.

With my companions, wandering about the grounds, I found a German heavy machine gun on its side, and three dead Germans immediately above where we had been in the shelter – a matter of a mere two metres, apparently knocked out by mortar fire. A Russian mortar platoon arrived and set up the largest mortar I had seen right next to the hospital. We thought it was a token of protection, but as soon as they were ready, started firing off at some target across the town. We lent a hand, carrying boxes up from the road, but soon came on the receiving end of heavy artillery fire (I am deaf as a result). The platoon smartly packed up and left. The Germans were mounting a counterattack and we had to round up carts from the locality, load the bed cases and move out, pushing and pulling them.

The journey took several days, during which at least one died from exposure each day, and through this stage of our travels, we were too occupied to notice anything but our efforts. Arriving at a large hospital in Rosenburg, all were taken in except we three – the padre who had volunteered (a Captain King), and the two medics. We were told that no help was available – we were to go home, but stay on the roads, or be shot. The padre was given a piece of paper with one

Russian word written in pencil, to show at check points. After one night in a warehouse, we decided we would fare better if we split up, so, taking a copy of the paper, we three were alone again.

From there we walked to Deutsch Eylau, where we found a group of French POWs. Together we rounded up a stray cow, killed it cooked some – but were unable to eat it. We saw large numbers of civilian bodies lying spread out across the fields on either side, and some bodies crushed to mere imprints on the roads. At junctions there would be groups of civilians, mostly elderly, as many as 20, sitting or squatting, huddled together. They were dead too, but not shot. Apparently they had frozen to death, waiting for they knew not what. One still had his pipe in his mouth.

From Deutsch Eylau, the next part of the journey took us into Poland. Here there were no bodies and villages were occupied. We were told that leaflets had been dropped telling them to get out for 24 hours, then to come back. On return, each house had to display a little red flag and a central house had a large one. They were now communists.

One day we caught up with a column of slow-moving German POWs who were a pitiful sight. We had no wish to get involved and perhaps included with them, although by now we knew how to shout '*Ingliski Soyusniki!*' at any approach, while offering our bit of paper. Our caution was soon further justified when one German fell on the wayside. Without any compunction, one of the two Russians following behind, pulled a pistol and shot him through the head when his companion took the dead man's disc and wrote down his details in a notebook. We followed the column for several hours and counted 14 shot in the same way. We decided that some fell out, not from exhaustion, but as a deliberate act of suicide. Eventually we arrived at Thorne and stayed the night in the main railway station. We moved on again until we came to Warsaw. Through all this, we had no idea of direction, but continued as directed at the various checkpoints on presentation of our piece of paper. At Warsaw we were again billeted with civilians and stayed for three days in a suburb.

Unfortunately, one of my companions was unable to continue. His boots were completely worn out, and his feet were in a bad way, so we left him there in the good hands of our hosts and did the next part to Lubin.

Here we were taken to a railway goods siding where we were taken over by three American civilians who gave us a K ration and handed us a cigarette apiece. They apologised for the circumstances and we bedded down for the night on straw. The next morning, with others assembled there of various nationalities, we boarded a troop train.

Each wagon had a small stove in the centre and there was a small amount of coal. A sack of dried bread pieces was also there. The train journey took nearly a week, with one stop at Tarnapol, where we received a large bowl of soup. We were also transferred to another wagon because the fierce blizzard we were travelling through had ripped the roof loose, and we had been holding it down by attaching scarves etc. to the hooks. We arrived in Odessa, where we were given a delousing and a shower, then were taken to a British boat that had a Red Cross boat alongside, transferring new uniforms and clothing.

As an NCO, I was at the head of the group, having been called out by names and numbers taken earlier, when a brass band playing *Colonel Bogey* arrived with a few more strays behind. At the head of these was Captain King, the padre. Naturally he took precedence and half way up the gangway he turned and put up two fingers in a victory sign, saying 'I beat you after all!'. He was a fine man and an inspiration.

During our journey via Port Said, Naples to offload Italians, and Marseilles to offload French, we joined a convoy at Gibraltar, and docked at Liverpool. There was a platform with the mayor and dignitaries, a large band playing and a huge crowd on the quayside. I believe we were the first POWs to return."

Trooper Jack Border of the 22nd Dragoons had miraculously survived the D-Day assault, in which he had been a wireless operator/loader in a flail tank. Moving to scout cars, he followed the Allied advance up to Holland, where he spent the last part of the war, just south of Nijmegen.

"In May I was stood down – we were resupplying, but on the 2nd May one of our sergeants was killed, the last one of ours to be killed during the war from our squadron. Then the news came that it was all over, and there was just a flood of relief. Nobody had wanted to go on, we had been through a miserable winter that year – it had been so cold. I had never felt so cold in all my life.

In the towns there was euphoria – flowers, people cheering – but all this really belonged to the men who had gone before, they had done the hard work.

Our tanks were handed over in June because the 22nd Dragoons were going to be disbanded. The first thing the officers did – because we were a cavalry regiment – was to swan off to get some horses. I'd opened my mouth and had told one of the officers that I used to ride, and another of my colleagues said that he was a blacksmith, so the next thing we know, we are looking after 21 horses, even though I was a driver. I still had my scout car and was billeted with a German family where the mother had lost her husband and the daughter's husband was a POW somewhere – and of course, we were in their home.

The first night, I don't think I shut my eyes. We had been forced on to them, and I quite thought they would get at us because of all the tragedies they had probably faced because of the Allies. But they were no different from us. We're all human beings, after all's said and done.

I stayed in Germany from June to the end of the year before being shipped home, and then on to Egypt and Palestine – but that's another story."

Stoker Bill (Chalky) White survived the sinking of his landing craft in the Channel late in 1944 and was then sent out to the Pacific, where he was when the Japanese surrendered in summer 1945. Following the bombing of Hiroshima, he and some other crewmen went to see the site of the first A-bomb.

"I was on the mine-laying cruiser HMS *Manxman*, which was the fastest ship in the Royal Navy. I went up to Tokyo and went to look at Hiroshima about three months after the bomb had been dropped – and I couldn't believe the sight.

It was devastating. We didn't know anything about the bomb – we had no idea what an atomic weapon could do, and we had picked up photos from Hong Kong, taken more or less directly after the explosion had occurred. When we went ashore in Japan, all the Japanese would bow to us. They had surrendered – the very thing the Emperor had always said they wouldn't do.

Hiroshima looked like a hurricane had gone through, followed by a fire. I thought, 'How could one bomb do this – just one bomb?'. We didn't discuss it because we were so glad the war was over, but when I saw Tokyo, it was just as bad – and that had only been fire-bombed and not touched by nuclear bombs.

You know, nobody had warned us or spoken about radiation. It was just an atomic bomb that had ended the war. People say it was a dreadful thing to do, but you can only die once – it doesn't matter how, and of course war is total war. Women and children are involved. This is what some people don't seem to recognise. The bomb saved many many lives. Can you imagine what would have happened if we had invaded Japan?

I wouldn't have missed the war for the world. It let me come to terms with myself and it taught me discipline – how to live. The Navy, the ship, was a home. We were always together. I had joined up at 17, prompted by my brother who had recently joined. I went to Lewisham where they asked me how old I was. I had said 18. They said not, but if I came with a birth certificate, I could then prove I was. So I went home and, with my young sister's help, I altered it and then went back. I spotted an old petty officer wearing thick glasses, so I pushed it under his nose, he took one look at it, and I was in. It was the best thing I ever did."

Able Seaman Gunner Len O'Keefe was aboard the destroyer HMS *Rotherham*, which had been involved in the Fourteenth Army's taking of Rangoon, when news came of the liberation of Europe. While the ship was docked at Trincomalee, Ceylon, where the fleet was based, Lord Mountbatten came to address the men.

"Lord Louis Mountbatten, the C-in-C South East Asia Command, came aboard, stood on the fo'c'sle, said, 'Gather round, lads,' and thanked us for our past efforts. He said the next job was the invasion of Singapore. Well, the dropping of the atom bombs altered everything, and turned the invasion planning into one big rescue operation, because of the plight of our people who were Japanese prisoners of war.

As we left Ceylon, the fleet made an impressive sight. It included merchant ships and two big white hospital ships with their distinctive red crosses. During the voyage we were despatched with two motor launches to take the surrender of Singapore Naval Base. Our first lieutenant said, 'Let's show the Japs smart British tars,' and asked us to dress in our No 1s, which was our best tropical going-ashore rig.

As we steamed up the Jahore Straits, at that moment we never trusted the Japs, so the 4.7 in guns were loaded, but trained fore and aft. I can see the lads now, in line of the fo'c'sle – the water as flat as a pond with only our bow wave and those of the two MLs disturbing the water. It was so peaceful – but we were all thinking the same thing. Were those 15 in naval guns going to open up on us?

Thankfully nothing shattered the peace and as we came alongside, there were Japs with white armbands to take our lines and help us tie up. Some of us went ashore as landing parties and met some of our POWs from Changi Jail. They were overwhelmed to see us.

One man hugged me and said he was a regular soldier who had finished his tour of duty and they were going back to the UK when war was declared, so his regiment had to stay. He was taken prisoner and had been away from home nearly 10 years. He hugged me again and said, 'It's OK now – the Navy is here.'. And he started crying. We took them back to the ship and the lads gave them their rum tots and food.

In the warehouses were found crates of cutlery, plates, cups etc – all untouched by the Japs who had no use for them, so every mess deck was supplied with new cutlery and china. Some lads even brought back a piano and asked permission to bring it aboard – eventually we presented it to the fleet canteen in Trincomalee.

Our captain, Captain Beeks, DSO, RN, took over a large house nearby and I was detailed one morning to don my best uniform and stand outside the house. A big black car pulled up in the driveway and our stepped the Japanese Admiral, Fukudome, the C-in-C. He walked down to me and I saluted, which he returned, then I took him inside and handed him over to our chief petty gunnery officer, who took him to the captain and other officers to sign the surrender."